JOSEPH STALIN AND THE ART OF TYRANNY

JOSEPH STALIN AND THE ART OF TYRANNY

ONE OF HISTORY'S MOST FEARED DICTATORS

WILLIAM NESTER

FRONTLINE
BOOKS

JOSEPH STALIN AND THE ART OF TYRANNY
One of History's Most Feared Dictators

First published in Great Britain in 2025
by Frontline Books
An imprint of
Pen & Sword Books Ltd
Yorkshire - Philadelphia

ISBN 978 1 03613 129 6

A CIP catalogue record for this book is available from the British Library

Typeset by Lapiz Digital

Printed and bound in the UK by CPI Group (UK) Ltd,
Croydon, CR0 4YY.

Printed on paper from a sustainable source by
CPI Group (UK) Ltd, Croydon, CR0 4YY

For a complete list of Pen & Sword titles please contact
PEN & SWORD BOOKS LTD
47 Church Street, Barnsley, South Yorkshire, S70 2AS, England

E-mail: enquiries@pen-and-sword.co.uk

Website: www.pen-and-sword.co.uk
or
PEN & SWORD BOOKS
1950 Lawrence Rd, Havertown, PA 19083, USA

E-mail: uspen-and-sword@casematepublishers.com

CONTENTS

LIST OF PLATES

ACKNOWLEDGEMENTS

I would like to express my deep gratitude and pleasure at having had yet another opportunity to work with the outstanding publishing team of John Grehan, Lisa Hooson, Stephen Chumbley and Martin Mace, who were always as kind as they were professional.

LIST OF TABLES

INTRODUCTION

> '[T]he people need a Tsar, whom they can worship and for whom they can live and work.' (Joseph Stalin)

> 'To choose one's victims, to prepare one's plans minutely, to slake an implacable vengeance and then to go to bed . . . there is nothing sweeter in the world.' (Joseph Stalin)

> 'What happened? Why did it happen? How could it have happened?' (Hannah Arendt)

The Art of Tyranny is real. Successful tyrants provoke comfort and terror, love and fear in those they rule arbitrarily without restraint. They indoctrinate populations to believe that they are infallible demigods dedicated to the people's well-being, guarding them from dangerous enemies within and beyond the regime. Tyrants, of course, do not act alone. They hold and assert unchallenged power from atop a pyramid of institutions packed with fawning sycophants and cowed submissives.

Joseph Stalin was not just any tyrant, but perhaps history's most genocidal dictator.[1] Guided by Communist ideology, he established a totalitarian political system for the Soviet Union that nationalized all business and farm property; directed and struggled to develop the economy through five-year plans that determined all prices, wages and production; and murdered or imprisoned in slave labour camps all 'enemies of the people'. His policies killed at least 11,000,000 people by bullets, famine, disease and being worked to death.

That is clear enough. Yet, Stalin is among history's greatest paradoxes. In Western liberal democracies, knowing people view Stalin with horror as a vicious dictator and mass murderer who brutally ruled the Soviet Union from 1929 until his death in 1953. Yet, in Russia, Stalin often tops lists of the most popular historic figure in Levada opinion surveys.[2]

How could descendants of those who survived Stalin's regime adore the man responsible for repressing, exploiting and possibly imprisoning or even murdering their ancestors? And what explains Stalin's willing executioners, literally millions of bureaucrats, police and soldiers in the Soviet government and Communist Party organizations carrying out his commands.

A key element of the art of tyranny is getting people to love their ruler. Stalin formed a personality cult for himself as the beloved great leader of the Soviet Union and the world communist movement. Stalin made himself the people's *Vozhd* or 'Leader' just like Adolf Hitler and Benito Mussolini respectively became Germany's *Führer* and Italy's *Duce*. Nearly eight decades after his death, Stalin's personality cult continues to inspire and sooth countless followers in Russia and around the world.

***

Joseph Stalin created himself. He was christened Joseph Vissarionovich Djugashvili in 1878 but from 1913 appropriately called himself Stalin or 'Steel'. He had an implacable, ruthless will buttressed by a messianic, infallible universal creed. At age 19, he committed himself to overthrowing the Russian empire with a communist revolution. From 1889 to 1917, he worked his way up revolutionary ranks, with the turning point being his election to the communist Bolshevik Party's Central Committee in 1913. During those years, authorities arrested and exiled him to towns in Siberia or above the Arctic Circle four times. He tried to escape seven times and succeeded three times. Then, in March 1917, a liberal coalition forced Tsar Nicholas II to abdicate, then formed a government. Among that government's first acts was to amnesty political prisoners. Stalin was soon in Petrograd with his fellow communists, determined to overthrow that liberal government. Later that year in November, Stalin was among the Bolshevik elite, led by Vladimir Lenin, that carried out the coup d'etat and imposed an increasingly tyrannical communist regime.

Biographer Adam Ulam summarized Stalin's stunning political development during the Russian Revolution's first decade:

> In 1917, Stalin's transformation within a few weeks from a misanthropic recluse into a man acknowledged by a sizable group as their leader marked him as a skilful politician. By the mid-1920s and in the context of Soviet politics he became a superb one. He had all the essential ingredients: an excellent sense of timing, simple but effective oratory

> in which certain crudity was reassuring to the average Party member; the appearance . . . of a man free of internal complexes and problems, zestfully playing the political game . . . The tyrant lay dormant in the politician.[3]

Lenin recognized Stalin's abilities as a nearly inexhaustible workhorse and wielded him as his key administrator and troubleshooter. Stalin dutifully fulfilled each post and mission, at times ruthlessly and literally performing that role. Lenin got the Central Committee to approve Stalin as a member of the Politburo and the Ogburo; as the commissar or head of the Nationalities, State Control and Worker and Peasant commissions (departments); as a political commissar beside the commanding generals of four Fronts during the civil war; and, most vitally, as the Communist Party's General Secretary or head.

After Lenin died in 1924, Stalin eliminated his rivals in a series of prolonged struggles to emerge as the Soviet Union's undisputed leader in 1929. That done, he completed the communist revolution by nationalizing all private property, developing the economy through Five-Year Plans and amassing all vital political, police, economic, military and cultural power in his hands, with the death toll at least 11,000,000 people.

Stalin's tyranny faced only one true threat during its existence. It came not from Stalin's imagined millions of enemies lurking among the Soviet people, but from rival tyrant Adolf Hitler. The German army's onslaught that began on 22 June 1941, nearly destroyed the Soviet Union. After a week of stunned inaction as sweeping German mass tank-led offensives circled and destroyed one Soviet army after another, Stalin asserted himself as the Red Army's Supreme Commander-in-Chief.

That was a new role for Stalin. Before then, he had little experience, took little interest and interfered little in military matters. He had no military training. His withered left arm exempted him from conscription during the First World War. During the Civil War, he was an army political commissar who mostly requisitioned supplies and enforced order behind the lines. By observing and asking questions, he did learn basic strategy, tactics, training, logistics, weapons and morale. For the next two decades, his only significant role in military affairs was ordering hundreds of thousands of officers purged and tens of thousands murdered.

As supreme military commander, Stalin was central for all key planning and made all key decisions. So how did he do? Stalin grew into that role. The most vital strength he brought to it was total power and will. He also understood that military operations depended on mobilizing and training soldiers and workers; producing and transporting supplies; gathering, analysing and using intelligence; enticing foreign aid and allies; and getting Soviet civilians willingly to do anything he deemed vital for victory. Stalin was or became adept at all those key elements of war.

***

So, what dynamic of nature and nurture, choices and circumstances made Stalin the man and the tyrant? Alas, beyond his grave there is probably no reliable source of his genes to determine his genetic makeup. Scientists who map the human genome discover ever more ways that genes determine each individual's uniqueness. Some things like intellect, appearance and sexuality cannot fundamentally be changed, only groomed or neglected. Others give us tendencies like being relatively more open or close minded, introverted or extroverted, potentially skilled or interested in some things and unskilled or uninterested in others, empathic or uncaring and laid back or assertive.

Children who suffer repeated humiliations and beatings while being denied affection, understanding and encouragement tend to bear lifelong smouldering anger, a sense of inferiority and a lust for vengeance. They often become bullies who scapegoat and vent their rage on others. They also often become dogmatic believers in creeds, groups and movements that promise justice and provide a sense of belonging, purpose and empowerment. They see the world in stark good-versus-evil warring dichotomies in which they embody the former and their enemies the latter. Stalin exemplified all that.

Stalin certainly had an unhappy childhood. He was the only child of a couple whose alcoholic father berated and beat him and his mother, who also scolded and smacked him. He had physical imperfections that likely bolstered his feelings of inadequacy, inferiority, rage and retribution. He was 5ft 4in and heavyset. He was born with two toes fused on his left foot. At age five, a poorly-set broken left arm stiffened and later kept him from being drafted into the army. A childhood bout with smallpox left his face and body heavily pockmarked. He had rotten teeth and lost many of them over the years. He had dark brown eyes and thick dark brown hair. He was an outsider in the Russian empire. He was born and grew up in a small, remote city in Georgia, learned Russian at an early age and eventually became fluent although he never lost his Georgian accent.

He was very bright and sought outlets for his intelligence. As the Soviet ruler, he enjoyed movies, concerts, plays and ballets. Among his favourites was *Swan Lake* which he saw a score or more times, including the night before his fatal stroke. He was an avid reader and enjoyed discussing books and essays for both pleasure and power: 'If you want to know the people around you, find out what they read.'[4] He especially relished biographies of 'great men'. Not surprisingly, his role model and 'teacher' was Ivan the Terrible, closely seconded by Peter the Great. He insisted that 'the people need a Tsar, whom they can worship and for whom they can live and work'.[5]

Although Stalin wrote a lot of essays on Communism, they were pedantry, not poetry, dull and plodding. Nor was he a gifted orator although with practice he became proficient. Comrade Lion Feuchtwanger observed: 'Stalin is definitely not a great speaker. He speaks slowly and without any brilliance in a slightly muffled voice and with difficulty. He develops his arguments slowly, appealing to people's common sense so they will grasp them not quickly but firmly.'[6] Indeed, among Stalin's political skills was reducing complex issues to simple maxims that most people could grasp. The trouble came when those maxims became ideological shibboleths that justified genocidal measures like collectivization and purges.

Stalin was a hard worker who put in long daily hours. During meetings, he usually said little but listened intently as he chain-smoked and doodled wolf heads with a red pencil on a pad. He developed into an adept politician. Biographer Ulam explained: 'Stalin was careful to stage his appearances according to the occasion: at an audience with a military officer, he would be an impassive man of steel, at a youth or workers' meeting a jovial father of his people, to a foreign journalist an unpretentious and businesslike politician.'[7]

Patience was among his strengths. Much like a motionless crocodile on a riverbank, he waited until the perfect moment to lunge and clamp his jaws on his victim. Stalin explained: 'To choose one's victims, to prepare one's plans minutely, to slake an implacable vengeance and then to go to bed . . . there is nothing sweeter in the world.'[8] His plots for eliminating rivals could take months or even years to execute. For instance, a Soviet agent did not ingratiate his way into the armed Mexico City compound of Leon Trotsky and drive an icepick into his skull until 1940, 11 years after Stalin exiled his most hated rival.

Historian Roy Medvedev offers yet another dimension of Stalin's character: 'A man of strong will, Stalin was at the same time extremely cautious and, on occasion, indecisive as well. In difficult political situations he often didn't know what to do, but he was able to conceal his indecisiveness, frequently preferring to act after the event rather than providing leadership.'[9] One key way that Stalin steadily amassed power was by seeming to be as obsequious, cooperative and non-threatening as possible. Isaac Deutscher explained his method: 'In the Politburo, when matters of high priority were under debate, he never seemed to impose his views on his colleagues. He carefully followed the course of the debate to see which way the wind was blowing and invariably voted with the majority unless he had assured his majority beforehand. He was therefore always agreeable to the majority.'[10] His colleagues rewarded him with more posts and thus power. Eventually, he controlled enough institutions and followers that he could openly isolate and eliminate his rivals for total power.

Although Stalin at times erupted in rage at failures and setbacks, he was mostly calm and soft-spoken. When he chose to do so, he could be charming in a low-key, smiling, reassuring way. Most Americans who met Stalin were struck by how down-to-earth he was. Secretary of State Cordell Hull recalled: 'I thought to myself that any American having Stalin's personality and approach might well reach high public office in my own country.'[11] Stalin's humour was mostly scatological but occasionally sardonic. Yugoslav communist Milovan Djilas observed that: 'Stalin had a sense of humour – a rough humour, self-assured, but not entirely without finesse and depth.'[12] For instance, during the 1945 Yalta conference, Prime Minister Winston Churchill worried about his Conservative Party's fate in an election scheduled later that summer, then noted that 'Marshal Stalin has a much easier political task. He has only one party to deal with.' Stalin replied, 'History has shown that one party is of great convenience to a leader of a state.'[13]

Stalin was twice married and had sporadic, fleeting affairs, mistresses and prostitutes. Yet he was no ladies' man. He was awkward, bashful around attractive women. As he rose in power, he received ever more fawning letters often with photos from women who wanted to be his wife or lover. After his second wife's death, Stalin did not pursue romantic relations and likely had few sexual relations.

***

Stalin fathered three known children, Yakov with his first wife, Ekatarina, and Vasily and Svetlana with his second wife, Nadya. He also adopted Artyom Sergeev, a deceased friend's orphan and preferred him over his two natural sons. He both pampered and berated his daughter during his fleeting home visits. After his death, Svetlana managed to escape the Soviet Union for freedom in the United

States. Tuberculosis killed Ekatarina and a gunshot killed his second wife, Nadya. Most likely Nadya, who was neurotic and depressed, pulled the trigger after Stalin publicly humiliated her. Yakov tried to kill himself, but the gunshot grazed his chest. He was captured during the Second World War. When the Germans offered to swap him for General Friedrich Paulus, captured at Stalingrad, Stalin refused, not wanting to appear to have taken advantage of his power when the sons of millions of other Soviet parents had been captured. Vasily was an alcoholic and womanizer, who became a pilot and general during the Second World War.

Stalin's material needs were Spartan. He dressed simply, usually just a peasant-style tunic, shirt, trousers and boots. After naming himself a marshal amidst the Second World War, he wore a military uniform during work days until his death. He lived in a series of sparsely furnished apartments, even at the Kremlin where he spent a couple of decades. He had three similarly austere dachas within 20 miles of Moscow. His only taste of luxury was sojourning at a Sochi palace above the Black Sea during his rare vacations.

He rarely drank alcohol to excess. During banquets with their incessant toasts, he usually had his glass refilled with coloured water from a vodka bottle. Yet he loved gathering his coterie for prolonged alcohol-soaked banquets and getting them drunk to blow off steam while he played them against each other with vulgar jokes and behaviour. He was often childishly crude. During state banquets, he might seek someone's attention by throwing a bread roll at him or her.

Stalin's life spanned 74 years until a cerebral haemorrhage killed him in 1953. That longevity seems astonishing given his tobacco addiction, near constant hyper stress and paranoia and disdain for exercise. He chain-smoked cigarettes but liked to be publicly seen and photographed with a pipe for the cerebral image. As he aged he suffered worsening neurosis, sciatica, rheumatism and gout.

***

Above all, Stalin had a pathological character that was brutal, paranoid, cruel, devious, cunning, jealous and sadistic and those traits worsened the more power he amassed and asserted. No matter how old he got, Stalin remained a 12-year-old bully. He was hot-tempered and often erupted with curses and threats at anyone who made a mistake, including contradicting him. Emotionally, he had to harden himself as he had more people tortured and murdered or locked up in slave labour camps. His pathologies were not unlimited – he avoided torture sessions and executions, yet relished hearing his henchmen's accounts of how the victim behaved during his final minutes.[14]

Stalin projected his own vilest traits on enemies and allies alike. He was deeply paranoid. Soviet Premier Nikita Khrushchev later recalled:

> Stalin was a very distrustful man, sickly suspicious; we knew this from our work with him. He could look at a man and say: 'Why are your eyes so shifty today?' or 'Why are you turning so much today and avoiding looking me directly in the eyes?' The sickly suspicion created in him a general distrust even toward eminent Party workers whom he had known for years. Everywhere and in everything he saw 'enemies', 'double-dealers,' and 'spies'.[15]

Stalin was a deeply jealous man, not for ostentatious wealth or beautiful women, but for power and prestige. Bolshevik theorist Nikolai Bukharin explained: 'Stalin cannot live unless he has what someone else has. He cannot live without it.'[16] Stalin hated those more intelligent, knowledgeable, sophisticated, articulate, attractive and confident than himself, which characterized most Bolshevik leaders. He sought to destroy those he was incapable of emulating. Above all, he detested Leon Trotsky, intellectually brilliant and arrogant, who never veiled his contempt for Stalin. In his 1930 memoir, Trotsky sneered that Stalin 'was the most outstanding mediocrity in our Party'.[17] A decade later, Stalin got his vengeance when one of his assassins planted an icepick in Trotsky's skull. Stalin genuinely respected Lenin but sought not just to follow but to surpass him as the unquestioned, all powerful, all knowing god-like leader of the Soviet Union and world communism.

Stalin at once demanded and detested sycophancy. Historian Simon Montefiore described how Stalin's tyranny manipulated his immediate advisors in his lair:

> They studied Stalin like zoologists to read his moods, win his favour and survive. The key was to understand Stalin's unique blend of supersensitive discomfiture and world-historical arrogance, his longing to be liked and his heartless cruelty: it was vital not to make him anxious . . . There are certain key rules which resemble the advice given to a tourist on how to behave if he is unlucky enough to encounter a wild animal on his camping holiday. The first is to look him straight in the eyes. Otherwise he asked, 'Why don't you look me in the eye today.' . . . The visitor has to maintain calm at all times: panic alarmed Stalin . . . Visitors must show respect by taking notes.[18]

Transport commissar Ivan Kovalev explained how Stalin made others inwardly tremble in his presence: 'One felt oppressed by Stalin's power but also by his phenomenal memory and the fact that he knew so much. He made one feel even less important than one was.'[19]

Through mass arrests and executions, Stalin terrified the Soviet people, those in his inner circle, down through the Communist Party's ranks and 150 million or so ordinary workers and pensioners. Khrushchev recalled: 'In those days anything could have happened to any of us. Everything depended on what Stalin happened to be thinking when he glanced in your direction . . . Without warning he could turn on you with real viciousness.'[20]

Biographer Adam Ulam explained the complex, twisted psychology behind Stalin's persecution, torture and murder or enslavement of millions of human beings:

> The mechanics of terror, like the mechanics of collectivization, soon acquired its own momentum. The more he killed, the more he was bound to suspect. Since his mind evidently made no distinction between actual and potential treason, slander became a prima facie proof . . . Considerations of personal vengeance played an increasing role. Stalin had always been a vile tempered and dangerous man to cross . . . Stalin's inhumanity fed on the idea of his own historic mission. He was the embodiment of the Revolution, the foundation on which Soviet power rested.[21]

Stalin transformed himself into a semi-divine figure who personified the glories of the Soviet Union, the Communist Party and the unfolding communist utopia. Ideologically, personality cults are anathema to communism which insists that perennial struggles among economic classes, not individual leaders, determine history. But under first Lenin then Stalin, communism had morphed from a political ideology into an atheistic theology of worship and devotion. Stalin did not truly believe the ideal version of himself propagated ceaselessly, but he insisted that everyone else did. Historian Dmitri Volkogonov summarized Stalin as an intellect and cult leader:

> While Stalin may . . . have had an exceptional intellect, he was far from being a genius. Nor was he at all realistic about his own capabilities . . . For the most part, his views were those of an amateur, if not of an outright ignoramus, but the chorus of praise that greeted his every utterance raise those views to the rank of the highest revelation.[22]

***

What did Stalin believe in other than himself and his obsession with power and death? No mere tyrant could commit such vast atrocities on his own. Stalin needed a totalitarian ideology and political system to inflict such evil on so many people. The ideology of communism justifies a Communist Party's seizure of a country to amass all political, economic, social, cultural and religious power in its hands.[23] He was a hardcore communist by zealous conviction, not cynicism. His mother got him schooled in a seminary and hoped he would become a priest. Instead, during his late teens, he lost faith in Christianity and became first an atheist then a committed communist and revolutionary.

As an ideology, communism is simple to understand and so, for simple-minded people, to believe and zealously follow. Communists split all of humanity into two economic classes, the minority rich 'haves' (bourgeoisie) and majority poor 'have nots' (proletariat) and assert that the rich got rich by suppressing and exploiting the poor. That suppression and exploitation justifies the poor revolting against the rich, eliminating them, confiscating their wealth and distributing it equally among themselves.

In practice, communism is a totalitarian system in which a tiny elite – the Communist Party – suppresses and exploits everyone else. Communists justify their suppression and exploitation by claiming the opposite – that they have liberated the downtrodden masses from their former oppressors. Communists manipulate the vilest of human emotions – jealousy, greed, hatred and vengeance. Communism promises a future utopia to justify all their mass confiscation, torture, imprisonment and murder.

Communism is a secular religion that demands from its adherents unquestioning belief in a set of abstract ideals. The Communist Party is for communist true believers as the pope is for conservative Catholics – infallible. For communists, individuals are insignificant, fallible, interchangeable, expendable and mortal, but the Communist Party is the immortal and infallible engine of human progress. Trotsky explained:

> None of us desires or is able to dispute the will of the Party. Clearly the Party is always right . . . We can only be right with and by the Party, for history has provided no other way of being in the right . . . We have . . . historical justification in saying, whether it is right or wrong in certain individual cases, it is my party . . . And if the Party adopts a decision which one or other of us thinks unjust, he will say, just or unjust, it is my party and I shall support the consequences of the decision to the end.[24]

The Communist Party promptly punishes those who falter in their faith, with the harshest fate for those heretics who refuse to recant.

Paranoia pervades every communist system. 'Informants' (*Seksots*) are crucial to communist totalitarianism. The Soviet regime enlisted tens of millions of informants or around one of every five people to spy on their fellow workers, neighbours and even family members and report any heretical anti-communist words or deeds. The existence of that secret army of informants was known to all. The terror of being charged with being a counterrevolutionary kept virtually everyone tensely within the regime's straitjacket of permissible behaviour and attitudes. Konstantin Shteppa, a Soviet professor of ancient history, expressed the prevailing mindset: 'I was naturally sorry for my friends, but I was . . . also afraid of them . . . the trivial criticisms and grumbles and expressions of resentment and disappointment which occurred in every conversation forced every Soviet citizen to feel guilty.'[25]

Stalin was a communist zealot yet subjected interpretations of that creed to political circumstances. Bolshevik leader Nikolai Bukharin explained: 'He changes his theories according to the need he has of getting rid of somebody at such-and-such a moment.'[26] Communist Milovan Djilas elaborated: 'All in all, Stalin was a monster who, while adhering to abstract, absolute and fundamental utopian ideas, in practice had no criterion but success – and this meant violent and physical and spiritual extermination.'[27] Whenever anyone guardedly raised the issue of his policies' human costs, Stalin's most frequent responded with the bromide, 'You can't make an omelette without breaking eggs'. Yet Stalin merely fulfilled totalitarian and genocidal policies that Lenin initiated. Lenin repeatedly proclaimed that: 'A revolution without firing squads is meaningless.'

***

Tyrants are as old as humanity. Tyrants wield capricious, murderous, uninhibited and often unhinged power over others. Prince Vlad the Impaler of fifteenth-century Wallachia was an especially cruel and murderous tyrant who earned his soubriquet by having all those who resisted him along with their families impaled on giant stakes inserted through their rectums. Aztec kings triumphantly watched thousands of naked war captives pulled up temple stairs and stretched across an altar, where a priest sliced open their chests, pulled out the still beating hearts and stuffed them into the gaping mouth of a stone deity.

Totalitarian tyranny is a twentieth-century phenomenon and was confined to Joseph Stalin's Soviet Union and the communist puppet regimes he imposed in Eastern Europe along with Mao Zedong's China, the Kim dynasty's North Korea, Pol Pot's Cambodia, Ho Chi Minh's Vietnam and Fidel Castro's Cuba. Never before had tyrants completely controlled not just the government but virtually all economic and social relations.[28] Four related revolutions empowered those tyrants to construct and rule their totalitarian regimes: an ideological revolution of Communism that justified their 'Dictatorship of the Proletariat' over everyone and everything; a mass communications revolution of telephone networks; a surveillance revolution of tiny listening and eventually camera devices planted in walls, vehicles and telephone receivers; and a transportation revolution of gasoline-powered vehicles on roads and steam locomotives pulling scores of box cars on rails.

Stalin perfected a totalitarian system that Vladimir Lenin began and developed. Lenin in turn got the idea from Karl Marx who invented but did not elaborate the notion of a 'Dictatorship of the Proletariat'. Lenin seized that concept and made it central to his version of communism. The Communist Party was a hierarchy of power that was concentrated at the pinnacle with an elite of committed, ruthless, farsighted revolutionaries. They issued commands that each layer and section below them dutifully fulfilled.

After seizing Russia's government, Lenin and his comrades established a pyramid of government power parallel to and overlapping the Communist Party's pyramid of power that extended to every factory, village, apartment building, school faculty and other workplace across the Soviet Union. Although Lenin was the supreme leader, his power was not total. He was brilliant at asserting soft psychological power to get others to follow him by the sheer weight of his domineering intellect and personality. The communist dictatorship possessed and wielded collective power with Lenin the first among equals. Those in the elite checked each other to prevent any one of them from amassing all power.

Yuri Pyatakov was among that revolutionary elite and explained the dictatorship's justification and powers:

> According to Lenin, the Communist Party is based on the principle of coercion which doesn't recognize any limitations or inhibitions. And the central idea of this principle is not coercion by itself but the absence of any limitation whatsoever – moral, political and even physical . . . Such a party is capable of achieving miracles and doing things which no other collective of man could achieve . . . A real Communist . . . that is a man who was raised in the Party and had absorbed its spirit deeply enough becomes himself a true miracle worker.

Unquestioning faith was the key to that miraculous empowerment:

> For such a Party a true Bolshevik [Communist] will readily cast out from his mind ideas in which he has believed for years. A true Bolshevik has submerged his personality in the collectivity, 'the Party', to such an extent that . . . [t]here is not life for him . . . outside the ranks of the Party and he would be ready to believe that black was white and white was black, if the Party required it. In order to become one with this great Party he would fuse himself with it, abandon his own personality, so that there is no particle left inside him which was not at one with the Party.[29]

What Stalin did was transform that collective dictatorship into a one-man tyranny. He ruled from the pinnacle of a power hierarchy in which each person dutifully performed his role and faced arrest, prison and even execution if he failed, was disloyal or merely suspected.

***

Like the totalitarian system, Stalin initiated neither the slave labour camps nor mass murder system, Lenin did. What Stalin did was to perfect the existing system's scale organization and efficiency. Historian Robert Conquest explained that: 'camps seem to have been in existence as early as mid-1918, but decrees legalizing them were passed in September 1918 and April 1919. The first true death camp seems to have been at Kholmogori near Archangel in 1921.'[30] By 1922, the Main Administration of Forced Labour governed a system of sixty-five slave or death prison camps. In October 1922, Lenin decreed that the Commissariat of Justice of the People's Commissariat of Internal Affairs (NKVD) would run the system now called the Main Administration of Places of Detention, better known as the Gulag. The number of inmates rose slowly, steadily to 30,000 by 1928, when Stalin victoriously ended his five-year campaign against his rivals. His power now surpassed that of Lenin before his first stroke in 1922. Over the next decade, he made his power totalitarian through a series of purges that imprisoned or executed ever more people. The Gulag's inmates soared to 2,000,000 by 1932 then doubled to 4,000,000 by 1937, when the number plateaued through 1942 as deaths roughly matched new inmates, then gradually subsided with fewer arrests during the Second World War. Overall, the Gulag warehoused as many as 20,000,000 slave labourers from Lenin's decree in 1918 to Stalin's death in 1953. Of those, at least one of four died from murder, disease and despair while the survivors existed in utter misery.[31]

***

Joseph Stalin brilliantly mastered the art of tyranny. He systematically eliminated his political rivals and amassed power until he established the world's first totalitarian system, known as Stalinism. He completed the Soviet Union's communization by nationalizing all industries, land and natural resources and developed the economy through command Five-Year Plans. He had millions of real or imagined enemies murdered or enslaved in labour camps. In alliance with America and Britain, he led the Soviet Union to victory over Nazi Germany in the Second World War. He expanded the Soviet Empire to engulf Eastern Europe and imposed communist regimes in East Germany, Poland, Czechoslovakia, Hungary, Romania and Bulgaria along with Estonia, Lativia, Lithuania and Moldova that were incorporated into the Soviet Union. The Red Army also imposed a communist regime on North Korea, but Stalin let tyrant Kim Il-sung rule independently. He began the nuclear weapons programme that successfully tested an atomic bomb in 1949 and eventually surpassed that of the United States in sheer destructive power. He remained a tyrant until his last breath, feared by his inner circle's sycophants and hundreds of millions of other repressed and exploited people across the Soviet empire and beyond. And, finally, he died not from an assassin but a stroke on 5 March 1953.

Joseph Stalin was as unique an individual as everyone else who has ever existed. So too was the scale of the crimes he committed. Yet Stalin was just the latest tyrant in a crowd that extends through humanity to its earliest and latest days. As such, Stalin is a face for a distinct type of tyrannical personality. In her pioneering book *The Origins of Totalitarianism,* which first appeared in 1949 when Stalin remained firmly in power, Hannah Arendt sought to answer these three key haunting questions: 'What happened? Why did it happen? How could it have happened?'[32]

Those questions guide *Joseph Stalin and the Art of Tyranny,* but they do not end with his totalitarian regime. Although Stalin is long dead, Stalinism lives on in three crucial ways, as a political system, as a bundle of political strategies and tactics and as a personality cult that is perhaps the key political strategy.

Stalinism the totalitarian political system was the model for the Eastern European countries and North Korea that the Soviet Union conquered during the Second World War and for the Communist Parties that later took power in China, Vietnam and Cuba. For complex reasons to be explained, thereafter the totalitarianism of those Stalinist regimes gradually diminished, most to the point where democratic revolutions transformed them from 1989 to 1991. Yet, a few like Russia,

China, Belarus and Vietnam are authoritarian regimes. Only North Korea and Cuba retain Stalinist regimes. Stalinism as a model bundle of political strategies and tactics along with the art of creating a personality cult has inspired actual dictators around the world including Saddam Hussein, Vladimir Putin, Xi Jinping, Hugo Chavez, Francisco Madero and Daniel Ortega, to name the best known of hundreds of recent ones; and would-be dictators like Viktor Orban, Rodrigo Duterte, Donald Tusk and Donald Trump.

An exploration of Stalin and Stalinism is critical to comprehending global politics not just during his lifetime but ever since and for the foreseeable future. *Joseph Stalin and the Art of Tyranny* reveals critical lessons for understanding tyrants and those realms of human nature that make them possible.

Chapter 1

RADICALIZATION

> 'We Georgians have our own code of a tooth for a tooth, an eye for an eye, a life for a life . . . No Georgian ever forgives an offense or an insult to himself, his family or to his forbearers, ever!' (Joseph Stalin)

> 'From his experience at the seminary he had come to the conclusion that men were intolerant, coarse, deceiving their flocks in order to hold them in obedience, that they intrigued, lied and as a rule possessed numerous faults and few virtues.' (Svetlana Alliluyeva)

> 'To become a good socialist, one must reject all tender, soft feelings of kinship, friendship, love, gratitude and even honour itself . . . A revolutionary knows only one science – the science of destruction and extermination.' (Sergei Nechaev)

> 'I would advise you to discard the "principle" of devotion to individuals. It is not the Bolshevik way. Be devoted to the working class, to its party, its state . . . But don't get it mixed up with devotion to people, which is just an empty and superfluous fad of intellectuals.' (Joseph Stalin)

Joseph Stalin was the revolutionary alias that Joseph Vissarionovich Djugashvili adopted in 1913. He was born on 6 December 1878, not on 21 December 1879, as he later claimed to confuse the secret police. Those dates are in the Julian calendar that will be used until 31 January 1918, when the Bolsheviks adopted the Gregorian calendar 13 days ahead.

Stalin was born and raised in Gori, a small Georgian city of 45,000 people.[1] His parents were Vissarion 'Besso' Djugashvili, a shoemaker, and Ekaterina 'Keke' Geladze Djugashvili, a laundress. His father was a rage-filled alcoholic who often beat him and his mother, who also at times hit and scolded him while also adoring him. When Stalin, nicknamed Soso, was five in 1883, his mother, backed by the village priest, forced his father to leave; he went to work in a shoe factory in Tbilisi, Georgia's provincial capital then called Tiflis.

Nature and nurture, genes and experiences, shape every person's character. Stalin is infamous for being paranoid, cruel, ambitious, spiteful, envious and vindictive, exacerbated by a deep inferiority complex.[2] How much genetics determined that, is impossible to say. Certainly his father's brutality, belittlement and, finally, abandonment was critical. Atop that, Stalin was small for his age and grew to just 5ft 4in. During his boyhood, he had two near-death experiences that further marred his appearance. Smallpox pitted his face and body. During a religious procession, a horse-drawn carriage struck him and broke his left arm; poorly set, his arm atrophied. Offsetting all that was the knowledge that he was the last born and only survivor of two brothers who died shortly after their births. His mother often reminded him that God blessed them with his miraculous survival so he should be a good boy. He was a rambunctious child who believed that somehow he was special and destined for great things. He grew up with an unquenchable drive to beat others figuratively and at times literally in any struggle.

Stalin may have loved his mother more than anyone else in his life. After he left home, he was affectionate and apologetic in the rare letters he wrote her with lines like: 'Dear Mother, please live for 10,000 years. Kisses, Soso' and 'I know you're disappointed in me but what can I do? I'm busy and can't write often.'[3] He invited her to Moscow in 1935, when they had this amusing, bittersweet exchange: '"Why did you beat me so often?" "That's why you turned out so well," she replied, before asking: "Joseph, what exactly are you, now?" "Well, remember the tsar? I'm something like a tsar." "You'd have done better to become a priest," she said, a comment that delighted Stalin.'[4]

Stalin grew up in Georgia, a remote province of the Russian empire with a language and culture distinct from that of the rulers. Georgia had been an independent kingdom until Russia annexed it in 1800. Stalin began learning Russian at a young age and eventually mastered it although his Georgian accent persisted. He later admitted one Georgian cultural trait deeply imbedded in his psyche. Like many clannish societies, blood feuds and vendettas were integral to Georgia's culture. Stalin explained: 'We Georgians have our own code of a tooth for a tooth, an eye for an eye, a life for a life . . . No Georgian ever forgives an offense or an insult to himself, his family or to his forbearers, ever!'[5]

Stalin was bicultural throughout his life, with his Russian and Georgian sides morphing from one to the other depending on circumstances. Historian Simon Montefiore described Stalin as a Potemkin Russian with a Georgian soul: 'His lifestyle and mentality remained Georgian. He talked Georgian, ate Georgian, sang Georgian, personally ruled Georgia through the local bosses, becoming involved in parochial politics, missed his childhood friends and spent almost half his last eight years in his own isolated fantasy Georgia.'[6]

Having been born into poverty as a Georgian, Stalin hated Russia's tsar, nobility, industrialists, financiers, merchants and landowners that controlled the economy and enriched themselves by exploiting masses of urban and rural labourers. Yet, he embraced the Russian side of his upbringing because Russia was politically, economically and culturally powerful and Georgia was so weak.

Stalin loved to read. His favourite teenage book was the novel *The Parricide*, by Alexander Kazbegi. Stalin never killed his real abusive father but dedicated his life to destroying the Romanov dynasty and Tsar Nicholas II, then ruling the Russian empire.

***

Russia's tsar was an absolute monarch whose decrees were laws. He had an advisory Council of State with ministers for the army, navy, foreign affairs, interior and secret police (Okhrana). He appointed all provincial governors. There was no national assembly and political parties were outlawed. Through the state body Holy Synod, he controlled the Russian Orthodox Church and its head the Patriarch. Alexander II did initiate two reforms in 1861, with decrees that emancipated the serfs and let villages govern themselves through local assemblies (*zemstrovs*). Nearly all Russians and other ethnic groups viewed the tsar as a near divine father figure, expressed through sayings like: 'Through God and Tsar Russia is strong'; 'Only God and the Tsar know'; 'Everything is under the power of God and the sovereign'.[7]

Political culture includes those elements of a group's culture – beliefs and behaviours – that shape politics. Russian political culture is characterized by deep-rooted authoritarianism, xenophobia and communalism formed by 1,600 years of violent history.[8] Russia began as a state imposed by Viking chief Rurik with his capital at Novgorod in 862. His son Oleg moved the capital to Kiev. Grand Prince Vladimir adopted Orthodox Christianity as Russia's faith in 988. The Russians had their own Orthodox Patriarch and developed the Cyrillic alphabet to translate the Bible into their own language. The Mongols invaded

Russia in 1236 and by 1242 had destroyed Kiev and overrun the entire realm. For two and a half centuries Russian Grand and regional princes paid tribute to the Mongolian empire. The Russians faced invaders from the west. Prince Alexander Nevsky of Novgorod defeated a Swedish army in 1240 and a Teutonic Knights army in 1242. The Russian Grand Prince established a new capital at Tver in 1315. Yuri, the prince of Moscow, fought to become the Grand Prince; he was killed in battle but his son Ivan won that title in 1328. Grand Prince Dmitry led a revolt and destroyed a Mongol army in 1380 and asserted power over the regional princes by 1382. After the Ottoman Turks captured Constantinople, the capital of the Byzantine emperor and the Orthodox patriarch, Russians insisted that their own Patriarch headed Orthodox Christianity and that Moscow was the Third Rome or capital after Rome and Constantinople. Grand Prince Ivan the III or the Great declared independence from the Mongol empire in 1480. After marrying the last Byzantine princess in 1472, Ivan III elevated himself to Tsar, a Russian version of Caesar. Ivan IV took title to all land (*oprichnina*) and distributed it as fiefs to his loyal followers (*oprichniki*). He earned the sobriquet 'the Terrible' as he and his followers tortured and murdered thousands of real or imagined enemies. Stalin would model his rule on that of Ivan the Terrible.[9] The Romanov dynasty took power in 1613 and would rule Russia until 1917.

During his reign from 1689 to 1725, Peter I or the Great tried to transform Russia from an Asiatic into a European culture. He toured north-west Europe for two years and brought back ideas, engineers and artists to lead that cultural revolution. He forced Russian nobles and merchants to shave their beards and trade oriental robes for Western suits. He established industries like shipbuilding, gun-making and cannon-casting. He founded the city of St. Petersburg on the Neva River just a few miles upstream of the Baltic Sea in 1703 and moved his capital there from Moscow in 1713. He had schools established for all noble and merchant children. He had Cyrillic reformed to make it easier to spell and understand and introduced Roman numerals. He set up the first Russian newspaper. He introduced the Table of Ranks in which anyone who wanted to become an official or officer started at the bottom and worked his way to the top. The Great Northern War lasted from 1701 to 1721 and Russia emerged the victor, surpassing in power the Swedish and Polish kingdoms.

Peter's reforms provoked a political tug-of-war between 'Westerners' and 'Slavophiles' that has persisted ever since. Westernizers who want to emulate and integrate with Europe and America began with Peter and prominently included Catherine the Great, Alexander I for his rule's first few years, Alexander II, Nicholas II and Boris Yeltsin. Prominent Slavophile leaders who shun the West and want Russia or the Soviet Union to be autonomous, authoritarian, conservative and dominant among Slavic peoples included Alexander I for most of his reign's last two-thirds, Nicholas I, Alexander III, Joseph Stalin and Vladimir Putin. Most tsars expressed a mix of western and Slavophile sentiments and policies.

Catherine I or the Great was a German princess who married Peter III, had her husband murdered in 1762 and from then until her death in 1796, brought in foreign writers, wits, painters, architects, composers and other artists and encouraged creative Russians to emulate them. She forced nobles at court to converse in French rather than Russian. Military campaigns expanded the Russian empire, most notably the conquest of Crimea and southern Ukraine in 1783. The term 'Potemkin Village' as an ideal façade masking a harsh reality arose during her reign. During a voyage down the Volga River, her chief advisor Prince Grigory Potemkin had an ideal artificial village with 'peasants' dismantled each night and set up downstream for the tsarina later to inspect so that she never saw a real Russian village's poverty and squalor.

Russian high culture peaked in the nineteenth century and the twentieth century's first 14 years.[10] Brilliant Russians excelled in each creative field such as fiction with Nikolai Gogol, Ivan Turgenev, Fyodor Dostoevsky, Leo Tolstoy and Maxim Gorky; poetry with Alexander Pushkin, Mikhail Lermontov and Fyodor Tyuchev; playwrights with Anton Chekov, Pushkin, Gogol, Gorky and Tolstoy; short story writers with Pushkin, Turgenev, Gogol, Tolstoy, Dostoevsky, Chekov; painters with Ilya Repnin, Valentin Serov, Vasily Surikov and Issac Levitan; and composers with Mikhail Glinka, Pyotr Tschaikovsky, Modest Mussorgsky and Nikolai Rimsky Korsakov. Undoubtedly, Russia could have produced just as many distinguished twentieth-century creators but the communists murdered, drove into exile or drove into mediocrity most of them.

Late nineteenth century Russia steadily modernized. An industrial revolution was transforming the economy as small craft production gave way to factories mass-producing goods. From 1860 to 1914, the number of newspapers soared from 13 to 856; literacy expanded from around one in ten to four in ten people; lower schools rose from 250 to more than 16,000; and the number of universities expanded from one to eight and students from 5,000 to 69,000.[11] Although the urban population expanded from 7,000,000 to 28,000,000, seven out of ten Russians remained peasants. Poverty was as pervasive as ever. In cities, the gap widened between the growing masses of working poor and the rich elite and comfortable middle class that employed them.

Unions and strikes were illegal, but labourers secretly organized and frequently stopped work to demand better pay and conditions. The government responded with laws that prevented women and children from night work in the textile industry; limited work hours to eight daily for 12 to 15-year-olds; limited work hours to eleven and a half daily for businesses with more than twenty employees; forbade work on Sundays and holidays; and made employers liable for workplace injuries. Those reforms did not appease radicals who demanded ever more sweeping ones.

***

Stalin was very bright with an excellent memory. His mother enrolled him in the Gori Church School when he was eight. He needed six years to finish the four-year course, although he graduated with an honours certificate in July 1894. Stalin's mother hoped he would become a priest. At age 14, Stalin passed the entrance exam for the Tbilisi Theological Seminary.

The seminary gave Stalin an monthly five-rouble stipend. Stalin recalled that: 'My father found out that along with the scholarship, I also earned money (five roubles a month) as a choirboy . . . and once I went out and saw him standing there: "Young man, sir," said Besso, "you've forgotten your father . . . Give me at least three roubles, don't be as mean as your mother."' With the seminary's authority behind him and now a teenager, Stalin felt powerful enough to resist: '"Don't shout!" replied Soso. "If you don't leave immediately, I'll call the watchman." Besso slunk away.'[12] He was stabbed to death in a drunken tavern brawl in 1909.

A seminary classmate recalled Stalin's mid-teenage piety: 'he was very believing, punctually attending all the divine services, was the leader of the church choir. I remember that he not only performed the religious rites but also always reminded us of their meaning.'[13] Yet Stalin soon lost faith in Christianity and embraced a secular, atheistic, revolutionary creed that demanded the total devotion of its followers.

In her memoirs, Stalin's daughter Svetlana insightfully interpreted his stories about that time of his life:

> A church education was the only systematic education my father ever had. I am convinced that the parochial schools in which he spent more than ten years played an immense role, setting my father's character for

> the rest of his life, strengthening and intensifying his inborn traits . . . From his experience at the seminary he had come to the conclusion that men were intolerant, coarse, deceiving their flocks in order to hold them in obedience, that they intrigued, lied and as a rule possessed numerous faults and few virtues . . . This lack of compromise, this inflexibility, this inability to agree with an opposing opinion even if it was obviously a good one, I also attribute to his experience at the seminary, where students had been imbued with fanaticism and intolerance.[14]

Students complained that the seminary authorities spied on them, searched their belongings, censored what they could read and dismissing and expelled them for trivial offenses. They condemned the authorities for teaching the glories of Russian history and culture while denigrating Georgian history and culture. The agitation peaked in 1883 with student protests and strikes that provoked the administration to expel eighty-seven students, with twenty-three of them exiled from Tiflis. The agitators did score a victory when the administration approved a course on Georgian history and culture. Other student strikes erupted in 1890 and 1895. Radical views penetrated the Tbilisi Theological Seminary. Ever more students abandoned the Orthodox Church's theology and embraced Marxism. And Stalin was among them.

***

What was the Marxist creed that so greatly inspired Stalin and countless others?

Karl Marx and his partner Friedrich Engels developed Communism as an ideology in reaction to the industrial revolution's worst excesses of exploited labour. Their key writings were the *Communist Manifesto* of 1848 and *Das Kapital* (published in three volumes in 1867, 1885 and 1894); Marx died in 1883 and Engels finished the last two volumes.

Marx was influenced by philosopher George Hegel's belief that history is driven by conflicts or dialectics among conflicting ideas worth fighting for, in which a dominant idea or thesis is challenged by an alternative or anti-thesis. That conflict leads to a synthesis between them which becomes the latest thesis and so on. Marx substituted classes for ideas as the reason for struggle. He insisted that history would have five critical stages. The first was primitive communism when people lived in small hunter-gatherer bands and shared what little they gathered to sustain themselves. The domestication of first animals, then plants let populations expand in numbers and live in one place. That resulted in a rigid pyramid of economic, political, social and religious power as a tiny elite suppressed and exploited masses of people who produced food along with a small class of people who made things like tools, weapons, dwellings and so on and a tiny class of merchants who exchanged things. There have been three stages of this pyramid of power and class conflict, one ancient based on slaves, another medieval based on serfs and, with industrialization, the contemporary one where the ruling bourgeoisie repressed and exploited the proletariat class of factory workers and other labourers. In each stage, the revolution inevitably came when the elite got richer and fewer and the masses poorer and more desperate. Marx claimed that the first two pyramids were briefly transformed when the oppressed overthrew their rulers, only to result in a restored pyramid of exploitation with slightly different characteristics. He claimed that inevitably the present-day proletariat would overthrow the bourgeoisie and lead humanity to its final historical stage, communism, where everyone shared the wealth and lived prosperous, happy lives. That revolution would begin in the most advanced industrial countries where the proletariat was the most numerous and thus powerful, places like Germany, Britain, France and America; a communist revolution in Russia could not occur because the proletariat was too small.

That simple creed inspired then and since countless people to embrace it, organize or join communist parties and fight for its fulfilment. In 1864, Marx himself helped organize the First Socialist International of political parties dedicated to working together for a global communist revolution, but the movement dissolved in 1876 in a bitter split as ever more parties embraced the related ideology of anarchism developed by Mikhail Bakunin. The Second Socialist International emerged in 1889 and lasted until 1914, when the socialist parties in Germany, Britain, France, Italy and Belgium failed to revolt against their ruling classes, but instead supported their countries in joining the First World War.

Marx claimed to ground his theories on history and that his history was scientific. That, of course, is false. Marx and his adherents have practised pseudo-history and pseudo-science. Marxists are polemicists who cherry-pick historical facts to justify their core ideological assertion that class warfare propels history. In reality, a myriad of related human and natural forces shape history, of which at times class conflict is one of many. The historian's task is to identify the most vital forces and explain the dynamic among them over time.

Marxism seeped into Russia through the state censorship.[15] Translated copies of *The Communist Manifesto* had circulated shortly after Marx published it. The first volume of Marx's *Das Kapital* was translated into Russian in 1872 and smuggled in. Articulate, charismatic Russian Marxists emerged during the mid- to late century, although most wrote and agitated in foreign exile. The first was Alexander Herzen who advocated agrarian populism called Narodnikism. The threat of arrest forced him to flee to London where he penned more essays that were smuggled into Russia and distributed. More than anyone, he inspired Alexander II to free the serfs in 1861. His *My Life and Thoughts* (1870) was a lyrical and profound memoir. Nikolai Chernyshevsky asserted a version of Marxism that emphasized agrarian socialism. He explained Marxism's key tenets and called for a revolution based on democracy, land reform, women's rights and a classless society in his 1862 novel *What Is To Be Done?: Stories about New People*. He was imprisoned from 1862 to 1883 and died in 1889. German Eduard Bernstein advocated a peaceful Marxist revolution that took power through ballots rather than bullets. Of course, that was only possible in countries with parliaments that let Marxist parties compete for seats. In contrast, Mikhail Bakunin advocated a violent overthrow of not just the monarchy but all authoritarian institutions, the abolition of private property and power to the people in their villages and neighbourhoods, a revolution he called anarchism. Bakunin euphemistically called assassinations, uprisings and other terrorist acts, 'propaganda by the deed'. Georg Plekhanov was the leading Russian Marxist during the 1890s. To evade arrest, he fled to Geneva where he formed the Emancipation of Labour Group and wrote the influential tract *Socialism and the Political Struggle* (1883).

Inspired by these ideas, radicals formed in Russia an array of revolutionary groups like People's Will, Land and Liberty, People's Freedom and Black Distribution. People's Will agents assassinated Tsar Alexander II on 1 March 1882. Sooner or later, the secret police destroyed those groups with arrests and executions or imprisonment. Then one group emerged that would not just endure but spearhead a communist revolution in Russia.

Nine delegates from three Marxist groups held what later was called the First Congress in Minsk from 13 to 15 March 1898. Among the delegates were Vladimir Lenin and Julius Martov from their Saint Petersburg League of Struggle for the Emancipation of the Working Class. They elected a three-man Central Committee of Stepan Radchenko, Boris Eidelman and Araki Kremer. They founded the journal *Iskra* (*The Spark*). They failed to agree to a common name for their movement.

***

Stalin attended Marxist study circles in Gori. Sylvester Djibladze led the local Marxist movement with its weekly journal *Kvali* (*The Furrow*) in Tbilisi. Stalin joined the group in 1898. Djibladze became Stalin's first mentor who encouraged and guided him with revolutionary duties and readings. Diehard revolutionaries like Sergei Nechaev inspired Stalin and countless others to emulate them with assertions like this: 'To become a good socialist, one must reject all tender, soft feelings of kinship, friendship, love, gratitude and even honour itself . . . He is not a revolutionary who pities anything in this world . . . A revolutionary knows only one science – the science of destruction and extermination . . . Poison, the knife, the noose – the revolution consecrates everything.'[16]

The seminary expelled Stalin in 1899, not for radical political agitation but because he failed to take the exams. For three months he worked as a clerk for the Tbilisi Geophysical Observatory where he had a small room. Stalin was involved in a railway strike in July and August 1900. After police raided his room but failed to catch him, he went underground and devoted his life to imposing a communist revolution on Russia.

Tbilisi's twenty-five leading Marxists voted to form a nine-man steering committee with Stalin a member in November 1901. Stalin received the mission to organize a Marxist movement in Batum, a Black Sea port and terminus of an oil pipeline from Baku on the Caspian Sea. He began writing essays for the underground press in Tbilisi. In one, he offered these encouraging words to his fellow revolutionaries: 'The sacrifices we make today in street demonstrations will be compensated a hundred-fold. Every militant who falls in the struggle or is torn out of our ranks rouses hundreds of fighters.'[17]

Stalin helped provoke a strike by 900 oil refinery workers in February 1902, when the company fired 389 of them. The Okhrana or secret police arrested and jailed thirty-two strike leaders. On 8 March, Stalin organized a march on the jail and demanded that authorities either release those incarcerated or incarcerate them all. The protester ranks swelled that day and into 9 March. When they refused to disperse, troops opened fire, killing fourteen and wounding fifty or so of them. Stalin escaped without injury.

The Okhrana arrested Stalin on 5 April 1902. He lingered in prison until 9 July 1903, when he received his first of four sentences of exile through 1917, during which he made five escape attempts of which three succeeded, two temporarily and one permanently. They sent him to the village of New Ida in the Balagan region of Irkutsk Province in Siberia. He arrived on 27 November 1902. Around this time, Stalin adopted the *nom de revolution* Koba, the name of the rebel hero of Alexander Kazbegi's novel *Parricide*.

Among the many reasons why a communist revolution eventually engulfed Russia was that, while the Tsarist regime was extremely corrupt and inept, it was not brutal enough. Exile to Siberia or the Arctic Circle involved being transported to some small town where the miscreant worked and lived under the often-myopic observation of local officials. The tsarist regime had a revolving-door penal system that let revolutionaries slip through their fingers to further undermine their authority. A communist revolution would never have happened if the tsarist regime was as systematically ruthless as the communists who overthrew them.

The communists eventually took power and imposed a totalitarian system on Russia because they were utterly ruthless and either murdered or imprisoned all those who opposed them. That merciless disregard for human life was among communism's appeals for Stalin. He later wrote: 'I would advise you to discard the "principle" of devotion to individuals. It is not the Bolshevik way. Be devoted to the working class, to its party, its state . . . But don't get it mixed up with devotion to people, which is just an empty and superfluous fad of intellectuals.'[18]

Stalin escaped in January 1904 and returned to Tiflis and the underground. He led planning for a series of armed robberies committed by others to finance the party, operations euphemistically called 'expropriations'. The Tiflis State Bank robbery yielded a hundred thousand rubles.[19]

Stalin was a delegate to the Bolshevik conference in Tammerfors, Finland, where he first met Lenin in 1905. Two decades later, he confessed his initial disappointing impressions:

> Lenin had long been drawn in my imagination as a giant, stately and imposing. How disenchanted I was to see a most ordinary man, below average height, in no way . . . different from ordinary mortals. Usually, a 'great man' is expected to arrive later at a meeting so that the members of the meeting should wait for his appearance with baited breath . . . How disenchanted I was when I learned that Lenin had arrived at the meeting before the delegates and, hiding in the corner, was simply having a conversation, a very ordinary conversation with very ordinary delegates. I won't conceal . . . that at the time this seemed to me at the time a kind of violation of necessary rules.[20]

That memory revealed a lot about both Stalin and Lenin, the former's idealist and pedantic notion of leadership and the latter's down-to-earth personality and political skills.

***

Among Marxism's shibboleths is that grand economic forces and class struggle determine history, not individuals. Theoretically, Marxists condemn the notion that 'Great Men' shape history as an illusion. Yet, history belies that belief with countless examples of how leadership – good, bad and mediocre – crucially effects the outcome of political struggles.

Ironically, among history's most influential leaders was Vladimir Lenin.[21] Without his leadership, a communist revolution would not have engulfed Russia when and how it did; the ongoing social democratic revolution that Lenin destroyed most likely would have succeeded. If so, the history of Russia and the world beyond would have sharply differed from what actually happened, with tens of millions of lives saved rather than exterminated.

Instead, Lenin elaborated Marx's ideas, established and led a communist party and wielded it to overthrow Russia's government and impose a communist dictatorship. How did he achieve all that? Varying mixes of character, choices and chance explain his life like any other.

Lenin exuded authority with his razor-edged intellect, oratory, confidence and demands. Although of average height, he stood out with his bald dome, pointed beard, fierce brown eyes, scowl and, most vitally, impassioned speeches justifying violent revolution. Although he was an authoritarian, he mostly sought to dominate others by convincing rather than forcing them to yield to his commands and beliefs. He was willing to forgive past differences for the sincere devotion of his followers going forward: 'It is wrong to recall mistakes that have been completely set right.'[22]

Lenin's real name was Vladimir Ilich Ulyanov, bestowed shortly after his birth on 10 April 1870. He was born in Simbirsk, a town on the Volga River a thousand miles south-east of Moscow and into an upper middle-class family whose father was the province's Inspector of Popular Schools. He was the third of six children, with the oldest Alexander.

Lenin was one-eighth Jewish from his mother's side but was raised an Orthodox Christian. He took pride in the Jewish part of his ancestry. Writer Maxim Gorky later recalled that Lenin considered Jews superior in intellect, enterprise and progressiveness to Russians: 'I feel sorry for those people who are intelligent. We don't have many intelligent persons. We are a predominately talented people, but we have a lazy mentality. A bright Russian is almost always a Jew or a person with an admixture of Jewish blood.'[23]

Lenin was a very bright but rambunctious child, critical, demanding, sarcastic and short-fused. He won admission to the city's elite Classical Gymnasia school where he got the highest grades for most of his classes. The crucial event of Lenin's youth came when he was 16 and his brother Alexander was executed along with four others on 8 May 1887, for a plot to assassinate Tsar Alexander III. Alexander was then a 20-year-old student at Saint Petersburg University, when he joined a radical group that embraced Marxist and anarchist ideals. The date they chose for the assassination was 1 March 1887, the sixth anniversary of Alexander II's murder by another radical group. An Okhrana or secret police informer supplied the plot's evidence.

His brother's execution radicalized rather than intimidated and shamed Lenin. Around that time, his previous questioning of Christianity turned to atheism and Marxism increasingly attracted him. He sought and achieved admission to Kazan University in 1887. He joined a Marxist study group, was arrested on 5 December 1887 and was expelled along with thirty-nine others the next day.

Lenin did not immediately join the revolutionary underground. With both his father and older brother dead, he became the family's head as they moved to a large farm his mother bought near Samsara. He managed the farm and its peasant labourers poorly. He spent much of his time teaching himself English and translating Marx's *Communist Manifesto* into Russian. He and his family sold the farm and moved to Samsara where Lenin formed a local Marxist circle and amassed a library of Marxist books and pamphlets. He also studied university subjects by reading the course curriculums. His petition was accepted to take Saint Petersburg University's gruelling series of final examinations in July and September 1889 and he earned a First Class Degree with honours. He returned to Samsara where he studied jurisprudence and practiced law in 1892 and 1893. He moved to Saint Petersburg in August 1893, where he joined a law firm and Marxist study group. He made his first trip abroad, to Geneva where he met George Plekhanov in May 1895, then journeyed to Paris where he hobnobbed with an array of Marxist revolutionaries. After he returned to Saint Petersburg, he tried to unify in organization and thought an array of Marxist groups, with Yuli Martov's Youngsters the most popular and dynamic. They formed the Union of Struggle for the Emancipation of the Working Class with Lenin and Martov the most prominent among the five-man steering committee. The Okhrana cracked down in August 1896, with arrests of the group's leaders including Lenin and Martov and sentences of three years to remote Siberian towns on 26 January 1897.

Lenin turned his exile into a sabbatical in which he developed his own version of Marxism eventually called Leninism. Among the scores of essays he wrote during his life, the key texts were *The Development of Capitalism in Russia* (1899), *What Is to Be Done?* (1902) and *Imperialism: The Highest Stage of Capitalism* (1916) and *The State and Revolution* (1917). He rejected one key Marxist concept, embraced a concept that Marx introduced but did not develop and made both central to Leninism.

Marx insisted that that communist revolutions were impossible without preceding 'bourgeois' or liberal democratic revolutions that overthrew authoritarian regimes. The most advanced industrial societies with the largest proletariats would first realize communist revolutions. Lenin realized that the elite in advanced industrial societies could avoid revolutions by paying off workers with higher wages and better conditions. He argued that revolutions were most likely in countries like Russia where industrialization was just beginning and the work conditions were the harshest. Even then, owners could co-opt disruptive workers with superficial handouts.

What was vital was Marx's related notion of a 'Dictatorship of the Proletariat' embodied by the Communist Party as history's vanguard, leading the way through a revolutionary struggle to a classless utopia. Lenin conceived the 'Dictatorship of the Proletariat' as an elite guard of farsighted zealots committed to a communist revolution at all costs. The Communist Party would be a dictatorship that its members would unquestionably obey and after taking power, would wield total power to transform that country into a classless utopia. He explained that: 'Only the Communist Party is capable of unifying, educating and organizing a vanguard of the proletariat and not the whole mass of the working people that alone will be capable of withstanding the inevitable petty bourgeois vacillations of this mass.'[24]

After being released, Lenin left Russia for 15 years of foreign exile that included prolonged residences in Zurich, London, Geneva and Paris along with shorter stints in other cities. He devoted those years to developing and leading a revolutionary communist movement for Russia. He switched his last name to Lenin as a cover, although the police soon learned about the change.

Fifty-one delegates from several Marxist groups convened the Second Congress at Brussels from 29 July to 6 August 1902, with Lenin, George Plekhanov and Martov contending for leadership. When Belgian authorities shut them down, they moved their Congress to London until 23 August. They formally adopted the name Russian Social Democratic Workers Party.

They split over their goals, with Lenin advocating a violent revolution led by a Dictatorship of the Proletariat and Plekhanov and Martov calling for peaceful change by demanding a Russian parliament, free elections and civil rights. Lenin scored a crucial propaganda victory when he called his faction 'Majoritarians' or Bolsheviks after winning a procedural vote and he labelled the moderates as 'Minoritarians' or Mensheviks. Actually, Mensheviks outnumbered Bolsheviks then and thereafter until the 1917 revolution. A third faction was the Jewish Bund whose five delegates walked out after Lenin and Martov rejected their demand to have more representatives.

Nonetheless, the Bolsheviks and Mensheviks kept a shaky alliance. During that Congress and each subsequent one, the delegates elected an eight-man Central Committee that governed the Party, with five Mensheviks including Martov and Plekhanov and three Bolsheviks, including Lenin. Lenin did ensure that his own followers dominated the Party journal, *Iskra*.

***

An insurrection erupted in Russia in early 1905.[25] The previous year, Japan went to war against Russia to secure its economic privileges in China's north-eastern region of Manchuria. That war worsened existing mass poverty with soaring prices as food and other vital goods dwindled as the government mobilized them for the army. The army and navy suffered humiliating defeats and wretched conditions that diminished morale and authority.

Orthodox Priest George Gapon sought to transform Russia into a constitutional monarchy that alleviated harsh factory wages and conditions, lowered prices for food and other goods and distributed land to the peasants.[26] He worked with the Union of Russian Factory Workers of Saint Petersburg to draft and sign a petition that called on Nicholas II to embrace those reforms. The petition read: 'Sire – We, the workers and inhabitants of Saint Petersburg . . . come to . . . seek justice and protection. We are impoverished; we are oppressed, overburdened with excessive toil, contemptuously treated . . . We are suffocating in despotism and lawlessness.'[27]

Gapon led several thousand men, women and children in a march to the tsar's Winter Palace to present him the petition on 9 January 1905. The tsar and his family were not there. Nervous troops opened fire and killed or wounded scores of protesters as the survivors fled.

That slaughter transformed the tsar's image from a benign father-figure into a malevolent despot in countless minds. It also provoked mass strikes, demonstrations and destruction. In the countryside, peasant mobs attacked, looted and destroyed over 3,000 estates while the army crushed over 2,700 peasant uprisings. There were mutinies in the army and navy. The most serious was a mutiny by the battleship *Potemkin*'s crew in Odessa harbour as a mass revolt erupted ashore. Loyal troops killed over 2,000 rioters and wounded another 3,000 before they smothered that uprising.[28]

In Saint Petersburg, the Menshevik Social Democrats led by Leon Trotsky formed the Soviet (Council) of Workers' Deputies on 17 October 1905. To propagate their view, they began a newspaper, *Izvestia* (*News*). The authorities arrested Trotsky and other key leaders on 3 December and in the following days crushed an uprising by their followers.

Nicholas II signed on 17 October, a Manifesto that promised a parliament or Duma and civil rights. That inspired liberal leaders to found the Party of Constitutional Democrats (Kadets), conservatives the Union of 17 October Party (Octobrist) Party and labour unionists the Labourite Party (Trudoviks). The tsar approved other reforms including easing press censorship and strengthening the legal authority of village councils (*zemstrovs*) that Alexander II had authorized in 1862.

For the Duma election held from 26 March to 20 April, the Kadets, Trudoviks and Octobrists ran candidates while the Social Democrats and Social Revolutionaries boycotted it. The Kadets, Trudoviks and Octobrists respectively won 184, 124 and 38 of 497 seats. The Duma convened in the Winter Palace's Coronation Hall on 27 April 1906. The Duma could pass laws but required approval of the State Council and tsar before they could take effect. The tsar retained his absolute powers including being able to suspend the Duma or any laws. Nicholas first appointed Ivan Goremykan as prime minister but when he proved ineffective replaced him with Peter Stolypin on 21 July 1906.

Stolypin initiated land reform that divided communal land among peasant families and let them own their share. Agricultural production soared with the private ownership and initiatives it encouraged. The trouble was that only about three of ten peasants were landowners while the rest remained tenants. Stolypin survived nine assassination attempts until the tenth succeeded on 18 September 1911. The tsar responded to Stolypin's death not with a eulogy but a warning: 'Now there will be no more talk about reform.'[29]

***

During the 1905 revolution, Lenin and his Bolsheviks could only sit restlessly in their foreign perches, reading newspaper stories about the turmoil and violence. Lenin would carefully study the events of 1905 as a dress rehearsal for a later revolution, trying to extract critical lessons about what worked and what failed.

Lenin and thirty-three Bolsheviks convened the Russian Social Democratic Workers Party's Third Congress at London from 25 April to 10 May 1905. He did so in defiance of the Mensheviks who convened their own conference in Geneva. The Bolsheviks formed a Combat Committee to prepare for a future violent revolution by infiltrating the army, navy, factories, mines and other organizations and mobilizing their members.

Stalin was among 112 delegates who attended the Fourth Party Congress in Stockholm from 8 to 25 May 1906. Nearly three times more delegates – 300 – attended the Fifth Congress in London from 13 May to 1 June 1907. There were 105 Bolsheviks representing 33,000 members, 97 Mensheviks for 43,000 members, 59 General Jewish Labour Bundists for 33,000 members, 44 Polish Social Democrats for 28,000 members, 29 Latvian Social Democrats for 13,000 members and four non-faction delegates. Stalin was a delegate but mostly observed in the proceedings. Each Congress and the Central Committee that its delegates selected had two types of members, 'full' who spoke and voted and 'candidates' who only spoke.

Stalin married Ekatarina 'Kato' Svanidze, a seamstress, in June 1906 and they had a son, Yakov, born on 31 March 1907. To evade increasingly suspicious authorities, they moved to Baku. Tuberculosis or typhus killed his wife on 22 November 1907 and he left Yakov with her family to raise.

The Okhrana recaptured Stalin on 25 March 1908 and returned him to Solvychegodsk. He escaped in 1911 and this time fled to Saint Petersburg's underground. There Stalin became close to Sergei Alliluyeva, an electrician, and his wife Olga Fedorenko, a beautiful, passionate women who enjoyed many lovers. Both backed the revolution and provided a safe house for agents. Among their children was Nadya Alliluyeva, Stalin's future second wife. The Okhrana recaptured Stalin on 22 April 1912 and this time sent him to the town of Narim in the Arctic Circle province of Tomsk. He escaped on 1 September, first to Moscow's underground then to Saint Petersburg. His freedom was fleeting.

During the Social Democratic Workers Party's conference in Prague from 6 to 11 January 1912, Stalin was elected to the ten-man Central Committee. Missions took him to Vienna then Krakow. He adopted the last name, 'Stalin', or 'Steel', in 1913. He won accolades for his article, 'Marxism and the National Question' published in the party's journal *Pravda* in January 1913. Lenin enthusiastically embraced Stalin for his years of dedication to the revolution capped by his article. According to Stalin, Lenin asked him if he wrote the whole article. Stalin said yes and asked if he made any mistakes. Lenin replied, 'No, on the contrary, splendid'.[30]

The Okhrana arrested Stalin in February 1913 and this time exiled him to Turukhansk in Siberia, where he spent four years. While he languished in the wilderness, cataclysmic events engulfed Europe and created upheavals ideal for revolution.

Chapter 2

REVOLUTION

'There is dogmatic Marxism and creative Marxism . . . It is quite possible that Russia will be the country that will show the path to socialism . . . One should reject the obsolete concept that only Europe can show us the right path.' (Joseph Stalin)

'Had I not been present in 1917 in Petersburg, the October Revolution would still have taken place – on the condition that Lenin was present and in command. If neither Lenin nor I had been present in Petersburg, there would have been no October Revolution.' (Leon Trotsky)

'In a period of revolution it is impossible to halt, you have to move – either forward or backward. Therefore whoever tries to halt in time of revolution must inevitably lag behind. And whoever lags receives no mercy: the revolution pushes him into the camp of counterrevolution.' (Joseph Stalin)

'The remedy invented by Lenin and Trotsky, the general suppression of democracy, is worse than the evil it is supposed to cure.' (Rosa Luxemburg)

'We are exterminating the bourgeoisie as a class. During the investigation, do not look for evidence that the accused acted in deed or word against Soviet power. The first question that you ought to put are: to what class does he belong? What is his origin? What is his education or profession? And it is these questions that ought to determine the fate of the accused. In this lies the significance and essence of the Red Terror.' (Felix Dzerzhinsky)

A revolution rapidly and systematically changes something into something else, related but distinct. Probably most people think of political revolution when they mull the notion.[1] Vivid examples come to mind of revolutions that transformed monarchies into republics as in France; authoritarian regimes into communist regimes as in China; communist regimes into liberal democracies as in East Germany, Poland, Czechoslovakia, Hungary, Bulgaria and Romania; democracies into fascist regimes as in Italy, Japan and Germany; communist into authoritarian regimes as in Russia and China; a republic into a monarchy as twice in France; a secular authoritarian regime into an Islamist authoritarian regime as in Iran. There are half-revolutions like those of England and France from absolute into constitutional monarchies. There are nationalist and liberal movements that transform colonies into independent nations with a republic like the United States from Britain's constitutional monarchy and empire. And there are two-stage revolutions like Russia's; swift change first from an absolute monarchy into a republic and then from a republic into a communist regime. And these are just the more prominent illustrations.

Nonetheless, political revolutions are quite rare. Severe and worsening human conditions like poverty, repression, exploitation, corruption, brutality, violence and incompetence may undermine an existing political system's authority and legitimacy, but alone are not enough to provoke a revolution. For a political revolution to have a chance of success, four ingredients are crucial – an alternative, appealing ideology; a revolutionary movement with a military wing that fights the regime and a political wing that builds a rival political, economic, social and cultural system; adaptive, ruthless leaders; and some triggering event like a massacre, natural disaster or defeat in war. Around the globe at any time there are scores of countries with revolutionary conditions but little chance of revolutions because they lack one or more of those four keys.

***

Russia was certainly ripe for revolution in 1917.[2] For nearly two and a half years, Russians had been fighting an unwinnable war, suffering humiliating defeats, millions of dead and wounded and worsening food shortages, poverty, soaring prices and despair. Tsar Nicholas II was an absolute monarch and an utterly inept ruler. His throne rested atop bureaucratic, army and secret police pyramids of power riddled with corruption, incompetence and sloth.[3]

The First World War made the Russian Revolution possible.[4] The governments of Russia and the other Great Powers had no intention of going to war in August 1914, but did so anyway. No one country caused the war, but to varying degrees each Great Power was responsible for failing to take decisive diplomatic measures that might have prevented it. Two alliances split the continent. The Central Powers included Germany and Austria-Hungary and the Alliance included France and Russia. Britain was aligned if not formally allied with France and Russia. Russia and Serbia were allied.

An assassination provoked a crisis that the Great Powers failed to resolve. Bosnia-Herzegovina had been an Ottoman empire province with roughly equal numbers of Orthodox Serbs, Catholic Croatians and Muslims. In 1908, Austria annexed Bosnia-Herzegovina that neighbouring Serbia had wanted for itself. The Serbian government sponsored the terrorist group Black Hand to undermine Austrian rule. On 28 June 1914, Black Hand member Gavrilo Princip murdered visiting Austrian Archduke Franz Ferdinand and his wife Sophia. Austrian police swiftly arrested Princip and other Black Hand members who, under harsh interrogation, admitted their link with Serbia's government.

Austria's government issued to Serbia's government a ten-point ultimatum on 23 July. Serbia's government agreed to nine of the demands but refused to let Austrian police shadow Serbian police in investigating the conspiracy. Austria declared war on Serbia on 28 July. That set off a chain reaction among the alliances. Russia mobilized its army against Austria on the 30th which provoked Germany to mobilize against Russia, then France against Germany. The war began on 4 August, when the German army attacked France and neutral Belgium. That provoked Britain to join France, Russia, Serbia and now Belgium against Germany and Austria. The war soon stalemated on all three fronts, Western, Eastern and Serbian.

When the war began, Russia's army numbered 5,971,000 men in 115 infantry and 38 cavalry divisions.[5] It was and remained the world's largest army even as its ranks steadily diminished but was plagued by a vicious cycle of bad leadership, supply, intelligence and morale. About half the army was posed to march west in August 1914 and the sheer weight of all those troops might have steamrolled the outnumbered German armies facing them. But German General Paul von Hindenburg was as brilliant as Russian General Alexander Samsonov was clueless. He outmanoeuvred and crushed the Russian army at the Battle of Tannenberg from 21 to 30 August, inflicting 90,000 casualties while suffering only 14,000; Samsonov committed suicide. Hindenburg then outmanoeuvred General Paul von Rennenkampf at the Battle of Masurian Lakes from 2 to 16 September, inflicting 125,000 casualties while suffering another 14,000.

The Germans pushed the Russians back nearly a hundred miles before their offensive ground to halt. On the Eastern Front as on the Western, Serbian and, from May 1915, Italian Fronts, two technologies, machine guns and barbed wire, transformed the initial brief war of manoeuvre into a stagnant war of increasingly elaborate networks of trenches. Within sandbag bunkers, two men with a machine gun, one firing and the other feeding it long belts of ammunition, could slaughter literally hundreds of enemy soldiers struggling to advance through coils of barbed wire.

As Austrian and Turkish armies joined German armies against Russia, the Eastern Front stretched along a shifting 600-mile line between the Baltic and Black Seas. It was less rigid than the Western Front because it was longer, with more opportunities for creative generals to punch through relatively thinly defended stretches of the enemy front. But every offensive, however initially successful, inevitably ground to a halt against hastily dug-in enemy troops.

Nicholas II committed a fateful act on 5 September 1915, that would weaken Russia's already fraying political and military fronts. He left Petrograd for the front-line headquarters where he would act as commander-in-chief. That was a disastrous decision. He knew nothing about military affairs and his presence would slow the high command's decision-making. The Russian people would attribute any subsequent defeats to their tsar's incompetence even though he merely signed off on strategies devised by consensus among his generals.

Meanwhile, in Petrograd, Tsarina Alexandra came under the influence of Grigori Rasputin, a long-haired, wild-eyed, bearded mystic and womanizer whose alleged healing powers seemed to alleviate her son Alexei's haemophilia. Rumours spread that Rasputin had seduced Alexandra and her four daughters. A coterie of army officers murdered Rasputin during a drunken orgy they invited him to on the night of 30 December 1916. Yet the damage to Alexandra's reputation could not be repaired.

***

Russia's revolution went through two stages in 1917. In March, a social democratic coup forced Nicholas II to abdicate then formed a democratic government. In October, a communist coup drove out the social democrats and formed a dictatorship.

The government announced on 19 February that bread rationing would begin on 1 March. Several thousand workers, mostly female, protested the war, worsening shortages, rising prices, abysmal pay, harsh conditions and the tsar's inept rule in Petrograd's Vyborg industrial district on Woman's Day, 23 February. That inspired tens of thousands of protesters, including workers, students, army deserters and radicals, many waving red flags and banners with 'Down with the Tsar' and 'Down with the War', to clog central Petrograd and converge on Nevsky Prospect the next day. That led to a general strike with protesters surging through the streets on 25 February. All three days, the police and Cossack officers kept their men from lowering their rifles and firing, despite some protesters shouting vile insults and looting stores.

From his headquarters at Pskov, Tsar Nicholas ordered General Sergei Khabalov, the Petrograd Military District commander, to suppress the protesters on 26 February. Officers ordered their mostly reluctant troops to open fire. Most pulled triggers, some aiming upward. The fusillades killed or wounded hundreds of people and the fleeing crowds trampled scores more. Several hundred soldiers of the Pavlovsky Regiment mutinied and tried to join the mob. Khabalov ordered Cossacks to surround the mutineers, who surrendered. Khabalov had the mutineers disarmed, nineteen ringleaders arrested and the rest confined to their barracks.

A coalition of Menshevik, Social Revolutionary and Bolshevik leaders formed an Executive Committee and announced on February their establishment of the Petrograd Soviet in a Tauride Palace wing opposite from that occupied by the Duma. They called on labourers, soldiers and sailors to elect deputies to the Petrograd Soviet for an assembly the next day. That inspired swift elections in workplaces and barracks with 3,000 delegates, two-thirds soldiers and sailors, packed into Tauride Palace's Catherine Hall on 28 February. The Soviet's Executive Council included six Mensheviks, two Bolsheviks, two Social Revolutionaries and five independent socialists. Their first act was to change the assembly's name to the Petrograd Soviet of Worker and Soldier Deputies.

Meanwhile, a coterie of generals in Petrograd agreed that the tsar must abdicate and sent him a telegram urging him to do on 1 March. Nicholas I meekly agreed to abdicate in favour of his 12-year-old son Aleksei. Doctors told Nicholas that Aleksei was so weak from haemophilia that he would not survive the year. Nicholas then abdicated in favour of his younger brother Grand Duke Mikhail.

Word of the crown's transfer from one Romanov brother to another provoked howls of rage among the protesters packed within and outside Tauride Palace. That intimidated Mikhail into announcing he would not accept the crown after all. The end of Romanov rule inspired radicals in Petrograd and other cities to swarm into government offices to tear down any royal symbols and hoist red flags atop the roofs or unfurl them from top-floor windows.

The Duma's assemblymen voted to form a provisional government with Prince Georgy Lvov as prime minister, Alexander Kerensky as justice minister and other prominent members to head the other ministries. Kerensky was the government's only avowed socialist.[6] He was renowned for his compassion, eloquence and call for sweeping civil rights, and industrial and agrarian reforms. Over the next several months, Kerensky worked with the Duma's leaders to devise and pass those reforms. Like the French Revolution, the traditional formal language yielded to equalitarian expressions as the people were now 'citizens' (*grazhdanin*) rather than subjects, with 'comrade' (*tovarich*) the salute among working class (*trudiakhshchisia*) citizens in their 'democracy' (*demokratiia*).

The provisional government committed two acts, one generous, the other honourable, that proved to be self-destructive. It pardoned and released political prisoners and upheld its alliance and thus the ongoing war. The first mass anti-war protest against the new government occurred on 20 and 21 April and more would follow through the spring, summer and autumn.

A parallel revolution spread across the countryside. Peasant tenants on thousands of estates confiscated the land from its owners and split it among themselves. The Social Revolutionary Party's leaders announced their formation of the First All-Russian Peasant Assembly and election for delegates from 4 to 25 May.

***

Where was Bolshevik leader Vladimir Lenin when Russia's revolution erupted? He had spent most of the war years in Zurich, writing and struggling to inspire his followers in exile or underground in Russia. Published in 1916, his book *Imperialism: The Highest Stage of Capitalism* explained why the working class did not unite across national borders when war erupted in August 1914, but instead dutifully fought for their respective countries. He argued that over previous generations European governments used profits from their foreign colonies to pay for political and economic reforms at home that alleviated working conditions that let them co-opt the proletariat. He predicted that the stalemated war would worsen economic and social conditions that made revolution increasingly likely, especially in Russia. In that, he was prescient.

During his Swiss exile, Lenin's right-hand men in Petrograd were the Bolshevik Party's Russian Bureau of Alexander Shlyapnikov, Pyotr Zalutsky and Vyacheslav Molotov. The Bolshevik Party's armed militia were called the Red Guards whose companies stockpiled arms stolen or bought from the black market. The Russian Bureau issued Order Number One on 1 March, that called on troops in every regular army regiment to form their own soviets that would obey the Petrograd Soviet's orders and reject those of the provisional government. By July, the Bolsheviks had over 20,000 armed Red Guards in Petrograd, Moscow and other cities.

Joseph Stalin and Lev Kamenev were among thousands of political prisoners released by the provisional government's amnesty. On 12 March, they arrived in Petrograd and presented themselves to the Russian Bureau. Stalin and Kamenev received editorial posts alongside Molotov at *Pravda*. Stalin's key job was writing unsigned editorials that explained the Bolshevik position on the unfolding revolution.

Molotov and Kamenev squabbled over policy, with Molotov opposed and Kamenev conciliatory toward the provisional government. Stalin backed Kamenev and the two got the Politburo to fire Molotov as *Pravda*'s top editor as well as his membership on the Presidium, Politburo and Petrograd Soviet's executive committee, with Stalin replacing him in all those powerful positions. Stalin had scored a stunning victory in his first open political fight against a rival. Ironically, he would later have his ally, Kamenev, purged and eventually executed, while Molotov, his political enemy at the time, became one of his most devoted sycophants and retained power until after the tyrant's death.

Yet the Russian Bureau made Stalin a conditional rather than full member. The Bolshevik leaders were concerned about a rumour that he had been and perhaps remained a police informer.[7] An official Soviet history published in 1962 observed: 'Concerning Stalin it was reported that he had been an agent of the Central Committee in 1912 and therefore it would be desirable to include him, but in view of certain personal characteristics of his, the Bureau decided to invite him only in an advisory capacity.'[8] Stalin angrily denied the rumour and insisted on his devotion to the Bolshevik Party and future communist revolution.

Among the provisional government's reforms was to legalize all political parties. From 27 March to 2 April, the Bolsheviks held a conference in which they debated how to respond to the ongoing revolution. Stalin was among those who advocated cooperating with the provisional government and other parties and reuniting with the Mensheviks. The conference ended without a consensus.

During these months, Stalin stayed with the Alliluyev family, who he had befriended during his previous sojourn in Petrograd. Sergei was an active party member and his daughter Nadya was a typist at Bolshevik Party headquarters. Stalin and Nadya would later marry.

Meanwhile, Lenin got the German government's permission to cross Germany with thirty-one followers en route to Russia. The Germans clearly had an interest in helping a group of revolutionaries return to their homeland and overthrow its government. Lenin insisted that each member paid his or her own fare and other expenses to avoid appearing like German agents. However, the rumoured transit price Lenin may have paid Berlin was peace at any price once the communists took power. That is certainly what happened.[9]

Lenin's entourage included Grigori Zinoviev, Karl Radek, and his wife Nadezhda Krupskaya, who retained her maiden name. The revolutionaries embarked at Zurich on 17 March, changed trains at the border where they received their own car, although the train was not 'sealed' or locked as is popularly believed. It took six days for them to reach the German Baltic Sea port of Sassnitz, where they took a ferry to Trelleborg, Sweden, then trains to Stockholm and Helsinki. A delegation of Bolsheviks, Mensheviks and Social Revolutionaries greeted Lenin and his entourage when they reached Petrograd on 3 April.

Over the next several months, Lenin committed a series of controversial acts that undercut the power of himself and the Bolshevik Party. On 4 April, he asserted his ten-point 'April Theses'. The Bolshevik Party would rename itself the Communist Party, dedicated to overthrowing the provisional government and imposing a communist government. To that end, the Bolsheviks would take over all soviets and expel members from other parties. The Second Socialist International would give parties the choice to join the Communist Party or be expelled. Rural soviets would confiscate all land from their owners and transfer title to the peasants residing there. He denounced Mensheviks, Kadets and Social Revolutionaries for collaborating with rather than fighting the provisional government.

The Petrograd Bolshevik Committee, led by Zinoviev and Kamenev, voted overwhelmingly against Lenin's April Theses by thirteen to two on 8 April. The opponents condemned Lenin's slogans 'all power to the soviets' and 'all land to the peasants' as impractical and premature. Those policies violated the Marxist creed that a bourgeois revolution should proceed a proletariat revolution and that peasants were peripheral rather than central to either revolution.

For the initial Bolshevik Party headquarters, Lenin chose Kschessinska Mansion, the former home of the famed ballerina Maria Kschessinska who was Nicholas II's mistress. Lenin's inner circle included Yakov Sverdlov and Stalin. With Lenin's backing, Stalin published a *Pravda* editorial on 14 April that defied those who opposed the rural revolution: 'We urge the peasants, the country poor of all Russia, to take this business [changing ownership of land] into their own hands and to move it ahead.'[10]

Despite these controversies, within a month of Lenin's return, Bolshevik Party membership soared from around 30,000 to 80,000. On 24 April, the Bolshevik Party Congress convened with 109 delegates. The first vote approved Lenin's proposal to expand the Central Committee from nine to thirteen members. During the subsequent election, Stalin won 97 votes, just behind Lenin and Zinoviev with 104 and 101 respective votes and ahead of Kamenev with 95.[11]

The next issue was highly controversial. Lenin had Stalin propose a resolution with contradictory principles. The first was that 'every nation forming a part of Russia must be recognized as having the right to secede freely and to form an independent state'. The second was that the 'interests of the working class demand the merging of the workers of all nationalities of Russia into unified proletariat organizations . . . Only such an amalgamation of the workers of different nationalities into single organizations enables the proletariat to wage a victorious struggle against international capital and bourgeoisie nationalism.' The delegates approved the resolution by 56 to 16 with 18 abstentions.[12]

The Central Committee met after Congress dissolved itself. Lenin proposed and the Central Committee approved a four-man steering bureau later called the Political Bureau. It included Lenin, Stalin, Zinoviev and Kamenev. Within two months of arriving as a poorly-known comrade who had languished for years in Siberia, Stalin had won a series of political contests that carried him into the Bolshevik Party's executive elite alongside Lenin himself.

Lenin periodically used Stalin as a troubleshooter to resolve conflicts that arose within the Bolshevik Party. During the months before the Bolshevik coup, Stalin's main work was editing and writing articles for *Pravda*. In a May article entitled 'Lagging behind the Revolution', he wrote these words inspired and praised by Lenin: 'In a period of revolution it is impossible to halt, you have to move – either forward or backward. Therefore whoever tries to halt in time of revolution must inevitably lag behind. And whoever lags receives no mercy: the revolution pushes him into the camp of counterrevolution.'[13] With that imperative, Lenin would pressure his mostly reluctant comrades to initiate a revolution they believed was premature until he finally won them over.

***

The most famous Russian revolutionary after Lenin reached Petrograd on 17 May.[14] Until then, Leon Trotsky had asserted himself as a committed communist who spurned and criticized Bolsheviks and Mensheviks alike. He was highly intelligent, articulate, charismatic, self-confident, ambitious and ruthless. Unlike most dreary communist pedants, his prose is readable and at times lively, even if his theories are just as obtuse. Yet he suffered weaknesses that ultimately were self-destructive. He was a much better rabble-rouser than organizer. He was arrogant and condescending toward those he deemed less intelligent than himself, which was nearly everyone. So, he alienated far more potential followers than he enticed. Communist Milovan Djilas offered this first glowing then damning portrait: 'Trotsky, an excellent speaker, brilliant stylist and skilled polemicist, a man cultured and of excellent intelligence, was deficient in only one quality: a sense of reality.'[15]

Trotsky's worst mistake was dismissing Stalin as a mere brute and drone. After Lenin died, Stalin outsmarted Trotsky along with the rest of the communist elite to eliminate those rivals and assert total power. Stalin systematically stripped Trotsky of his government and party positions, depleted his followers with threats and arrests, got him expelled from the party, exiled him to Siberia, expelled him from the Soviet Union and finally had him assassinated in Mexico City.

Trotsky was named Lev Davidovich Bronstein at birth and embraced his revolutionary name when he was 23. He was born into a Jewish peasant family in a small town in southern Ukraine. His intelligence earned him a scholarship at Odessa's Royal School. No trauma radicalized him, just worsening indignation at the pervasive poverty, exploitation and degradation of most peasants and urban labourers. Marxism's simplistic bromides about class struggle and revolution armed Trotsky, like countless others, with an explanation and cure for those inequities and injustices.

He studied engineering at the University of Odessa for a year but dropped out to organize the South Russia Workers Union. The Okhrana arrested him with 200 other radicals in January 1898 and exiled them to small Siberian towns. During his years of exile, he married his first wife,

Aleksandra, and they had two daughters. Of the smuggled Marxist tracts that he devoured, Lenin's *What Is to Be Done?* most influenced him. He embraced Lenin's idea that communism was impossible unless a 'Dictatorship of the Proletariat' of committed revolutionaries led the way. In August 1902, he escaped and eventually reached Vienna, the first of a series of varying foreign sojourns that included London, Munich, Nice, Paris, Zurich and New York. He earned money for himself and his family as a freelance journalist who wrote articles not just for Social Democratic publications like *Pravda* and *Iskra* but less radical newspapers. His first marriage ended in divorce in 1902. His second marriage, with Natalia, endured to his death; they had a son and a daughter.

Trotsky first met Lenin in London in October 1902. Trotsky's intellect and zeal greatly impressed Lenin, although they heatedly debated Marxist theory and revolutionary strategy whenever they got together then and thereafter. Like most other Marxists, Trotsky's views and interpretations of the creed changed over time. Initially, he embraced Marx's 'historical law' that communist revolutions would occur first in the most advanced industrial countries. Since Russia was only partly industrialized, its revolution would have to wait. He eventually reconciled that belief with Lenin's insistence that revolution was most likely in Russia, which could provoke revolutions elsewhere in Europe. Trotsky contrived this explanation: 'Russia cannot of course come to socialism independently. But having opened the era of socialist transformations, she can give a push to the socialist development of Europe and in this way be brought to socialism by the tugboat of the advanced countries.'[16] Vital for achieving that was a 'permanent revolution' by communist elites in each country that coordinated their efforts to subvert and destroy existing regimes and erect communist utopias in the ruins.

When an insurrection erupted in Saint Petersburg in January 1905, Trotsky slipped back into Russia to transform it into a communist revolution. In the 3 March 1905 edition of the Social Democratic newspaper *Iskra*, he called for a revolt to establish first a provisional government then a constituent assembly. The government crushed the revolt with Trotsky among those jailed. He received another Siberian exile and eventually escaped to settle in Vienna in 1907.

He attended Social Democratic conferences as an independent voice that resisted joining a faction. He explained: 'Menshevik? Bolshevik? I personally am equally close to both of them, I work closely with each of them and am equally proud of every revolutionary achievement of the party regardless of which faction played the leading role.'[17]

During the First World War, the Trotskys left Vienna and eventually settled in New York. He was there when he learned of the coup that forced Nicolas to abdicate and formed a provisional democratic government. He embarked on a series of ships and trains that took him to Petrograd where he was determined to lead a communist revolution.

***

The All-Russian Congress of Soviets convened from 3 to 24 June. The Bolsheviks remained a minority with only 130 of the 777 delegates. Mensheviks and Social Revolutionaries had most delegates. The Congress elected a Central Committee with 123 Mensheviks, 119 Social Revolutionaries and 57 Bolsheviks.

When his time came at the podium, Lenin demanded that the Congress embrace a hardline policy that arrested leading financiers and industrialists and negotiated the war's end with Germany. He insisted that the Bolshevik Party would take power and rule alone if the other parties did not follow it. That provoked stunned silence then laughter and catcalls by delegates from the other parties.

The failure of a Russian offensive then success of a German counteroffensive that captured a swath of territory in western Ukraine provoked a crisis for the provisional government in late June. Tens of thousands of protesters paraded through the streets and massed outside Tauride Palace. The coalition of parties dissolved and for three weeks anarchy prevailed.

Thousands of protesters led by soldiers and sailors massed before the Palace demanding the war's end on 3 July, but the ministers within could only send out word that they were still struggling to form a government. The next day, on 4 July, nearly 20,000 protesters, of whom thousands were sailors from the Kronstadt naval base, gathered before Bolshevik headquarters at Kschessinska Mansion and demanded that Lenin lead them in overthrowing the provisional government and establishing a communist government.

Here was an opportunity that Lenin had dreamed of for decades. Yet he was tongue-tied when he appeared at the balcony before them. He gave a rambling speech with the message the time was not yet ripe then disappeared inside. The protestors surged back to Tauride Palace where they joined forces with other massed protesters. Violence and looting erupted. Trotsky appeared on Tauride Palace's central balcony to harangue the mob that the time was not yet ready for an uprising, but they should patiently await the signal when the Bolsheviks would lead them to power. The protesters dispersed as rumours spread that loyal regiments were converging to repel them. Military authorities disarmed the sailors and arrested their leaders when they returned to Kronstadt. Lenin was relieved that he had backed down rather than led that uprising. Otherwise, that failure would have discredited him and his Bolshevik Party.

Prince Lvov resigned as the provisional government's prime minister on 8 July. Alexander Kerensky managed to patch together a coalition government with himself prime minister. He cracked down on the chaos by issuing decrees that restricted public protests, restored the military death penalty for desertion and mutiny, and forbade soldiers and sailors from joining soviets. He named General Lavr Kornilov the army's commander-in-chief.

Kerensky also ordered the arrest of Bolshevik Party leaders. Police raided *Pravda*, smashed its printing press and arrested those present; Stalin and Kamenev were elsewhere at the time. The Petrograd Soviet decided to shut down the Bolshevik Party headquarters. On 5 July, Lenin and Zinoviev fled to the underground to avoid arrest. Stalin invited them to reside with him at the Alliluyev home.

Through runners carrying his messages, Lenin directed the Bolshevik Party. He had the Bolshevik Party move its headquarters to the spacious Smolny Institute, a former school for daughters of the nobility. The Bolsheviks secretly held their Sixth Party Congress from 26 July to 3 August, with 276 delegates representing 100,000 members. The delegates were diverse with 55 per cent Russians or Ukrainians, 17.5 per cent Jews, 10 per cent Latvians, 4 per cent Poles, 3.5 per cent Estonians and Lithuanians and 3 per cent Georgians and Armenians. The Congress elected a Central Committee with twenty-eight members including sixteen Russians or Ukrainians, six Jews, two Georgians, two Latvians and one Armenian.[18]

Stalin and Yakov Sverdlov chaired the Conference. Stalin presented the report summarizing revolutionary conditions and what the Party had done and would do to accelerate them. He concluded with these provocative observations:

> There is dogmatic Marxism and creative Marxism . . . It is quite possible that Russia will be the country that will show the path to socialism. No country until now has enjoyed such freedom as Russia does . . . The base for our revolution is broader than in Western Europe . . . In Germany the state . . . apparatus functions incomparably more efficiently than do these untried leaders from our own bourgeoisie . . . One should reject the obsolete concept that only Europe can show us the right path.[19]

Kerensky asked Kornilov to gather the region's regiments and prepare to rush to Petrograd and oust the Bolsheviks if they took over. Instead, Kornilov marched his corps toward Petrograd intending to take power for himself from 10 to 12 September. Agitators within the army ranks sowed hesitation among their comrades. Kornilov sheepishly ordered his troops to return to their base. Kerensky had Kornilov and thirty of his top officers arrested.

Kerensky announced on 14 September, the establishment of the Russian Republic and formation of a Provisional Council to prepare elections for a Constituent Assembly to be held in December. He authorized the Bolshevik Party to participate in the elections. He formed a five-man Directory with himself the head and members of the Kadet, Menshevik and Social Revolutionary Parties. He also had himself named the Supreme Commander-in-Chief although he had no military experience. On 17 September, he dissolved the Duma and moved his government to the Winter Palace.

***

With Lenin and most other top Bolsheviks in hiding, Trotsky became the dominant leader. The government had arrested him on 7 August, but released him along with hundreds of other revolutionaries after Kerensky declared the Russian Republic on 2 September. That enabled the Bolsheviks to establish a majority on the Petrograd Soviet.

The Central Committee assigned Trotsky, Stalin, Kamenev, Alexi Rykov and Vladimir Milyutin to draft a call for the provisional government to transfer power to Petrograd Soviet at the next Democratic Conference. On 22 September, after Trotsky read the proclamation before the Democratic Conference, the delegates voted in favour by 77 to 50. On the 25th, the Petrograd Soviet elected Trotsky as its chair.

Dead set to provoke a violent revolution, Lenin slipped back into Petrograd on 10 October. The Central Committee secretly convened the next day, with only twelve of its twenty-one members. Lenin proposed and the Committee voted ten to two for an armed revolt as soon as conditions were right; Zinoviev and Kamenev were the dissenters. The Petrograd Soviet established a Military Revolutionary Committee to prepare the uprising.

Lenin instigated the Bolshevik takeover of Petrograd on 25 October (7 November). Red Guards, now 40,000 strong, took over all government offices except the Winter Palace where Kerensky's government was housed. Meanwhile, with 390 delegates, the Bolsheviks enjoyed a slender majority of the 649 delegates that convened at the Second Congress of Soviets that met from 25 to 27 October; Social Revolutionaries and Mensheviks had only 160 and 72 respective delegates. After Congress approved the takeover, Lenin had it dissolved. Red Guards overran the Winter Palace on 26 October. Kerensky escaped with a handful of advisors and found refuge at the army's headquarters in Pskov 180 miles south-west of Petrograd.

At the Smolny Institute, Trotsky announced that: 'The Provisional Government, headed by Kerensky, was dead and awaited only the broom of history to sweep it away.'[20] He explained the revolution's brutal immediate means and goals:

> We're introducing the dictatorship of the proletariat. We'll force people to work. Why did sabotage exist under the terror of the past? Well, here we don't merely have terror but rather the organized violence of the workers applied to the bourgeoisie . . . It is necessary to say clearly . . . to the workers that we are not in favour of coalition with the Mensheviks and others . . . We have a coalition with the workers and the soldiers who are fighting . . . We seized power and now we must also carry responsibilities.[21]

That provoked protests by Mensheviks and Social Revolutionaries. Trotsky demanded that they join the Bolsheviks as junior partners. A few lingered but most angrily stormed out. Menshevik chief Yuli Martov stayed to propose a resolution for a coalition government. That enraged Trotsky, who shouted: 'You are miserable bankrupts, your role is played out; go where you ought to go – into the dustbin of history!'[22] Martov and his comrades hurried away. By not standing firm and demanding a coalition, the Mensheviks and Social Revolutionaries let the Bolsheviks solely control the new government. Menshevik Nikolai Sukhanov later ruefully admitted that terrible folly: 'By our own irrational decision, we ensured the victory of Lenin's whole "line".'[23]

The Bolsheviks mass printed and distributed this declaration:

> To the Citizens of Russia, The Provisional Government has been overthrown. State power has passed into the hands of the organ of the Petrograd Soviet of Workers' and Soldiers' Deputies, the Military-Revolutionary Committee which stands at the head of the Petrograd proletariat and garrison. The cause for which the people has struggled: the immediate proposal of a democratic peace, the abolition of the gentry's landed property, workers' control over production, the creation of as Soviet Government – victory for this cause has been secured. Long live the revolution of workers, soldiers and peasants.[24]

Lenin's iron will enabled his Bolshevik Party to take power. He was zealously committed to a coup d'etat and browbeat virtually every one of his reluctant comrades to join him, with only Zinoviev and Kamenev refusing. Trotsky later explained: 'Had I not been present in 1917 in Petersburg, the October Revolution would still have taken place – on the condition that Lenin was present and in command. If neither Lenin nor I had been present in Petersburg, there would have been no October Revolution.'[25]

The Bolsheviks had seized power in Petrograd over two days in a near bloodless coup. That was the first crucial step. The next was far more daunting – taking over the rest of Russia and imposing a communist revolution for what would be called the Soviet Union.[26]

Red Guards took over city halls and army barracks across Russia, usually against no or little resistance. Red Guards exterminated any 'White' or Tsarist forces they encountered. The worst immediate threat was from General Peter Krasnov who marched from Pskov with 700 Cossacks against Petrograd. Red Guards surrounded him and his men and forced their surrender on 15 November.

Lenin explained the essence of the political system that he and his comrades were constructing: 'Dictatorship is iron authority, authority that is revolutionarily audacious as well as rapid and merciless in its suppression of both exploiters and hooligans.'[27] To that end, their political system had overlapping party and government hierarchies often with the same cadres occupying two equivalent seats, with the Bolshevik Party, renamed the Communist Party on 8 March 1918, firmly in charge, as a state within a state. Lenin had the Congress of Soviets declare the formation of Russia's new government called the Council of People's Commissars with the acronym Sovnarkom, on 26 October 1917. Lenin would be Sovnarkom's Premier or Chairman from 1917 to 1924. Thirteen of the fifteen commissars headed existing government ministries. To that Lenin added the Nationalities Commissar and State Control Commissar and tapped Stalin to head both. He later established the Worker and Peasant Inspection Commissar with Stalin as its chief. He named Trotsky Foreign Affairs Commissar. On 29 November, the Sovnarkom established an temporary 'Foursome' including Lenin, Trotsky, Stalin and Sverdlov to decide all 'emergency questions,' with other delegates then present at the Smolny Institute.

The communists sought to win the loyalty of workers, peasants and lower middle class with their simple but enormously appealing slogan 'Peace, Bread and Land'. They fiercely debated just how to realize each of those goals before reaching a consensus. Sovnarkom issued a series of decrees that led to sweeping reforms.

Sovnarkom began regulating the economy and nationalizing industries with four initial decrees. The Decree on Land declared the confiscation of all state, royal, noble, church, business and gentry-owned land to be distributed to the peasants or the soviets. The Decree on the Eight Hour Day came on 29 October. The Decree on Workers Control of 14 November empowered a committee of workers and managers to run each business or institution. On 1 December, Sovnarkom established the Supreme Council of the National Economy to manage industry, finance, agriculture and trade. On 15 December, Sovnarkom nationalized the banking and financial industry and formed the Supreme Economic Council to manage the economy.

Two key related pillars of the communist regime's power were providing people with basic needs in a system that constantly monitored and either mobilized or persecuted every man, woman and child. Lenin explained:

> The objective of this registration and supervision is clear and universally understandable that everyone should have bread, go about in sturdy footwear and decent clothing, should have a warm dwelling and should work conscientiously; that no scoundrel (including anyone who shirks doing any work) should be free to roam about but should be held in prison or should work off his sentence in forced labour of the heaviest kind; and that none of the wealthy, evading the rules and laws of socialism, should be able to evade the same fate as the scoundrel – the fate that in justice ought to be become the fate of wealthy people.[28]

Feeding the population was a daunting problem. Malnutrition and famine plagued Russia. The war had engulfed much of Russia's western and most productive agrarian lands. Soaring prices for existing food kept millions of people from buying all they needed for sustenance. Anticipating ever higher prices, peasants and speculators promoted them by hoarding rather than selling what they had.

To break that vicious price-supply cycle, Lenin issued this decree on 15 January 1918:

> [Sovnarkom] proposes to the All-Russian Food Supplies Committee and the Commissariat of Food Supplies to intensify the dispatch not only of commissars but also of numerically strong, armed detachments for the most revolutionary measures for the movement of loads, the collection and distribution of grain . . . and also for a merciless struggle with speculators right through to the proposal for local soviets to shoot discovered speculators and saboteurs on the spot.[29]

Lenin drafted and signed, along with Stalin, the 'Declaration of the Rights of the Peoples of Russia' on 1 November 1917. Those 'rights' included equality for all people, abolition of all national and religious privileges and self-determination or autonomy for all national groups and independence for any that demanded it. However, the communist regime eventually would brutally, cynically and systematically violate those 'rights'. Yet Lenin, Stalin and the Bolshevik elite sincerely believed in those rights when they initially declared them.

***

As the Bolsheviks amassed power for themselves, they tried to eliminate all enemies and rivals alike. Sovnarkom issued a decree on 27 October that banned all opposition newspapers while Red Guards arrested Menshevik, Social Revolutionary and Kadet leaders. The All-Russia Executive Committee of the Railwaymen's Union threated to strike if the Bolsheviks did not form a coalition. On 4 November, Kamenev and four followers resigned from the Central Committee and Sovnarkom with the same demand.

Hoping to win a Bolshevik majority, Lenin let the scheduled Constituent Assembly elections take place in mid-December. The Bolsheviks garnered only one of four votes or 24 per cent of the total. When the 44,433,000 votes were finally counted, the Social Revolutionaries won most seats with 299 followed by the Bolsheviks with 168, the Ukrainian Social Revolutionaries with 81, the Left Social Revolutionaries with 39, the Mensheviks with 18, the Constitutional Democrats with 15 and the remaining 83 seats split among an array of tiny parties or individuals.

The Constituent Assembly convened in Tauride Palace's Catherine Hall on 5 January. Bolshevik Red Guards ominously surrounded the palace and heckled the opposition deputies as they entered. Social Revolutionary Viktor Chernov chaired the Assembly but keeping order and decorum was virtually impossible as Bolsheviks issued resolutions and jeered opponents. Their most important resolution was for a vote to ratify all the decrees that Lenin had issued. They lost by 237 to 138 votes. The Bolsheviks condemned the Assembly for being dominated by 'counterrevolutionaries', and stormed out, later followed by the Left Social Revolutionaries. The remaining deputies debated what to do until late at night when Chernov adjourned the Assembly.

The next day, Sovnarkom decreed the Constituent Assembly's abolition and had Red Guards bar the deputies from entering. Russia would not have another democratically-elected national assembly for 74 years.

***

As for the ongoing war against the Central Powers, on 26 October 1917 Sovnarkom issued this Peace Decree:

> The [Soviet] government proposes to all the governments and peoples of all the warring countries to conclude a truce immediately . . . for no less than three months for . . . the completion of negotiations on peace with the participation of representatives of all peoples and nations . . . that have been dragged into the war or compelled to take part in it.[30]

The Bolshevik leaders debated how to extract Russia from the war. Lenin demanded peace at any price to free resources to consolidate communist rule. Trotsky favoured an ambiguous policy of 'neither war nor peace' as Russia withdrew from the fighting without making any concessions to Germany in a treaty. Stalin backed Lenin's position. Sovnarkom sent a diplomatic delegation to negotiate with a German delegation led by General Maximilien Hoffman at Brest-Litovsk on 16 November. They signed an armistice on 2 December.

For a formal peace treaty, Sovnarkom dispatched Foreign Commissar Trotsky to Brest-Litovsk in mid-December. The Bolsheviks had no bargaining power since desertion, short supplies and abysmal morale plagued the Russian army while the Red Army was being expanded. On 11 January, the Central Committee overwhelmingly voted to back Trotsky's plan. On 10 February, Trotsky announced that Russia would withdraw from the war and demobilize its army without signing a peace treaty. On 16 February, Hoffman warned that Germany would launch an offensive. On the 18th, the Central Committee voted by seven to six and one abstention in favour of seeking a formal peace treaty. That same day, the German offensive began and within a week had advanced over 125 miles through the demoralized Russian army. The furthest German advances were to Narva, 100 miles from Petrograd and Mogilev, 300 miles from Moscow.

In the Treaty of Brest-Litovsk, signed on 3 March 1918, the Communist regime surrendered Russia's provinces of Estonia, Latvia, Lithuania, Poland, Belarus and Ukraine to Germany in return for peace. Those cessions included 34 per cent of the Russian empire's population or 55 million people, 32 per cent of its farmland, 54 per cent of its industry and 89 per cent of its coal mines.[31]

The Bolshevik's Seventh Congress convened from 6 to 8 March. The delegates included forty-seven voting plenipotentiaries and fifty-nine non-voting consultatives. Nicolai Bukharin led the faction that rejected the humiliating peace treaty and sought to keep fighting the Germans. Lenin's Resolution on War and Peace endorsed the treaty. The delegates voted thirty in favour and twelve opposed with four abstentions. The All-Russian Congress of Soviets ratified the treaty during its session from 14 to 16 March.

Meanwhile, the Central Committee approved two more revolutionary measures. They voted to abandon the Julian calendar and adopt the Gregorian calendar on 14 February 1918, which advanced dates by thirteen days. They also voted to move Russia's capital from exposed Petrograd to much more secure and central Moscow. Lenin convened the government in the Kremlin on 12 March 1918.

***

For Lenin, wielding violent terror against counterrevolutionaries was essential for the communist regime's survival and eventual unlimited power over Russia and other countries. He initiated the first communist reign of terror with mass roundups of suspected 'enemies of the people', who were tortured for confessions, tried and executed. Mingled rage, fear and vengeance motivated him and his henchmen.

Lenin carefully studied the French Revolution for lessons in how to take and hold power. He saw himself as the Russian Revolution's Maximilian Robespierre, ideologically pure and utterly ruthless in realizing his utopian vision. He embraced Robespierre's reign of terror to eliminate any opposition and consolidate the revolution's power. Trotsky justified terrorism in Marxist terms:

> The Red Terror is a weapon utilized against a class, doomed to destruction, which does not wish to perish . . . Without the Red Terror, the Red bourgeoisie, together with the world bourgeoisie, would throttle us long before the coming of the revolution in Europe . . . The man who recognizes the revolutionary historic importance of . . . the Soviet system must also sanction the Red Terror.[32]

Regicide was a key assertion of communist terror. Lenin hated the Romanov dynasty that had ruled Russia from 1613 to 1917. Among the communist murder victims was Tsar Nicholas II, his wife, four daughters and son. After being deposed, the tsar and his family had moved several times, finally seeking refuge in a mansion called Ipatev

House in Yekaterinburg near the Ural Mountains. On 30 April 1918, the local communist cadres received Lenin's orders to imprison the royal family in their home. The execution command came on 18 July 1918. A communist hit squad herded the family into a room, shot them to death, then incinerated the bodies.

Six weeks later Lenin himself was nearly murdered. Fanny Kaplan had devoted a dozen years to the Social Revolutionary Party, including a prison stint. Like her comrades, the Bolsheviks' worsening dictatorship enraged her. On 30 August 1918, Lenin gave a speech at the Hammer and Sickle Arms Factory in Moscow. As he emerged, Kaplan called his name. As Lenin faced her, she fired three shots before guards subdued her. One bullet clipped his jacket, another lodged in his neck and the third pierced his left shoulder and stopped near his collar bone. He was rushed to a hospital where doctors decided that trying to extract the bullets near arteries was more dangerous than leaving them alone. Lenin slowly recovered.

That assassination attempt became Lenin's excuse to assert terror against all 'enemies of the people'. The Bolshevik regime reinstated the death penalty whose abolition was among the reforms initiated by the liberal democratic government it overthrew. Kaplan was executed on 3 September, the first of hundreds of thousands of 'enemies' killed in the first round of terror over the next two years. The result was a vicious cycle. The communist regime indiscriminately prosecuted and executed ever more suspects whether or not they were guilty. Tortured confessions led to more arrests and killings. With nothing to lose, ever more people resisted, which worsened the communists' paranoia and retribution.

Trotsky asserted this justification for terrorism: 'The man who repudiates terrorism in principle – i.e. repudiates measures of suppression and intimidation against a determined and armed counter-revolution – must reject any idea of the political supremacy of the working class and its revolutionary dictatorship. The man who repudiates the dictatorship of the proletariat is also repudiating socialist revolution and digging the grave of socialism.'[33]

A bureau within the Commissariat of the Interior spearheaded the terror. Felix Dzerzhinsky had founded the 'Extraordinary Commission for Combating Counterrevolution and Sabotage' (Cheka) on 17 December 1917. Dzerzhinsky had this public proclamation issued:

> We are exterminating the bourgeoisie as a class. During the investigation, do not look for evidence that the accused acted in deed or word against Soviet power. The first question that you ought to put are: to what class

> does he belong? What is his origin? What is his education or profession? And it is these questions that ought to determine the fate of the accused. In this lies the significance and essence of the Red Terror.[34]

Over the next seven decades, the Communist Party's reign of terror within the Soviet empire and beyond varied in its number of victims along with the name of the terror organization. Dzerzhinsky changed the name to the 'State Political Administration' (GPU) on 6 February 1922, then the 'United State Political Administration' (OGPU) on 15 November 1923 and ran it until a heart attack killed him on 20 July 1926. The name changed to the 'People's Commissariat of Internal Affairs' (NKVD) on 10 July 1934, the 'Ministry for State Security' (MGB) on 15 March 1946 and the 'Committee on State Security' (KGB) on 13 March 1954, which persisted until 3 December 1991.

No matter how often the name changed, the organization's mission remained the same – gathering intelligence and eliminating 'enemies of the people' at home and abroad. Assassination of 'enemies of the people' abroad was a vital task. For that, assassins wielded whatever weapon was appropriate. Smersh, the acronym for 'Death to Spies,' specialized in such 'wet operations.' When a gunshot would provoke too much attention, the assassin might slip a poison into the victim's tea or soup. Poison was silent but deadly until the victim began groaning or screaming. No one contributed more to the NKVD's repertoire of poisons than Dr Grigory Maironovsky who headed its Laboratory Number One from 1938 to 1946, having previously led the Bach Institute of Biochemistry in Moscow from 1928 to 1935.

The Kremlin officially inaugurated the Soviet Union's concentration camp system on 15 April 1919.[35] By December 1919, the Communists had established and filled 7,500 concentration camps, 21,700 prisons and 4,100 labour camps. From its inception to its official abolition on 4 April 1956, the Main Administration of Corrective Labour Camps and Colonies, best known for its acronym, the Gulag, enslaved at least 18,000,000 victims, of whom at least 1,600,000 died from execution, disease, suicide or being worked to death.[36]

***

Russia's civil war began the day the Bolsheviks seized power.[37] The first phase involved Red Guards taking over cities and regiments, imposing Soviets and executing or imprisoning anyone who resisted. Fighting was sporadic and limited. The shock of the Bolshevik coup paralyzed Russian generals on the front line against the enemy German, Austrian and Ottoman armies. They hated and opposed the new regime but had no alternative government to support. Sovnarkom dispatched commissars to their headquarters to pressure them into backing the Bolsheviks while ever more soldiers embraced communism.

Russia's army and navy respectively numbered 6,300,000 soldiers and 750,000 sailors on paper when the Bolsheviks took power. Desertion severely depleted those ranks while seeping communism won the loyalty of ever more men who remained. Five million soldiers and sailors voted in the Constituent Assembly election of December 1917 and more than four of five voted either for Social Revolutionaries or Bolsheviks or an astonishing 41 per cent for each.[38]

With the peace treaty, the stream of deserters became a river. But that also freed Russian generals to turn their armies' loyal remnants against the Communist regime. Collectively they became known as the 'Whites' in their war against the 'Reds'. General Mikhail Alexseyev got the allegiance of Cossack Ataman or Head Chief Alexey Kaladin at Rostov on the Don River in southern Russia to form first the Alexseyev Organization then the Volunteer Army. General Larv Kornilov joined them. In April 1918, the Volunteer Army tried to capture Ekaterinodar, capital of the Kuban Soviet Republic, but the Red Guards repelled them and Kornilov was among the dead.

Ironically, the one Russian army corps that remained intact was the 35,000-man Czech Legion composed mostly of Czechs and Slovaks residing in the western Russian empire. Petrograd formed the Czech Legion in November 1914 in return for the promise to help them liberate their compatriots living in the Austrian Empire and forming the new state of Czechoslovakia. During the war, the Czech Legion expanded its ranks with volunteers among captured Austrian troops who were Czechs and Slovaks. Tomas Masaryk chaired the Czech National Council, the exiled government for a future Czechoslovakia. After Russia exited the war, Masaryk took command of the Czech Legion. On 25 March, he negotiated at Penza a deal with the Communist regime for the Czech Legion to journey east on the Trans-Siberian Railway to Vladivostok then board a ship bound for France. In mid-May, the Czech Legion was scattered along the railway from Penza to Vladivostok. At Cheliabinsk in the Ural Mountains fighting broke out on 14 May, when Red Army troops tried to confiscate a Czech Legion regiment's weapons. On the 25th, Trotsky issued the order to local soviets that: 'Every armed Czechoslovakian found on the railway is to be shot on the spot.' That provoked Masaryk to ally the Czech Legion with the White Army. He deployed the Czech Legion at cities on the Trans-Siberian Railway from Samsara on the Don River to Irkutsk near Lake Baikal. Trotsky typically appreciated the irony: 'At first sight it might seem incomprehensible that some Czechoslovak Corps which has wound up with us in Russia through the tortuous ways of the World War, should at the given moment prove to be almost the most important factor in deciding the question of the Russian Revolution.'[39] What Trotsky did not note was his responsibility for driving the Czech Legion into the ranks of the White army by failing to defuse the crisis with diplomacy and instead trying to crush it with brute force.

***

Eventually, four foreign countries entangled themselves in the civil war to support the Whites. Russia's separate peace with the Central Powers imperilled the Western Allies France, Britain, America, Belgium and Italy. Berlin and Vienna could transfer most of their troops from the now peaceful Eastern Front to the Western and Italian Fronts and those reinforced armies could overwhelm the defenders. That was the worst fear among the Allies. There was another. Huge stockpiles of war supplies that the Allies had donated Russia awaited transportation from the ports of Archangel and Murmansk on the northern White Sea and at Vladivostok the Siberian Railway's terminus on the Pacific. What if the Bolshevik regime sold those supplies to the Central Powers for desperately-needed hard cash?

Washington, London and Paris agreed to send troops to protect those supplies. Meanwhile, Tokyo's government was overjoyed at the Bolshevik revolution, chaos and the Russian army's depletion. They dispatched 20,000 troops to Vladivostok to annex not just that port but eastern Siberia with its rich natural resources to Japan's Empire.[40]

Around 150 British troops secured Murmansk on 3 March 1918. In June, 600 British reinforcements secured the railway south for 300 miles, scattering Red Guard units along the way. On 1 August, around 600 British and French secured Archangel. In both ports, the foreign troops allied with local White troops. British troops from the captured Ottoman provinces of Basra, Baghdad and Mosul advanced north as far as Baku on the Caspian Sea. Contingents of American troops eventually deployed in Archangel, Murmansk and Vladivostok.

The British funnelled an enormous amount of supplies to White armies. At Vladivostok, the British sent 79 ships packed with 97,000 tons of supplies including 600,000 rifles, 346 million ammunition rounds, 6,831 machine guns, 192 field guns and uniforms and equipment for 200,000 troops. A British military mission to General Denikin's army in Ukraine distributed 198,000 rifles, 6,200 machine guns, 1,121 field guns, 1,900,000 shells, 500,000,000 rounds of ammunition, 60 tanks, 168 warplanes, 460,000 greatcoats and 645,000 pairs of shoes. The White armies that received those supplies made poor use of them.[41]

***

The Supreme Revolutionary War Council commanded the Red Army during the Civil War.[42] It established a War Council for each front that included generals and commissars. Vladimir Antonov-Ovseenko initially was the War Commissar. Lenin did not believe he was smart and tough enough for such a vital post. On 14 March, Lenin named Trotsky War Commissar and Supreme War Council chair with the key mission of destroying the counterrevolutionaries. Trotsky fulfilled that role with utter ruthlessness and flexibility. What Trotsky called 'War Communism' was the mobilization of all available human and economic resources to defeat the White armies. To fill the Red Army's ranks, Sovnarkom instituted conscription in June 1918. The Red Army expanded swiftly to 1,000,000 troops by December 1919, 3,000,000 by December 1920 and 5,300,000 by December 1921. The Red Army's first commander-in-chief was General Jukums Vacietis, appointed on 2 September 1918, then Sergei Kamenev on 8 July 1919, after Vacietis was cashiered for being an alleged White agent.

The initial 'Red Army' was an oxymoron. The communists had undermined the Russian army with agitators that resisted discipline and mutinied against officers. The army eventually collapsed with regiments depleted or dissolved. Trotsky knew that the Red Army would not win unless he transformed it from an ill-disciplined collection of armed militias into a professional army. For that, he enticed as many former Tsarist officers as possible to restore order, discipline and esprit de corps. To ensure their loyalty, he assigned each officer a political commissar and held their families as hostages. Eventually he got 60,000 former officers and 200,000 former non-commissioned officers to join the Red Army.[43] Meanwhile, to demoralize the enemy, he ordered captured White army officers interrogated, tortured and shot. Stalin backed Trotsky's call for transforming a revolutionary army into a professional army: 'Facts show that the concept of a volunteer army does not withstand criticism, that we shall not be able to defend our Republic if we do not construct another regular army imbued with discipline.'[44] Lenin lauded Trotsky's accomplishments: 'The game is won. If we have succeeded in establishing order in the army, it means we shall establish it everywhere else. And the revolution – with order – will be unconquerable.'[45] In an armoured train, Trotsky travelled from one front to another to supervise military operations.

The Communists eventually won the Civil War. Four related reasons explain that victory. First, the Reds had a unified government while the Whites had no central command to coordinate operations among their armies. Second, the Reds enjoyed interior transportation and communication lines that emanated from Moscow, while the White armies were dispersed on the Russia's empire far fringes. Third, the Reds controlled Russia's most industrialized cities and most fertile farmlands while the Whites persistently struggled to mass enough munitions, provisions and other vital war supplies. Fourth, Communist slogans and ideology appealed to downtrodden people even if the Communists actually exploited them more systematically and harsher than anyone else.

***

The Communist regime faced major White army threats in southern Russia, central Siberia on the trans-Siberia railway and the Baltic States and eventually defeated each. The fighting was the most sustained on the southern front that extended across Ukraine and lower Don and Volga River regions. At Samsara on the Don River, the Social Revolutionaries allied with a Czech Legion regiment to rout the Communists and on 9 June 1918, declare the Committee of Members of the Constituent Assembly (Komuch) as Russia's legitimate government. General Mikhail Tukhachevsky led the First Red Army to capture Kazan on 10 September, Simbirsk on 12 September and Samsara on 7 October 1918. As the Komuch fled it dissolved itself.

General Alexander Rodzyanko commanded a small army in Estonia, with his headquarters at Tallinn. That front was dormant until September 1919, when General Nikolai Yudenich replaced him, expanded the army to 17,000 troops and marched on Petrograd. The Red Army routed his army and pursued the remnants to the Estonia border. Russian and Estonian diplomats signed an armistice on 3 January 1920 that ended fighting and the threat on that front

Admiral Alexander Kolchak commanded a White army that seized power at Omsk in November 1918 and declared himself chief of state of the Provisional All-Russian Government. White army troops under his command peaked at 200,000 and included the Czech Legion. Despite those numbers, Kolchak was an indecisive commander who mostly defended the region from Red Army attacks. The Red Army repulsed his only significant offensive at Ufa in June 1919. A Red Army offensive drove Kolchak and his troops from Omsk on 14 November 1919 and the White army retreated to Irkutsk. There General Maurice

Janin, the Czech Legion's commander, cut a deal with the Red Army to capture and turn over Kolchak. The Communist executed Kolchak on 7 February 1920. That same day, Janin signed an armistice with the Communists that let the Czech Legion journey unmolested to Vladivostok where they would board a ship bound for western Europe.

Generals Anton Deniken and Pyotr Wrangel commanded White armies on the southern front through much of 1918 and 1919. Wrangel led an offensive that captured Tsaritsyn on 19 June 1919, but the Red Army recaptured the city on 1 July. The Red Army crushed Denikin's army at Orel from 11 October to 18 November 1919. Deniken withdrew to Crimea with his remaining troops. Wrangel replaced Deniken in April 1920 and launched an offensive into Ukraine that got as far as Mariupol before being defeated. Wrangel withdrew back into Crimea where the Red Army eventually overwhelmed him. The civil war effectively ended when he and his inner circle abandoned their remaining troops and packed aboard a ship at Sevastopol bound for western Europe and foreign exile on 14 November 1920.

***

During the Civil War, Stalin served as political commissar on half a dozen fronts. His role was to accompany the armies and debate then accept or reject military plans submitted by the generals, oversee requisition of all necessary supplies and eliminate any 'enemies of the people'. Stalin returned to Moscow between missions.

His first mission to Tsaritsyn was the most successful; in 1925, the Central Committee renamed the city Stalingrad because of his feats. Tsaritsyn was a prosperous city on the Volga River 550 miles south-east of Moscow; Tsaritsyn's wealth came from a diversified dynamic economy as a rail centre with munitions factories, regional grain trade and oil refined from Baku. White armies tried to take Tsaritsyn several times during the civil war. In June 1918, Tsaritsyn was defended by 20,000 Red Guards commanded by Klimenti Voroshilov, seconded by Semyon Budyonny, the cavalry commander. Lenin sent Stalin and 400 Red Guards by armoured train to Tsaritsyn. Lenin armed Stalin with martial law powers and instructed him to be 'merciless' and 'ruthless' in crushing counterrevolutionaries and requisitioning and sending back to Moscow grain, munitions, oil and other supplies. Stalin promised Lenin: 'Be assured our hand will not tremble.'[46] En route, White Russian troops shot at the train, the only time Stalin ever came under fire in his entire life.

During his five months in Tsaritsyn, Stalin and Voroshilov bonded and later Voroshilov became one of Stalin's key followers. Stalin also fell in love. Among his entourage was Sergei Alliluyev, a Petrograd friend and his daughter Nadya, who served as a typist. During this time, Stalin and Nadya became lovers. He was 41 and she was 17 when they married in February or March 1919. Their son Vasily was born in 1921 and their daughter Svetlana in 1926. They had a tempestuous marriage that ended in tragedy. That was partly because he was rarely home and during his brief sojourns was as autocratic and abrasive as he was elsewhere.

General Pyotr Krasnov's 40,000-man White army began a siege of Tsaritsyn in July 1918. Voroshilov and Stalin built up the garrison and its supplies and the Red Guards eventually drove off Krasnov's army in September. During that time, Stalin and Voroshilov got into a rancorous dispute over tactics with War Commissar Trotsky, Army Commander-in-Chief Vacietis and regional army commander General Pavel Sytin. Trotsky sent Lenin a letter criticizing Stalin for being too ruthless in executing the merchants handling grain and other products and called for his dismissal. Lenin recalled Stalin on 19 October, then sent him to Perm in December 1918 to oversee Red Army operations against Admiral Alexander Kolchak's White Army. In January Stalin returned to Moscow where he stayed until May 1919 when he was sent to Leningrad to supervise operations until July. After returning to Moscow he stayed there until May 1920 when he received orders to hurry to the Southwest Front to oversee Red Army forces fighting an invading army.

***

General Josef Pilsudski was Poland's Chief of State and Commander-in-Chief. His army routed the Red Army from Vilnius, the capital of the Lithuanian-Belorussian Soviet Republic, in April 1919.[47] He followed up that victory the next year by invading Ukraine on 23 April, capturing Kiev on 7 May and advancing eastward. The Poles soon outran their supplies. General Mikhail Tukhachevsky commanded the Red Army facing the Poles. He launched a counter-attack that drove them back.

Lenin made Stalin political commissar to General Alexander Yegorov who commanded another army in the region. With supplies dwindling, Pilsudski withdrew his army back to Poland. Lenin insisted that if the Red Army invaded Poland the Poles would rise and overthrow their government. Stalin warned that the Poles were too numerous and united to be defeated. Lenin's view prevailed. He had Commander-in-Chief Sergei Kamenev order Tukhachevsky on 23 July to open an offensive toward Warsaw. Meanwhile, Yegorov, accompanied by Stalin, attacked south-west to capture Lvov. Had the armies combined against either city they would have captured it, but divided, they failed.

The Poles counter-attacked on 16 August and routed both armies which retreated to Russia. Tukhachevsky blamed Stalin for his defeat. Earlier Stalin disobeyed Kamenev's order to transfer an infantry corps and a cavalry corps to Tukhachevsky's command. He wrote Lenin these excuses for his blatant insubordinations:

> The Politburo should not occupy itself with trifles. I can remain at the front for a maximum of two weeks more. I need rest, look for a substitute. I do not for a moment believe the promises of the commander-in-chief, he always lets one down with his promises. As for the mood of the Central Committee in favour of peace with Poland, it seems to be an inescapable fact that our diplomacy sometimes very successfully destroys the results of our military victories.[48]

Stalin's request for leave was approved on 29 August.

Had Stalin obeyed that command, Tukhachevsky might have staved off rather than succumbed to the onslaught. Pilsudski followed, advancing his army as far as Minsk by 15 October. Russian and Polish diplomats signed an armistice on 12 October 1920 and the Treaty of Riga on 18 March 1921. Under the Treaty of Riga, Poland recognized Soviet sovereignty over Ukraine and Belorussia in return for 30 million gold rubles and 29 million rubles of railway equipment, tracks and trains.

Lenin was ultimately responsible for that debacle. He had insisted that Poland was ripe for revolution and Russia's Red Army could liberate the Poles from the regime that ruled them. He also dominated the collective decision to split the armies between Warsaw and Krakow, rather than concentrating them against Warsaw, which likely would have fallen. On each front, Tukhachevsky and Yegorov made strategic and tactical mistakes that compounded the initial fatal campaign decision.

Stalin's next missions were first to supervise the conquest of Armenia and then Georgia, which the Red Army respectively completed by December 1920 and June 1921. Apparently, no document exists that reveals Stalin's feelings about Georgia's conquest, but most likely he was triumphant at crushing his fatherland and imposing a communist regime on it.

***

Lenin and Trotsky believed that Russia's communist revolution would only succeed if communist revolutions engulfed other countries in Europe and beyond. Trotsky explained:

> Now, after the so very promising start of the Russian revolution, we have every reason to believe that in the course of this war a mighty revolutionary movement will develop throughout Europe. It is clear that that this movement will be able to develop successfully and achieve victory only as a European-wide movement. If it remains isolated within national boundaries, it is doomed to destruction. The salvation of the Russian revolution lies in its extension to all Europe.[49]

Because of that, Trotsky dismissed any need for traditional diplomacy. As People's Commissar for Foreign Affairs, 'I will issue a few revolutionary proclamations to the peoples of the world, then shut up shop.'[50]

Russian foreign policy subsequently proved to be a bit more complicated than that.[51] The Kremlin often nurtured trade and diplomatic relations with a foreign government on one level while trying to destroy it by nurturing a revolutionary movement on another level.

To facilitate those revolutions, Lenin had Radio Moscow broadcast an appeal for all communist parties and their affiliates around to unite in the Third Communist International on 24 January 1919.[52] Fifty-one delegates of various groups attended the First Congress of the Communist International (Comintern) at the Kremlin from 2 to 6 March 1919. During his speech before the Congress, Foreign Commissar Trotsky proclaimed: 'We are ready to struggle and die for the world revolution!'[53] He also drafted Comintern's 'Manifesto' or programme of ends and means. The delegates voted to establish an Executive Committee and elected Grigory Zinoviev the president with Nikolai Bukharin and Karl Radek his assistants.

Comintern never lived up to the dreams of Lenin and its founders. Comintern agents did not instigate and could not save the Spartacist rebellion led by Karl Liebknecht and Rosa Luxemburg in Germany in January 1919, crushed by the German army; or the Hungarian Soviet Republic established by Bela Kun from 21 March to 1 August 1919, crushed by the Romanian army. Comintern distributed 5.2 million rubles as seed money among Communist Parties in Hungary, Czechoslovakia, Germany, Italy, Austria, Yugoslavia, Poland, the Netherlands and the United States from March to August 1919 alone, but none of those parties blossomed.[54]

Comintern established three affiliates, the Young Communist International in 1919; the Department of International Communications responsible for supplying foreign Communist Parties with money and arms in 1921; and the Red International of Trade Unions (Profintern) in 1921. Comintern invited foreign Communist Party cadres to Moscow for training to become revolutionary leaders.

Soviet foreign policy's first clear triumph was not some Comintern-led communist revolution but came from traditional diplomacy of careful negotiation and compromise. Under the Treaty of Rapallo, signed by Foreign Ministers Georgii Chicherin and Walther Rathenau on 22 April 1922, the Soviet Union and Germany agreed to mutual recognition, cooperation and trade. A secret relationship soon developed whereby the German military evaded restrictions imposed by the Treaty of Versailles by training air force pilots in the Soviet Union.

As for Comintern, the one place around the globe where it nurtured a viable Communist Party was in China. Chen Duxiu, Li Dazhao, Chen Tu-hsiu and other Marxists along with Comintern agents founded the Chinese Communist Party (CCP) in Shanghai in July 1921. Leninism was the model with its Dictatorship of the Proletariat of elite, committed, ruthless, yet flexible and collegial communists with the best among them the chair; two-stage bourgeois then proletariat revolution; and short-term alliance with the most powerful bourgeois organization, in China's case the National Party (Kuomintang, KMT). Traditional Chinese culture influenced the CCP like Confucianism with its pragmatism, conformism, hard study and work; redemption through self-criticisms; and unequal yet familial relations. Chinese communists viewed relations with the Soviets as that between younger and elder brothers whereby the latter instructs, leads and aids the former in return for loyalty and obedience.

In two key ways, the Marxist-Leninist model was inappropriate for China. China's proletariat was a miniscule part of the population with just one in fifty Chinese working in factories, mines and other modern industries, while nine in ten Chinese were peasants. Likewise, the KMT simply provided its generalissimo Chiang Kai-shek an army and organization for his dictatorship and was incapable of leading a bourgeois revolution. Indeed, the alliance proved to be a death-trap when Chiang launched his troops against the CCP in cities across eastern China in 1927 and slaughtered or routed nearly all of them.

***

Meanwhile, the Communists changed Imperial Russia's name. They declared the Russian Socialist Federative Soviet Republic (RSFSR) of Russia, Ukraine, Belorussia and Transcaucasia on 25 January 1918 and the Union of Soviet Socialist Republics (USSR) on 30 December 1922. Eventually by conquest or designation of existing regions the Soviet Union would have fifteen 'republics' that were all brutal communist dictatorships ruled by the Kremlin.

The Eighth Party Congress convened in Moscow from 18 to 23 March 1919, with 301 delegates who could speak and vote and 102 others who could only speak. The Communist Party had 313,766 members. Congress elected the Central Committee with nineteen full and eight candidate members. The Central Committee then approved Lenin's proposal to create two elite groups at the Communist Party's pinnacle, the Political Bureau (Politburo) for devising policies and the Organizational Bureau (Orgburo) for implementing policies. Lenin chaired both. He split the Politburo between a three-man Secretariat that ran the Party and Government and a War Cabinet that devised military strategy and mobilized human and material resources.

Stalin was elated to be among those elected to the Politburo along with Lenin, Trotsky, Lev Kamenev and Nikolai Krestinsky as full members and Grigory Zinoviev, Nikolai Bukharin and Mikhail Kalinin as half members. Stalin was also re-elected to the Central Committee and elected to the newly established Ogburo in charge of administration and personnel.

***

From November 1917 to June 1921, the Soviet government and the Communist Party that controlled it expanded respectively to 5,400,000 officials and 1,400,000 members. During that time the regime hijacked the Russian empire, imposed a harsh dictatorship, confiscated most of the realm's wealth and destroyed or routed any enemies who opposed them. They did all that to 'liberate' the 'proletariat' from the 'bourgeoisie' that suppressed and exploited them. They promised to establish a communist society in which everyone was wealthy, healthy and happy. Alas, that lofty goal eluded them.

Instead, the Communist Revolution was catastrophic. Eliminating the rich and middle classes and confiscating their wealth decimated the economy, leaving nearly all the survivors except the Communist Party elite poorer, hungrier and angrier. During the four and a half years from the Communist takeover to the extinction of the last armed resistance, around 3,000,000 people died from fighting, execution, starvation and disease. As for the Red Army, at least 632,000 died in action and 581,000 from disease. Those deaths were atop the 2,200,000 military and 730,000 civilians that Russia suffered from August 1914 to March 1918 in the First World War. From 1914 to 1920, around 10,000,000 people lost their homes and became refugees. Around 7,000,000 children became orphans and most of them became street urchins (*besprizorniki*). Around 3,000,000 Russians fled into foreign exile, including most of the realm's most enterprising and creative individuals.[55]

What Soviet history books either avoided or downplayed was that American food aid saved millions who otherwise would have starved to death.[56] In February 1919, Congress formed the American Relief Administration with $100 million in funds to purchase and distribute food and medicine to needy people in Europe. President Woodrow Wilson appointed Herbert Hoover, who had earlier led a relief effort for Belgium, to head the American Relief Administration. Hoover raised another $100 million in private donations and, from 1919 to 1921, distributed aid to twenty-three European countries. Word of the horrific famine afflicting Russia prompted Congress to allocate $20 million for its relief. The American Relief Administration operated in Russia from November 1921 to June 1923, employed 300 Americans and 120,000 Russians and daily fed an average of 10,500,000 people. Congress terminated that aid programme after learning that Lenin was actually selling Russian and pilfered American grain to foreign countries for the hard currency. History's ironies never cease.

Chapter 3

POWER STRUGGLE

'[T]he New Economic Policy meant the restoration of private property and the revival of the middle class . . . Naturally, this was . . . a retreat on the ideological front. As soon as the NEP was instituted, the confusion and famine began to subside. The cities came back to life. Products started to reappear in the market stalls, and prices fell.' (Nikita Khrushchev)

'Stalin . . . wanted to influence us psychologically, to undermine our limitless love for Lenin and to increase his own stature as the uncontested leader and great thinker of our era.' (Nikita Khrushchev)

'Trotsky is making another . . . attempt to prepare the ground to substitute Trotskyism for Leninism. Trotsky badly needs to dethrone the party and the cadres that went through the uprising, so that, having dethroned the party, he can proceed to dethrone Leninism.' (Joseph Stalin)

'Comrade Stalin, having become General Secretary, has accumulated enormous power in his hands and I am not quite sure that whether he will always be able to use this power carefully enough.' (Vladimir Lenin)

'The time has come to replace the slogan, "Long live Leninism!" with the slogan "Long live Stalinism!"' (Lazar Kaganovich)

Communism worsened rather than alleviated conditions for most Soviets as the communists exploited workers and peasants worse than the bourgeois managers and landowners they had eliminated and replaced. Nikita Khrushchev vividly described what life was like:

> Those first years of Soviet power were years of struggle and hardship and self-sacrifice. But the People still believed in the Party; even the most illiterate of our citizens understood the Party's slogans and rallying

> cries . . . We told ourselves that no matter how bad things were, they had been worse . . . before the Revolution. Actually, that wasn't true for everyone. The most highly skilled miners in the pits where I worked . . . had been better off before the Revolution . . . I lived worse after the Revolution when I was deputy manager of mining operations than before the Revolution when I was a simple metalworker.[1]

Karl Radek was among those who worried whether communism's ruthless ends justified the means. He especially regretted the hypocrisy whereby the Communist Party repressed and manipulated the proletariat and peasants to 'liberate' them. He recognized the irony that the Communist Party was alienating the very people that it was supposed to inspire:

> The Party is the politically conscious vanguard of the working class. We are now at a point where the workers, at the end of their endurance, refuse any longer to follow a vanguard which leads them to battle and sacrifice . . . Ought we to yield to the clamours of the workingmen who have reached the limit of their patience but do not understand their true interests as we do? But the Party has decided that we must not yield, that we must impose our will to victory on our exhausted and dispirited followers.[2]

The tragic mix over six years of world war then civil war and communism devastated the economy and the lives of most Russians. The economy of 1920 was 40 per cent that of 1913. The value of finished industrial products in 1921 was 16 per cent that of 1912 and semi-finished products 12 per cent.[3]

3.1 Production in Key Sectors, 1913 and 1921[4]

	Coal	Steel	Rail Freight	Grain
1913	29,000,000	4,000,000	132,000,000	80,100,000
1921	8,900,000	200,000	39,400,000	37,600,000

Hatred of the communist regime was widespread, but the Red Army and Cheka swiftly eliminated any dissent. After the defeat of the White and Polish armies, the most serious threat to communist rule was the revolt of 15,000 sailors and workers at the Kronstadt naval base on the Gulf of Finland near Petrograd from 1 to 8 March 1921. The rebels formed soviets and demanded the abolition of the communist regime and the implementation of democracy with freedom of speech, assembly, the press and free elections with multiple parties. Lenin had the Red Army brutally crush the revolt.

Every dictator is unique in how he asserts power. Biographer Louis Fisher explained Lenin's style:

> Lenin was a dictator, but not the kind of dictator that Stalin later became. He employed maximum violence with minimum mercy against people he considered his political enemies . . . Inside the Bolshevik power apparatus, however, he wore out and argued down his communist opponents, at worst he demoted or dismissed them, sometimes excluded them from the Party . . . but did not send them to an executioner's dungeon. He dictated by force of will, persistence, vitality, superior knowledge, executive talent, political vigour, practical sense and persuasion.[5]

The Communist Revolution's failures discouraged Lenin. He sought a major reform from the Tenth Party Congress that convened from 8 to 16 March 1921. During a speech, he admitted that: 'We have failed to convince the broad masses.' He also deplored the moral and intellectual shortcomings of countless communists, but explained: 'No profound and popular movement in all history has taken place without its share of filth, with adventurers and rogues, without boastful and noisy elements . . . A ruling party inevitably attracts careerists.' As bad was the Soviet Union's 'bureaucratic deformities' and 'the prevalence of personal spite and malice'. Later he lamented that: 'We are living in a sea of illegality' and the Communist Party 'lacks general culture'.[6] German communist Rosa Luxemburg argued that Lenin's dictatorship caused those and other problems: 'The remedy invented by Lenin and Trotsky, the general suppression of democracy, is worse than the evil it is supposed to cure.'[7]

Lenin recognized that the communism that confiscated private property and businesses, imposed industrial and agricultural production quotas and imprisoned or executed any opponents had devastated the economy. He proposed and eventually forged a consensus for a New Economic Policy (NEP) that encouraged entrepreneurs to profit by investing in businesses with production and prices determined by supply and demand – in other words, the very system of private property and free markets that communism was dedicated to destroying. Khrushchev explained Lenin's logic:

> This was a bold, decisive and dangerous – but absolutely necessary – step for him to take . . . In essence, the New Economic Policy meant the restoration of private property and the revival of the middle class . . . The

> commercial element in our society was firmly back on its feet. Naturally, this was . . . a retreat on the ideological front, but it helped us recover from the Civil War. As soon as the NEP was instituted, the confusion and famine began to subside. The cities came back to life. Products started to reappear in the market stalls and prices fell.[8]

Meanwhile, the Communist Party targeted a rural scapegoat to blame for the famine, poverty and exploitation there. Four out of five Russians were peasants. Poverty afflicted most peasants who sheltered in hovels, worked small plots of land and struggled to harvest enough food to feed themselves. Kulaks were enterprising peasants, adept at buying and selling land, crops, livestock and equipment. They lived in larger, better furnished houses and farmed more acres than most of their neighbours. The Communists condemned kulaks as a peasant bourgeoisie that exploited the peasant masses. Lenin declared: 'Merciless mass terror against the kulaks . . . Death to them!'[9]

***

The Communist Party's Eleventh Congress convened at Moscow from 27 March to 2 April 1922, attended by 522 delegates with speaking and voting rights and 165 with just speaking rights. They elected a Central Committee with twenty-seven full and nineteen candidate members. The Central Committee then elected the Politburo with seven full members – Vladimir Lenin, Leon Trotsky, Joseph Stalin, Lev Kamenev, Grigori Zinoviev, Alexei Rykov and Mikhail Tomsky and three candidates – Nikolai Bukharin, Vyacheslav Molotov and Mikahil Kalinin.

Stalin was among those the Central Committee re-elected to both the Politburo and Orgburo. Atop those posts, the Central Committee conferred on Stalin another position that he would steadily exploit eventually to become the Soviet Union's totalitarian ruler. On 3 April 1922, the Central Committee appointed Stalin to be General Secretary of the Communist Party, with Vyacheslav Molotov and Valerian Kuybyshev as his deputies.

Molotov soon became Stalin's most devoted follower.[10] They first met when they worked together on *Pravda* in 1917. Molotov's real name was Scriabin, but like Stalin he adopted an alias to help dodge the police. Like Stalin, Molotov was ruthless and relentless. Lenin thought little of Molotov, accusing him of the 'most shameful bureaucratism and the most stupid'.[11] Although Molotov was merciless toward 'enemies of the people', he adored and let himself be manipulated by his wife,

Polina Karpovskaya. She was a devoted revolutionary whose alias was Zhemchuzhia or 'Pearl.' Polina and Nadya, Stalin's wife, became best friends.

***

Unexpectantly, a power vacuum appeared at the apex of Soviet power that Stalin was eager to fill.

At age 52, Lenin suffered a stroke on 26 May 1922, that paralyzed his right side and rendered him speechless. By July, he had regained the ability to speak and write, but remained feeble. On 15 December 1922, the Politburo established a committee of Stalin, Lev Kamenev and Nikolai Bukharin to oversee Lenin's medical care and daily activities. They imposed these restrictions: 'Vladimir Ilyich has the right to dictate every day for five or ten minutes, but this cannot have the character of correspondence and Vladimir Ilyich may not expect to receive any answers. He is forbidden [political] visitors. Friends or those around him may not inform him about political affairs.'[12]

Stalin committed an act that severely aggravated Lenin's stress after he learned about it. He telephoned his wife Nadezhda Krupskaya and severely criticized her. On 23 December 1922, she wrote Kamenev and Zinoviev that: 'Stalin allowed himself yesterday an unusually rude outburst directed at me . . . During all these thirty years I have never heard from any comrade one word of rudeness . . . I beg you to protect me from rude interference with my private life and from vile invectives and threats.'[13]

Stalin's belligerence bolstered Lenin's growing worries about his ambitions. From 23 to 29 December 1922, Lenin dictated to his secretary Lydia Fontiyeva a 'Testament' that assessed the Communist Party and its key leaders. His worst criticism was of Stalin and he called for his dismissal as General Secretary. His Testament was to be read after his death by the next Congress.

Meanwhile, Lenin dictated a letter to Stalin on 5 March 1923, that read:

> You permitted yourself a rude summons of my wife to the telephone and a rude reprimand of her . . . I have no intention to forget so easily that which is being done against me and I need not stress here that I consider as directed against me that which is being done against my wife. I ask . . . that you weigh carefully whether you are agreeable to retracting your words and apologizing or whether you prefer the severance of relations between us.[14]

Stalin's reply or whether he made one is unknown. What is clear is that Lenin's debilitation emboldened him to commit acts that he would never have done when Lenin was healthy and firmly in charge. Nikita Khruschev later astutely explained that:

> I think Stalin's attitude toward Krupskaya was just another instance of his disrespect toward Lenin himself . . . Stalin never let himself breath a word against Krupskaya in public, but in the inner circle he allowed himself to say all sorts of outrageous things about her . . . He wanted to influence us psychologically, to undermine our limitless love for Lenin and to increase his own stature as the uncontested leader and great thinker of our era. To this end, he cautiously but deliberately sprinkled into the consciousness of those around him the idea that privately he wasn't of the same opinion about Lenin that he professed publicly.'[15]

Lenin was moved from Moscow to his home at Gorki in May 1923.

Stalin now felt confident enough to launch a systematic campaign to amass total power in his hands.[16] That campaign's first phase targeted Leon Trotsky, his strongest rival, for destruction. Stalin and Trotsky despised each other and over the years exchanged increasingly biting criticisms. Trotsky distained Stalin as an unsophisticated boor and thug, good for carrying out brutal or tedious missions, but unworthy of being among the Bolshevik Party's inner circle. He repelled Stalin's early attempts to forge a friendship between them. He understood Stalin's warped psyche that made him potentially dangerous:

> Being enormously envious and ambitious, he could not but feel his intellectual and moral inferiority every step of the way . . . Only much later did I realize that he had been trying to establish some sort of familiar relations. But I was repelled by the very qualities that would strengthen him . . . namely the narrowness of his interests, his pragmatism, his psychological coarseness and the special cynicism of the provincial.[17]

Stalin was jealous of Trotsky's superior intellect, eloquence and worldliness and bristled at his condescension. He was dead set to drive Trotsky from the Communist Party and take his power and prestige. He denounced Trotsky in speeches at both the Twelfth Congress in April and the combined plenum of the Central Committee and the Central Control Commission in October 1923.

Stalin's aggression bewildered rather than alarmed Trotsky. At one point, Trotsky pleaded to Lenin that: 'There must be an immediate and radical change . . . It is necessary that Stalin . . . revise his behaviour. Let him not overreach himself. There should be no more intrigues, but honest cooperation.'[18] Stalin was not the only target of Trotsky's sneering contempt. He had also alienated most top communists, especially Lev Kamenev and Grigori Zinoviev. Zinoviev and Trotsky both wanted to replace Lenin as leader. Stalin would enlist Kamenev and Zinoviev as allies to destroy Trotsky, before turning on them. He knew his campaign would take years to realize in a series of prolonged battles that steadily eliminated enemies and friends alike and enhanced his institutional, legal and cultural power.

As General Secretary, Stalin packed the Communist Party's ranks with devoted followers. Biographer Robert McNeal revealed that extent of his power:

> In 1924, two years after Stalin had assumed his post, 90.6 per cent of the secretaries in 55 provinces had been in the job less than two years and 69.2 per cent less than one year. In addition, it appears that the Secretaries controlled the budgets of the regional party commands, disbursing to them the largess that the party received secretly from the state. Finally, the Secretariat exercised substantial control of the party's organs, especially *Pravda* and the network of agitprop workers. The power to suppress opposition propaganda was equally important. In September 1927 the party forbade publication of a long 'platform' that the opposition had prepared and this goaded the dissidents into establishing an underground printing press, a step that enabled Stalin to accuse them of treason.[19]

***

A massive stroke killed Lenin on 21 January 1924. He had wanted to be buried near his mother in his hometown, but the Central Committee plenum convened the following day to discuss how to honour Lenin in death. They decided to immortalize Lenin, a decision confirmed unanimously by the Second All-Union of Soviets that met on 26 January. In doing so, his colleagues ignored Lenin's wishes to be quietly buried with no ceremony in a remote place. Instead, the Communist Party established a 'Lenin Cult' with heroic statues and paintings of him across the country and constant paeans by members to his alleged genius and leadership. Lenin's writings were published to be extolled and studied by all.

The state funeral took place on 27 January. The regime entombed Lenin in a small wooden mausoleum at the base of the Kremlin wall on Red Square. Stalin was among the pall bearers that carried Lenin's coffin to the vault. Stalin gave this eulogy for Lenin: 'Comrades, we Communists are people of a special cut . . . We are those who form the army of the great proletarian strategist, the army of Comrade Lenin. There is nothing higher than the honour of belonging to this army. There is nothing higher than the title of member of the party whose founder and leader was comrade Lenin.'[20] Later that year, Stalin lengthened his rather skimpy list of written works with *The Foundations of Leninism* and *On Lenin and Leninism* that at once extolled the great man and himself for understanding and carrying on his great work.

The question on everyone's mind was who should follow Lenin as the Soviet Union's leader. The ideologically and politically correct response was that no one could fill Lenin's place and that collective leadership should prevail. That did not stop Stalin and other ambitious comrades from struggling to take his place.

***

Stalin's drive for power was nearly stillborn. The Thirteenth Congress convened from 23 to 31 May 1924, with 748 delegates with full rights to vote and speak and 416 delegates who could only speak. Nadya Krupskaya submitted Lenin's 'Testament' to the Congress and it was read before the delegates. The first part included this: 'I would strongly advise that this Congress adapt several changes in our political system', with the most important expanding the Central Committee from fifty to a hundred members. Lenin clearly favoured Trotsky over Stalin: 'Comrade Stalin, having become General Secretary, has concentrated unlimited power in his hands and I am not convinced that he will always manage to use this power with sufficient care. On the other hand, Comrade Trotsky . . . is characterized by outstanding talents. To be sure, he is personally the most capable person in the present Central Committee.' Then came this bombshell warning:

> Stalin is too crude and this defect, which is entirely acceptable in our milieu and in relations among us as communists, becomes unacceptable in the position of General Secretary. I therefore propose to comrades that they should devise a means of removing him from this job and should appoint . . . someone . . . who is distinguished . . . by . . . more tolerant, more polite, more attentive toward comrades, less capricious.[21]

Stalin reacted to the those unexpected, damning and embarrassing charges with public contrition and decisive behind-the-scenes manipulation. In a speech, he declared: 'We have Lenin's instructions . . . and I think it is now time to carry them out. I therefore request the plenum to release me from the post of General Secretary.'[22]

The Central Committee failed to act on Lenin's prescient views and accept Stalin's offer to resign. In his three preceding years as the Communist Party's general secretary, Stalin had packed the national and regional ranks with supporters. Now his influence was powerful enough to get most delegates to agree to keep it secret. Much to their later regret, his allies Kamenev and Zinoviev led the effort to reconfirm Stalin in all his power positions.

Stalin then counter-attacked with a speech that exposed 'Comrade Trotsky's six principal errors'. Stalin invented and condemned what he called 'Trotskyism'. He repeatedly insisted that: 'The task of the Party is to bury Trotskyism as an ideology.'[23] But when Kamenev and Zinoviev called for Trotsky's expulsion, Stalin shrewdly knew that drastic step was premature so he opposed it. He sought to be the calm, moderate, wise voice between histrionic extremes.

He unleashed another barrage against Trotsky during a Trade Union plenum on November 1924. With his speech pointedly titled 'Trotskyism or Leninism?' he warned that: 'Trotsky is making another . . . attempt to prepare the ground to substitute Trotskyism for Leninism. Trotsky badly needs to dethrone the party and the cadres that went through the uprising, so that, having dethroned the party, he can proceed to dethrone Leninism.'[24] Of course, while accurately describing Trotsky's ambitions he also expressed his own. Eventually, Stalin would replace Leninism with Stalinism.

Stalin's January 1925 attack on Trotsky was especially searing:

> Trotsky does not understand and I doubt whether he will ever understand, that the Party demands of its former and present leaders not diplomatic evasions but an honest admission of mistakes. Trotsky, evidently, lacks the courage frankly to admit his mistakes. He does not understand that the Party's sense of power and dignity has grown, that the Party feels that it is the master and demands that we should bow our heads to it when circumstances demand.[25]

Of course, what Stalin really sought was that he rather than the Communist Party would hold all power and loyalty.

The Central Committee voted to fire Trotsky as Army and Navy Commissar on 25 January 1925. Kamenev proposed Stalin to replace him. A majority rejected that proposal and instead appointed Mikhail Frunze. When a heart attack killed Frunze on 26 October 1926, Stalin got the Central Committee to approve Kliment Voroshilov, a key ally, for that post.

The Fourteenth Party Congress convened from 18 to 31 December 1925, with 665 delegates with speaking and voting rights and 641 with just speaking rights. They represented 643,000 Communist Party members and 445,000 member applicants. Stalin had wielded his General Secretary powers to ensure that most delegates were his own handpicked supporters. He got them to approve the Central Committee's expansion to sixty-three full and forty-three candidate members, then filled most of those seats with his own followers.

Stalin's growing power unnerved most of his comrades. During a speech, Kamenev issued this warming on behalf of those troubled by his rise:

> We are against creating a 'leadership' theory. We are against making a 'leader.' We are against having the Secretariat which in practice unites both policy and organization, standing above the political organ. We are for having the Politburo so organized internally that, while it unites all the politicians of the Party, our top body genuinely has full power; and we are for the Secretariat being subordinate to the Politburo and carrying out its instructions. I personally suggest that our General Secretary is not the person to unite the old Bolshevik staff around him . . . I have said it countless times to Comrade Stalin and I have said it countless times to the group of Leninist comrades.[26]

Stalin kept his face expressionless as he inwardly burned at Kamenev's denunciation. Kamenev was now high of his list of those eventually to completely destroy. In a rebuttal speech, Stalin denied any ambition for more power and only admitted that: 'I am coarse, comrades. I am coarse and heavy-handed toward those who perfidiously try to divide and destroy the Party. I have not concealed it. Perhaps you need a certain softness in dealing with rebels. But that is not in my nature.'[27] Congress reappointed Stalin to the Central Committee, which, now mostly packed with Stalin's allies, tabled Kamenev's proposal to replace Stalin as General Secretary.

Stalin steadily built a personality cult around himself. Among the measures that he got the Communist Party to endorse in 1925, on 10 April his comrades voted to change Tsaritsyn's name to Stalingrad to honour his services there during the Civil War. Another was the Communist Party's approval of Deputy General Secretary Molotov's motion that Stalin's Marxist writings be collected and published in a book. Even as Stalin now allied with Bukharin, he sought to undermine and replace him as the Communist Party's theoretician. He sought to socialize his comrades to believe this critique of Bukharin: 'As a theorist, he is not completely Marxist, he is a theorist who needs to study some more if he wants to be a Marxist theorist.' Among the later trumped-up charges against Bukharin that justified murdering him was he was not a pure communist in thought as well as deed.[28]

Stalin got Central Committee plenums to fire Zinoviev as Leningrad's Communist Party chair on 26 March 1926 and replace him with Sergei Kirov, among his most devoted followers, then fire Zinoviev as Comintern's chair on 22 November 1926 and replace him with Bukharin. He got Kamenev fired from the Politburo on 1 January 1926, as deputy chair of the Council of People's Commissars on 16 January 1927 and from the Central Committee on 19 November 1927. He got the Central Committee to expel Trotsky and Zinoviev from the Communist Party on 15 November. The Fifteenth Party Congress that met from 2 to 19 December 1927 ratified those expulsions. Nearly all of the 898 delegates with speaking and voting rights and 711 delegates with just speaking rights were Stalin's followers.

One criticism that Stalin hurled against Trotsky, Zinoviev and Kamenev was their belief that the Soviet Union would only survive if communist revolutions erupted in other countries. To that end, they had supported the Communist International (Comintern) and diverted scare money, men and other resources to foreign countries. Stalin argued that Comintern had failed but also the European countries posed no immediate threat. So the Communist Party should devote itself to perfecting 'Socialism in One Country'. During the Fifteenth Party Congress, he reassured the delegates that 'Socialism in One Country' was not incompatible with provoking communist revolutions elsewhere: 'To win fully, to win definitely, we must see to it that the current capitalist encirclement be changed to a socialist one; we must strive for the proletariat's winning in at least a few other countries. Only then will our victory be full and final.'[29]

Stalin followed up his Fifteenth Congress victories with his latest false offer to resign as General Secretary in the next Central Committee plenum. He declared: 'I think that until recently there were circumstances that put the party in the position of needing me in the post as person who was fairly rough in his dealings, to constitute a certain antidote to the opposition . . . Now the opposition has not only been smashed, it has been expelled from the party . . . Therefore I ask the plenum to relieve me of the post of general secretary.'[30] The Central Committee voted unanimously to retain him as General Secretary.

***

Stalin now led the Soviet Union, although his powers were not yet absolute. How was Stalin able to outfox and eliminate all his rivals and allies alike to become the Soviet Union's totalitarian ruler?

Stalin was not content to systematically expel his rivals from their government and party posts and eventually have them arrested and executed. Accompanying and justifying those purges was his rewriting of history. For instance, amidst his campaign against Trotsky, he asserted: 'Trotsky did not play any special role in the October uprising, nor could he do so, being chairman of the Petrograd Soviet, he merely carried out the will of the appropriate party bodies, which directed every step Trotsky took . . . This talk about Trotsky's special role is a legend being spread by obliging "party gossip".'[31]

Stalin's rivals empowered him by consistently underestimating his abilities and ambitions. Biographer Adam Ulam explained:

> Whatever their respect for his guile and internal manoeuvrings, his enemies were always sure of one thing: Stalin could never become the leader of international Communism. He had hardly been abroad, he had not mastered a single foreign language, his pretensions as a theorist were ridiculous. How could a man like that step into Lenin's shoes or people like Zinoviev and Bukharin? Yet here again he fooled them.[32]

Stalin was a master political strategist and tactician. He outfoxed his rivals time after time. As General Secretary he steadily deepened and broadened his following within the Communist Party at the national, regional and local levels. None of his foes could muster more than handfuls of comrades because they lacked an institution for a power base to nurture over time. And none of them could match Stalin in sheer ruthlessness, jealousy and hatred, in his drive to eliminate anyone who appeared more intelligent, articulate or charismatic than himself.

Chapter 4

STALINISM

> 'To gain a final victory of socialism in our country, we must catch up with and pass capitalist countries in technology and economy.' (Joseph Stalin)

> 'The history of Old Russia shows . . . that because of her backwardness, she was constantly being defeated . . . Beaten because of backwardness – military, cultural, political, industrial and agricultural backwardness . . . We are behind the leading countries . . . We must make up this gap distance in ten years.' (Joseph Stalin)

Stalinism was Joseph Stalin's transformation of the Soviet Union from an authoritarian into a totalitarian tyrannical regime where with unrestrained power he controlled the Communist Party and government to determine virtually all key political, economic, social and cultural relations and outcomes.[1] He justified totalitarianism with typical Orwellian Communist double-talk during a speech at the 1930 Sixteenth Party Congress:

> We are for the withering of the state. But at the same time we stand for the strengthening of the proletariat dictatorship, which constitutes the most powerful, the mightiest of all governing powers that have ever existed. The highest development of government power for the purpose of preparing the conditions for withering away of governmental power, this is the Marxist formula. Is this 'contradictory?' Yes, it is contradictory. But this contradiction is life and it reflects completely the Marxist dialectic.'[2]

Stalin's literal seat of power was an office on the Central Committee building's fifth floor on Old Square until 1930 when he shifted to another office in the Kremlin's Yellow Palace, also called the Sovnarkom or Council of Ministers building. Within the vast Kremlin fortress, he lived at Poteshny until his wife Nadezhda's death then swapped apartments with Bukharin to live at the 'Little Corner.' Half a dozen miles from the Kremlin he had a dacha he named 'Nearby,' another named Volinskoe beside a lake a few miles further in the village of Kuntsevo, a third named Zubalovo on the Moscow River 20 miles from Moscow and a dacha overlooking the Black Sea in Sochi.

Stalin's daily routine compounded the stress for those who worked directly with him and faithfully executed his commands.[3] He was a night-owl who rose around noon then worked at his Kremlin office until around six or seven in the evening. He then usually invited his closest advisors for dinners that often morphed into alcoholic binges extending late into the night. He enjoyed getting his sycophants drunk and urging them to commit humiliating antics and crude jokes.

***

Stalin essentially completed the communist revolution from 1928 to 1933, with the First Economic Plan that nationalized all property, eliminated open markets and assigned each industry production quotas.[4] He promised that would initiate a virtuous cycle of ever greater communism, modernization, industrialization and global power: 'To gain a final victory of socialism in our country, we must catch up with and pass capitalist countries in technology and economy.' For a precedent and model, he looked back two centuries: 'When Peter the Great, competing with the more developed Western countries, feverishly constructed industrial works and factories to provide for supplies for the army and to strengthen the country's defences, this was an attempt to eliminate backwardness.' He gave the Soviet Union a decade to achieve communism and darkly warned what would happen if that effort failed: 'We are fifty or a hundred years behind the advanced countries. We must make good this distance in ten years. Either we do it or we shall go under.'[5]

Stalin announced the first Five-Year Plan from 1929 to 1933 to communize the economy during the Fifteenth Party Congress, held from 2 to 19 December 1927. The Supreme Economic Council and the State Planning Commission (Gosplan) devised and implemented the Five-Year Plan with vast arrays of quotas and subsidies that targeted key industries like iron and steel, machine tools, tractors, trucks, aircraft, automobiles, petroleum, chemicals and military weapons like tanks, artillery and warships. Industrial muscle is only as strong as the infrastructure skeleton that embeds it. The Five-Year Plan improved or built bridges, ports, canals, railways, electrical power plants, transmission lines, water and sewage systems, hospitals, schools, warehouses and other structures. The most celebrated was Moscow's Metro or subway system with many stations encased in marble and displaying works of art, whose construction Nikita Khruschev supervised.

Stalin's most ambitious infrastructure project was the 141-mile, nineteen-lock Baltic-White Sea Canal constructed mostly by 126,000 slave labourers from January 1931 until its opening on 2 August 1933. Officially, of those workers, the state freed 12,484 and shortened the sentences of 59,526, while 12,300 died during its construction; the unofficial estimates of the death roll are around 25,000 workers. That human and financial toll produced a canal just 11½ft deep that could be transited by small vessels no larger than 600 deadweight tons, far short of the 2,000 to 3,000 deadweight tons of ocean-going vessels. The canal was supposed to be 17½ft deep, but funding shortfalls forced engineers to that shallower level.[6]

The Communist Party exploited workers much worse than their predecessors.[7] Workers detested the Communist managerial class or 'bosses' (*nachalstov*) for their arrogance, corruption and incompetence. To those who worried that communism actually recreated a system in which the ruling elite enjoyed virtually all wealth extracted from the exploited masses, Stalin retorted: 'These people think that socialism requires equality, equality in the needs and personal life of the members of society. These are petty bourgeoisie views of our left-wing scatterbrains . . . The left-wingers do not understand that money and moneyed economy will remain with us for a long time.'[8] Defence Commissar Klimenti Voroshilov complained bitterly to Stalin about the workers: 'I no longer know what to do to make these people assume some of their responsibilities, to work differently in our way, our socialist way. I cannot say that these people do not work; on the contrary they work until they are exhausted, but with no results.'[9]

The communization of industry devastated the economy. From 1928 to 1933, economic production fell short of quotas or outright plummeted. The Five-Year Plan promised to expand steel production from 4 million to 10.4 million tons but only reached 6 million tons; coal from 35 million tons to 75 million tons with 64 million actual tons; electricity from 500 million kilowatts to 22 billion with 13 billion actual kilowatts; chemical fertilizer from 175,000 tons to 8 million tons with 1 million actual tons.[10]

There were some successes. From 1926 to 1939 the urban population increased by 30,000,000 or from 18 per cent to 24 per cent of the total population. The salaried labour force of industrial workers and administrators rose from 10,800,000 to 22,600,000. For better or worse, the number of bureaucrats soared from 2,767,000 in 1924 to 8,780,000 in 1935 and exceeded the number of factory workers.[11]

***

One vast challenge that Stalin promised communism would resolve was agricultural – peasants hoarding crops and high food prices. The worst problem was grain production which had plummeted from an average annual 1,000,000,000 poods from 1909 to 1913 to 514,000,000 poods from 1923 to 1927. Yet, communist policies of imposing low prices on grain and confiscating grain hordes provoked those shortages by robbing peasants of incentives either to plant or sell what they sowed; instead, peasants converted fields to crops without price controls and either fed what grain they produced to their livestock or hid it in hope of higher future prices.[12] The food shortages led to a famine that killed millions in some regions like Ukraine and strict rationing across the Soviet Union. Ignoring their ideological commitment to 'equality', the Communist Party actually imposed a food rationing system with fifteen grades depending on the relative caloric requirements of one's work; miners and factory workers got 'priority' portions.[13]

Typically, rather than look in the mirror, the communists identified a scapegoat to blame and destroy. Communism condemns kulaks or wealthy peasants as rural bourgeoisie, who allegedly get rich suppressing and exploiting poor peasants, the rural proletariat. The trouble was establishing criteria for differentiating rich peasants from other peasants. How many more cows or chickens did a peasant have to own more than his neighbours to be a detested kulak? Stalin puzzled over that key question: 'What does kulak mean?'[14] Neither he nor any fellow communist ever definitively answered that. Instead, they finessed it by empowering communist cadres to simply denounce, arrest and prosecute kulaks as they imagined them. The most common charge was 'speculation' or hoarding to drive up prices with the penalty confiscation of the property and at least three years as a slave labourer in the Gulag. Another critical charge was 'wrecking' or sabotage by destroying the economic means of production in agriculture, industries, infrastructure and sales outlets.

Stalin warned that kulaks prosed an existential threat to the revolution. In December 1929, he commanded 'the liquidation of the kulaks as a class', tapped Molotov to destroy them and had the Politburo empower him with the decree 'On the Means for the Liquidation of

Kulak Farms in Areas of Complete Collectivization'. Molotov and his staff estimated that kulaks numbered from 5,000,000 to 7,000,000 people. They split the kulaks in three classes, with the richest to be murdered, the middling sort to be sent to slave labour concentration camps and the lowest level to be exiled in scattered underpopulated towns in Siberia or the Arctic Circle.

Stalin's regime rounded up and deported 1,680,000 peasants to slave labour camps or isolated towns in 1930 and 1931. The army and police ruthlessly massacred those that resisted. With nothing to lose, over 800,000 peasants engaged in over 2,000 revolts against the communist system. Stalin's regime confiscated their crops and livestock. Peasants killed their livestock rather than surrender it to the communists. Crop production plunged from an index of 100 in 1928 to 81.5 in 1933; livestock was 65 per cent of its 1913 level, with horses plummeting from 32.1 million to 15.4 million, cattle from 60.1 million to 33.5 million, sheep from 97.3 million to 32.9 million and pigs from 22 million to 11.5 million. Atop that the Soviet Union exported grain to earn desperately needed hard currency with 1 million poods shipped abroad in 1928, 13 million in 1929, 48.3 million in 1930, 51.8 million in 1931, 18 million in 1932 and 10 million in 1933.[15] The result was food shortages across the Soviet Union and famine in southern Ukraine, middle Volga, northern Caucasus and Kazakhstan.

Meanwhile, the Communist Party nationalized all farmland and herded peasants into vast collective farms (*kolkhoz*) where families inhabited rooms with communal toilets in hastily constructed buildings, ate in cafeterias, performed daily quotas of work and were severely punished if they protested and worse if they resisted.[16] The communization of agriculture, the elimination of private property and markets and the imposition of a command economy was a catastrophe that killed as many as 8,500,000 million people, 7,500,000, including 3,000,000 children, from starvation and another 1,000,000 who died from execution, disease or suicide.[17] During one of their summits, Winston Churchill asked Stalin about collectivization. Stalin complained that: 'it was a terrible struggle' and they had to murder 'ten million . . . It was fearful. Four years it lasted. It was absolutely necessary . . . It was no use arguing with them.'[18]

Collectivization also destroyed the lively peasant village cultures of Russians and other ethnic groups to replace them with brutal uniformity and conformity. Historian Moshe Lewin explained that tragic transformation: '"We are not our own men but the *kolkhoz*'s." the peasants often repeated. This summed up the whole process. Before they had been their own men, now they belonged to the *Kolkhoz*, but the *Kolkhoz* did not belong to them.'[19]

***

Naturally the chasm between what the Communists promised and what they delivered enraged countless people. Nikita Khrushchev explained:

> Many workers were worse off than they had ever been under capitalism. They were starving. Although the workers were making great sacrifices for the sake of industrializing and fortifying our country, they were under the impression that with the victory of the Revolution, their lives would improve materially . . . We had been taught by the Party to believe that once we set about building Communism, the means of consumption would be evenly distributed among all those who toiled. Yet here were bourgeois specialists being singled out for special privileges and high wages while the workers were being paid less than in the old pre-Revolutionary days.[20]

To those who, given communism's cataclysmic results, timidly suggested that Stalin was trying to modernize the Soviet Union too fast, he warned that national security was critically at stake: 'To slow down the tempo [of industrialization] means to lag behind. And those who lag behind are beaten. The history of Old Russia shows . . . that because of her backwardness, she was constantly being defeated . . . Beaten because of backwardness – military, cultural, political, industrial and agricultural backwardness.'[21] He insisted that his imposition of pure communism was a brilliant success: 'We have built heavy industry under socialism. We have converted the middle peasant to socialism. The main things from the point of view of [socialist] construction have already been done. Relatively little is left for us to do: to learn technology, to master science. And when we accomplish that, we shall have rates of industrialization of which right now we do not even dare dream.'[22]

Yet, despite communism's victorious emergence, Stalin warned that the Soviet Union still harboured countless 'enemies of the people' who had to be unmasked and destroyed. He identified them as:

> The remnants of dying classes – industrialists and their servants, private traders and their stooges, former nobles and priests, kulaks and their henchmen, former White officers and NCOs, former gendarmes and policemen – they have wormed their way into our factories, our

> institutions and trading bodies, our railway and river transport enterprises and . . . our collective and state farms . . . Of course, they have brought with them their hatred of the Soviet regime.'[23]

They sabotaged the economy by burning, breaking, exploding, diseasing, derailing and killing. They must be exposed and destroyed.

Stalin and his fellow zealots could never admit that communism itself inevitably caused mass economic destruction and human suffering and death. Instead, he masked communism's inevitable catastrophes with scapegoats. He had the Communist Party's ranks purged from 3,000,000 members in January 1933 to 2,700,000 in December 1933. Most were simply expelled, but tens of thousands were charged and convicted of various crimes and thousands were executed.[24] Those mass murders were merely a harbinger of the genocide of millions to come.

***

Stalin's wife Nadya was among countless Soviets for whom the despair of existing within a totalitarian communist state eventually overwhelmed her. She bore the double burden of marriage to Stalin. They had a stormy relationship, with frequent shouting matches and separate bedrooms.

Four children crowded Stalin's Kremlin apartment complex: Yakov born with his first wife in 1907; two children of their own, Vasily and Svetlana, born respectively in 1921 and 1926; and Artyom Sergeev, a comrade's baby orphaned and adopted in 1921.[25] What is astonishing is the children did not turn out worse. Being the child of anyone famous can be a terrible burden as mingled privileges, expectations and demands can warp the child's development. Having a famous father who is also the feared tyrant of a totalitarian communist regime can compound those potential problems. Atop that, the children had to endure a demanding, critical and untender mother and an infrequently seen father who was mostly remote or scornful and rarely affectionate.

Despite those handicaps, two of the four had relatively successful lives. Svetlana was a bright, chubby, red-haired freckled girl and later woman. Khrushchev observed this about the father-daughter relationship: 'He loved her but he used to express these feelings in a beastly way . . . . He broke the heart first of a child, then of a young girl, then of a woman and mother. It all resulted in Svetlana's gradual psychic breakdown.'[26] They fought bitterly over many issues, especially her choices of husband.

Svetlana defected to the United States in 1966 and wrote a revealing memoir. She described her hellish existence engulfed by Stalin's black shadow at the Kremlin: 'And over it all a wasted, obdurate man . . . who with his accomplices had turned the country into a prison, in which everyone with a breathe of spirit and mind was being extinguished; a man who aroused fear and hatred in millions of men – this was my father.'[27]

Stalin preferred his adopted son to his two natural sons because his natural character was stronger. Artyom rose steadily in the army eventually to become a general. His career bore neither distinction nor controversy. Stalin's two natural sons disappointed him in their personal lives and military careers. Yakov was a slender, sensitive, insecure, sickly boy and later man. Stalin felt he was weak in character and bullied him, believing that would strengthen him. Instead, he merely exacerbated his son's neuroses. When Vasily was 18, he fell in love with and married Zoya, an Orthodox priest's daughter. That enraged Stalin who verbally blistered him whenever he saw him. Yakov tried to shoot himself, but the bullet grazed his chest rather than killed him. That provoked his father's latest cruel quip, that he 'couldn't even shoot straight'.[28] Yakov finally succumbed to his father, divorced Zoya and rejoined the Stalin household. Stalin got him an artillery captain's commission. Yakov was captured during the German invasion and died in captivity. Vasily was an angry trouble-making child who became an angry trouble-making and alcoholic adult; despite wretched military reports about his mean, reckless conduct, he rose to general because no one with authority dared cashier him.

Nadya was quite bright but also neurotic, bipolar and narcissistic and suffered long bouts of deep depression, exhaustion and listlessness. She was aloof to and critical of her natural and adopted children. An abortion in 1926 damaged her uterus. She had a defective heart valve and suffered from angina and rheumatism. Svetlana explained how Stalin ruined her life: 'She was only sixteen when my father took shape in her eyes as a Hero of the Revolution. When she matured, she realized how mistaken she had been. Her own principles ran afoul of his political cynicism and savagery. Everything around her followed what she felt was the wrong path and my father was no more the ideal.'[29]

Nadya died from a gunshot to her heart on the night of 8 November 1932. She had recently read Michael Arlen's book *The Green Hat* that extolls suicide. That evening was the annual banquet and ball for the regime's elite that celebrated the anniversary of the communist takeover of Russia. Stalin flirted with Galina Yegorov, the wife of General

Alexander Yegorov. Perhaps to make him jealous, Nadya danced somewhat suggestively with Abel Yenukidze, a womanizer especially fond of ballerinas. After Stalin rebuked her, Nadya stormed out of the ball. That night Stalin may have gone off with Galina to his dacha. The next morning, their maid found Nayda dead in bed with a bullet wound in her heart. Most likely, she killed herself although naturally gossipers whispered that Stalin had her murdered. There were fresh bruises on her face. Did he return enraged, argue with, punch then shoot her, then go to his dacha? The official medical cause was death from appendicitis. No neighbour admitted to hearing the gunshot that might have provoked a rush to the apartment and perhaps witness who held the smoking gun.

Regardless of how she died, Nadya's death deeply depressed Stalin. With Molotov present, he complained bitterly that 'she left me like an enemy' and 'I didn't save her'.[30] To escape constant reminders of her, he left his children for nannies to raise in their Poteshny Palace apartment complex while he moved to an apartment in the Kremlin's nearby Yellow Palace. He rarely saw his children after that. Later he scapegoated his wife and her suicide for problems that their children suffered: 'Children growing up without their mother can be raised perfectly by nannies, but they can't replace the mother.'[31]

Chapter 5

COMMUNIST CULTURE

> 'The cultural revolution would now suffice to make our country a completely socialist country.' (Vladimir Lenin)

> 'The artist ought to show life truthfully. And if he shows our life truthfully he cannot fail to show it moving to socialism. This is and will be, Socialist Realism.' (Joseph Stalin)

> 'The official art of the Soviet Union – and there is no other over there – resembles totalitarian justice, that is, it is based on lies and deceit. The goal of justice, as of art, is to exalt the 'leader', to fabricate an heroic myth. Human history has never seen anything to equal this in scope and impudence.' (Leon Trotsky)

Culture is a group's distinct values, traditions and aspirations. A cultural group's size can vary from a handful of people to nations or even a group of nations called a civilization. One element of every culture is a group's distinct notion of aesthetics. A group's cultural values and creative ways to express them usually evolve with time.

Vladimir Lenin understood the dynamic among related political, economic, social and cultural revolutions whereby each dimension bolstered the others. He sought a cultural revolution for Russia that transformed its traditional culture into a communist culture.[1] He explained:

> Our opponents told us repeatedly that we were rash in undertaking to implant socialism in an insufficiently cultured country. But they were misled by our having started from the end opposite to that prescribed by theory (the theory of pedants of all kinds), because in our country the political and social revolution preceded the cultural revolution, that very cultural revolution which nevertheless now confronts us. The cultural

> revolution would now suffice to make our country a completely socialist country.[2]

Historian Sheila Fitzpatrick explained Lenin's vision: 'Lenin had rejected the idea that cultural power, like political power, could be seized by revolutionary action. Culture, in his view, had to be patiently acquired and assimilated; Communists must learn from "bourgeois specialists" despite their identification with an alien social class; and refusal to learn was a sign of "Communist conceit".'[3]

Lenin believed that a communist political and cultural revolution were entwined, with one impossible without the other. Having established a Dictatorship of the Proletariat, the Communist Party had to impose a cultural revolution from above on the masses. Yet that involved a dilemma. His wife Nadezhda Krupskaya explained: 'Socialism will be possible only when the psychology of the people is radically changed. To change is the task standing before us.'[4] Leopold Averbakh, who headed the 'Revolutionary Association of Proletarian Writers', elaborated that process: 'The cultural revolution is a lengthy epoch during which human material will be transformed, the toiling masses themselves will be re-educated and a new type of man produced. In this work a great and serious task falls to the lot of art, with its specific means of influencing the whole human psyche.'[5]

A Central Committee resolution in 1928 explained the ends and means of the communist cultural revolution: 'Literature, the theatre and the cinema should all be brought forward and into contact with the widest circles of the population and should be utilized in the fight for a new cultural outlook, a new way of life, against bourgeois and petit-bourgeois ideology, against . . . the resurrection of bourgeois ideology under new labels . . . against a slavish imitation of bourgeois culture.'[6]

Joseph Stalin's policy on art, music and literature was clear – all creative endeavours should glorify the Communist Party and Communism and vilify its enemies. He demanded that: 'The artist ought to show life truthfully. And if he shows our life truthfully he cannot fail to show it moving to socialism. This is and will be, Socialist Realism.'[7] Most of his comrades zealously supported that policy. Indeed, Lenin had Stalin launch the Communist Party's first campaign against free thinkers and artists in August 1922, when he oversaw the expulsion of 160 intellectuals, scientists and artists as 'counterrevolutionaries'.[8] They were lucky to escape with their lives to exile in foreign countries where most were embraced for their creativity.

***

To promote that vision of culture, the Communist Party established a series of institutions. Lenin issued a decree that Russia's artistic heritage be preserved. To that end, Sovnarkom expanded the number of museums from 30 in 1917 to 87 by December 1918 and by 1920, the State had nationalized 550 old mansions and 1,000 private art collections to be museums.[9]

Tsar Peter the Great established the Russian Academy of Sciences in February 1724. For two centuries, the Russian Academy of Sciences promoted scientific and cultural development. The Communist Party set up the Socialist Academy of Socialist Sciences in June 1919 to supersede the Russian Academy of Sciences, renamed it the Socialist Academy in April 1919 and the Communist Academy in April 1924, then merged the two rival institutions into the Soviet Academy of Sciences in February 1936.

The Communist Party founded the 'Russian Association of Proletariat Musicians' (RAMP) in June 1923 and the 'Russian Association of Proletariat Writers' (RAPP) in January 1925, with the latter explicitly required 'to scourge and chastise in the name of the Party'. When those organizations appeared to promote views that seemed to challenge his own, Stalin issued the Decree on the Reformation of Literary and Artistic Organizations in April 1932 that abolished them both. To reward creative people, Stalin established the Stalin Prize for Science and Engineering and for Literature and Art in 1941. Thereafter, he annually presided over the awards ceremony until his death in 1953 and the awards continued until 1956.

***

As for communist painting and other visual arts, Averbakh explained the values that must guide them: 'Proletarian art is not a form of art which must necessarily be created by a proletarian. Proletarian art is such art as aids the proletariat in the building of socialism and organizes our feelings and thoughts in the direction of building of a Communist society.'[10] Forcing artists to conform to that communist 'aesthetic' created a distinct form of 'art'. The result was to render 'Communist culture' a derisive oxymoron for those who equate culture with individual artistic creations within a group of people sharing an aesthetic tradition. As the saying goes, 'there is no accounting for taste'. A stroll through the leading art museums of Moscow or Leningrad reveals the stark divide of 1929. For a dozen years before then, Russian painting was revolutionary with the abstract, jagged images of Constructivists and Supremacists. Thereafter came the endless procession of canvases filled with muscular men and hardy women smiling as they toiled at their machines or in their fields in the workers' paradise. Those with sophisticated tastes may mock 'Soviet Realism' with its cliched human cartoon images that epitomized the ideal 'Soviet Man' and 'Soviet Woman' that the communists were trying to realize. Yet those images comforted and inspired countless Soviets.

Leon Trotsky genuinely thrilled at modern art as revolutionary and abhorred Soviet realism as philistinism personified:

> The October Revolution gave a magnificent impetus to all types of Soviet art [but] the bureaucratic reaction . . . has stifled artistic creation with a totalitarian hand . . . The official art of the Soviet Union – and there is no other over there – resembles totalitarian justice, that is, it is based on lies and deceit. The goal of justice, as of art, is to exalt the 'leader,' to fabricate an heroic myth. Human history has never seen anything to equal this in scope and impudence.[11]

***

As for revolutionary literature, Averbakh explained its essence: 'Proletarian literature we understand as that literature which comprehends the world from the viewpoint of the proletariat and influences the reader in accord with the tasks of the working class.'[12] To that end, the Communist Party forced writers to celebrate proletarian triumphs in their class warfare against the bourgeoisie, surpassing their Five-Year Plan quotas, joyous peasants being collectivized, and related uplifting themes. The Central Committee elaborated that standard with 'On Publishing Work' in August 1931:

> The content and character of the book should in every way respond to the demands of socialist reconstruction; it should be militant and deal with political themes of the present day; it should arm the broad masses of the builders of socialism with Marxist-Leninist theory and with technical knowledge. The book should be the mightiest means of educating, mobilizing and organizing the masses for the tasks of economic and cultural building . . . Imaginative literature . . . should reflect . . . the transformation of social relations and the growth of new people – the heroes of socialist construction.[13]

Prominent novels of 'proletarian literature' included Boris Pilnyak's *Naked Year* (1922), *Tale of the Unextinguished Moon: Murder of the Army Commander* (1926), *Mahogany* (1929), *The Volga Flows into the Caspian Sea*

(1930) and *Birth of Man* (1935); Valentin Kataev's *The Embezzlers* (1929), *Time Forward!* (1933) and *Peace Is Where the Tempests Blow* (1937); Leonid Leonov's *Sot* (1931), *The Thief* (1931) and *Soviet River* (1931); Fyodor Gladkov's *Cement* (1925) and *Energy* (1932); Marietta Shaginian's *Hydrocentral* (1932); Mikhail Sholokhov's *Virgin Soil Upturned* (1932); and Fyodor Panferov's *Brusski: A Story of Peasant Life in Soviet Russia* (1933).

Pilnyak became the All-Russian Union of Writers' president in 1929. His *Tale of the Unextinguished Moon* was a veiled conspiracy story in which, with pseudonyms, Stalin had Defence Commissar Mikhail Frunze murdered and replaced with his devoted supporter Kliment Voroshilov. Stalin banned *Tale of the Undistinguished Moon* in 1926.

Like Stalin, Andrei Zhdanov was a Georgian who entered a seminary and dropped out a communist. He joined the party at age 15, became a political commissar during the civil war and thereafter rose through the ranks through hard work and loyalty. He was very bright and a voracious reader of history and literature. Stalin tapped him to chair the first Congress of Writers in 1934. Zhdanov's mission was to ensure that every novel, poem, play and essay conformed to strict communist correctness.

5.1 Number of Newspapers Before and After the Revolution[14]

	Dailies	2–4 Times Weekly	Weekly	Total
1914	824	240	691	1,767
1928	201	254	47	702

5.2 Production of Books and Pamphlets Before and After the Revolution[15]

	All Titles	All Copies
1913	34,600	133,562,000
1917	13,100	140,000,000
1918	6,100	77,700,000
1927	27,700	212,000,000

Soviet censorship was far worse than under the tsar. Russia had a flourishing semi-free press before the First World War with 824 daily and 1,767 total newspapers in 1914. Wartime censorship and shortages of paper and ink cut back the number of newspapers. On 26 October 1917 Sovnarkom issued the Decree on the Press that warned the state would suppress any publication that resisted Sovnarkom rule. By 1928, there were just 201 daily and 702 total newspapers and they all parroted the Communist Party line. Likewise, the number of bookstores in 1927 was less than in 1914, with 259 in Moscow and 161 in Leningrad compared to around 500 and 341 respectively before the war. And the Communist regime ensured that all those books published were ideologically correct.[16] Stalin purged books and essays along with his political enemies who wrote them. On 7 March 1935, after trials found Leon Trotsky, Grigori Zinoviev and Lev Kamenev guilty of various crimes, Stalin had their written works purged from all libraries and bookstores and made it a crime for people to own copies. He issued the same decree for written works from a bevy of other 'enemies of the people' on 21 June 1935.

Stalin targeted one writer that he wanted to lead the Soviet Union's literary revolution. Maxim Gorky was then Russia's greatest living writer, celebrated for his novels, short stories, plays, memoirs and essays and eventually recipient of five Nobel Prize for Literature nominations. In September 1921, as the Communist Party's terrorism worsened, he fled to exile in Sorento overlooking Naples Bay, Italy. Stalin genuinely admired Gorky as a writer and from 1928 tried to entice him back ideally to glorify his regime. When Gorky explained he needed Italy's healthy climate to relieve his tuberculosis, Stalin offered to send him medical experts to treat his disease or, better yet, give him the best of care in the Soviet Union. He promised him a Moscow townhouse and numerous honours. Gorky could return to Sorento for the winters while enriching the Soviet Union with his brilliance the other three seasons.

Gorky finally agreed to return in 1932. Stalin got Gorky to write essays justifying the elimination of kulaks and other enemies of the people. Hoping that Gorky would write his biography, he had an assistant send him boxes of often doctored materials about his life. Gorky found excuses to postpone beginning that project.

Privately, Gorky deplored the regime's 'stupid habit of raising people up into high positions only to cast them down into the mud . . . These dramas were generally the work of obyvateli (obtuse philistines) and one is reminded of them every time one sees with what delight people throw themselves on to a man who has made a mistake, in order to take his place.'[17] Gorky tried to help out imperilled fellow artists when he could avoid being prosecuted himself. He finally succumbed to being among Stalin's henchmen in 1933 when the tyrant forbade him from leaving the Soviet Union. In an essay about anti-communists for *Pravda*, Gorky asserted: 'If the enemy does not surrender, we must exterminate them.'[18]

Stalin issued the Decree on Artistic and Literary Organizations that abolished the 'Russian Association of Proletariat Musicians' and the 'Russian Association of Proletariat Writers' on 23 April 1932. He then established the 'Union of Soviet Writers' and insisted that Gorky head it. When he renamed the Moscow Art Theatre after Gorky, Ivan Gronsky, one of his head art bureaucrats, dared observe that the venue was better associated with Anton Chekhov. Stalin replied, 'That doesn't matter. Gorky's a vain man. We must bind him with cables to the Party.'[19] Gorky became the central figure for official Communist literature in which the inner circle of truly gifted writers included Boris Pasternak, Isaac Babel, Boris Pilniak and Vasily Grossman.

Stalin was less intolerant of writers than any other career. He eventually soured on Gorky for failing to write his biography and other offenses, but never had him imprisoned, let alone murdered. Of Pasternak, he wrote: 'He's doubtless a great talent. He is very capricious but that's the character of gifted people. Let him write what he wants and when!' Later he rejected advice to have Pasternak arrested: 'Leave that cloud-dweller in peace.'[20] Stalin's favourite writer and for a while drinking buddy was Damian Bedny, the 'Proletariat Poet', whose madcap escapades finally got him booted out of the Kremlin.

Stalin's theatre and film critiques could be deadly and not just at the box office. He walked out of Alexi Tolstoy's play *On the Rack* about Peter the Great, quipping: 'A splendid play. Only it's a pity Peter was not depicted heroically enough.' Stalin summoned Tolstoy, commanded him to write a novel about Peter the Great, then gave him the tsar's 'correct' characteristics and achievements to reveal.[21] He condemned Andrei Platonov's *Higher Command* that dared to satirize collectivization, but did not purge him because he remained a zealous communist.

***

For Lenin, 'Of all the arts, for us the cinema is the most important'.[22] For a population in which only two out of five people were literate before the revolution, cinema was the best medium for indoctrinating them with propaganda.

Lenin initially put his wife Nadezhda Krupskaya in charge of Sovnarkom's Cinema Sub-section, then renamed it the All-Russian Photography and Cinematographic Section headed by Dmitri

Leshchenko in 1919. A Sovnarkom decree nationalized the film industry on 27 August 1919. Sovnarkom established the State Film School in Moscow with Vladimir Gardin its first director in 1919. The initial emphasis was on producing agitational (*agitki*) or propaganda films, with ninety-two filmed from 1918 to 1920.[23]

The State Film Board ensured that all movies were ideologically correct. Although Boris Shumiatsky nominally led the Film Board, Stalin actually micromanaged his duties by editing scripts, interviewing and advising directors and actors and critically watching the final products. What especially discomforted Stalin on the screen and in public places beyond was sexuality. He ensured that the State Film Board censored any passionate or prolonged kisses. For various violations, the Film Board stopped production on thirty-four films in 1934, fifty-five in 1936 and thirteen in 1937, while another twenty films were withdrawn after they were publicly shown.[24]

Nonetheless, Stalin's favourite way to relax was in a darkened theatre watching a movie, engrossed with its humour or pathos. His favourite film was *Chapaev* about Vasily Chapaev, a heroic Red Army commander during the Civil War. He also enjoyed Grigory Alexandrov's musical comedies *The Jolly Fellows Circus, Volga, Volga* and *Tanya,* all starring his wife, Lyubov Orlova. He loved the dramatic films of Sergei Eisenstein, especially *Battleship Potemkin, Bzehin Meadow* and *Alexander Nevsky*. He ordered the film industry to create biopics of Russian tsars Alexander Nevsky, Ivan the Terrible, Peter the Great, generals Alexander Suvorov and Mikhail Kutuzov and admiral Fyodor Ushakov.

***

Stalin enjoyed attending plays at the Moscow Arts Theatre, ballet at the Bolshoi Theatre and classical music concerts at several venues. Of singers, he especially adored soprano Natalya Schpiller and mezzo Vera Davydova. His favourite play was Mikhael Bulgakov's *The Days of the Turbins,* about Russia's Civil War and based on his novel *The White Guard*.[25]

Vsevolod Meyerhold was a leading playwright, actor and director who deplored communism's devastation of that art:

> The painful and wretched thing that pretends to the title of the theatre of socialist realism has nothing in common with art . . . Where once there were the best theatres in the world, now . . . everything is gloomily well regulated, averagely arithmetical, stupefying and murderous in its

> lack of talent. Is that your aim? If it is . . . you have done something monstrous! . . . you have eliminated art.[26]

The communist regime executed Meyerhold on 1 February 1940.

Among Stalin's favourite operas was Mikhail Glinka's *Ivan Susanin* (*A Life for the Tsar*, 1836), about a Russian hero who resisted Poland's invasion in 1613. He especially relished the scene where the Russians slaughter the Poles in a forest. His daughter Svetlana speculated that post-war performance likely reminded him of the Katyn massacre of 21,000 Poles he ordered.[27]

***

Communist culture transformed architecture. The goal was to create an oversized heroic style as inspiring as the New Soviet Man and New Soviet Woman. Svetlana, Stalin's daughter, describes one typical result: 'The House of Rest, built . . . in that pseudo-classical style of "Socialist Realism" with columns, frescos and statues at every step, was a miracle of bad taste and pretentiousness.'[28] To remake cities with Socialist Realist buildings, the communists bulldozed old districts. In Moscow alone, the cadres destroyed over 3,000 historic, mostly lovely buildings. Across the Soviet Union, the communists gleefully demolished over 25,000 churches and 500 monasteries during the 1930s.[29]

***

Education is a key way to realize Western Civilization's core value of humanism or enlightened individual. The idea is that every individual is born a unique bundle of potentialities, mostly positive and some negative. Humanity's practical and moral duty is to nurture or bring out the best in each individual to realize his or her full potential as a unique individual in a community of fellow humanists. A humanist education involves teachers developing open minds, critical thinking skills and a joy in learning fundamental history, science, art, music and literature.

Communists seek not education but schooling for children and young adults. Schools teach the skills of reading, writing and mathematics along with communist pseudo-versions of the social and natural sciences. Communists indoctrinate children from their first year in communist dogma and persist in that socialization each year thereafter through lower schools and for those who went to universities. Outside school, children were encouraged to join the Little Octobrists from age six to nine, the Young Pioneers from 10 to 14 and the All-Union Leninist Young Communist League (Komsomol) from 15 to 23. Each organization had uniforms, oaths, songs, activities and books to promote proper communist beliefs and behaviours.

The Soviet regime faced a vast challenge for schooling. Under the Tsarist regime in 1914, 91 per cent of children went to school. During the First World War, that share dropped to 62 per cent by 1918, then the civil war and communism further depressed enrolled students to 49 per cent in 1919 and 24 per cent in 1920.[30] The challenges for expanding university schooling were also formidable. The Communist Party had only 8,000 members with university degrees and only 138 engineers were Communist Party members.[31]

The Communist Party was successful at expanding the numbers of lower schools, technical schools and universities.[32] During the First Five-Year Plan from 1927–8 to 1933–4, preschools and their students increased tenfold from 2,155 to 10,611 institution with from 107,500 to 1,061,700 pupils enrolled; primary and secondary schools from 118,558 to 166,272 with from 7,896 to 9,656,000 enrolled; secondary specialized schools from 1,037 to 3,509 institutions with from 189,400 to 723,700 enrolled; and universities and colleges from 148 to 714 with from 168,500 to 458,300 enrolled. The quality of those new schools varied considerably.

5.3 Expansion of Schools and Students, 1927–1934[33]

	1927–8	1933–4
Preschool		
Institutions	2,155	19,611
Students	107,500	1,061,700
Primary and Secondary		
Institutions	118,558	166,272
Students	7,896,000	9,656,000
Secondary Specialized		
Institutions	1,037	3,509
Students	189,400	723,700
Universities and Colleges		
Institutions	148	714
Students	168,500	458,300

Nonetheless, the regime did make progress. The Soviets gradually increased the literacy rate for children and adults to 56.6 per cent in 1926 and to 75 per cent in 1937. The regime helped working-class students receive advanced schooling. From 1928 to 1931, the number of children from working-class families going to universities rose from 40,000 to 120,000. From 1928 to 1932, the number of engineers rose from 18,000 to 74,000 and the number of professional managers in government and industry rose from 63,000 to 119,000.[34]

***

What the Communist Party created with one iron fist, it destroyed with the other. Engineers, scientists and professors did not escape Stalin's purges. The first show trial was the so-called 'Shakhty Affair' with fifty-three engineers and technicians on trumped-up charges of sabotage and espionage in May 1928; all were found guilty, with eleven condemned to death and six actually executed while the others were imprisoned or had their sentences commuted. That was just the beginning. Historian Nicolas Wirth counted

> 3,000 engineers arrested in 1928-1929 in the Donbass [Ukraine's eastern industrial region]; 5,000 to 7,000 functionaries and cadres arrested in 1930 in the central economic administration; 4,500 railways functionaries arrested in 1930-1931 for 'sabotage,' including 1,300 engineers (around 25 per cent of all cadres at this level); 140,000 functionaries dismissed during the purge of administrations in 1930; plus another 135,000 in 1932-1933. At the same time more than 140,000 workers were promoted 'on the job' to administer positions in 1929-1931.[35]

Of the Kiev Academy of Sciences' thirteen secretaries (presidents) from 1921 to 1938, every one was arrested. Of the Institute of Red Professors, 85 of 183 suffered arrest and enslavement or execution during the late 1930s. Twenty-seven leading astronomers disappeared during those years. Of 700 writers who attended the First Congress of the Union of Soviet Writers in 1934, only 50 were alive 20 years later in 1954. Of over 2,000 writers, 1,500 died from execution or disease, overwork or suicide in the Gulag.[36] Isaac Babel was a brilliant short-story writer who was executed on 27 January 1940.

Atop the genocide of 'enemies of the people', Stalin tried to ethnically cleanse or destroy the cultures of various ethnic groups by having their intellectuals, writers, painters, composers and other artists arrested and executed.[37] For instance, he had forty-five of Ukraine's cultural leaders arrested and tried on various trumped-up charges for a conspiratorial 'Union for the Liberation of Ukraine' in April and May 1930, then executed. That was the first prosecution round. Eventually nearly all the several hundred members of Members of the Ukrainian Union of Writers were wiped out.[38]

***

Stalin understood that soft or psychological power was essential to successfully asserting hard physical power over the long term. That reality, of course, was as vital to realizing Moscow's foreign policies as it was domestic policies. The Soviet Union abroad was as strong as those who believed in communism and embraced communist culture.

One vital source of Soviet power was the array of prominent foreign sympathizers who were not openly communists or secretly Comintern agents. A key dimension of Russian political culture is the 'Potemkin Village'. Lenin, Stalin and the rest of the Communist Party elite established Potemkin Villages or fake idealized versions of communist utopia for factories, collectives, schools and courts. They gleefully ushered naïve, ignorant, hopeful foreign idealists from one Potemkin fantasy to the next. The foreign sympathizer then returned to his or her country to write glowing accounts of the progressive, brave new society the communists had established in the Soviet Union.

Among the prominent leftists who visited Stalin's Soviet Union and returned with radiant reports of the utopia the Great Leader was developing were Fabian Socialists Sidney and Beatrice Webb, philosopher Betrand Russell, writer Andre Gide, playwright George Bernard Shaw and playwright Bertold Brecht. Shaw naively remarked: 'I find it just as hard to believe that [Stalin] is a vulgar gangster as that Trotsky is an assassin.'[39] In contrast, Brecht embraced Stalin's war against the 'enemies of the people.' He expressed the Orwellian madness and depravity of Stalin's genocide with these words: 'The more innocent they are, the more they deserve to die.'[40]

British author Herbert George 'H.G.' Wells was president of the International Poets, Essayists and Novelists (PEN) Club, founded in London in 1921. Among the most prominent initial members were Wells, Shaw, Joseph Conrad and John Galsworthy, its first president. PEN's members dedicate themselves to developing a global community of writers and protecting them against any enemies who would silence or stunt them. That should have made the Soviet Union the number one target for PEN's condemnation, but most members instead celebrated what they believed was Stalin's enlightened leadership.

Wells visited the Soviet Union in 1934 amidst the famine and mass murders that were killing millions of Soviets. Like all foreign visitors he saw only a series of 'Potemkin' groups of writers and other artists, factories and farms that appeared progressive. In his memoir, he recalled that:

> I confess that I approached Stalin with a certain amount of suspicion and prejudice. A picture had been built up in my mind of a very reserved and self-centred fanatic, a despot without vices, a jealous monopoly of power . . . I have never met a man more candid, fair and honest . . . I had thought before I saw him that he might be where he was because men were afraid of him, but I realize that he owes his position to the fact that no one is afraid of him and everybody trusts him.[41]

To his credit, Wells later he had second thoughts and issued this warning: 'we live in an age in which the autonomous individual is ceasing to exist – or perhaps one ought to say, in which the individual is ceasing to have the illusion of being autonomous . . . When one mentions totalitarianism one thinks immediately of Germany, Russia, Italy, but I think that one must face the risk that this phenomenon is going to be world-wide.'[42]

Tragically, numerous bright Americans were Stalinist dupes.[43] The highest ranking American 'fellow traveller' was Joseph Davies, America's ambassador to the Soviet Union from 11 November 1936 to 11 June 1938. No American official was a worse 'useful idiot', an intelligence term, for believing and spreading communist propaganda. His book, *Mission to Moscow*, published in 1941 and made into a 1943 Hollywood movie, extolled Stalin and his regime. For instance, he witnessed the show trials and genuinely believed that:

> They disclose the outlines of a plot which came very near to being successful in bringing about the overthrow of this government . . . those charged in the indictment were established by the proof and beyond a reasonable doubt to justify the verdict of guilty of treason . . . All of these trials, purges and liquidations, which seemed so violent at the time and shocked the world, are now quite clearly a part of a vigorous and determined effort of the Stalin government to protect itself from not only revolution from within but from attack from without. They want to work thoroughly to clean up and clean out all treasonable elements within the country. All doubts were resolved in favour of the government.[44]

His stint as ambassador was not his last 'mission to Moscow'. President Franklin Roosevelt sent that communist sympathizer back to Moscow along with London and other places during the war. Stalin awarded him the Order of Lenin for his priceless work promoting Soviet interests.

Wendell Willkie was a rich corporate lawyer and financial wizard who ran as the Republic Party's presidential nominee against Franklin Roosevelt in the 1944 election. In his bestselling 1943 book, *One World,* having visited the Soviet Union, he reassured readers that: 'Russia is neither going to eat us or seduce us . . . I believe it is possible for Russia and America, perhaps the two most powerful countries in the world, to work together for economic freedom and the peace of the world.'[45] Willkie was obvious to the reality that the communists had eliminated economic freedom and all other freedoms in the Soviet Union, nationalized all industries and property, suppressed and exploited all workers and developed the economy through Five-Year Plans.

The list of other American dupes was long. Among the most prominent were journalists John Reed, Louise Bryant and Max Eastman. Political scientist Harold Laski attended one of the show trials and after returning to the United States declared: 'basically I did not observe much difference between the general character of a trial in Russia and in this country'.[46] Theologian Reinhold Niebuhr fervently believed that: 'Ideally, collaboration between the Communist and the democratic world might lead to a wholesome exchange of political experience . . . We have . . . more liberty and less equality than Russia has. Russia has less liberty and more equality. Whether democracy should be defined primarily in terms of liberty or of equality is a source of unending debate.'[47]

In American communist and other far left circles, surrogates fought out the rivalry between Stalin and Trotsky.[48] That debate raged in the pages of weekly or monthly journals like *The New Republic, Partisan Review* and *The Nation*. Members of the American Civil Liberties Union (ACLU) bizarrely questioned whether the right of free speech should extend to communist regimes or be confined to democratic governments. Communists Philip Williams and Philip Rahv founded the bimonthly *Partisan Review* as an outlet for radical essays in 1934. The Moscow show trials and rumours of vast purges, combined with Moscow's Popular Front strategy, provoked a bitter debate between Stalinists and sceptical critics in 1936. Williams and Rahv suspended *Partisan Review*'s publication that year, then resumed publication in December 1937 with a solid sceptical outlook. John Dewey and Sidney Hook, respectively a University of Chicago professor and *Partisan Review* editor, founded the Committee for Cultural Freedom as a more sceptical leftist view on 1 January 1938; the members renamed their organization the American Committee for Cultural Freedom on 14 May 1951. All along the Moscow-based Communist International (Comintern) worked closely with America's Communist Party, affiliates like the John Reed Club and League of American Writers and scores of other front organizations to nurture spies and propagandists.

A few sympathizers eventually became apostates and repentants. Among them was Max Eastman. In *The New Republic*'s October 1939 issue, he admitted and warned that: 'We were wrong. You cannot serve democracy and totalitarianism'. Eastman elaborated that theme in his book, *Stalin's Russia and the Crisis of Socialism* (1940).[49] Dewey was another defector who once lauded the Soviet Union before learning enough about it to publicly loath it. He attended the same show trials that Ambassador Davies did, but saw through the Potemkin. He warned that the show trials 'may serve the interests of Soviet propaganda' but do 'not serve the interests of truth about Russia'.[50]

***

Personality cults are as old as the first narcissistic leader with the political skills to pull it off.[51] Traditional Russian political culture revered tsars as benevolent father-figures. After taking power, the communists tapped into and bolstered the political culture with their personality cults for Lenin and Stalin.[52]

Crucial to Stalin's power was creating a personality cult whereby he was celebrated as a heroic, all-knowing, wise, benevolent, decisive demigod to be worshiped and obeyed by all. Doing that would have been impossible had Stalin not first spearheaded the drive to make Vladimir Lenin into a personality cult.[53] He did so literally over Lenin's dead body.

Lenin sought to transfer the Russian people's traditional faith and devotion to Orthodox Christianity and other religions to the Communist Party. Yet, he would have opposed what Stalin and his other comrades did to him after he died, transform him into a demigod that the masses and Communist Party elite could worship. The Central Committee ordered the construction of a massive dark red granite mausoleum beneath the Kremlin's wall on Red Square. In 1929, the mausoleum was completed and Lenin's coffin with a glass top was displayed within it. During visiting hours, a long line of Soviet and foreign visitors waited patiently to shuffle past and briefly gaze in adoration at their embalmed demigod. During communist holidays like the revolution's anniversary and May Day, leading officials would stand atop the mausoleum and watch troops, tanks, workers, youths and other groups parade by, the soldiers goosestepping.

Lenin's tomb was the ultimate site of worship. Elsewhere across the Soviet Union were hundreds of bronze statues, paintings and posters of him along with Lenin streets and squares to inspire the masses. All his written works were collected, sorted in chronological order and published in volumes for people to buy and study. Communist Party officials sprinkled Lenin quotes in their speeches while *Pravda* and other newspapers did so in their editorials. No matter what the subject, teachers had to help students understand how Lenin influenced it.

As Stalin led the effort to deify Lenin he and his lackeys steadily constructed a personality cult for himself.[54] He wanted everyone to believe that he was Lenin's natural successor as the 'Great Leader' or '*Vozhd*'. Ever more statues, paintings and posters of Stalin adorned squares and office walls. Stalin justified his personality cult as conforming to traditional Russian political culture: 'Don't forget we are living in Russia, the land of the tsars. The Russian people like to have one man standing at the head of state. Of course, this man should carry out the will of the collective.'[55] Among Stalin's key strategies was to get his followers publicly to celebrate or propose more power for him after which publicly he would pretend modestly to reject those statements. For instance, Lazar Kaganovich, among his devoted followers on the Ogburo, proclaimed: 'Comrades! It's time for us to tell the people the truth. Everybody keeps talking about Lenin and Leninism. We've got to be honest with ourselves. Lenin died in 1924. How many years did he work in the Party? Compare it with what has been accomplished under Stalin! The time has come to replace the slogan, "Long live Leninism!" with the slogan "Long live Stalinism!"'[56] Stalin pretended angrily to repudiate that notion while inwardly glowing.

Stalin's Cult surpassed Lenin's Cult by the October Revolution's 1933 anniversary. Journalist Eugene Lyon counted the busts or portraits of Soviet leaders on just six blocks of a parade route in central Moscow. Those glorifying Stalin numbered 103, nearly double Lenin's 58, with 56 for Deputy General Secretary Lazar Kaganovich, 33 for Defence Commissar Kliment Voroshilov and just five for Karl Marx. A poem in *Pravda* captured Stalin's usurpation of Lenin's revered place: 'Now when we speak of Lenin, It means we are speaking of Stalin.'[57]

Chapter 6

TERROR

'This era in which we live . . . will be known in history as the era of Stalin, just as the preceding era entered history as the time of Lenin.' (Lev Kamenev)

'Mount your prisoner and do not dismount until they have confessed.' (Joseph Stalin)

'The more innocent they are, the more they deserve to die.' (Bertold Brecht)

'The closer we get to socialism, the sharper becomes the character of class war.' (Joseph Stalin)

'By raising their hand against Comrade Stalin, they raised their hand against all the best that humanity has because Stalin is hope . . . Stalin is our banner. Stalin is our will. Stalin is our victory.' (Nikita Khrushchev)

Joseph Stalin had been the Communist Party's General Secretary for a dozen years and was 55 years old in 1934, when he asserted the final elements of totalitarian power for himself in a series of crucial steps. The first came during the Seventeenth Communist Party Congress with 1,225 voting and 736 just-speaking delegates from 26 January to 10 February 1934. The Congress's last and most vital act was to elect the Central Committee's seventy-one members. Each delegate received a ballot list prepared by Stalin's Secretariat. They voted by crossing out the names of those they opposed. The most prominent candidates were Politburo members Stalin, Sergei Kirov, Vyacheslav Molotov and Lazar Kaganovich. Kirov won overwhelming support with only a couple of cross-outs, Kaganovich and Molotov received around a hundred negative votes each. Stalin got from 123 to 292 cross-outs.[1]

Stalin acted decisively to transform that humiliating vote against him into an overwhelming false vote for him. He had Kaganovich destroy the negative votes and replace them with positive ones. On 10 February, the Secretariat released the list of 71 Central Committee members with Stalin winning 1,056 of 1,059 votes cast and Kirov second with 1,055 votes. Stalin then got Kirov to issue this paean for all good communists everywhere to echo:

> It is hard to conceive such a gigantic figure as Stalin. For years past starting with the time when we worked without Lenin, we have not known one turning in our work, not one great initiative, slogan, direction in our policy, the author of which was not Stalin . . . .[T]his relates not only to the building of socialism as a whole but to the separate questions of our work . . . [O]ne must underscore this with all one's might that all our successes . . . we owe . . . completely to Stalin.[2]

That resolution was unprecedented. Never before had Congress singled out one man for such adulation, not even Lenin. During the Congress, Lev Kamenev noted how critical this transformation was: 'This era in which we live . . . will be known in history as the era of Stalin, just as the preceding era entered history as the time of Lenin.'[3]

Stalin later avenged himself against those who opposed him during that Congress. During his secret speech before the 1956 Twentieth Party Congress, Premier Nikita Khruschev revealed that of the 1,966 delegates to the Seventeenth Communist Party Congress, Stalin eventually had 1,108 of them arrested, seven of ten of them executed and the rest sent to the Gulag. Of the 139 Central Committee members and 15 Politburo members that Congress elected, Stalin respectively had 98 and five executed.[4]

***

Stalin soon had the perfect excuse to perpetuate the prosecution and execution or imprisonment of his Communist Party opponents and millions of other victims, known as the 'Great Terror'.[5] The key murder in Soviet history took place on 1 December 1934.[6] That afternoon Sergei Kirov arrived for work at the Smolny Institute, where he headed both Leningrad's government and Communist Party. As he ascended the steps to his third-floor office, Leonid Nikolaev stepped behind him, pulled a revolver from his pocket and shot him in the head, killing him instantly. Guards tackled Nikolaev and took him to police headquarters for questioning.

When Stalin learned of the murder, he had Abel Yenukidze, the Central Executive Committee's Secretary, sign a 'Charter of Terror' that empowered authorities to speed up trials, expand 'evidence' to include hearsay and rumours, and immediately imprison or execute the guilty without appeal. The Charter of Terror inaugurated Stalin's latest rounds of purges whereby more than 2,000,000 people were arrested and either murdered or imprisoned in slave labour camps over the next three years.

Stalin led a delegation to Leningrad to supervise the investigation of Kirov's murder. He interrogated Nikolaev, a disgruntled and suspended Communist Party member, who claimed that Ivan Zaporozhets, the Leningrad NKVD's deputy chief, had forced him to commit the murder. Stalin ensured that all 'evidence' supported a plot by Grigory Zinoviev and the 'left opposition'.

Kirov's assassination has been as contentious a whodunnit for Russians as President John Kennedy's assassination has been for Americans. Conspiracy theories proliferated with the most prominent that Stalin himself ordered the death of his chief political rival. According to the theory, Stalin secretly ordered NKVD chief Genrikh Yagoda to have Zaporozhets arrange the murder. He later had Kirov's bodyguard, who was not with Kirov at his death, killed in a car wreck, then the deaths of the two who murdered the bodyguard.

In his death-obsessed, vengeful, paranoid mind, Stalin had plenty of reasons to have Kirov eliminated. Kirov was a decade younger than Stalin and was renowned for being highly intelligent, charismatic and kind-hearted. The Seventeenth Communist Party Congress election revealed how much the delegates favoured Kirov and despised Stalin. Indeed, a group of high party officials secretly tried to talk Kirov into replacing Stalin as General Secretary, but he refused. Stalin soon learned and fumed about that offer. He tried talking Kirov into giving up his powerful posts as Leningrad's mayor and party chief and working alongside him in the Kremlin. Kirov insisted on retaining those positions. The Central Committee held a Plenum from 25 to 28 November 1934, during which problems of collectivization, eliminating the kulaks and grain rationing were debated. Stalin insisted on accelerating the pace for each policy. Kirov initially called for fewer controls and more grain shipped to Leningrad to feed the hungry population, but eventually, reluctantly backed Stalin's hardline position. On 28 November, Stalin saw Kirov off at Moscow's central station where he boarded a train bound for Leningrad.

If Stalin's guilt for Kirov's death can never be proven beyond a reasonable doubt, what is clear is that he exploited the murder as the excuse to wipe out the Communist Party's venerable Bolsheviks along with their followers and replace them with young protegees devoted to himself.[7] He made Nikolaev the trigger man for a vast conspiratorial web across the Soviet Union with Zinoviev and Kamenev central.

The first trial included Nikolaev and fourteen co-conspirators who had been tortured into signing confessions of treason and other 'crimes against the people' and were shot on 29 December. Over the next month, another 6,501 people were tried and executed in Leningrad alone and by March 1935 as many as 100,000 people were sent to the Gulag.[8] The next key trial included Zinoviev, Kamenev and seventeen alleged co-conspirators, dubbed the 'Moscow Centre', in Leningrad. The trial opened on 15 January 1935 and ended late the next day, with Vasily Ulrikh the presiding judge and Andrei Vyshinsky the state prosecutor. Vyshinsky presented evidence obtained by torture from the Nikolaev trial that resulted in convictions and incarcerations for the accused, with kingpin Zinoviev getting ten years, his deputy Kamenev five years and various terms for the others. That was just the first show trial for Zinoviev and Kamenev. As the 'evidence' massed from other investigations and trials, they would find themselves in the dock again, this time with unbeatable charges that would result in their executions. On 29 July 1935, Stalin issued the decree that the terrorist counterrevolutionary underground movement known as the 'United Trotskyite-Zinovievite Centre' had assassinated Kirov and sought to murder Stalin and his close advisors like Voroshilov, Kaganovich, Zhdanov and other prominent Communist leaders. Zinoviev, Kamenev and the other others were interrogated, forced to sign confessions, then brought to trial where they received death penalties and were executed on 25 August 1935. Stalin did not have Zinoviev and Kamenev physically tortured, but instead had them informed that if they did not confess, he would have their loved ones suffer the same fate.

***

The 'Potemkin Village', an idealized façade to mask a squalid real village, is a crucial element of Russian political culture. Ironically, amid the mass arrests and executions, Stalin had the Soviet Union's third constitution drafted and implemented. The 1936 Constitution was a classic Potemkin. The text enshrines such liberal democratic rights as due process, free elections and freedom of speech, assembly and religion. Stalin had the constitution written and promulgated as he had millions of people prosecuted, tortured into false confessions of various 'crimes against the people', then either shot or sent to a slave labour camp. Indeed, any arrested suspect who appealed to his or her constitutional rights was usually eliminated more quickly.

Stalin expanded the powers against, and charges and penalties for 'enemies of the people'. He issued a decree on 7 April 1935, that lowered the age of those who could be charged, tried and executed for such crimes to children as young as 12. Usually accompanying Trotsky-Zinoviev conspiracy charges were accusations of sabotage and espionage. Sabotage or 'wrecking' included crimes like derailing trains, poisoning food and monkeywrenching machines. As for espionage, Stalin's investigators 'uncovered' networks of Soviets who spied for the Germans, British or Japanese.

'Enemies of the people' had diverse positions, identities, motives and crimes. For instance, Railway Commissar Lazar Kaganovich reported that: 'In the political apparatus of the railway commissariat we have unmasked 220 people. In the transport division we have sacked 485 former gendarmes, 220 Social Revolutionaries and Mensheviks, 572 Trotskyites, 1,415 White officers, 285 wreckers, 443 spies. They were all linked with the counterrevolutionary movement.'[9]

Stalin ensured that nearly all executions and imprisonments were 'legal' by getting the accused to sign confessions of all their crimes. Of course, virtually all the accused were innocent of the charges against them. So Stalin ordered his police to torture confessions from 'suspects': 'Mount your prisoner and do not dismount until they have confessed.'[10] Torture included beatings, sleep deprivation and threats that their family would suffer the same harsh fate. Not all torture was applied physical pain. The 'conveyor' tactic was subjecting victims to a nonstop series of interrogators demanding answers and making various threats until they extracted confessions; few victims held out more than two or three days. Not everyone signed. Countless victims were beaten to death or suffered fatal heart attacks. In all, the police tortured false 'confessions' from millions of victims.

Why do people confess to crimes they do not commit? Of course, people enduring excruciating torture will say and do anything to stop the pain. Ironically, being a committed communist actually made confessing absurdities easier. Communism justifies every means to its utopian end of a classless society. Individual communists might fail but the Communist Party was infallible as it transformed the world for the better. Communist zealots exist in a bizarre alternate theoretical universe in which they must parrot the latest Party propaganda bromides even if they are false, illogical and contradict previous dogma. Zinoviev confessed this at his trial: 'My defective Bolshevism became transformed into anti-Bolshevism and through Trotskyism I arrived at Fascism . . . We filled the place of Mensheviks, Social Revolutionaries and White Guards who could not come out openly in our country.'[11] One survivor expressed the true communist believer's mindset:

> It is true that the interrogation methods, particularly when applied for months or years, are capable of breaking the strongest will. But the decisive factor is something else. It is that the majority of convinced Communists must at all costs preserve their faith in the Soviet Union. To renounce it would be . . . to renounce one's long standing, deep rooted convictions, even when these turn out to be untenable.

For Vagarshak Ter-Vaganyan, his duty and loyalty to the Communist Party made his confession inevitable:

> But in order to sign the testimony which is demanded of me, I must be sure first that it is really needed in the interests of the Party and the Revolution . . . I am unable to stop thinking. And . . . I come to the inescapable conclusion that the assertions that the oldest Bolsheviks have turned into a gang of murderers will bring incalculable harm not only to our country and the Party, but to the cause of Socialism all over the world.[12]

Nikolai Bukharin's existential need to justify his life eventually provoked him to confess:

> For three months I refused to say anything. Then I began to testify. Why? Because while I was in prison I made a re-evaluation of my entire past. For when you ask yourself: 'If you must die, what are you dying for?' – an absolutely black vacuity suddenly rises before you with startling vividness. There was nothing to die for, if one wanted to die unrepented . . . And then you ask yourself, 'Very well, suppose . . . by some miracle you remain alive, again what for? Isolated from everybody, an enemy of the people, an inhuman position, completely isolated from everything that constitutes the essence of life.[13]

When victims appeared in court, nearly all were broken, listless, glassy-eyed and mumbled their confessions. Just a few displayed defiance or gallows humour. For instance, Karl Radek reassured the court with this half-truth: 'The question has been raised here whether we were tormented while under investigation. I must say that it was not I who was tormented but I who tormented the examining officials and compelled them to perform a lot of useless work.'[14]

Some remained defiant even when promised prison rather than execution if they confessed. Nikita Khrushchev recalled an example:

'Before the execution [Alyosha] Svanidze was told that Stalin had said that if he asked for forgiveness he would be pardoned. When Stalin's words were repeated to Svanidze, he asked: "What am I supposed to ask forgiveness for? I have committed no crime." He was shot. After Svanidze's death, Stalin said: "See how proud he is: he died without asking for forgiveness."' When Mikhail Tomsky refused to confess and committed suicide, Stalin insisted that: 'his suicide confirms his guilt before the party'.[15]

Stress for those under suspicion but unindicted could also be debilitating. Sergo Ordzhonikidze was the People's Commissar for Heavy Industry from 5 January 1932 until 18 February 1937. He complained that: 'Stalin started a bad business. I was always such a close friend of Stalin's. I trusted him and he trusted me. And now I can't work with him. I'll commit suicide.'[16] After a bitter argument with Stalin, Ordzhonikidze went home and shot himself. The press announced his death as a heart attack.

The stress nearly overwhelmed Lev Mekhlis, *Pravda*'s editor from 1930 to 1937. To Stalin, he confessed his weaknesses and begged forgiveness:

> My nerves did not stand up. I did not comport myself as a Bolshevik . . . I can't be chief of *Pravda* when I'm sick and sleepless, incapable of following what is happening in the country, economics, art and literature, never getting the chance to go to the theatre . . . Forgive me, my dear Comrade Stalin . . . For me it's very hard to experience such a trauma.[17]

Mekhlis was among a handful of high officials that Stalin did not have murdered but kept in his inner circle until his demise.

Occasionally, passive acts of resistance saved lives, some prominent. One such was that of the novelist Boris Pasternak. He recalled that communist officials

> came to me . . . with something they wanted me to sign. It was to the effect that I approved of the Party's execution of the Generals. In a sense, this was a proof of their confidence in me. They didn't go to those who were on the list for liquidation. My wife was pregnant. She cried and begged me to sign, but I couldn't . . . I was convinced that I would be arrested . . . But nothing happened. It was, I was told later, my colleagues who had saved me indirectly. No one dared to report to the hierarchy that I hadn't signed.[18]

***

How did Stalin and his henchmen explain the existence of millions of 'enemies of the people' amidst the communist utopia they were forging? Stalin gave this Orwellian answer: 'The closer we get to socialism, the sharper becomes the character of class war.'[19] He did not elaborate why that was true. Of course, that was merely the absurd excuse. But under communism, believing and acting on absurdities is critical to emotionally preserving oneself often while eliminating others. Bukharin dared to issue this rebuttal: 'According to this strange theory, it would seem that the further we advance toward socialism, the more difficulties will pile up and the sharper the class struggle will become and at the very gates to socialism we apparently will either have to start a civil war or, perishing from hunger, lay down our bones to die.'[20]

***

Among Stalin's willing executioners during the purges from 1934 to 1939, three stood out.[21] The first was among the more depraved within the Communist elite. Genrikh Yagoda, the People's Commissar for Internal Affairs and NKVD chief from 10 July 1934 to 26 September 1936, gleefully conducted torture sessions. He had the bullets dug from the skulls of Zinoviev and Kamenev, mounted in glass cases and proudly displayed in his home amidst a huge collection of pornography and women's clothing. He reaped wealth from bribes and the black market. He was removed as NKVD chief in September 1936, but not arrested until March 1937. Tried with Bukharin and others a year later, he was executed immediately afterwards.

Stalin replaced Yagoda with Nikolai Yezhov, known as the 'Bloody Dwarf' for his short 5ft statue and all the people he tortured and executed during his overlapping stints as the People's Commissar for Internal Affairs from 26 September 1936 to 25 November 1938 and the NKVD's chief from 8 April 1938, to 9 April 1939. During the Terror, Stalin met with him over 1,100 times to review progress and plan greater results. Only Molotov merited more meetings during these years.[22]

Yezhov eventually and inevitably suffered the same fate as Yagoda, his predecessor. Stalin gradually had his inner circle arrested, charged and executed. He replaced Yezhov with Lavrenti Beria, the People's Commissar for Internal Affairs, on 25 November 1938. Beria was among the most violent, depraved and sadistic of Stalin's henchmen.[23] He gleefully presided over the execution of 413 high-ranking enemies of the people just from 24 February to 16 March 1939 and thereafter thousands more. He had scores of women he desired arrested on trumped-up charges, then raped them and often had them executed. Stalin proudly described Beria as 'our Himmler', referring to Heinrich Himmler to whom Hitler assigned the Holocaust.[24] Beria remained in power and briefly outlived Stalin.

Khrushchev explained the process at the top: '

> The rapid turnover among the main characters created by Stalin was very much part of Stalin's logic. He used henchmen to destroy honest men who he knew perfectly well were guiltless in the eyes of the Party and the people. Stalin stood above it all while the terror consumed its own executors. When one band of thugs got too embroiled in the terror, he simply replaced it with another.[25]

***

Two of the most distinguished Bolsheviks – Nikolai Bukharin and Alexi Rykov – were arrested on 27 February 1937. Bukharin had served as *Pravda*'s editor-in-chief from November 1919 to April 1929, Comintern's chief from November 1926 to April 1929 and on the Politburo from June 1924 to November 1929. Rykov's highest posts were being Premier and a Politburo member from 2 February 1924 to 19 December 1930. Then Stalin forced them to resign their posts for being allied with Zinoviev and Kamenev. After Stalin issued criticisms against Bukharin, the prelude to a formal arrest, Bukharin wrote Stalin that: 'I cannot live like this anymore. I am in no physical or moral condition to come to the Plenum . . . I will begin a hunger strike until the accusations of betrayal, wrecking and terrorism are dropped.'[26] Bukharin and Rykov were tried along with nineteen other 'co-conspirators from 2 to 13 March 1938 and executed on 15 March. That same day, before a crowd of 200,000 people packed in Red Square, Khrushchev explained that: 'By raising their hand against Comrade Stalin, they raised their hand against all the best that humanity has, because Stalin is hope . . . Stalin is our banner. Stalin is our will. Stalin is our victory.'[27]

***

Stalin conducted the purges as if mass murder or imprisonment was just another Five-Year Plan to develop the Soviet Union. He issued arrest quotas to Communist Party district chiefs and they sent him lists of suspects for his approval. Initially, he checked each name on each list but eventually finessed that tedious task by just signing the entire list.

The lists steadily lengthened. On 2 July 1937, Stalin had the Politburo issue a decree to local Communist Party chiefs to convene troikas of the Party Secretary, Procurator and NKVD chief to try and have executed all suspects. To assist that effort, on 30 July, Yezhov submitted to the Politburo the precise figures of 72,950 traitors to shoot and 259,450 to incarcerate in the Gulag, with those numbers divided among the Party districts. By the year's end, most districts had fulfilled or exceeded their quotas. Yezhov issued larger numbers of 386,798 executions and 767,397 imprisonments. In Ukraine, Khrushchev received a 50,000 quota, proudly had 55,741 people executed and asked for an additional 2,000-person quota; in 1938, he had 106,119 people arrested with half executed. The Communist Party chief for Stalinabad (Askabad) was ordered to kill 6,277 enemies of the people, but zealously doubled that to 13,259 executions. In the Transcaucasia Region, Beria soon fulfilled his quotas of 268,950 arrests and 75,950 executions, then requested a further 10 per cent.[28]

The purges led to rapid promotions for survivors up the depleted Communist Party hierarchy. Of regional secretaries, 88 per cent had been in the Communist Party since 1923 in 1938 and only 18 per cent in 1940. By 1939, 239 of the regional secretaries and 26,000 of the 33,000 senior cadres had occupied their seats for less than a year.[29]

Stalin widened the net from 'class' to 'nationalist' and 'religious' enemies. He ordered mass arrests of ethnic minorities like Poles, Germans, Georgians, Armenians, Kurds, Finns, Iranians, Estonians, Koreans, Chinese, Tajiks, Mongolians and others, with around 700,000 of them shot and 1,500,000 imprisoned, along with religious leaders of Orthodox Christians, Catholics, Jews and Muslims. The communists devastated Orthodox Christianity. From 1915 to 1941, the number of Orthodox buildings plummeted from 54,400 to 4,200, priests from 57,000 to 5,600, monasteries from 1,498 to 38, seminaries from 57 to 0 and bishops from 130 to 4. Muslims suffered nearly as much. From 1917 to 1990 the number of mosques fell from 26,000 to 450 and mullahs from 45,000 to 2,000.[30]

Stalin even waged a generational war by targeting Komsomol, the All-Union Leninist Young Communist League. In 1936, of Komsomol's Central Committee, he had 72 of 93 full members and 21 of 35 candidate members arrested along with 319 of the 385 provincial secretaries and 2,210 of 2,750 district secretaries. Stalin designated yet another category for prosecution on 5 July 1937, the wives and children of the enemies of the people. Wives and their children over 16 years old were imprisoned in slave labour camps for five to seven years while their children from birth to three years were put in orphanages along with those four to 15 years old unless they were 'socially dangerous' and imprisoned. Over a million children were raised either in orphanages or prisons.[31]

***

Having destroyed nearly all his imagined political opponents, Stalin targeted the military.[32] He most despised dashing Marshal Mikhael Tukhachevsky, renowned for his exploits as a hard-driving civil war general and womanizer. Tukhachevsky was a military visionary who called for replacing cavalry with massed tanks that swiftly punched through vulnerable parts of the enemy line to encircle and destroy entire armies. He called for masses of bomber and fighter aircraft to dominate the skies and destroy the enemy from above. He would likely have been invaluable in the Second World War.

Stalin's first step in Tukhachevsky's destruction was a rumour campaign that he was a traitor who conspired with German agents to overthrow the Communist Party and impose a Nazi regime on the Soviet Union. Then, Stalin demoted him from Deputy Commissar and transferred him to head the Volga District on 11 May 1937. Stalin met Tukhachevsky before he departed and promised him he would soon be back in Moscow. Stalin was good to his word. On 22 May, the NKVD arrested Tukhachevsky and imprisoned him in Lubyanka Prison where Yezhov personally tortured from him a treason confession and list of co-conspirators.

Stalin, backed by Yezhov and Voroshilov, addressed a hundred of the military's high command at the Kremlin on 1 June. He revealed Tukhachevsky's conspiracy and promised that the state would eliminate any counterrevolutionary agents anywhere including among their ranks. He charged Voroshilov and Yezhov with purging the military. The communist 'justice system' declared Tukhachevsky along with seven of his officers guilty and executed them on 12 June 1937. Stalin's hatred for Tukhachevsky was so unhinged that he had his wife, two brothers and one sister executed and three other sisters and his daughter sent to slave labour camps.[33]

Over the next year, Voroshilov and Yezhov supervised the arrests, trials and executions or prison for over 40,000 officers including murders of three of five marshals, 13 of 15 army commanders, eight of nine fleet admirals, 50 of 57 corps commanders, 154 of 186 division commanders, 16 of 16 army commissar, 25 of 28 corps commissars, 58 of 64 division commissars, 11 of 11 vice-commissars of defence and 98 of 108 Supreme Military Soviet members. Eventually, the communist regime purged 36,761 army officers and around 3,000 naval officers. Stalin's communist regime more severely purged political commissars from the military, with 125,000 eventually executed, imprisoned or cashiered.[34]

***

Stalin's deadly reach eventually became global.[35] Before December 1936, NKVD sporadically dispatched assassins against especially vocal and prominent anti-Soviet dissidents, with varying results. That month, NKVD Chief Yezhov organized the 'Administration of Special Tasks' that handpicked and trained assassins to operate as teams under deep cover in foreign countries, observe the target and pick the best method and time for his elimination. Assassins were experts in killing by hand, firearm, bomb, poison, knife or, in one infamous case, icepick.

After Stalin had him expelled from the Soviet Union in 1929, Leon Trotsky lived in Turkey and Norway before receiving political asylum in Mexico.[36] By 1936, Trotsky and his entourage had settled in an austere walled compound with manned guard towers and police contingents outside in Coyocan, a town a dozen miles south of Mexico City's plaza.

NKVD officer Leonid Eitingon received the mission to kill Trotsky in 1936.[37] He departed with an assistant for Mexico City where he devised a plan with Mexico's Communist Party, headed by Herman Laborde. The assassin team leader was David Siqueiros, the celebrated mural painter who was also a committed communist. Laborde and Eitingon mistook his zeal for competence. Siqueiros and twenty comrades dressed in army uniforms, armed themselves with machine guns and dynamite and incendiary bombs, packed into four cars and drove to Trotsky's compound on the night of 23 May 1940. By the time they arrived, other agents had lured away police guards posted outside with bribes and cut telephone lines. After arriving, the team killed the one remaining guard then tossed the bombs over the wall. The incendiary bomb exploded, starting a fire, but the dynamite bomb failed to detonate. Siqueiros and his men opened fire, then, rather than overwhelm the compound with an assault, jumped back into their cars and raced away. The fusillade of over 300 shots grazed Trotsky and a boy, while the fire singed his wife, but everyone else escaped harm.

Mexico's Communist Party condemned the attack and disavowed rumours of any link with it. Nonetheless, authorities identified and issued an arrest warrant for Siqueiros as the attack's kingpin on 17 June and finally captured him in September. The Communist Party organized mass protests that condemned the government for persecuting Siqueiros, a leading member of 'artists and men of science . . . considered . . . the bulwark of culture and progress'. During his trial, Siqueiros denied that he and his men were trying to murder Trotsky but had merely shot at him 'for psychological purposes only'.[38] After the court released him on bail, he fled to Chile where poet and communist Pablo Neruda invited him to paint a mural.

Meanwhile, Eitingon devised another plot. Ramon Mercader was a communist journalist, skilled alpinist and recent lover of acclaimed American Trotskyite, Sylvia Ageloff. With Ageloff's endorsement, Mercader got several interviews with Trotsky. Soon the guards stopped frisking him when he appeared at the compound. On 20 August 1940, he arrived with a pistol in one raincoat pocket, an icepick in the other and a dagger sewn in a sleeve. Trotsky greeted him in his office. To kill Trotsky, Mercader chose the silent icepick and slammed it into his skull. Trotsky screamed and guards rushed in to tackle Mercader. Trotsky died the next day. Mercader denied any NKVD link and received a 20-year term for murder. With Trotsky's murder, Stalin finally realized a dream that he had nursed for two decades.

***

Stalin completed his totalitarian power during the purges. Thereafter he rarely bothered with Communist Party institutions of governance. He held only two party congresses, one party conference and twenty-two plenums from 1934 to 1953, the year he died. When he did convene them, he merely had them rubber-stamp his decrees and personnel shakeups.

The exact number of people murdered or enslaved during Stalin's purges from 1936 to 1939 is unknowable. The general estimate is around one of twenty people or over 10,000,000 were arrested, with around 2,000,000 either murdered immediately after their trials and nearly all the rest incarcerated in slave labour camps where millions more died from overwork, disease and despair. During the peak years of 1937 and 1938, the best estimate is 8,000,000 imprisoned in the camps, of which 7,000,000 were formally arrested, 1,000,000 executed, and 2,000,000 who died from various causes. The Gulag's pre-war population was around 5,000,000 inmates and 2,126,000 administrators, transporters, suppliers and guards in 1939. In 1941, the Gulag's 3,500,000 slaves included 1,000,000 in mining, 200,000 in agriculture, 600,000 in construction and camp maintenance, 400,000 in lumbering, 1,000,000 deployed among various other state enterprises and the rest not designated. The high death rate reflected the callousness of a totalitarian system where slaves had no monetary value but could be endlessly supplied. During and after the war, the Gulag murdered fewer people and prevented more deaths with better food and medical care while arrests continued. The Gulag's population peaked at 12,000,000 in 1952.[39]

Stalin officially announced the end of purges before 1,900 cowed delegates during the Eighteenth Party Congress held from 10 to 21 March 1939. He had a vital reason to end the purges when he did. Europe appeared on the verge of a war that would likely engulf the Soviet Union.

Chapter 7

WORLD WAR

> 'Of course it's all a game to see who can fool whom. I know what Hitler's up to. He thinks he's outsmarted me but actually it's I who tricked him.' (Joseph Stalin)

> 'You have yourself to blame for all of this. You're the one who annihilated the old guard of our army. You had our best generals killed.' (General Kliment Voroshilov)

> 'Our victory means above all that our social system has won . . . Our political system has won.' (Joseph Stalin)

The chances for communist revolutions around the world rarely seemed riper than during the early 1930s. America's economy had imploded with New York's 1929 stock market crash, then Washington globalized the Great Depression with trade barriers that other countries emulated, collapsing international commerce. To varying degrees, a vicious cycle of poverty, joblessness, homelessness, bankruptcy and government impotence trapped every country. In democratic countries in western Europe and America, radical political movements attracted ever more desperate people.

Yet, in the Kremlin, Joseph Stalin shrugged at reports of these revolutionary possibilities. He pointed to even worse conditions a dozen years earlier following the First World War. Lenin and the other Bolshevik leaders had eagerly formed the Communist International (Comintern) to expand or found Communist Parties around the world. But the governments of those countries crushed every Communist movement. That did not surprise Stalin who was the only prominent leader sceptical of Comintern. He advocated 'Socialism in One Country', or achieving communism within the Soviet Union as a model for revolutions elsewhere and so powerful that it could thwart any foreign threats. After eliminating his rivals, he achieved that.

***

Meanwhile, the rival radical ideology of Fascism infected more countries.[1] Italian radical Benito Mussolini developed Fascism (Fraternalism) with these characteristics, a charismatic leader atop an authoritarian state that guided economic development, promoted ultranationalism, built an increasingly powerful military and conquered weak countries to exploit as colonies.[2] With those goals, Mussolini founded the Bands of Combat (Fasci di Combattimento) Party at Milan on 23 March 1919. The Fascist Party attracted so many members that Mussolini soon split it into two wings, one political that participated in elections and the other militant of black-uniformed thugs who intimidated rivals and the government itself. In October 1922, Mussolini had 20,000 Blackshirts in central Rome while he threatened 'to march on Rome' from Milan and lead them against the government. That spooked King Victor Emmanuel III into naming him prime minister on 30 October 1922. Mussolini formed a governing coalition between the Fascist Party and smaller nationalist parties. In June 1923, the coalition passed the Acerbo Law that would grant two-thirds of Parliament's seats to any party that won more than 25 per cent of the votes. The Fascist Party surpassed that threshold in the election held on 6 April 1924. With that power, Mussolini passed laws that gave the Fascist Party supreme power and outlawed other political parties. Mussolini's policies that developed the economy through investments in infrastructure and industries were highly popular. People rejoiced to receive paved roads, schools, hospitals, electricity, sewage and running water in their city districts and villages.

Japan was the next country where a fascist movement transformed a democracy into a dictatorship.[3] The turning point was 1925, when those in power began imposing ever more restrictions on elections and civil rights until eventually they abolished all political parties except the Imperial Rule Assistance Association. Japan's radicals never called themselves fascists, had no charismatic leader with supreme power, governed collectively and worshiped their semi-divine emperor with only symbolic power. Yet they had other key Fascist characteristics including authoritarianism, ultranationalism and imperialism, and eventually allied with Italy and Germany.

Anton Drexler founded the German Workers' Party in Munich in January 1919. Hitler joined the party in September of that year and rapidly rose through its ranks. On 24 March 1920 the Party was renamed the National Socialist German Workers Party (NSDAP). After Adolf Hitler took over the Nazi Party on 29 July 1921, he modelled it on Mussolini's Fascist Party in organization and strategy.[4] Hitler asserted that Germany would have won the First World War but was 'stabbed in the back' by a coalition of liberals, socialists, communists and Jews that agreed to surrender. He denounced the Weimar Republic formed after the war and called for Germany to become an ultranationalist authoritarian state. Under the Treaty of Versailles signed on 28 June 1919, Germany had to pay reparations to the Allied powers and restrict its army to 100,000 troops, its navy to small coast guard vessels and had to eliminate its air force. He repudiated that military and economic straitjacket. Hitler also called for expanding Germany's territory to encompass all German speakers elsewhere in central and eastern Germany and even in the Soviet Union.

Hitler's radical message initially repelled most Germans. The Nazis won 6.5 per cent of the vote and thirty-two seats in the May 1924 election, dropped to 3.0 per cent and fourteen seats in the December 1924 election and reached its nadir with 2.6 per cent of the vote and twelve seats in the 1928 election. Then Germany's economy collapsed with the Great Depression. The German government's inability to alleviate the mass poverty and joblessness boosted the Nazi Party's popularity as Hitler demanded decisive action to put people back to work. The Nazis won 18.2 per cent and 107 seats in the 1930 election, nearly one-third or 32.2 per cent of the vote and 230 seats in the July 1932 election and 33.6 per cent of the vote, and 196 seats in the November 1933 election. President Paul von Hindenburg named Hitler the chancellor (prime minister) since the Nazis were the largest party in the Reichstag (parliament). Hitler allied his Nazi Party with the Nationalist Party to pass two laws that transformed Germany from a democracy into a dictatorship. On 23 March 1933, following the Reichstag fire of 27 February, the Reichstag passed by 441 to 94 the Enabling Act granted the Chancellor the power to issue legal decrees that the Reichstag could not overrule. With that power, on 14 July 1933 Hitler issued the Law Against Formation of Parties that outlawed all but the Nazi Party. With that the Nazi Party won 92.1 per cent of the vote and all 661 Reichstag seats in the November 1933 election. Hitler proclaimed that Germany was now the Third Reich or empire that would last a thousand years.[5]

Mussolini coined the term totalitarian to describe what he aspired Fascism to be. But were the fascist regimes of Italy, Japan and Germany totalitarian? The simple answer is no, because none of those regimes abolished private property and markets. Their governments did nationalize some larger industries but mostly worked with business owners to manage production and prices. Germany's four-year plans indicated what Berlin hoped to achieve and where it would distribute subsidies to encourage business owners to invest there. Psychologically, Japan's system was totalitarian as the regime indoctrinated its soldiers and civilians alike to die fighting for their semi-divine emperor even when victory was impossible. Hitler's regime was totalitarian in its power systematically to arrest, transport to concentration camps and murder or enslave millions of people.

***

Joseph Stalin explained the Soviet Union's relationship with the Fascist countries during the 1934 Seventeenth Party Congress: 'Of course we are far from enthusiastic about the Fascist regime in Germany. But Fascism is beside the point, if only because Fascism in Italy, for example, has not kept the U.S.S.R. from establishing the best of relations with that country.'[6]

Stalin had mixed feelings about Hitler. Initially, he admired Hitler as a brilliant fellow tyrant then later hated him for the destruction he unleashed on the Soviet Union. After the war, when asked whether he thought Hitler was an adventurer or a lunatic, Stalin replied: 'I agree that he was an adventurer, but I can't agree that he was mad. Hitler was a gifted man. Only a gifted man could unite the German people. Like it or not . . . the Soviet Army fought their way into the German land . . . and reached Berlin without the German working class ever striking against . . . the Fascist regime. Could a madman so unite a nation?'[7]

Stalin only gradually recognized the growing threat that Nazi Germany backed by Fascist Italy posed to the Soviet Union from 1933 to 1939.[8] He pursued mostly constructive relations with the West. President Franklin Roosevelt recognized the Soviet Union on 16 November 1933 and the two nations soon exchanged ambassadors. The Soviet Union joined the League of Nations on 18 September 1934, but was expelled on 14 December 1939, for its imperialism against Finland. During those years, Stalin hoped war would erupt between the fascist and democratic countries. It did on 3 September 1939, but only after Stalin and Hitler formed a non-aggression pact and split Poland between them.

***

Of the three Fascist countries, Japan's was the first to challenge the League of Nations system that outlawed aggressive war, promoted collective security and sought the peaceful resolution of international disputes from its establishment in 1920. Japan's conquest of Manchuria in September 1931 was the latest stage in a series of imperialist thrusts that began four decades earlier.[9] The first was Japan's war against China from 1894 to 1895 that conquered the island of Taiwan. The second was Japan's war against Russia from 1904 to 1905 that won Korea as a colony and took from Russia its rights to run and defend the South Manchuria Railway, mines and the ports of Darien and Port Arthur in Manchuria, Sakhalin Island's southern half and the Kurile Islands. The third was during the First World War when Japan declared war against Germany to take over its Shantung Peninsula in China and its western Pacific island groups called the Carolinas, Marshalls and Marianas. Tokyo sought to carve a colony from eastern Siberia extending from Vladivostok during Russia's civil war from 1919 to 1922, but the Communist victory forced the Japanese to withdraw their army. Tokyo's next logical imperial step was to take advantage of the civil war devastating China and completely colonize Manchuria.

China's civil war began in 1927, when the Nationalist Party led by Chiang Kai-shek attacked its political ally the Communist Party, decimated its ranks and drove the remnants underground. On 18 September 1931, Japan's Kwangtung Army in Manchuria instigated the conquest by exploding a small bomb on the South Manchuria Railway, shooting several Chinese 'saboteurs', and claiming it must restore order to the entire region. Fighting erupted between Japanese and Chinese troops. Within months, the Japanese conquered most of Manchuria, renamed it Manchukou and established a puppet regime headed by Puyi.

Chiang Kai-shek's Nationalist government, then with its capital at Nanjing, protested to the League of Nations. The League of Nations issued two resolutions, one calling for Japan to withdraw its army and the other to send an investigative team to China to determine just what happened. The Lytton Commission, led by Victor Bulwer-Lytton, landed at Shanghai on 7 January 1932, for several months of investigation. On 2 October 1932, the League of Nations published the Lytton Commission's report which detailed Japan's blatant imperialism in Manchuria. Tokyo announced Japan's withdrawal from the League of Nations on 25 March 1933. The League of Nations did not issue economic, let alone military, sanctions against Japan for its imperialism. That appeasement encouraged Japan along with Italy and Germany to commit a series of aggressions over the next half-dozen years that culminated with the Second World War.[10]

Chiang Kai-shek did not attack the Japanese in Manchuria, but instead renewed an offensive against the Communist Party's stronghold in south-east China. That routed the Communists on their 'Long March' that began with 65,000 troops in October 1934 and followers and ended with 7,000 troops and followers at Yenan in northern China not far from Outer Mongolia in October 1935. At that point, Mao Zedong took over the Communist Party and infused it with his own variant of communism. Maoism was a distinct Marxist version in two key ways. Mao sought swiftly to realize pure communism by eliminating the traditional power elite and distributing its wealth as equally as possible to workers and peasants while providing them with rudimentary schooling and health care. He also emphasized a peasant-based revolution with parallel expanding political and military wings. Political commissars mobilized the people in each village and city district against the local officials, businessmen and landlords. All along the political and military wings destroyed the enemy's political and military forces while political commissars constructed a communist system that mobilized the population.

***

The Soviet Union was not the only great power that isolated itself during the 1930s. As the three fascist powers grew more militarily powerful and aggressive, the United States largely sat on the diplomatic sidelines. Most Americans believed that their relative isolation in the Western Hemisphere protected them from any aggressors in the Far East, Africa or Europe. That isolationist mindset was deeply rooted through multiple layers of America political culture and history.[11] During the colonial era from 1607 to 1775, the settlers were accustomed to economic, political and military autonomy and mostly fought Indians and their French and Spanish allies with little help from the mother country. During that era, English subjects transformed into free-born Americans, communitarianism into individualism and each of the eventual thirteen colonies became a quasi-republic with a elected assembly and civil rights for men of property along with a governor appointed by the king for eleven of them; the assemblies of Connecticut and Rhode Island elected their own governors. With independence, the young republic flourished economically in part by heeding President George Washington's sage advice to 'avoid entangling alliances'. Over a century and a half, America's trade globalized and its economy became the world's largest while its political leaders shunned involvement in European wars.

When Europe's great powers went to war in August 1914, President Woodrow Wilson followed tradition by keeping a strict neutrality even though nearly all trade was with the Allies. Wilson finally felt compelled to ask Congress for a declaration of war in April 1917 after German unrestricted submarine warfare sank three American merchant ships. Most Americans enthusiastically supported the war. Nearly four million men were drafted into the army and nearly two million of them served on the Western Front. Americans rejoiced in the decisive role their army played in defeating Germany in November 1918.

After the cheering receded, thoughtful Americans questioned the war's human, economic and moral toll. Around 110,000 Americans died, hundreds of thousands more suffered grievous wounds and the war cost $32 billion to fight. Wilson along with the British, French and Italian leaders designed a 'peace' treaty that scapegoated Germany as the war's initiator and forced it to pay a vast indemnity to the winners, even though to varying degrees each great power was responsible for blundering into a war that none of them wanted. The Treaty of Versailles also established a League of Nations dedicated to collective security for all countries to join. Wilson failed to get two-thirds of Senators to ratify the treaty so the world's greatest economic power and democracy did not join the League of Nations after the First World War.

Americans resumed enriching themselves from the global economy while doing little to help maintain it. Unregulated markets and greed led the New York stock market to soar to unsustainable heights in October 1929, then crash and engulf America in the Great Depression. Congress globalized that depression with the 1930 Smoot-Hawley Act that raised tariffs on imports by 50 per cent. International trade collapsed when other countries retaliated.

Although Washington spurned membership of the League of Nations, it did promote peace and prosperity with several policies through 1929. In 1924 and 1929, the White House worked with France, Germany and other countries to overcome a potential financial crisis when Germany threatened to default on its reparations payments; the American loaned Germany the money to pay the French and British so they could repay their own debts to the United States. Washington also sponsored a naval reduction conference from September 1921 to February 1922 whereby the great powers agreed to cap their numbers of warships and respect China's sovereignty. Finally, the American and French foreign ministers negotiated the 1928 Treaty of Paris that outlawed aggressive war and eventually forty-seven countries signed the treaty. Yet when Japan blatantly violated the Treaty of Paris, Secretary of State Henry Stimson merely announced on 7 January 1932 that the United States would not recognize its conquest of Manchuria.

After taking the presidential oath of office in March 1933, Franklin Roosevelt inaugurated his 'New Deal' of institutions, laws, subsides and programmes that stimulated the economy and provided people with employment.[12] Gradually America's economy revived. But American isolationism was as virulent as ever. Roosevelt was an internationalist who feared the Fascist powers but was politically straitjacketed from taking any decisive steps with Britain and France that might counter them. Indeed, Congress imposed 'neutrality laws' in 1935, 1936 and 1938 that prevented him from sending military or economic aid to the victim of an international aggressor. Eventually, Roosevelt would break those chains and transform American foreign policy from isolationism to internationalism.[13]

***

Hitler provoked the next international crisis in March 1935, when he announced that Germany would no longer adhere to the Versailles Treaty and would expand its army, navy and air force.

Prime ministers Ramsay MacDonald of Britain, Pierre Laval of France and Benito Mussolini of Italy met at Stresa, Italy, on 14 April 1935 and declared their opposition to any German violations of the Treaty of Versailles. Laval then flew to Moscow to sign a defence treaty with Stalin on 2 May 1935. That did not stop Hitler from beginning Germany's military build-up.

Then Mussolini provoked an international crisis when he ordered the army in Italy's colony of Somalia to invade neighbouring Ethiopia, then called Abyssinia, on 3 October 1935, after 14 previous months of sporadic clashes between Italian and Ethiopian troops on the frontier. Emperor Haile Salassie appealed for help from the League of Nation, which condemned Italy's aggression and imposed limited economic sanctions on 7 October. The sanctions did not include petroleum, and Britain, with its protectorate over Egypt, could have shut the Suez Canal and thus prevented any supplies or reinforcements from reaching Somalia. The British and French governments feared that imposing more than light economic sanctions would provoke Mussolini to ally with Hitler. The Italian army captured Addis Ababa, Ethiopia's capital, on 5 May 1936.

Meanwhile, Hitler again tested the League system when, on 7 March 1936, he ordered 20,000 troops to march into the Rhineland which the Versailles Treaty demilitarized. Prime Minister Stanley Baldwin admitted that Britain politically would not support a war against Germany for the violation. That forced French Prime Minister Albert Sarraut to accept the violation even though France's then million-man army vastly outnumbered Germany's. Hitler later remarked that: 'The forty-eight hours after the march into the Rhineland were the most nerve-racking of my life. If the French had then marched into the Rhineland we would have had to withdraw with our tails between our legs, for the military forces at our disposal would have been wholly inadequate for even a moderate resistance.'[14] What Hitler does not mention, possibly because he did not know, was that a group of generals was prepared to overthrow him if forced to make that humiliating retreat. And with Hitler gone, the chances of a future world war would have sharply diminished to near nothing.

***

Stalin had ignored the Communist International (Comintern) since its inception. He dismissed Comintern for its failure not merely to instigate any revolutions but even any viable Communist Parties. With his 'socialism in one country' policy, he essentially wrote off any hope that Comintern could fulfil its core revolutionary mission or perform any other acts that might enhance Soviet power.[15]

The worsening threat posed by fascist Japan, Italy and Germany forced Stalin to reconsider Comintern's potential usefulness. He authorized Comintern to promote a Popular Front strategy of forming coalitions of leftist political parties in France and other democratic countries to counter any right-wing political parties in those countries. The Popular Front strategy was most successful in France where the Communist Party's membership soared from 786,000 in 1935 to 3,960,000 in 1937.[16]

Comintern scored its first concrete victory when a Popular Front coalition in Spain won the election on 26 February 1936.[17] Manuel Azara became prime minster and began implementing such promised reforms as breaking up large farms and distributing land to peasants, better pay and work conditions for labourers and the confiscation and sale of Catholic Church property to help pay for reforms. That provoked worsening violence across Spain as strikes and looting erupted. A cabal of generals led by Franciso Franco conspired to launch a coup on 18 July, whereby all army units would take over nearby government buildings and crush any Popular Front forces. The civil war lasted until Franco's troops wiped out the last leftist forces and declared the nation unified on 1 April 1939.[18]

During those war, Hitler and Mussolini aided Franco with 16,000 and 50,000 respective troops and millions of dollars' worth of military supplies. Stalin sent 3,015 military advisors and 772 pilots along with 106 tanks, 60 armoured cars, 174 artillery pieces, 136 aircraft, 3,727 machine guns, 60,000 rifles and tons of ammunition to the Popular Front regime.[19] For Moscow, along with Berlin and Rome, Spain's civil war became a dress rehearsal for a future war as they tested strategies, tactics, weapons, equipment and leaders.[20]

***

Tokyo launched an all-out war to conquer China after a skirmish between their troops at the Marco Polo Bridge near Beijing on 7 July 1937.[21] Three armies with 600,000 troops among them invaded China, one from Manchuria, one from Shanghai up the Yangtse River Valley and a third that landed in south-east China to capture Canton. Those armies eventually linked up to take over most of eastern China. Initially, Chiang Kai-shek's Nationalists with its capital at Nanjing fielded 1,700,000 troops and Mao Zedong's Communists with its capital at Yenan fielded 600,000. The Japanese captured Nanjing in December 1937 and over the next month may have murdered 200,000 civilians there alone and eventually millions more across China.[22] Chiang and the remnants of his army withdrew up the Yangtse River to Chungking, where he established his new capital.

What ensured was a stalemate for the next eight years. The Japanese eventually fielded 1,125,000 troops along with 1,000,000 Chinese collaborators but that was never enough to conquer China. With increasing American aid, Chiang's army reached 5,700,000 but he refused to launch a massive offensive against the Japanese and instead waited for the war's end to instead attack Mao's army which reached 1,200,000 troops. The Communists fought and steadily drove back the Japanese in northern China.[23]

The Soviet Union and Japan fought an undeclared, sporadic frontier war in 1938 and 1939 that had decisive results.[24] Japan's war against China from July 1937 brought Japanese troops to stretches of the Soviet border with Manchuria. Marshal Vasily Blyukher commanded that front. In July and August 1938, his Red Army troops fought Japan's Kwantung Army near Lake Khasan. Both sides suffered heavy casualties before the Japanese withdrew. In 1938, the

Kwantung Army slowly advanced a few miles south of the Outer Mongolian border, building a railway along the way from Solon to Ganchzhur. In May, they invaded Mongolia by crossing the Khalkhin-Gol River. On 28 May, the Japanese attacked a joint Soviet-Mongolian army commanded by General Nikolai Feklenko but withdrew after two days of heavy fighting. When Feklenko failed to follow up his victory, Stalin replaced him with General Georgi Zhukov. Both sides reinforced their armies. On 3 July, the Japanese launched an offensive that Zhukov's troops eventually blunted, then on 20 August he counter-attacked and routed the Japanese. The Soviets, Mongolians and Japanese signed an armistice on 15 September 1939. This remote, obscure military campaign had global consequences. The decisive Soviet victory deterred further Japanese aggression against the Soviet Union. Instead, Tokyo shifted the direction of its imperialism to the south-west Pacific and Southeast Asia. That let Stalin focus on his own imperial ambitions for Eastern Europe.

***

Hitler's next violation of the Treaty of Versailles was Germany's annexation of Austria. He had nurtured an Austrian Nazi Party which Austrian Chancellor Kurt von Schuschnigg tried to suppress. Hitler summoned Schuschnigg to his mountain retreat at Berchtesgaden and demanded that he legalize the Nazi Party and appoint Arthur Seyss-Inquart the Minister of Public Safety. Schuschnigg agreed. Back in Vienna, Schuschnigg announced on 3 March 1938 that a referendum would be held on 13 March over whether Austria should remain independent or be a German province. Fearing a majority would favour independence, Hitler issued an ultimatum on 11 March that Schuschnigg accept annexation or face invasion. When Schuschnigg refused, Hitler ordered his army to invade Austria on the 12th. The Austrian army did not resist and Austrians packed the streets to welcome the German army. Schuschnigg resigned and Seyss-Inquart took his place as chancellor. Hitler began a victory procession through Austrian cities, starting with his birthplace at Brauna and culminating at Vienna on 15 March. The Nazi Party arrested over 70,000 people over the next month. In the rigged referendum on 10 April, 99.7 per cent voted for Germany to annex Austria.

Hitler then turned to Czechoslovakia whose western Sudetenland province's three million inhabitants were mostly ethnic Germans. On 28 March 1938, he demanded that Czech Chancellor Edvard Beneš cede the Sudetenland to Germany. When Beneš refused, Hitler began to build up German forces on the Czech border. Hoping to prevent a war, British Prime Minister Neville Chamberlain flew to meet Hitler at Berchtesgaden on 15 September. Hitler harangued Chamberlain for hours and refused to take anything less than all of the Sudetenland. Chamberlain flew back to London without a deal. Hitler issued Beneš an ultimatum on 24 September to yield the Sudetenland by 28 September or face an invasion. Chamberlain got Hitler to agree to postpone the invasion while the two of them along with French Prime Minister Edouard Daladier and Italian Prime Minister Benito Mussolini met in Munich to forge an understanding on 30 September. Beneš was summoned to Munich but not allowed to participate. The four drafted a treaty for Germany to annex the Sudetenland and ushered in Beneš, who reluctantly signed it with Hitler. Chamberlain flew back to London where he infamously waved his copy of the treaty before reporters and cheerfully proclaimed that he had secured 'peace in our time'.

That time was fleeting. The German army occupied the Sudetenland by mid-October. Then on 16 March 1939, Hitler ordered the German army to take over the rest of Czechoslovakia. Beneš ordered his army not to resist to prevent countless lives being lost and property destroyed before the ultimate German victory.

Hitler then turned his guns toward Poland and demanded that President Ignacy Mosciak yield the mostly ethnic German port of Danzig to Germany and subordinate the rest of his country to Germany. Prime Ministers Chamberlain and Daladier offered Poland a security guarantee on 26 March, which Polish Josef Beck eagerly accepted, but they did not draft that into a formal alliance treaty until 25 August. Meanwhile, Hitler massed troops along Poland's frontier and he and Mussolini formed an alliance that they called the Pact of Steel on 22 May 1939.

***

Stalin rebuffed efforts by the British, French and Poles to entice him into their security deal. He worried they were weak-willed and would once again bow to Hitler. He did not want to be on the losing side. He replaced Maxim Litvinov with Vyacheslav Molotov as Foreign Commissar on 3 May 1939. He did so to curry favour with Hitler since Litvinov was Jewish. He purged other Jews from prominent positions in the foreign ministry and embassies abroad as a sign he was interested in talking.

Hitler finally took the bait. On 14 August, he had German Ambassador Friedrich von Schulenburg present Molotov with a letter that read:

'The German government takes the view that between the Baltic and the Black Sea there is no question that cannot be settled to the complete satisfaction of both countries.'[25] Stalin eagerly embraced that offer. On 19 August, he had a trade treaty and non-aggression treaty drafted for Molotov to present to Schulenburg, who promptly sent them to Berlin. Hitler cordially wrote to Stalin on 20 August, welcoming the 'signing of the new German-Soviet trade agreement as a first step towards restructuring German-Soviet relations' whose highlight would be a 'pact of non-aggression'. He asked Stalin to receive Foreign Minister Joachim von Ribbentrop on 22 August. Stalin's reply was just as cordial: 'Thank you for your letter. I hope the German-Soviet agreement of non-aggression will be a turning point toward serious improvement of political relations between our countries.'[26]

Stalin warmly greeted Ribbentrop when he arrived on 23 August.[27] Ribbentrop assured him that Germany wanted nothing from Russia except peace and trade. Stalin and Ribbentrop then agreed to conquer and split Poland between them, with Germany taking the western two-thirds and the Soviet Union the eastern third. Elsewhere in Eastern Europe, they agreed to spheres of influence with Germany over Lithuania and the Soviet Union over Finland, Estonia, Latvia and Bessarabia in Romania. Stalin drew a different line when Ribbentrop suggested treaty words that extolled German-Soviet friendship. He bluntly told the ambassador:

> Don't you think we have to pay a little more attention to public opinion in our two countries? For many years now, we have been pouring buckets of shit over each other's heads and our propaganda boys could not do enough in that direction. Now all of a sudden, are we to make our people believe all is forgotten and forgiven? Things don't work so fast.'[28]

Molotov and Ribbentrop signed the Pact on 24 August. Stalin had champagne flutes distributed to the party, raised his and said: 'I know how much the German people loves its Führer. I should therefore like to drink to his health.'[29]

Stalin gloated over the pact and told his advisors: 'Of course it's all a game to see who can fool whom. I know what Hitler's up to. He thinks he's outsmarted me but actually it's I who tricked him.'[30] Nonetheless, Stalin sent Hitler an unrequested but happily-received gift. Several hundred German and Austrian communists had lived in exile in the Soviet after their attempted revolutions in those countries failed. Stalin ordered the NKVD to round them up and deliver them to Hitler, who sent them to concentration camps.

The German blitzkrieg began on 1 September, as 1,500,000 troops in 66 divisions with 2,700 tanks, 9,000 cannons and anti-tank guns and 2,315 warplanes attacked Poland defended by 1,000,000 troops in 39 divisions with 210 tanks, 4,300 guns and 800 warplanes.[31] The Soviet invasion of 750,000 troops in 33 divisions with 4,736 tanks, 4,949 guns and 3,300 warplanes began on 17 September. Astonishingly, the Poles valiantly held out until 5 October, when Warsaw finally surrendered. The Wehrmacht and Red Army inflicted enormous casualties on the Polish army, killing at least 66,000, wounding 133,700 and capturing 675,000 troops and also killed around 200,000 civilians and drove a million or more from their homes. Their victory was relatively cheap, with the Germans suffering 17,269 killed and 30,300 wounded and the Soviets 1,471 killed and 2,383 wounded.

Britain and France declared war against Germany on 3 September, but stayed securely in their positions. France's army numbered 5,000,000 troops and 3,200 tanks with most deployed in the Maginot Line of fortifications along the German border in September 1939. In addition, the British Expeditionary Force deployed in Flanders eventually numbered 390,000 troops. Had they attacked the Saarland, the sheer weight of numbers would have broken through the thinly-defended German lines, then advanced to the Rhine.

The so-called 'Phoney War' where all was quiet on the Western Front lasted from 1 September 1939 to 10 May 1940. The Germans and Soviets consolidated their parts of Poland, purging any potential enemies and requestioning anything of military or economic value. Each then attacked elsewhere.

***

Stalin's easy conquest of eastern Poland excited his desire for more conquests. Russia had conquered Finland from Sweden in 1809. After the Bolsheviks seized power in Russia in November 1917, the Finns declared independence and defeated a Red Army offensive to restore Russian rule. Stalin was determined to reconquer Finland once and for all.

Stalin issued an ultimatum to Finland's government on 12 October 1939, either to cede their naval base of Hango to the Soviet Union, a strip of frontier 20 miles deep on the Karelian Isthmus north of Leningrad and the Rybachi Peninsula that commanded the approach to Murmansk or go to war. The Finns rejected the demand. The war did not begin for another six weeks as the Red Army slowly massed troops and supplies along the border.

Stalin unleashed an assault by five armies with 760,000 troops, 2,514 tanks and 3,880 warplanes commanded by Marshal Kirill Meretskov at strategic regions of Finland's fronter on 30 November and they almost immediately bogged down.[32] The timing could not have been worse. Deep snow buried ground defended by Finland's 340,000 well-positioned troops wearing white camouflaged thick winter clothes; the Finns had only 32 tanks and 114 warplanes. Without anti-tank guns, the Finns hurled 'Molotov cocktails', gasoline-filled bottles with lighted cloth wicks, at enemy tanks. Troops on skies slipped around the front line and attacked Soviet convoys and supply depots. The Finns repelled the Red Army on each front, inflicting huge casualties while winter inflicted worse losses.

Throughout January 1940, Stalin built up the armies to vast numbers of now well-equipped and winter-clothed troops and launched a massive assault in mid-February. This time the Soviets overwhelmed most Finnish positions, although they suffered horrendous losses. When the Finnish government asked for a cease fire on 13 March, the Soviets had endured 126,875 killed, 188,671 wounded and 5,541 captured to 25,909 Finns killed, 43,857 wounded and 1,000 captured or five times more.[33]

The Finns signed a treaty on 13 March 1940, that ceded the port of Hango, the Karelian Peninsula and Lake Lagoda's north-eastern shore to the Soviet Union. Despite those gains, Stalin was enraged at the cost in time and manpower. In a classic case of 'projection', he martyrized himself and scapegoated Defence Commissar Kliment Voroshilov for those losses. In a rare case of confronting Stalin, Voroshilov shouted back: 'You have yourself to blame for all of this. You're the one who annihilated the old guard of our army. You had our best generals killed.'[34] On 28 March, Voroshilov admitted before the Central Committee that: 'I have to say that neither I nor General Staff . . . had any idea of the peculiarities and difficulties of this war.'[35] Khrushchev explained how Stalin's regime justified war against Finland: 'There is some question whether we had any legal or moral right for actions against Finland. Of course, we didn't have any legal right. As far as morality was concerned, our desire to protect ourselves was ample justification in our own eyes.'[36] Nearly three years later, while summiting at Yalta with Churchill and Roosevelt, Stalin admitted that in the Finnish War: 'The Red Army was good for nothing.'[37]

Stalin browbeat the governments of Estonia, Latvia and Lithuania to rejoin the Russian empire, now called the Soviet Union. The blunt choice for each was submit to Soviet rule or suffer conquest. When those leaders hesitated, Stalin ordered the Red Army and NKVD to systematically purges all enemies of the people in those countries. The mass murder and slave labour victims eventually included at least 60,000 Estonians, 34,250 Latvians and 75,000 Lithuanians before the Germans overran the region in June and July 1941. After the Red Army reconquered the Baltic states in late 1944, the Soviets murdered or enslaved 175,000 Estonians, 170,000 Latvians and 175,000 Lithuanians over the next nine years. After Stalin died, his successors ended the atrocities.[38]

After the dismal Finnish campaign, Stalin shook up his high command. He replaced Voroshilov with Semyon Timoshenko as Defence Commissar on 6 May 1940. He compensated Voroshilov by making him Deputy Chairman of the Council of Ministers and Chair of the State Defence Committee (GKO). Stalin restored the top rank of marshal, abolished during the revolution and bestowed that exulted title on victorious civil war generals Kliment Voroshilov, Semyon Budyonny, Alexander Yegorov, Mikhail Tukhachevsky, and Vasily Blyukher. On 6 June, the Sovnarkom approved a plan to create mechanized tank corps with two tank division and one motorized infantry division. Meanwhile, Stalin sought to weaken the NKVD by splitting it into two organizations led by lackies. In February 1941, the Eighteenth Party Congress approved his plan to have Lavrenti Beria retain control of the core NKVD while hiving off State Security (NKGB) as an independent entity led by Vsevolod Merkulov. Stalin did not actually implement that reorganization until 16 April 1943.

***

The Phoney War ended for the Germans on 9 April 1940, when the Wehrmacht invaded Denmark and Norway. The Danes surrendered without a fight. The 52,000 Norwegians, reinforced by an Allied task force with 38,000 British, French and Poles, fought 100,000 Germans. The Germans eventually repelled the British task force and the Norwegians surrendered on 10 June. In all, the Germans inflicted 1,819 British, 533 French and Polish, and 1,780 Norwegian casualties while suffering 5,296. Norway's conquest was more than a sideshow. Norway was vital to German security because a railway from northern Sweden carried iron ore to Narvik where it was shipped to Germany to feed its industries. If the British expedition and Norwegians had blunted the German invasion they would have severed that supply line.[39]

The Phoney War ended on the Western Front on 10 May, when 3,300,000 German troops in 141 divisions with 2,445 tanks, 7,376 guns and 5,638 warplanes attacked 3,300,000 French, British, Belgian and Dutch troops; the French and British fielded 4,071 and 700 tanks respectively and together flew 2,939 warplanes. The main German thrust was through the Ardennes Forest in Belgium then across northern France to the sea which they reached on 20 May, splitting the British army and a French army north and the rest of the French army south. The Netherlands surrendered on 15 May and Belgium on 28 May. The British managed to extract from Dunkirk 338,215 troops, two-thirds British and one-third French, by 30 May. The Germans routed the French armies elsewhere. An Italian army invaded south-eastern France on 10 June. The French government abandoned Paris for Bordeaux on 13 June. Marshal Philippe Petain asked for and received an armistice on 17 June and surrendered France to Germany at Compiègne on 25 June. The Germans conquered France as quickly as they had Poland, inflicted 73,000 killed, 240,000 wounded and 1,756,000 captured on the Allied forces and knocked out or captured 1,748 French and 700 British tanks and destroyed or captured 2,233 warplanes, mostly French. The Germans lost 27,674 dead and 111,034 wounded.[40]

Hitler's next two strategic steps were, first, to secure air superiority over the British Isles and superiority over the seas lanes supplying Britain from North America and then launch an invasion across the English Channel that conquered Britain. The Battle of Britain was the air campaign that lasted from the first major German bombing attack on 10 July until 31 October, when Luftwaffe commander Hermann Göring ordered a hiatus. The Royal Air Force shot down 1,977 German planes, killed 2,955 pilots, wounded 735 and captured 925, while losing 1,744 planes, 1,542 pilots killed and 422 wounded and 23,002 civilians killed and 32,135 wounded.[41] The Battle of the Atlantic lasted until the end of the war as German submarines prowled the ocean to sink over 3,500 merchant ships and kill 36,000 sailors, sink 175 warships and kill 36,200 sailors, with 751 Allied warplanes either shot down or crashed, while the Germans lost 753 submarines with 30,000 crewmen and 47 other warships.[42] Meanwhile, unable to conquer Britain, Hitler turned his gaze eastward.

***

Germany's blitzkrieg and conquest of France and the Low Countries alarmed President Roosevelt and other internationalists in Washington and across the United States. Yet, fearing the political wrath of isolationists, he did not speak out strongly against German and other fascist aggression until after he won re-election in the November

1940 election. On 17 December 1940, he proposed his Lend-Lease programme of giving military aid to victims of fascist imperialism. He was a master of political parables and explained that by helping others, Americans protected their own national security: 'Suppose my neighbor's home catches fire and I have a length of garden hose four or five hundred feet away. If he can take my garden hose and connect it with his hydrant, I may help him put out his fire.' In a radio broadcast on 29 December, he declared that the nation's security demanded that America become 'the arsenal of democracy' for Europeans fighting for their freedom.[43]

Congress passed the Lend-Lease Act by votes in the House of Representative of 250 to 165 and in the Senate by 60 to 31 and Roosevelt signed it into law on 11 March 1941. Two days later, Congress appropriated $11 billion for Lend-Lease and eventually the programme would dispense $51 billion. Britain received the largest amount, $36.4 billion, followed by the Soviet Union with $11.2 billion, France with $3.2 billion, China with $1.6 billion and the rest spread among thirty-two minor allies.[44] Churchill declared before Parliament that America's Lend-Lease programme was 'the most unsordid act in the history of any nation'.[45]

***

Germany's dazzling victories troubled Stalin. He knew that the Nazi-Soviet non-aggression pact would last only until Hitler believed the Wehrmacht was strong enough to conquer the Soviet Union. He sought to ensure that the Soviet empire's recent expansion was politically secure.

No East European country was strategically more important than Poland, the gateway for invasions from the west. Stalin capitalized on the Red Army's capture of Poland's eastern third by purging political and military leaders there. He had the NKVD round up, convey to the Katyn Forest near Smolensk, shoot and bury in mass graves 21,000 victims, including 14,000 leading intellectuals, politicians and landowners, 8,000 military officers and 4,000 police officers, in mass graves in April and May 1941.[46]

Stalin presented Romania's government, headed by King Carol, the agonizing choice to cede its eastern provinces of Bessarabia and Bukovina to the Soviet Union or else go to war. Romania with a larger population and army than that of the Baltic states, rejected that demand. Romania had taken Hungary's Transylvania region after the First World War. Stalin gained Hungary's gratitude by initiating an international conference at Vienna that returned Transylvania's northern half to Hungary. Hungary's leader Admiral Miklós Horthy released imprisoned communist leader Matyas Rakosi and sent him to Moscow. Meanwhile, Bulgaria succeeded in pressuring Romania into ceding its southern Dobruja region. Romania's government aligned with Berlin to prevent being extinguished by its aggressive neighbours.

***

Stalin ordered a military build-up in response to Hitler's belligerence and expansion of German territory and military power from 1936. Defence spending rose from an average 5.4 per cent of the economy from 1928 to 1934 to 43.3 per cent in 1941.[47] Soviet military personnel rose from 1,600,000 to 5,300,000 from January 1938 to June 1941 then to 11,400,000 by July 1945; the army soared from an average 2,800,000 in the last quarter of 1941 to 5,900,000 in 1943 then rose slower to average between 6,300,000 and 6,800,000 each quarter for the war's remainder. Of the 35,000,000 people who wore a uniform, 21,000,000 or 67 per cent were from the Russian Federation, 19,000,000 were ethnic Russians, 6,400,000 were Slavs mostly from Ukraine or Belarus and 6,900,000 were from the other twelve soviet republics. Around 1,000,000 women served, with 500,000 in combat units. Nearly all those who served were conscripted.[48]

On the eve of war with Germany, the Soviet military's paper strength was daunting, with 5,373,000 personnel, including 4,261,000 soldiers, 618,000 airmen, 183,000 anti-aircraft troops and 312,000 sailors. Supplementing that was the paramilitary People's Commissariat for Internal Affairs (NKVD) whose 379,782 troops included 167,582 border, 27,300 operational, 63,700 railway, 38,300 convoy, 29,300 installation and 44,600 other forces. The army was organized into 27 armies, 95 corps and 303 divisions, up from one army 38 corps and 138 divisions in January 1938.[49]

A Soviet infantry division numbered 14,483 troops split among three infantry regiments, two artillery regiments, with 144 guns including 54 anti-tank guns, 16 light tanks and various smaller support units. In June 1941, divisions averaged 9,648 troops or 67 per cent of the ideal strength. A motorized infantry division numbered 11,650 troops split among two infantry regiments and a tank regiment including 49 armoured cars, 275 light tanks and 98 guns and mortars. The standard rifle was the magazine-fed bolt-action 7.62mm Moison Nagant Model 1891/1930. A tank division numbered 10,940 troops split among two tank regiments, a motorized infantry regiment and an artillery regiment with 375 tanks, including 63 KV and 270 T-34 tanks and 60 guns and mortars.[50]

Tanks were among the key weapons that each side developed during the war in a race to outfight its enemies. The Soviets began the war with several light tanks including the 3.3-ton T-38, the 9-ton T-26 and the 11-ton BT-5, each with a 37mm gun, and the 45-ton KV-1 medium tank with a 76mm gun.[51] Soviet factories began producing the 31-ton T-34/76 with a 75mm in 1940 and its improved version, the 31-ton T-34/85 from 1942. The T-34/85 was the war's best all-round tank for firepower, armour, manoeuvrability and durability. Its wide tread let it advance across snow and mud that bogged down German Panzer IIIs and IVs. Eventually, the Soviets produced 35,120 T-34/76s and 48,950 T-34/85s. The Soviets also produced the 11-ton SU-76 tank destroyer with a fixed 76mm gun, with 1,900 in 1943, 7,200 in 1944 and 3,600 in 1945. During the war, the Soviets received 11,900 tanks and self-propelled guns from its allies, with the largest shipments 4,100 American 31-ton M4 Shermans with a short 75mm gun and 1,100 British 27-ton Matildas and 5,600 40-ton Churchills.[52] Standard Soviet artillery included 76mm, 107mm, 122mm and 152mm pieces and Katyusha multiple rocket launchers.

The Red Army had 272,000 motor vehicles when the Germans invaded and soon requisitioned 204,900 civilian motor vehicles. During the war, the Soviets produced tens of thousands of trucks and received tens of thousands more from the United States. Despite that, the Red Army still relied more on horses than motor vehicles to pull supply wagons and guns. The Soviets did not have a good half-track personnel carrier and instead the troops rode atop tanks or in trucks and horse-drawn wagons.

The quality of Soviet warplanes rose during the war although losses from combat and accident were enormous. Fighter-planes initially included the Yak-1, LaGG-3 and MiG-3, but their performance was so dismal in 1941 that the Kremlin rushed production of advanced Yak-9s and La-5s that were as good as German Me 109s and Fw 190s. The Il-2 with a pilot and rear-facing machine gunner was a first-rate light bomber. The Soviets never produced a good heavy bomber but eventually they reverse-engineered American B-29s that landed in their territory after raids against Japan and were interned with their crews because of Moscow's neutrality.

Despite the Red Army's rapid build-up, in May 1940, the officer corps was only 65 per cent filled; 70 per cent of them had served less than six months; and only 50 per cent of battalion commanders and 32 per cent of company and platoon had more than six months' training. Officers were mostly ill-schooled. In 1941, the officer corps included 7.1 per cent with higher military education, 55.9 per cent with secondary education, 24.6 per cent with military courses and 12 per cent with no education. The Soviet military's officer training system was extensive, with 203 schools for mid-level officers and nineteen army academies, seven naval academies and ten military departments at civilian universities for higher education. Despite the uniform curriculum, the quality varied considerably, with Frunze Military Academy in Moscow the most prestigious.[53]

Deficiencies riddled the Red Army. Stalin's purges rendered nearly all surviving Red Army officers and troops cowed novices from the lowest private to the highest marshal. The High Command never adequately adapted war plans to reflect the strategic and logistical challenges of pushing the frontier west a couple hundred or so miles after annexing the Baltic states, eastern Poland and western Bessarabia in 1939 and 1940. Compounding that was the commissar system where a Communist cadre shadowed each officer, noting and second-guessing everything he did; Stalin finally recognized how self-defeating the commissar system was and abolished it on 9 October 1943. Training, equipment, supplies and morale ranged from deficient to dismal. The top-down command system and harsh penalties for disobedience crushed initiative and enterprise as thoroughly in the military as it did in the economy. The Red Army doctrine of attrition warfare and mass frontal attacks inflicted millions more casualties on itself than if more prudent strategies and tactics were followed.

The Red Army was notorious for clearing minefields by ordering infantry regiments to charge through them. Marshal Georgi Zhukov explained to General Dwight Eisenhower the 'logic' of doing so: 'There are two kinds of mines; one is the personnel mine, the other is the vehicular mine. When we come to a minefield our infantry attacks exactly as if it were not there. The losses we get from personnel mines we consider only equal to those we would have gotten from machine guns and artillery if the Germans had chosen to defend the position.' Eisenhower imagined 'a vivid picture of what would happen to any American or British commander if he pursued such tactics'.[54]

Stalin pardoned 11,178 officers and restored them to appropriate commands in 1940. Among them was General Konstantin Rokossovsky, who Stalin noticed was missing his fingernails. 'Were you tortured in prison,' he asked. 'Yes, Comrade,' the general quietly replied. Stalin showed no pity but merely quipped: 'There are too many yes men in this country.'[55] Of course, Stalin's genocide had made them that way.

Ignoring the Red Army's array of obvious deficiencies, Stalin ordered his commanders to react to any German attack with an immediate counter-attack. In May 1941, Zhukov explained that strategy to the high command: 'Defending our country we must act offensively. From defence to go to a military doctrine of offensive actions. We must transform our training, our propaganda, our agitation, our press in an offensive spirit. The Red Army is a modern army and a modern army is an offensive army.'[56]

That doctrine unwittingly made the eventual German onslaught even more devastating. Rather than deploy its army with a light screen at the frontier followed by a defence in depth, the high command massed most troops behind the frontier. German panzer divisions punched through thin stretches of the Soviet defences to encircle and destroy entire armies.

Georgi Zhukov was the outstanding Soviet military leader of the Second World War.[57] He was born a peasant, drafted at age 18 into the army in 1915 and selected for training as a non-commissioned officer in the cavalry. He fought from 1916 through November 1917 and won a Cross of St. George for bravery. After the Bolsheviks took power, he joined a Red Army cavalry regiment, fought through the civil war, won the Order of the Red Banner and emerged as a regimental commander. In 1924, he studied at the Advanced Cavalry School in Leningrad. Thereafter he rose steadily in communist rank to command a brigade, then a division and finally a corps by 1938. He first achieved fame commanding the army that decisively defeated Japan's Kwantung Army at the Battle of Khalkhin-Gol in August 1939. Stalin transferred him to command the Kiev Special Military District in June 1940, then made him Chief of the General Staff and Second Deputy Defence Commissar in January 1941. Stalin used Zhukov as a troubleshooter, dispatching him from one imperilled front to the next where he mitigated defeats and launched counter-attacks. That earned Zhukov promotion to First Deputy Defence Commissar and Deputy Supreme Commander in August 1942. Stalin assigned Zhukov command of the First Belorussian Front in November 1944. Zhukov led his command in a series of campaigns coordinated with other Fronts that culminated with Berlin's capture in May 1945. His colleague Marshal Konstantin Rokossovsky described Zhukov as 'a person of strong will and resolution, brilliant, gifted, exacting, persistent and clear of purpose. All of these qualities undoubtedly are necessary for a strong military chief . . . True, sometimes his severity exceeded permissible limits.'[58]

***

Germany's military in June 1941 included 3,767,000 troops, 1,700,000 auxiliaries, 150,000 Waffen-SS troops, 680,000 air force personnel, 404,000 navy personnel, 7,200 guns, 4,000 tanks and 4,400 warplanes. Of 209 regular army divisions, Hitler massed 121 divisions on the Soviet frontier, 15 in reserve in Poland while deploying 38 in north-west Europe, eight in Norway, two in North Africa and seven in Greece.[59]

A German infantry division had 17,000 troops in three infantry regiments, one reconnaissance battalion, one artillery regiment and support units like headquarters, anti-aircraft, supply and medical. In October 1943, Berlin reduced the number of troops to 13,656 with the same fire power. The standard rifle was the 7.92mm bolt-action Karabin 98-K, renowned for being accurate, rugged and reliable. The standard panzer division had 11,792 troops in one panzer regiment of 118 tanks, two panzer grenadier or mechanized infantry regiments and an artillery regiment with 99 guns, including 45 anti-tank guns.

German tanks and their guns got larger during the war.[60] Spearheading the first German blitzkriegs were the 9-ton Panzer II with a 20mm gun followed by the 20-ton Panzer III with a 37mm gun and 25-ton Panzer IV with a short 75mm gun. Russia's T-34 proved superior in firepower and armour, so the Germans put a 50mm gun on the Panzer III and a long-barrel 75mm on the Panzer IV, then developed the 43-ton Panzer V Panther with heavier armour and a long 75mm gun and the 57-ton Panzer VI Tiger with an 88mm gun that appeared in 1943 along with the 46-ton Jagdpanzer 'tank destroyer' with a fixed 88mm gun. With thicker armour, Panthers and Tigers blew away T-34s in most duels. The trouble was that the Germans produced too few of either too late to win a decisive edge on the battlefield. The Soviets adapted their tactics against Panthers and Tigers by having T-34s avoid frontal attacks and instead swing wide to position themselves for shots at their treads and drive sockets that disabled them.

Most German troops were hardened, skilled veterans in 1941. They were trained at each level to take the initiative and react to circumstances rather than await orders. Their morale was sky-high given the series of victories they had scored over the previous two years. They had lost only 102,000 dead, wounded and missing in all the fighting on all the fronts from September 1939 to June 1941.[61] Yet some weaknesses burdened the German army. The worst was that the army was only partly mechanized. The armies that invaded the Soviet Union included 600,000 transport vehicles and 625,000 horses that drew supply wagons and guns.[62]

Göring had developed an excellent air force. The Germans had two first-rate fighter planes, the Me 109 and Fw 190. The Ju 87 Stuka was a first-rate dive bomber whose screaming sirens as it descended could distract and even demoralize anti-aircraft crews. The Ju 88 and He 111 were first-rate medium bombers. The four-engined He 177 heavy bomber was the German air force's only dud, deficient in range, payload and reliability. The air force's only deficit was that the Germans never produced a first-rate heavy bomber.

Germany had four severe hard-power weaknesses compared to the Soviet Union, people, space, production and natural resources. Germany's population was less than half that of the Soviet Union, with 80 million to 171 million. If Germany just fought the Soviet Union, it would have to score a rapid victory or else eventually lose a prolonged war of attrition as Stalin steadily mobilized twice as many soldiers and workers. As for space, the Soviet Union had 2,110,000 square miles of European and 6,460,000 square miles of Asian territory. In a war, the Red Army could sidestep a decisive defeat by withdrawing eastward, trading land for time and stretching German supply lines to the snapping point. At an inevitable point, the Soviets would enjoy an overwhelming advantage in position and troops over Germany and would punch steadily westward to victory. The Russians had pursued that grand strategy against Napoleon in 1812 and would repeat it against Hitler from 1941 to 1943. Although both sides had allies in both wars, the Russians enjoyed three that no foreign invader could overcome – the harsh, prolonged, deep-freeze winter preceded and followed by prolonged autumn and spring rains that soaked the earth that vehicles churned into axle-deep mud.

The Germans did enjoy one hard-power advantage. The mostly flat and open Russian plains were ideal for the mobile tank-led warfare of encircling and destroying enemy armies that the Germans had mastered. But that was a fair-weather strategy against the Soviet Union. At best, the Germans had half a dozen or so months of good weather to win decisively.

***

As for production, the Soviets churned out far more weapons and equipment in most categories than the Germans before and during the war. In 1943, Stalin boasted that: 'the lesson of the war are that the Soviet structure is not only the best form of the organization of the economic and cultural advance of the country in the years of peaceful development, but also the best form of mobilization of all forces of the people to drive off the enemy in wartime.'[63] That greater production was grounded in greater numbers of workers and natural resources to exploit. The Soviet Union had huge reserves of petroleum, iron ore, coal and other vital minerals. As for petroleum, the Soviets produced 33 million tons while the Germans produced 5.7 million tons, of which 3.9 million was high-priced synthetic oil, and they imported 5.5 million tons from Romania. Although wartime disruptions caused Soviet oil production to drop to 22 million tons in 1942 and 18 million tons in 1943, that was enough to fuel the Red Army while German oil production and imports fell short of demand. The Germans did outproduce the Soviets in steel which with the combined output of its domestic and conquered factories averaged 33.4 million tons from 1941 to 1944 compared to 11.3 million in the Soviet Union.[64]

One stunning Soviet feat was transferring an extraordinary number of factories from the path of the German onslaught to hopefully safe cities hundreds of miles eastward. By January 1942, an army of engineers, workers and transporters had dismantled and shipped the equipment, supplies and records of 1,523 factories, of which 1,360 produced defence products, out of harm's way, reassembled and manned them.[65] Around this time, Stalin expressed his appreciation for the critical related roles of industry and transportation in contemporary warfare with this axiom: 'Modern war is a war of motors. The war will be won by whichever side produces the most motors.'[66] Indeed, the Soviet Union outproduced Germany for most weapons throughout the war.

7.1 Soviet Pre-War Weapons Production[67]

	1937	1938	1939	1940	1941 Jan–Jun
Tanks	1,600	2,300	3,000	2,800	1,700
Artillery	5,400	12,300	17,000	15,100	7,900
Mortars	1,600	1,200	4,100	37,900	10,500
Rifles	567,400	1,224,700	1,396,700	1,395,000	792,000
Machine Guns	31,100	52,600	73,600	52,200	N/A
Aircraft	4,400	5,500	10,400	10,600	6,000
Shells/ Mines	N/A	13,000,000	20,000,000	33,000,000	19,000,000

7.2 German and Soviet War Production, 1941 and 1942[68]

	1941		1942	
	German	Soviet	German	Soviet
Rifles	1,359,000	2,421,000	1,370,000	4,049,000
Machine Guns	96,000	149,000	117,000	356,000
Artillery	22,000	41,000	41,000	128,000
Tanks/Self Propelled Guns	3,800	6,600	6,200	24,700
War Planes	8,400	12,400	11,600	21,700

7.3 German and Soviet War Production, 1943 and 1944[69]

	1943		1944	
	German	Soviet	German	Soviet
Rifles, Submachine Guns	2,509,000	4,081,000	3,085,000	3,006,000
Machine Guns	263,000	459,000	509,000	439,000
Artillery	74,000	130,000	148,000	122,000
Tanks/Self Propelled guns	11,000	24,000	18,000	29,000
Warplanes	19,000	30,000	34,000	33,000

7.4 Soviet Warplane Production and Losses[70]

	1941	1942	1943	1944	1945
Production	29,900	33,000	55,000	68,000	58,100
Losses					
Combat	10,300	7,800	11,200	9,700	4,100
Accidents	7,600	4,300	11,300	15,100	6,900

The Soviets were extremely wasteful of men, machines and equipment. The Red Army was notorious for launching mass infantry and tank attacks through minefields and against fortified enemy positions.

During just the war's first half-year, the Germans and their allies inflicted a stunning number of casualties on the Soviet military – 4,473,820, of which 3,258,673 were 'unrecoverable' killed, severely wounded or captured.[71]

Yet, despite frequent shortfalls the Soviets managed overall to expand the amount of men, machines and equipment. For instance, the Soviets lost and produced an extraordinary number of warplanes during the war. The warplane attrition rate worsened in a vicious cycle as the Soviets drafted more unqualified men as fliers and rushed them through more limited training so that ever more died from combat and accidents.

***

On 20 December 1940 Hitler ordered the Wehrmacht, to begin planning Operation Barbarossa, the invasion of the Soviet Union.[72] Within a week, spies conveyed word of that intention to Moscow.

That gave Stalin nearly seven months to prepare for the invasion. Instead, he trapped himself and thus the Soviet Union in his latest delusion.[73] He believed that Hitler did not want to attack earlier than 1942 at the earliest but would if he felt threatened. To avoid provoking that, he forbade not just the Soviet Union's full or partial mobilization but rejected repeated pleas by his generals to take such limited steps as fortifying the border, massing supplies and deploying troops to defendable positions. All along Stalin insisted that: 'Germany has a treaty of non-aggression with us. Germany is involved up to its ears in the war to the West; and I believe that Hitler will not risk creating a second front for himself by attacking the Soviet Union. Hitler is not such a fool as to think that the Soviet Union is Poland, that it is France, that it is England.'[74]

The first plea to prepare came during a General Staff meeting on 23 December 1940. General Georgi Zhukov, Kiev's Military District commander, called for a steady build-up of Soviet forces and endorsed a long-standing plan of General Mikhael Tukhachevsky, a show-trial murder victim, for the Red Army to attack the Germans if war erupted between them. Stalin rejected that plan as too provocative, but he did promote Zhukov to chief of staff on 1 February 1941. Zhukov, backed by Defence Minister Timoshenko, again asked for permission to mobilize the Soviet army to deter an attack. Stalin rejected that proposal, arguing that mobilization would instead provoke a German attack.

In the half-year before the attack Stalin received a series of warnings but refused to believe them. The first came on 29 December 1940, when

NKVD spies informed the Kremlin of Operation Barbarossa but gave no date for the invasion. Richard Sorge was a German journalist and NKVD spy. On 1 June, he passed word that the German invasion was scheduled for late June. Harro Schulze-Boysen was a NKVD spy, code-named 'Starshina', in Germany's Air Ministry. He gave two warnings that reached Moscow on 11 and 19 June. The first was that 'the question of the attack by Germany on the Soviet Union has been definitely decided'. The second was that 'all military preparations . . . are fully completed' and 'the blow can be expected at any time'.[75] On 13 June, Zhukov and Timoshenko warned Stalin of the steady build-up of Axis forces on the frontier and pleaded with him to order the Red Army's full mobilization. Stalin angrily rejected that intelligence, dismissing it as a gross exaggeration and insisting that, 'They'd be fools to attack us'.[76] Stalin also received two vague warnings from the British, the first from Ambassador Stafford Cripps on 11 April and the second from Churchill on 19 April. A German deserter crossed over on 21 June with word that the Wehrmacht would attack the next morning. The commander promptly sent that intelligence to the Kremlin. Stalin's reaction was: 'I think Hitler's trying to provoke us. He surely has not decided to make war.'[77]

***

Among the war's many 'what ifs' was the result had the Germans launched their onslaught seven weeks earlier. Hitler originally scheduled the invasion for 1 May 1941, but ended up delaying it for nearly two months. Ribbentrop's diplomacy had enticed Hungary, Romania and Yugoslavia into alliance with Germany and Italy. Then, on 26 March 1941, a military coup overthrew Yugoslavia's government and withdrew from the alliance. Although Yugoslavia's army would have contributed few forces to the invasion, Hitler called on Mussolini for a joint invasion of Yugoslavia to install a government committed to the alliance.

The Axis invasion included 337,000 German and 300,000 Italian troops, along with Hungarian and Bulgarian divisions. The invaders crossed the border on 6 April, and crushed the 700,000-strong but mostly ill-trained Yugoslav army, which surrendered on the 18th.[78] The Axis forces suffered less than 10,000 casualties. The Axis armies then invaded Greece, whose conquest took longer as they faced 450,000 Greek troops backed by 52,000 British, Australian and New Zealand troops. The Axis destroyed or captured nearly all the Greek army and many of the Allied troops by 1 June. The Germans suffered 7,784 dead and 10,752 wounded and the Italians 19,750 dead and 63,142 wounded.[79]

Had the troops, supplies and time devoted to conquering Yugoslavia instead been devoted to a 1 May invasion of the Soviet Union, the Axis onslaught would likely have captured Moscow and Leningrad in 1941 and the Caspian region's oil fields in 1942. Although Stalin would have moved his regime's capital to some city several hundred miles east, he might have been tempted to sign a treaty that traded territory for peace with Germany. Had that happened, Hitler could have transferred enough military forces to North Africa to conquer Egypt and then the Middle East with its vast petroleum deposits while building up Axis forces in western Europe and north-west Africa until the Reich was impregnable to an American-British invasion.

***

For most of the German-Soviet War, from five to seven million troops fought along a constantly shifting sinuous line snaking from 500 to 700 miles between the Baltic and Black Seas.[80] Each side organized its forces into army groups on multiple fronts as made most military sense. The Red Army's number of designated Fronts was five from June 1941, eight from October 1941, ten from May 1942, fourteen from November 1942 and twenty-six from October 1943 to the war's end.

Operation Barbarossa lasted from the Axis invasion on 22 June 1941 to the Soviet counter-attack that drove back German forces near Moscow on 5 December.[81] The Axis force initially numbered 3,800,000 troops, with 90 per cent German, 3,350 tanks, 3,030 armoured vehicles, 7,200 guns and anti-tank guns and 2,770 warplanes against 2,700,000 Soviets including 11,000 tanks and 9,100 warplanes. Over the next five months, the Axis inflicted 4,500,000 casualties on the Soviets, mostly captives, while suffering 1,000,000 casualties.

The Red Army deployed around 2,700,000 of its 5,500,000 on the western front in June 1941. Those troops were split among five Fronts, the Northern with one army commanded by General Markian Popov at Leningrad; the North-western with four armies by General Vasily Kuznetsov at Riga; the Western with four armies by General Dmitri Pavlov at Minsk; the South-western with four armies by General Mikhail Kirponos at Kiev; and the Southern with one army by General Ivan Tiulenev at Odessa.

The Germans deployed their troops in three Army Groups from the Baltic to the Carpathian Mountains, with General Ritter von Leeb commanding twenty-six divisions in two armies and one panzer group in Army Group North, General Feodor von Bock fifty divisions and one panzer group in Army Group Centre and General Gerd von

Rundstedt forty-one divisions and one panzer group in Army Group South. Another 600,000 Hungarian and Romanian troops lined their respective eastern frontiers on the Soviet Union.

On each front, the Germans launched their panzer armies to punch through weak stretches of the Soviet lines then circle and destroy entire armies. From 22 June to 30 September, the Germans suffered just 185,000 casualties while inflicting over 2,050,000 casualties on the Red Army, including 142,000 officers and 40 generals killed and 44 generals captured. During those months, the Red Army lost 14,900 tanks and 64,000 guns or mortars.[82]

Meanwhile, the Luftwaffe decimated the Soviet air force on the ground or in the air during the first month, destroying 3,990 warplanes while losing 550. Soviet losses worsened steadily as experienced pilots diminished and hastily trained pilots replaced them. That was just the dismal beginning. Of 31,000 aircraft when the war began, the Soviets lost 21,200, including 5,100 fighters and 5,200 bombers in battle and another 7,600 warplanes and 3,600 transport and trainer aircraft in accidents, while the Germans lost 2,180 warplanes in combat and 330 from accidents. That air battle over the Soviet Union far surpassed in numbers and losses than the Battle of Britain in which the Germans and Soviets respectively lost 1,290 and 790 warplanes from July to September 1940.[83]

***

News of the German onslaught devastated Stalin. For several days he was listless and could not make a clear decision. He had Molotov broadcast a message to the Soviet people. Molotov explained: 'Today at four in the morning, without any claims having been presented to the Soviet Union, without a declaration of war, German troops attacked our borders at many points and bombed our cities from the air . . . This unheard of attack on our country is perfidy unparalleled in the history of civilized nations.' He assured his fellow communist believers that: 'This war has been forced on us not by the German people, not by the German workers, peasants and intelligentsia, whose sufferings we can well understand, but by the bloodthirsty clique of Germany's fascist rulers.'[84]

After Zhukov learned of the attack, he called Stalin for instructions:

> No one answers. I keep calling. Finally I hear the sleep-dulled voice of the general on duty in the security section. I ask him to call Stalin to the phone. About three minutes later Stalin picked up the receiver. I reported

> the situation and requested permission to start retaliation. Stalin was silent. The only thing I could hear was the sound of his breathing. 'Do you understand me?' Silence again. Finally Stalin asked: 'Where is the defence commissar?'

Zhukov told him that Voroshilov was busy talking with the commanders. Stalin told Zhukov to summon the Politburo members for a meeting.[85]

Stalin pulled himself together by 30 June, to assert command over the military and its strategy.[86] That day he instituted the State Defence Committee (GKO) of Voroshilov, Georgi Malenkov and Beria with himself the chair; later he added Nikolai Voznesensky, Lazar Kaganovich and Anastas Mikoyan. GKO provided broad strategic oversight and decisions for the Supreme High Command (Stavka) to plan and implement. With Stalin in the chair, Stavka's initial members included Voroshilov, Semyon Timoshenko, Zhukov, Molotov, Budyonny and Evgeny Kuznetsov. Subordinate to Stavka was the General Staff with twelve directorates including Operations, Intelligence, Organization, Mobilization, Manning and Constructing, Communications, Auto-Road, Rear and Supply, Topography, Operational Rear and Supply, Construction of Fortifications and Ciphers along with the General Matters, Cadre and Military History departments. The wartime Chiefs of the General Staff included Zhukov, Boris Shaposhnikov, Andrei Vasilevsky and Aleksei Antonov. Overlap, red-tape, factions, incompetence and burnout plagued the Defence Commissariat, General Staff and their auxiliaries. Throughout the war, the High Command's personnel usually worked gruelling 16–18-hour days.

The Main Intelligence Directorate (GRU) or Second Directorate was initially attached to the General Staff then was transferred to the People's Defence Commissariat (NKO) on 23 October 1942; it was split between First and Second Directorates that respectively recruited spies in foreign and occupied lands. The State Committee on Defence then established a Directorate for Force Intelligence for the General Staff. The Main Directorate for Counterintelligence (GUK, later Smersh or Death to Spies) remained subordinate to the General Staff.

Stalin spoke on the radio to the Soviet people on 3 July, although his dull words and delivery were anything but Churchillian. He did call for ceaseless struggle against the invaders, including guerrilla or partisan attacks in the enemy's rear. He appointed himself Defence Commissar on 19 July and Supreme Commander on 8 August.

Stalin soon realized that he could rally the population if he appealed to them through nationalism rather than communism.

Visiting Yugoslav communist Milovan Djilas observed 'that Stalin used the term Russia and not Soviet Union, which meant that he was not only inspiring Russian nationalism but was himself inspired by it and identified himself with it'.[87] Eventually the titanic struggle with Germany and its allies was celebrated as Russia's 'Great Patriotic War'.

Nikita Khrushchev was astounded by Stalin's transformation from bewilderment, depression, denial and isolation during the German blitzkrieg's first weeks:

> I was called to Moscow to consult with Stalin. I found myself confronted with a new man. He was much changed from the way he'd been at the beginning of the war. He had pulled himself together, straightened up and was acting like a real soldier. He had also begun to think of himself as a great military strategist, which made it harder than ever to argue with him. He exhibited all the strong-willed determination of a heroic leader. But I knew what sort of hero he was.[88]

Stalin's flipflop from humiliation to hubris led to commands that inflicted more disasters on the Red Army. He played into German hands by ordering his generals to stand and fight rather than escape eastward. The result was a series of envelopments by German armies that cut off and captured millions of Soviet troops. Then, having made that possible, in rage and disbelief, Stalin demanded of his military entourage: 'How could it happen that our famous Red Army has surrendered so many of our cities and regions to the fascists?'[89] Amidst these disasters, Stalin learned that the Germans had captured Vasily, his son by his first wife. Later he would reject an offer to swap him for a captured German general.

***

A key German objective was Kiev, Ukraine's capital, situated on the Dnieper River and with 850,000 people the Soviet Union's third largest city. Kirponos and Budyonny asked Stalin for permission to withdraw from Kiev before the Germans surrounded it. Stalin angrily rejected that plea. The Germans captured the city with 103,000 prisoners on 19 September 1941, then staved off counter-attacks until the 24th. The Germans paused briefly to resupply and send the prisoners west then resumed their dash forward. The Soviets blunted the German advance at Rostov and the surrounding region. A German army overran most of Crimea except for the port of Sevastopol on the south-west coast; Sevastopol's defenders held out for nine desperate months.

German Army Group North's key objective was Leningrad, situated on the isthmus between the Baltic Sea and Lake Lagoda.[90] The city is mostly on the Neva River's south side a few miles upstream of the Baltic. Finland's border is just 20 miles north. Tsar Peter the Great founded the city in 1703 as Saint Petersburg and moved his capital there from Moscow. Saint Petersburg remained Russia's capital until 1919 when the Bolsheviks returned it to Moscow. They renamed the city Leningrad after Vladimir Lenin's death in 1924. In 1941, Leningrad sheltered 3,500,000 people and was the Soviet Union's second largest city after Moscow with 4,500,000.

After the German invasion, city officials began evacuating non-essential inhabitants. When the Germans got within artillery range, the population had dropped to 2,500,000. Zhukov commanded Leningrad's defence from 10 September to 7 October. Historian Otto Chaney calculated that for the city's defence

> 93 miles of anti-tank ditches, escarpments and counter escarpments were dug; 125 miles of wire entanglements were emplaced; 7,149 trenches for infantry squads and 389 miles of communications trenches were dug; 140 steel and cement and stone emplacements were constructed; 487 armour fire points were established; 176 tanks were placed in prepared firing points; 1,500 anti-tank obstacles . . . plus 1,395 . . . fire points were constructed; 809 firing points were set up in buildings; and 1,089 command and observation points and dugouts were prepared. About forty-five thousand persons worked on the defences each day. Much of this labour was performed by women who, like their families, were on near starvation diets.[91]

The German siege of Leningrad lasted 900 days. The Soviets sustained the diminishing defenders and inhabitants over Lake Lagoda by trucks over ice and boats over open water. The economy contracted with the population but somehow the Soviets managed to maintain most of the city's critical war industries; in April war industry workers numbered 254,000 including 181,000 women.[92] Leningrad's defence cost the lives of at least a million soldiers and civilians. Officially, the army suffered 144,800 dead in 1941, 83,700 in 1942 and 88,700 in 1943, while 632,000 civilians died but twice as many may have died. As on other fronts, many of those deaths were self-inflicted. The NKVD and city police arrested respectively 9,574 and 22,166 people on various 'crimes against the people' charges and executed 5,360 of them before October 1942.[93]

General Ivan Konev commanded the Central Front that included 1,250,000 troops, 1,700 tanks, 14,000 guns and 1,390 warplanes.

Hitler authorized Army Group Centre to resume its offensive on 30 September. Guderian's 2nd Panzer Group, Hoth's 3rd Panzer Group and Hoepner's 4th Panzer Group punched through the Soviet lines and their columns joined forces a hundred or so miles east, bagging 660,000 prisoners in the Viazma-Briansk pocket. Stalin rushed reinforcements to that front and called Zhukov from Leningrad to command the Moscow front on 10 October.

Zhukov struggled to form the shattered remnants of the army groups of Konev and Budyonny into a cohesive group at the front, while having hundreds of thousands of civilians construct Leningrad-type defences in an arc around 20 miles west of Moscow. Zhukov got a reprieve when Hitler refused to order Bock to follow up his latest stunning victory over Konev with a race to Moscow.

Stalin signed a decree on 15 October for officials to prepare to evacuate Moscow for Kuibyshev (Samara) 650 miles east on the Volga River. The Red Army's Political Administration (GPU) established itself in Kuibyshev while the General Staff set up in Arzamis, around 260 miles east of Moscow. Stalin may have briefly left Moscow but swiftly returned to bolster the morale on that beleaguered front.

Stalin ordered a 'scorched earth' strategy whereby withdrawing troops destroyed anything of military or economic value behind them. He initiated it on 17 November 1941, with these details: 'All inhabited locations up to a distance of 40-60 kilometres in the rear of the German troops and up to 20-30 kilometres on either side of the roads, are to be destroyed and burnt to ashes . . . Each regiment is to have a team of volunteers of 20-30 men to blow up and burn down inhabited locations.'[94]

Stalin telephoned Zhukov in mid-November and demanded: 'Are you sure that we will hold Moscow? I ask you about this with an aching heart. Tell me honestly as a communist.' Zhukov replied: 'We will, without fail, hold Moscow. But I need at least two more armies and 200 tanks.'[95] Stalin eventually scraped up enough troops and tanks to fulfil Zhukov's request.

Hitler authorized Bock to resume his offensive. As the Germans advanced Russia's two yearly allies emerged to retard them, first autumn rains and mud then winter snows and freezing temperatures. The Germans cracked but did not crush the northern and southern wings of the Moscow defences. One regiment got within 15 miles of Moscow and with binoculars could see church steeples. Guderian begged Bock to call off the offensive as subzero temperatures, Soviet firepower and a lack of food, fuel and munitions devastated his troops, tanks and trucks.

Stalin in 1900. (Wikimedia)

Stalin's identification card from the Secret Police files in St. Petersburg, 1913. (Wikimedia)

Lenin speaking in Moscow, 1918. (Wikimedia)

Trotsky in Red Square, 1921. (Wikimedia)

Lenin and Stalin, 1922. (Wikimedia)

Soviet famine from collectivization in Ukraine. (Wikimedia)

Soviet Gulag slave labour and death camps. (Wikimedia)

Hitler planning military operations with his generals. (Wikimedia)

Anniversary of the Revolution Red Square Parade 1941. (Wikimedia)

Red Army armoured attack in the Battle of Kursk 1943. (Wikimedia)

Stalin, Roosevelt, and Churchill at Yalta. (Wikimedia)

American and Soviet Troops meet at Torgau on the Elbe River in central Germany, 25 April 1945. (Wikimedia)

Soviet soldier raising the Red Flag over Berlin, 1945. (Wikimedia)

Stalin and Mao, 1950. (Wikimedia)

Stalin in death. (Wikimedia)

Nikita Khrushchev at the Twentieth Communist Party Congress. (Wikimedia)

Fall of the Berlin Wall, 9 November 1989. (Wikimedia)

Vladimir Putin at a parade in Red Square. (Wikimedia)

By early December, Zhukov's Western Front included 388,000 troops and 550 tanks versus 240,000 German troops and 900 tanks. On the 6th, he launched attacks on the German lines' southern and northern wings and eventually broke through. Hitler aided the Soviets on 18 December with his 'Standfast Order': 'Commanding generals, commanders and officers are to intervene in person to compel the troops to fanatical resistance in their positions without regard to the enemy broken through on the flanks or in the rear. This is the only way to gain the time necessary to bring up the reinforcements from Germany and the West that I have ordered.'[96] The result was that the Soviets eventually cut off and captured hundreds of thousands of Germans that might have escaped westward.

By the time Zhukov halted his offensive on 1 January 1942, the Germans had withdrawn to a defensive arc 50 miles westward. The Battle of Moscow was the Red Army's first strategic defeat of the Wehrmacht. Zhukov gave Stalin credit for the victory as he 'did a great job in organizing the strategic reserves and the material and technical means needed for armed combat. In the period of the battle around Moscow he was always attentive to advice, but, unfortunately, he sometimes made decisions that the situation did not call for.'[97]

***

During the six months that the Soviets desperately fought to survive the German onslaught, President Roosevelt and Prime Minister Churchill forged an informal alliance between their nations that began massively aiding the Soviet Union. They also developed a deep friendship grounded on their common crusade, upper class background and humanist values.[98]

Roosevelt explained how critical American aid to Moscow was in an August 1941 letter to Secretary of War Henry Stimson: 'I deem it to be of paramount importance for the safety and security of America that all reasonable munitions help be provided for Russia, not only immediately but as long as she continues to fight the Axis powers effectively.' According to Ambassador Averell Harriman, Roosevelt viewed Stalin's intentions as mostly realistic: 'He looked upon Stalin's policy as combining an ideological drive to promote world Communism with more traditional aspects of Russian imperialism. I believe he felt that the revolutionary fervour would gradually recede after the war and that the self-interest of the Russian people increasingly would become the guide to Soviet policy.'[99]

Churchill reacted to the attack on 22 June with a brilliant radio speech in which first he declared: 'The Nazi regime is indistinguishable from the worst features of Communism . . . It excels all forms of human wickedness in the efficiency of its cruelty and ferocious aggression. No one has been a more consistent opponent of Communism than I have for the last twenty-five years.' Yet, Germany's invasion of Russia required the British to ally with the lesser of two evils against the more dangerous evil:

> We are resolved to destroy Hitler and every vestige of the Nazi regime . . . It follows therefore that we shall give whatever help we can to Russia and the Russian people . . . The Russian danger . . . is our danger and the danger of the United States, just as the cause of any Russian fighting for his hearth and home is the cause of free peoples in every quarter of the globe.[100]

More succinctly, in explaining how he could forge a relationship with Stalin, he replied: 'If Hitler invaded hell, I would make at least a favourable reference to the devil in the House of Commons.'[101]

Yet Churchill always remained leery of the tyrant. He feared that allying with the Soviet Union to crush German imperialism would give Moscow the opportunity to expand its own communist empire as they already had in eastern Poland, Latvia, Lithuania, Estonia and southern Finland. He wrote Stalin a letter on 9 July with a rather mixed message. He promised that Britain and America would send the Soviet Union what needed military and economic they could but warned that in any peace settlement 'our line would be that territorial frontiers will have to be settled in accordance with the wishes of the people who live there . . . and that these units . . . mut be free to choose their own form of government and system of life, so long as they do not interfere with the similar rights of neighbouring peoples.'[102]

All along Churchill did what he could to forge a warm, trusting, working relationship with a man he viewed as a mass-murdering tyrant.[103] After the invasion, he wrote Stalin these encouraging words: 'We are all glad here that the Russian armies are making such strong and spirited resistance to the utterly unprovoked and merciless invasion of the Nazis. There is a general admiration for the bravery and tenacity of the Soviet soldiers and people. We shall do everything to help you that time, geography and growing resources allow.'[104]

To that end, Churchill had Ambassador Stafford Cripps negotiate and sign with Molotov 'The Agreement for Joint Action between Great Britain and the USSR' on 12 July. The key tenets forged a bilateral alliance to fight Germany with neither making an armistice or peace treaty with Germany without the other's consent. On 19 July, Stalin wrote Churchill the first of a series of demands that Britain open a 'second front' in north-west Europe to divert German troops from the Soviet Union.[105] On 20 July, Churchill replied with the first of a series of letters that patiently explained that neither Britain nor the Western Alliance was then capable of invading north-west Europe.[106]

Churchill gave this glowing letter of introduction for Harry Hopkins, Roosvelt's personal diplomat and troubleshooter:

> Mr. Harry Hopkins has been with me these days. Last week he asked the President to let him go to Moscow. I must tell you that there is a flame in this man for democracy and to beat Hitler. A little while ago when I asked him for a quarter of a million rifles, they came at once. He is the nearest personal representative of the President . . . He is your friend and my friend. He will help you to plan for the future victory and the long term supply of Russia.[107]

Fortunately, Hopkins lived up to Churchill's accolade. He met Stalin in late July and assured him that President Roosevelt would soon send Lend-Lease shipments to the Soviet Union.

Sailing from their homelands in naval flotillas, Roosevelt and Churchill met at Argentia, Newfoundland, Canada for a three-day summit from 9 to 12 August 1941. This was the first of many summits between the two of them and then together or separately with other national leaders.[108] On the last day, they signed the Atlantic Charter, the 'common principles' that they would fight for if America joined Britain in the world war. Those values included 'no aggrandizement, territorial or other', 'no territorial changes that did not accord with the freely expressed wishes of the peoples concerned', 'the right of all peoples to choose the form of government under which they will live', 'sovereign rights and self-government restored to those who have been forcibly deprived of them', freedom of commerce and navigation, and freedom from want and fear.

For the leaders of two liberal democracies, composing and asserting those principles was easy enough. However, realizing them would prove to be a Sisyphean struggle. Communist tyrant Joseph Stalin would thwart every effort they made to apply those principles to Eastern Europe and many other regions around the globe.

Roosevelt and Churchill sent Stalin a joint letter that explained their summit's understandings and pledged support with this caveat: 'The war goes on upon many fronts and before it is over . . . further fronts . . . will be developed. Our resources, though immense, are limited and it must become a question of where and when those resources can best be used to further to the greatest extent our common effort.'[109]

To greatly varying degrees, Roosevelt and his advisors worried about the geopolitical and moral dilemmas of allying with the Soviet Union. Roosevelt and Churchill had committed themselves to the Atlantic Charter that renounced territorial gains from the war and sought post-war free trade and elections. Secretary of State Cordell Hull anticipated that

> the Soviet Union has tremendous ambitions with regard to Europe and the US and Great Britain will be forced to state that they cannot agree, at least in advance, to all of its demands. It would seem that it is preferable to take a firm attitude now, rather than to retreat and to be compelled to take a firm attitude later when our position had been weakened by the abandonment of the general principles.[110]

Ironically, the war's only joint Anglo-Soviet military operation was the takeover of Iran. Reza Shah Pahlavi voiced sympathy for Hitler after the German invasion of the Soviet Union. To prevent him from allying with Germany, Churchill and Stalin cut a deal whereby each sent an army into Iran, with the Soviets and British respectively occupying the country's northern and southern halves. They did so from 25 to 31 August and subdued the Iranian army with light casualties. The Allies forced the shah to abdicate in favour of his son, Mohammed Reza Pahlavi, on 16 September. The bilateral agreement required each side to withdraw its troops from Iran within six months of the war's end.

***

America's Lend-Lease programme filled the chasm between what the Soviet Union produced and what it needed. Roosevelt announced the first Lend-Lease donation – $1 billion – to Moscow on 4 November 1941. Eventually, America gave $11.2 billion in Lend-Lease aid to the Soviet Union. Initially the aid was a no-interest loan for the Soviets to repay within five years of the end of the war. On 11 June 1942, the White House announced that its Lend-Lease programme for the Soviet Union, like that for Britain, was free.

America shipped an astonishing amount of war material to the Soviet Union. Especially vital to the Red Army were 1,683 light tanks and 5,488 medium tanks which along with 5,218 British tanks was 16 per cent of the 99,150 tanks that Soviet factories produced during the war. Soviet factories produced 205,000 second-rate trucks and other vehicles while the United States shipped over twice as many vehicles – 401,000, including 77,972 Jeeps, 24,902 three-quarter-ton Dodge trucks and 351,715 medium trucks. The 14,589 aircraft that the Americans flew to the Soviet Union was around 11 per cent of total Soviet production. Lend-Lease supplied around 4,300,000 tons of food and fodder or 10 per cent of total Soviet production.[111]

America's Lend-Lease donations to the Soviet Union prevented its military collapse and surrender. Without Lend-Lease, not just the Soviet Union would have lost the war. A peace treaty between Berlin and Moscow would probably have detached Estonia, Latvia, Lithuania, Ukraine, Belorussia and the oil-rich Caucasus region from the Soviet Union to Germany as satellite states. Peace on the Eastern Front would have let Hitler send most troops deployed there elsewhere, with the most vital dispatched to North Africa to overwhelm British forces, capture Egypt and eventually the oil-rich Persian Gulf. That would have led to a stalemate in Western Europe. American troops would have poured into Britain to protect that realm and prepare for an Allied invasion of northern France. Meanwhile, the Americans would have concentrated on defeating Japan. An invasion of north-west Europe might not have occurred until after the Americans developed atomic bombs, with one targeted on Hitler at Berlin.

***

America openly allied with Britain and the Soviet Union after the devastating Japanese attack against the fleet at Pearl Harbor, Hawaii on 7 December 1941. The following day, Roosevelt asked Congress for a war declaration which the Senate approved by 82 to 0 and the House of Representatives by 388 to 1. Germany and Italy declared war on the United States on 11 December and Congress reciprocated later that day by 88 to 0 in the Senate and 300 to 0 in the House.

Churchill and his Chiefs of Staff visited Washington to begin planning a common strategy from 22 December to 14 January 1942. One key decision was to create a Combined Chiefs of Staff to plan grand strategy with equal numbers of American and British service chiefs in Washington. They also decided to concentrate their forces on defeating Germany and Italy first and then defeat Japan.

That Europe-first decision came despite increasingly dire reports from the Pacific. Japan's attack on Pearl Harbor opened a series of offensives whereby Japanese task forces invaded America's colony the Philippines on 8 December and conquered it by 8 May 1942; British

Malaya and Singapore from 8 December to 16 February 1942; the Dutch East Indies from 10 January to 8 March 1942; and British Burma from 14 December to 28 May 1942. That required the Allies temporarily to reverse their priorities. By late 1942, a series of American offensives had turned the Pacific theatre's strategic tide against the Japanese. During the Battle of the Coral Sea from 4 to 8 May, an American fleet turned back a Japanese fleet trying to sever the most direct sea lane between the United States and Australia. During the Battle of Midway from 4 to 7 June, an American carrier fleet sank four Japanese carriers while losing one of its own. American marines captured Guadalcanal on 7 August and held it against repeated Japanese assaults until the last on 9 February 1943.

Roosevelt made a fatal decision that delayed victory in Europe and so caused vast and unnecessary casualties in both Europe and the Pacific and let the Red Army conquer Eastern Europe and East Germany. The logical Pacific strategy was for Admiral Chester Nimitz to lead the island-hopping campaign across the central Pacific from Hawaii to Japan while General Douglas MacArthur held the south-west Pacific with minimal forces. Roosevelt succumbed to MacArthur's demand for him to command enough forces for an advance through the Solomon Islands, New Guinea, the Philippines and beyond. That squandered vast numbers of troops, weapons, supplies, warships, warplanes and, most critically, landing craft that were desperately needed in Europe.

Had the landing craft allocated to MacArthur be given instead to Eisenhower, Allied forces could have realized their original plan of simultaneous invasions of northern and southern France on 1 May 1944. Those armies would have swiftly routed the Germans, joined forces in eastern France then reached the Rhine River by mid-autumn rather than half a year later. They might then have crossed the Rhine and fought their way to Berlin and beyond while the Soviets were stalled on the Vistula River 350 miles away. The western Allies could have continued east to liberate most of the countries that the Red Army actually conquered. Tragically, that did not happen.

***

During the long winter, Stalin's system rebuilt and expanded the Red Army to vast numbers by the time large-scale offensives resumed. In May 1942, the Soviets numbered 5,600,000 troops, 3,882 tanks, 44,000 guns and heavy mortars, 21,450 50mm mortars and 2,221 warplanes between the Baltic and Black Seas. The trouble was that the Germans and their allied forces was just as powerful. They numbered 6,000,000 troops, including 810,000 non-Germans, 3,229 tanks, 57,000 guns and mortars and 3,395 warplanes.[112]

The Germans had two key weaknesses. Victory was possible only if they could encircle and destroy Soviet armies as systematically as they had the previous year, then capture Leningrad, Moscow, Stalingrad and, ideally, the oil-rich Caspian Sea region as far as Baku. If so, the shattered Soviets would have to withdraw to the Urals for a last stand and probably peace talks that would yield Belorussia and Ukraine to the Axis. But that was unlikely. The previous year's German blitzkrieg shock and awe that decimated Soviet armies and demoralized surviving officers and soldiers had dissipated. With the brilliant Marshal Zhukov in command, veteran generals led the Red Army and prepared elaborate in-depth defences designed to slow and eventually blunt German offensives. The Germans undoubtedly would break through in some sectors and inflict horrific losses, but inevitably would literally run out of gas. And that was the second weakness. Gasoline along with most other vital supplies were limited. Most gasoline came from Romania's Ploesti oil fields and refineries. The further east the Germans advanced the further their supplies stretched along the wretched roads and railways. Along the way partisan groups swelled in numbers and boldness to destroy supply columns and tie down ever more troops diverted from the front lines.

The first major German offensives opened along the southern front where their armies circled and destroyed Russian armies and overran most of the Donbass industrial region of eastern Ukraine. On 18 May, after a two-week battle, they captured Kharkov, the region's key manufacturing city with a pre-war population of 840,000. That latest debacle cost the Soviets 270,000 casualties, 1,200 armoured vehicles and 2,600 guns.[113] The Soviets landed an army at Kerch in Crimea, to retake the peninsula and relieve Sevastopol, besieged since 31 October. The Germans devastated the attackers and captured the rest of Crimea, with Sevastopol's remaining defenders surrendering on 4 July. Over the previous ten months, the Soviets suffered 240,000 casualties defending Crimea, including 150,000 at Sevastopol. Over the next two months, the Germans overran the lower Don River valley and captured Rostov on 25 July. Soviet and German casualties from January to June 1942 were respectively 1,400,000 and 180,000, a seven-to-one ratio.[114]

To all these disasters, Stalin could only demand more troops mobilized and more war goods produced. He issued his latest 'no retreat' order on 28 July1942: 'Not a step backwards! This must be our main slogan. It is necessary steadfastly, to the last drop of blood, to defend each position, each metre of Soviet territory and to hold it as long as possible.'[115]

Hitler and his generals turned their eyes to the oil-rich Caucasus region with the key city Baku on the Caspian Sea. They believed they could bring Stalin's regime to its knees if they deprived it of petroleum and used it to fuel their own further advances. They launched their campaign with two million troops on 28 June. By late November, the Germans had overrun a vast region all the way to the Caucasus Mountain foothills and Grozny's outskirts, but still 350 miles from Baku.

Meanwhile, General Friedrich Paulus's 250,000-man Sixth Army crossed the Don River at Kalach and fought its way 50 miles to Stalingrad on the Volga River's west bank. Stalingrad was the new name for Tsaritsyn, bestowed in 1925 to honour Stalin's role in its defence during the civil war. Stalingrad was the region's manufacturing centre with a pre-war population of 445,000. German troops began fighting their way into Stalingrad on 23 August.

Stalin split the Stalingrad front between two army groups, General Vasily Gordov's for the city and northward and General Andrei Yeremenko's south-east, with Marshal Konstantin Rokossovsky in overall command. The battle within Stalingrad raged until 13 November as the Germans fought their way from the rubble of one building to the next until they wiped out most of the defenders. Meanwhile, Zhukov launched an offensive on the central front ideally to divert resources from the German armies on the southern front. The Germans blunted that offensive.

***

Meanwhile, the Americans and the British heatedly debated strategy for Europe during a summit at the White House from 19 to 24 June 1942. The Americans wanted to mass forces in Britain and cross the English Channel to northern France as soon as possible. The British wanted Allied forces systematically to capture the Mediterranean Basin, starting with an American army landing in North Africa. Word of a catastrophe decided the issue.

In North Africa, General Erwin Rommel had launched his Afrika Korps against British General Neil Ritchie's Eighth Army, routed it and captured Tobruk with 33,000 defenders on 21 June. Rommel then pursued Eighth Army to El Alamein where it made a stand just 70 miles west of Alexandria. Upon learning of that disaster, Roosevelt immediately embraced the North African strategy. They braced for Stalin's enraged reaction.

Churchill flew to Moscow for his first meeting with Stalin on 12 August. Along the way 'I pondered on my mission to this sullen, sinister Bolshevik State I had once tried so hard to strangle at its birth and which, until Hitler appeared, I had regarded as the mortal foe of civilized freedom.'[116] He delivered Stalin the news that the Allied 'second front' for 1942 would be in North Africa, not northern France and explained why. The tyrant's reaction did not surprise him: 'Stalin, who had begun to look very glum, seemed unconvinced by my argument and asked if it was impossible to attack any part of the French coast.' Churchill replied that: 'War was war but not folly and it would be folly to invite a disaster.' To that,

> Stalin, who had become restless, said that his view about war was different . . . that troops must be blooded . . . If you did not blood your troops you had no idea what their value was . . . There was an oppressive silence. Stalin at length said that if we could not make a landing in France this year he was not entitled to demand it . . . but was bound to say that he did not agree with my arguments.

Finally, Churchill achieved a breakthrough: 'Stalin seemed suddenly to grasp the strategic advantage of "Torch". He recounted four main reasons for it: first, it would hit Rommel in the back; second, it would overawe Spain; third, it would produce fighting between Germans and Frenchmen in France; and forth, it would expose Italy to the whole brunt of the war.'[117]

Churchill's victory was fleeting. The next day Stalin fired off this angry, pointed letter to Churchill demanding that he fulfil a vital bilateral promise:

> It will be recalled that the decision to open a second front in Europe in 1942 was reached at the time of Molotov's visit to London and found expression in the agreed Anglo-Soviet Communique released on June 12 last . . . Needless to say the Soviet High Command, in planning its summer and autumn operations, counted on a second front being opened in Europe in 1942. It will be readily understood that the British Government's refusal to open a second front . . . delivers a mortal blow to Soviet public opinion . . . complicates the position of the Red Army at the front and injures the plans of the Soviet High Command.[118]

To that, Churchill replied that the pending American invasion of French Morocco and Algeria and eventual drive east to join forces with Britain's Eighth Army fighting westward constituted that year's 'second front'. The two armies would trap the German and Italian forces between them. Meanwhile, the threat to invade Europe diverted vast numbers of German forces there instead of the Russian front. However, the Germans would defeat an actual premature invasion with inadequate forces with severe losses. The British and Americans would only invade the continent after massing enough troops and supplies to win.[119]

They then met and Churchill recalled that: 'We argued for about two hours, during which he said a great many disagreeable things, especially about us being too much afraid of the Germans . . . I repulsed all his contentions squarely, but without taunts . . . I suppose he was not used to being contradicted repeatedly, but he did not become at all angry or even animated.'[120] Churchill stayed for another day of frustrating talks followed by an amiable state banquet.

The next morning Churchill flew to Cairo for a week and learned late on 19 August about the latest disaster. At dawn that morning the British had launched a raid with 10,500 mostly Canadian troops to capture the French port of Dieppe. The result was a disaster as the 1,500 German defenders killed 907 Canadians, wounded 2,460 and captured 1,946, killed 247 British troops, sank a destroyer and 33 landing craft with 550 sailors dead and shot down 100 aircraft.[121]

Within two months, the Allies racked up the first of a series of victories in North Africa. General Bernard Montgomery took command of the devastated Eighth Army at El Alamein and soon replenished its ranks, supplies and morale. He launched Eighth Army in a series of attacks from 23 October to 11 November that finally routed the Afrika Korps. On 8 November, three corps commanded by General Dwight Eisenhower landed in North Africa, one with 35,000 Americans in Morocco, another with 33,000 Americans at Oran and the third with 39,000 Americans and British at Algiers. Within days, they forced the French defenders to surrender. Eisenhower combined the two corps in Algeria along with a French African corps into the First Army led by British General Kenneth Anderson. As Montgomery's Eighth Army pursued Afrika Korps' remnants west to southern Tunisia, Anderson pushed First Army east against a German and Italian army led by General Hans-Jurgen Arnim. Gradually, the Allied armies squeezed and punched back the Axis forces. On 13 May 1943, Arnim surrendered around 250,000 troops; those losses were atop the 150,000 casualties the Axis had previously suffered in the campaign starting with El Alamein seven months earlier. That was a crushing victory over the Axis.[122]

***

Amidst the campaign, Roosevelt, Churchill and the Combined Chiefs of Staff held their latest summit, this one at Casablanca in Morocco from 14 to 24 January 1943. They made two critical decisions. One was to delay an invasion of France until May 1944, while they invaded Sicily, and perhaps Italy ideally, to defeat Mussolini's regime. The other came during a press conference, when Roosevelt made a startling and controversial statement. He announced that America and Britain were committed to warring against the Axis powers until they unconditionally surrendered. Churchill backed Roosevelt but wished the president had held his tongue about such a key strategy. Knowing they had nothing to lose might encourage the Axis powers to fight to the death.

Stalin's latest barrage against the Americans and British was their decision to invade Sicily and delay Normandy. He wrote to Churchill that:

> Your decision creates exceptional difficulties for the Soviet Union, which, straining all its resources, for the past two years has been engaged against the main forces of Germany and her satellites and this leaves the Soviet Army, which is fighting not only for its country but also for the Allies, to do the job alone . . . against an enemy that is still very strong and formidable.[123]

Of course, the notion that the Red Army was solely fighting Germany and its allies was absurd. The Americans and British had just concluded a brilliant campaign that killed tens of thousands of Axis troops and captured a quarter of a million in North Africa, while their fleets battled German submarines in the Atlantic and their bomber crews were steadily increasing their devastating attacks on German cities while suffering terrible losses.

Yet Stalin certainly had a powerful point that Sicily was an unnecessary sideshow that delayed for a year the vital invasion of northern France. In that, Churchill was mostly to blame. Roosevelt and his advisors wanted to invade northern France as soon as the Allies massed enough troops and supplies for it to be successful. Churchill feared that the Germans would defeat any invasion there, no matter how powerful it was. He replied to Stalin that:

> if we threw away a hundred thousand men in a disastrous cross-Channel attack . . . with forces too weak to exploit any success . . . even if we got ashore, be driven off as the Germans have forces already in France superior . . . I cannot see how a great British defeat and slaughter would

> aid the Soviet armies. It might, however, cause the utmost ill-feelings here . . . The best way for us to help you is by winning battles and by not losing them.[124]

Throughout most of the war, Churchill insisted on a Mediterranean strategy of a series of attacks against what he called the Axis's 'soft underbelly'. He wanted first to invade Italy, then the Balkans. The Americans countered that mountainous southern Europe was actually ideal for defence and the best place to fight was the northern European plain from Brittany to Berlin, ideal for a rapid tank division led war. Of course, that was the obvious winning strategy but time after time Churchill talked Roosevelt into backing his strategy, first with the American invasion of North Africa, then their joint invasion of first Sicily then mainland Italy.

***

Meanwhile, the Soviets scored their own decisive victory over the Germans. By late November 1942, Soviet forces on the Central and South Fronts numbered 2,530,000 and 1,100,000 troops, 4,260 and 930 tanks and 1,400 and 900 warplanes, respectively.[125] The decisive battle would come on the southern front. Stalin, Zhukov and other key commanders agreed that cutting off and destroying Paulus's Sixth Army at Stalingrad should be the priority.

Rokossovsky launched his two army groups against either flank of Paulus's army on 19 November and within two weeks they had linked up to cut off the Germans in Stalingrad.[126] Paulus surrendered on 2 February 1943. The Germans lost 291,000 troops at Stalingrad, with 91,000 killed and 200,000 captured, but altogether the six-month campaign in the region probably cost the Axis at least 1,000,000 casualties with two-thirds Germans and the rest Romanians, Hungarians and Italians. The Soviets suffered far worse losses, at least 1,300,000 casualties, but Stalin and his commanders deemed destroying an entire German army was worth that cost.

Stalin issued a declaration on 23 February 1943, that succinctly explained Stalingrad's critical importance to the war: 'Three months ago the Red Army began an offensive on the approaches to Stalingrad. From that time the initiative of military action has been in our hands and the tempo and force of the offensive operations are not weakening.' In a different speech a few days later, he observed that: 'The correlation of forces on the Soviet-German front has changed. The fact is that Fascist Germany is more and more exhausted and is becoming weaker and the

Soviet Union is deploying its reserves more and more and is becoming stronger.'[127]

Indeed, Stalingrad was the Eastern Front's strategic fulcrum. Thereafter, the Soviets mostly attacked and advanced and the Germans mostly defended and retreated all the way to Berlin and eastern Germany and Austria.

Hitler recognized how catastrophic Stalingrad was. Days before the surrender on 30 January 1943, he issued this dire warning that the Russians sought to 'conquer Europe, to destroy its culture, to exterminate its people and to gain slave labour . . . Either there is a victory of Germany . . . of our allies and of Europe or the Asiatic-Bolshevik wave will break into our continent where our culture is the world's most ancient.'[128] Of course, with slightly changed wording, Stalin could have expressed the same warning about Hitler and the Nazis. And if so, then each tyrant would have projected his regime's most evil aspects on the other.

The Germans suffered another devastating defeat in July and August 1943, this one the campaign of Kursk-Orel, history's largest tank battle.[129] On 5 July, two Army Groups, General Erich von Manstein's on the southern front and General Gunther von Kluge's on the central front, launched offensives against the Red Army forces before them, led by Generals Nikolai Vatutin and Konstantin Rokossovsky respectively. The combined German forces initially included 780,000 troops, 2,900 tanks, 10,000 guns and anti-tank guns and 2,100 warplanes versus 2,100,000 Soviet troops, 5,100 tanks, 25,000 guns and anti-tank guns and 7,300 warplanes. The plan was for the army groups to break through and join forces far in the Soviet rear. Each attack soon stalled as the Soviet defence in depth destroyed hundreds of German tanks. The Soviets then counter-attacked. Both sides rushed reinforcements to the vast front. By the time, the campaign ended on 23 August, the Soviets had inflicted at least 430,000 casualties and destroyed 1,200 tanks and 600 warplanes while suffering 710,000 casualties, 7,000 tanks and 4,200 warplanes. The Soviets could soon make up their horrendous losses, the Germans could not.

***

Throughout the war, Stalin celebrated nationalism and patriotism more than communism and idealism to inspire Soviets. Indeed, he called the ongoing struggle the 'Great Patriotic War'. Yet he also bolstered the Communist Party's ranks to double loyalty to him and his regime. The Communist Party expanded from 2,600,000 full and 1,210,000 candidate members in July 1941 to 4,290,000 full and 1,660,000 candidate members four years later. During that time, the party admitted 5,230,000 full and 3,620,000 candidate members, while a couple of million died from combat or execution.[130]

Stalin had the army and Communist Party organize partisan or guerilla bands behind enemy lines.[131] On 29 June 1941, he issued this decree:

> In the districts occupied by the enemy [there are to be set up] partisan and sabotage groups for the struggle with the units of the enemy armies, to ignite a partisan war everywhere, to blow up bridges, roads, to damage telephone and telegraph links, to burn warehouses and so on. In the occupied regions to create intolerable conditions for the enemy and all his henchmen, to pursue and destroy them at every step and to block all their efforts.[132]

Partisan groups mushroomed behind enemy lines and inflicted increasingly serious damage by destroying German military infrastructure, inflicting casualties and diverting or slowing the advance of countless troops. Although Stalin appreciated those efforts, the Red Army's desperate fight against the German blitzkrieg occupied nearly all his time. He did not set up a Central Staff of the Partisan Movement to supply and coordinate the groups attached to his headquarters until May 1942. By July 1942, of 82,000 partisans, 63,000 fought behind the centre front, 12,000 in Ukraine and 5,000 on the Leningrad front. The partisans peaked at around 200,000 in the summer of 1943.

The Germans cracked down harshly on partisans. Field Marshal Wilhelm Keitel issued an order in September 1941 that: 'Since the beginning of the campaign against Soviet Russia, Communist insurrection movements have broken out everywhere in the areas occupied by Germany. The type of action taken . . . is growing into open rebellion and wide-spread guerrilla warfare.' The 'solution' was to execute from 50 to 100 enemy soldiers or civilians for every German soldier killed.[133]

***

Stalin saw a golden opportunity to dominate Eastern Europe after the war. Less than two weeks after the German onslaught, he invited the Polish, Yugoslav and Czechoslovakian governments-in-exile in London to transfer to Moscow which would help them reconquer their countries and restore their rule. He got no takers, so he had communist governments-in-exile formed among refugees from those and other Eastern European countries in Moscow. Eventually, each communist exile government had a radio station beaming propaganda to the homeland and swelling ranks of a military and secret police eventually to take power in the wake of the Soviet Red Army.

Stalin sought to mask his strategy to impose communist regimes across Eastern Europe after the war. To that end, he viewed as expendable the most obvious institution that promoted revolution, the Communist International or Comintern. He announced Comintern's demise on 28 May 1943: 'The dissolution of the Communist International is both appropriate and timely for it will ease the organization of pressure by all peace-loving nations against the common foe, Hitlerism and expose the lie of the Hitlerites that Moscow allegedly intends to interfere in the life of other states and "Bolshevize" them.'[134] Stalin did not regret that decision. His heart was never in Comintern. He had little interest or knowledge of foreign countries, governments, communist parties and potential revolutionary conditions.

Comintern's termination was a brilliant diplomatic act. The Roosevelt and Churchill administrations applauded that decision as solid evidence that their wartime alliance of convenience could persist into the post-war years. Actually, Comintern did not die, it disappeared. In every country the Red Army conquered, Soviet commissars joined forces with and nurtured existing Communist Parties to take power. In countries beyond the Red Army's reach, Soviet agents conspired with their Communist Parties to take power. The most powerful allies were the Communist Parties of France and Italy that led guerrilla wars against Germany's occupying armies.

Berlin reaped a stunning propaganda victory against Moscow in 1943. The German army acted on local rumours about a massacre in the Katyn forest near Smolensk and uncovered mass graves in March 1943. The Soviets had murdered 21,857 people, two-thirds officers and one-third other 'enemies of the people'. Joseph Goebbels, the Reich's Propaganda Minister, saw the Katyn massacre as an excellent chance to tip the free world's opprobrium balance between Nazism and Communism toward Moscow. On 13 April, Radio Berlin announced the gruesome discovery, blamed the Soviets and invited the European Red Cross to investigate. Poland's exiled government in London called on Stalin to endorse that investigation. On 15 April, Polish diplomat Edward Raczynski and General Wladyslaw Sikorski met with Churchill to inform him that the Soviets had indeed massacred those Poles. That revelation posed the latest dilemma for Churchill in having an ally that was as genocidal as the Nazis they were fighting.

Stalin angrily denounced the accusations and any investigation that 'interrupted' relations with the exiled Polish government in London. In a letter to Churchill, he condemned the 'behaviour of the Polish Government toward the U.S.S.R.' as 'contrary to all rules and standards governing relations between two allied states'. He dismissed the charges as Nazi propaganda and accused them of perpetuating the massacre.[135]

Churchill consulted with Roosevelt and the two reluctantly agreed to give their ally the benefit of the doubt. Churchill replied to Stalin that: 'We shall certainly oppose vigorously any "investigation" by the Red Cross or any other body in any territory under German authority. Such investigation would be a fraud.'[136] He added that he hoped Stalin's 'interruption' of relations with the exiled Polish government would be brief

Actually, the interruption would be permanent. Stalin used the Katyn massacre accusation to support a Moscow-controlled communist exiled government to embed in Polish territory as soon as the Red Army liberated it. Learning of Stalin's intention from a Goebbels broadcast, Churchill informed Stalin that: 'So far this business has been Goebbels' triumph. He is now suggesting that the U.S.S.R. will set up a Polish Government on Russian soil and deal only with them. We should not, of course, be able to recognize such a Government and would continue our relations with' the London Polish government that was the 'most helpful . . . for the common cause'.[137]

***

On 9 July 1943 two armies, the American Seventh and the British Eighth, led respectively by Generals George Patton and Bernard Montgomery, invaded Sicily. When their armies met at Messina on 17 August, they had inflicted 155,000 Italian and 25,000 German casualties, mostly prisoners.[138]

Amidst that campaign, Mussolini was overthrown. The dictator's decision to go war with Nazi Germany in June 1940 had led to one humiliating disaster after another. On 25 July, Mussolini's own Grand Council of Fascism voted to depose him by 19 to 9 votes and ordered him present the result to the king. Victor Emmanuel III accepted the resignation, had Mussolini arrested and named Pietro Badoglio, the nation's most distinguished general, Italy's prime minister.

Had the king then declared that Italy would withdraw into neutrality and ordered German forces to leave the country, he would have spared Italy enormous future death and destruction. Instead, he and Badoglio dithered for nearly seven weeks as Hitler sent ever more German divisions into Italy to intimidate them into remaining allies. In Lisbon in neutral Portugal, secret talks were held between Eisenhower's chief of staff General Walter Beddell Smith and British liaison General Kenneth Strong with General Giuseppe Castellano. On 31 August, they shifted their talks to a villa at Cassibile, a small town near Syracuse, Sicily. On 3 September, they signed an armistice whereby Italy would lay down its arms and Allied troops would occupy the country. That same day, Montgomery sent a division across the Straits of Messina to undefended Reggio. Despite this, Victor Emmanuel hesitated to publicly announce the armistice. Eisenhower had the armistice announced on 8 September and the next day, the American Fifth Army landed at Salerno and the British Eighth Army at Taranto. As the Allies disembarked, the king, prime minister and their entourages fled Rome for safety behind Allied lines. Tragically, neither Victor Emmanuel nor Badoglio ordered Italian generals to resist the Germans. Instead, the Germans disarmed nearly the entire Italian army and sent the men to work in German factories.

The American and British decision to invade Italy was their worst strategic blunder. Italy's mountainous terrain is perfect for defence. The Allied armies slowly, sporadically ground their way up the peninsula and got no further than the Po River valley's southern rim when the war ended. That campaign diverted nearly two million Allied troops, sailors and airmen and cost 375,000 casualties. Had the Allies avoided Italy's peninsula and instead committed those immense forces to southern France while an ever greater force invaded northern France, they likely would have defeated Germany at least half a year earlier.[139]

***

Stalin predicted that catastrophic result and castigated Roosevelt and Churchill for their blunder, first with letters then face to face in late November 1943. Stalin agreed to meet Roosevelt and Churchill at Tehran, Iran. That summit was preceded by two others.

Foreign ministers Vyacheslav Molotov, Cordell Hull and Anthony Eden met in Moscow from 18 October to 11 November 1943. Their most important decision was to establish the European Advisory Commission (EAC) on 31 October. Unwisely, Roosevelt and Churchill accepted Stalin's insistence that the European Advisory Commission draw their occupation zones for Germany long before any Allied armies touched German soil, let alone joined forces after overrunning it. Averell Harriman replaced Admiral William Standley as America's ambassador to Stalin on 18 October 1943.

Roosevelt, Churchill and Chinese Generalissimo Chiang Kai-shek met in Cairo from 22 to 26 November, along with the Combined Chiefs of Staff. Roosevelt and Churchill tried to prod Chiang into launching his huge but poorly trained and equipped army against Japanese forces in China and neighbouring Burma. Chiang gave them vague assurances that he had no intention of realizing. He was saving his army to fight the Communist Party after the Americans defeated Japan. Roosevelt wanted to promote Chiang and China as one of the Four Policemen who impose order in their respective spheres of influence and work together in the future United Nations after the war.

Roosevelt, Churchill, their entourages and the Combined Chiefs then flew to Tehran to meet with Stalin from 28 November to 1 December.[140] Roosevelt accepted Stalin's invitation to stay in a cottage within the Soviet embassy compound rather than a mile away at America's embassy. The stated reason was to avoid possible assassination attempts as Roosevelt's car daily made its way slowly back and forth between the embassies through the crowded narrow streets. More important for Roosevelt was to nurture relations with Stalin by showing his trust and holding frequent informal talks with him.[141]

One critical issue the Big Three agreed on was post-war trials for Axis war criminals. However, they differed over whether publicly to announce that. Churchill called for a joint declaration of their intent to prosecute all war criminals that might 'exert a deterrent effect on the enemy terrorism'.[142] Stalin argued that declaring that would instead encourage the Axis leaders to fight to death to avoid prosecution. Stalin feared Germany's eventual post-war resurgence to threaten Europe again. To prevent that, he called for 'liquidating' at least 50,000 German officers. That appalled Churchill who insisted that Britain would never support mass murder. Roosevelt tried to make light of Stalin's remark, saying only 49,000 should be killed. That swelled Churchill's anger. Stalin defused the tension by changing the subject.[143]

Poland was another crucial issue. Two exiled Polish governments were determined to take power in Warsaw, one pro-democratic in London and the other pro-communist in Moscow. The London Poles had constructed an actual government-in-exile headed by Prime Minister Stanislaw Mikolajczyk. Roosevelt was largely indifferent to Poland's fate if it did not affect his popularity with seven million Polish-American voters in the November 1944 presidential election. Roosevelt readily and Churchill reluctantly agreed to Stalin's demand that Poland's borders be shifted 150 miles westward. The concessions on Poland deeply troubled Churchill. Britain had gone to war with

Germany after it invaded Poland in September 1939 and now was acquiescing to the Soviet imposition of a puppet regime on Poland.

Stalin forced Roosevelt and Churchill to settle a strategic stalemate by asking when they would invade northern France and who would command the campaign. Churchill had always opposed what was now called Operation Overlord, fearing that the Germans would destroy an invasion on the beaches. Instead, he insisted on his 'soft underbelly' strategy of attacking Axis positions throughout the Mediterranean Basin. Roosevelt and his Joint Chiefs condemned Churchill's strategy for frittering away Allied power with literal and figurative dead ends instead of striving for a knockout blow to Hitler's regime by landing in Normandy and fighting east across France, the Low Countries and Germany all the way to Berlin.

Churchill recalled that: 'Stalin looked at me across the table and said, "I wish to pose a very direct question to the Prime Minister about Overlord. Do the Prime Minister and the British Staff really believe in Overlord?"' Churchill responded ambivalently.

What did Stalin think of Roosevelt and Churchill? Ambassador Harriman observed that Stalin clearly preferred one ally over the other:

> When the president spoke . . . Stalin listened closely with deference, whereas he did not hesitate to interrupt or stick a knife in Churchill whenever he had the chance. I felt . . . that Stalin's attitude was motivated not only by the greater power of the United States but also by his understanding that Roosevelt represented something entirely new; his New Deal was reforming capitalism to meet the needs and desires of the working class. There was nothing about that in Communist dogma.[144]

That said, Stalin harboured very mixed feelings of respect and contempt for both. For instance, Stalin described Churchill as: 'A powerful and cunning politician. In the war years, he behaved as a gentleman and achieved a lot. He was the strongest personality in the capitalist world.'[145] Mostly, he scorned not just Roosevelt's flattery and Churchill's bluster, but what he believed was their intention somehow to extract concessions from him: 'Churchill is the kind who, if you don't watch him, will slip a kopeck out of your pocket! . . . And Roosevelt? Roosevelt is not like that. He dips his hand only for bigger coins.'[146] If they had known his views, Roosevelt and Churchill would certainly have bristled at Stalin's ingratitude, paranoia and delusion. Yet they might have made fewer concessions to him had they better understood his mind.

In the Big Three's joint communique released on 6 December, they committed themselves and the United Nations to goals beyond the destruction of the Axis powers, including to 'banish the scourge and terror of war for many generations . . . the elimination of tyranny and slavery, oppression and intolerance. We will welcome them . . . into a world family of democratic nations . . . we look forward to the day when all peoples of the world and live free lives, untouched by tyranny.'[147] The world's worst tyrant undoubtedly smiled sardonically as he cynically signed a set of principles that would abolish his life's purpose. As long as Western military aid and campaigns continued he would cheerfully pretend to embrace their values.

***

Amidst the war, Stalin's children exacerbated his stress and anxiety. The worst came from his son with his first wife, Yakov, an artillery captain who was captured at Smolensk on 16 July 1941. Stalin's reaction to that news was not sorrow but rage that he had not died fighting. Yakov resisted pressure by the Germans to make treasonous statements. The Germans eventually interned him in Sachsenhausen concentration camp. In February 1943, after the Red Army captured General Friedrich Paulus with his army's remnants at Stalingrad, Berlin offered to swap Yakov for him. Stalin refused, still enraged that Yakov had surrendered like millions of other Soviet soldiers rather than died fighting. Yakov died on 16 July 1943, most likely shot by a guard when in despair he tried to climb the fence. When Stalin was told that his son Jacob had been killed, he replied, 'I have no son called Jacob'.[148]

Vasily began the war as a pilot and colonel. He flew twenty-seven sorties during which he shot down an enemy fighter plane. Despite that rather meagre feat, he was promoted to general and received several medals for heroism. The favouritism and false adulation warped him. A superior's report described him as

> hot-headed and excitable by nature, lacks self-control; there have been incidents of physical violence against subordinates. In his private life he has behaved in ways unbecoming . . . [like] tactless behaviour during with flying staff and rudeness toward individual officers . . . His health is not good, especially his nervous system. He is extremely irritable . . . All the above listed shortcomings significantly diminish his authority as a commander and are incompatible with his duties as a divisional commander.[149]

Unmentioned in the report was Vasily's alcoholism. Despite those flaws, the army command did not dare cashier him until after Stalin's death a decade later; until then, they shuffled him between assignments that minimized his potential harm to national security.

Svetlana was 16 when she met dashing screenwriter Alexei Kapler, then 40 years old, after Vasily invited him to their home to discuss a film script about the air force. His best known scripts were *Lenin in October* and *Lenin in 1918*. Later at a party, Svetlana was smitten when Kapler asked her if she knew the foxtrot, then taught her. He asked why she seemed so sad. She replied that the evening was a decade since her mother died. He expressed his condolences. Thereafter they got together many times. In her memoir, she recalled that: 'Kapler was the cleverest, kindest, most wonderful person on earth. He radiated knowledge and all its fascination.' Apparently, they exchanged no more than passionate kisses. Svetlana explained: 'Romantic and pure, I was brought up that sex was only for marriage. Father would not permit me anything outside of marriage.'

Stalin was furious when he received transcripts of their taped telephone conversations. He had Kapler arrested and sent to Lubyanka Prison on 1 March 1943, then confronted his daughter: 'Your Kapler is a British spy.' She blurted, 'But I love him!' Stalin erupted in fury: '"Love," screamed my father with a hatred of the very word [which] I can scarcely convey. And for the first time in his life, he slapped me across the face, twice. Apparently, the fact that Kapler was a Jew was what bothered him the most.' Stalin spared Kapler the fate of millions of other 'spies' and 'enemies of the people'. Instead, he received a five-year sentence to the Gulag.[150]

***

The Red Army juggernaut advanced westward from the Soviet Union, ever deeper into Eastern Europe throughout 1944. In every country, the Red Army 'liberated,' the Soviets imposed a pro-Mocow regime to eventually be replaced with a communist dictatorship. Stalin explained: 'This war is not as in the past; whoever occupies a territory also imposes on it his own social system. Everyone imposes his own system as far as his army has power to do so. It cannot be otherwise.'[151]

The Red Army fought its way into eastern Poland in January 1944. After capturing Lublin on July 24, the Soviets installed the communist Polish Committee of National Liberation as Poland's provisional government whose legitimacy Stalin recognized. Stalin justified all that in a letter to Churchill:

> We do not want to, nor shall we, set up our own administration on Polish soil for we do not wish to interfere in Poland's internal affairs . . . The Polish Committee of National Liberation intends to set up an administration on Polish territory and I hope this will be done. We have not found in Poland other forces capable of establishing a Polish administration. The so-called . . . Polish government in London, have turned out to be ephemeral and lacking influence.[152]

As the Red Army approached Warsaw, the underground Polish 'Home Army' led by General Tadeusz Bor-Komorowski prepared to revolt against the German occupiers. They wanted to liberate themselves with the Red Army's support. They hoped that simultaneous attacks by themselves within and the Red Army outside Warsaw would swiftly expel the Germans. They awaited word from Moscow to initiate that joint offensive. On 29 July, they excitedly heard radio messages by both the Union of Polish Patriots and Radio Kosciusko based in Moscow to prepare for 'active resistance'.

Warsaw is on the Vistula River's west bank with the suburb of Praga on the east bank. The bridge linking them was intact. On 31 July, the underground learned that Marshal Konstantin Rokossovsky's advanced guard was fighting its way into Praga. On 1 August, General Bor-Komorowski issued the order to revolt.

Stalin cynically ordered Rokossovsky to halt his offensive to let the Poles and Germans exterminate each other. The Red Army would then march in to occupy Warsaw's ruins and install the communist Polish government. Stalin rejected urgent calls by Roosevelt and Churchill to join forces with the revolt. He wrote Churchill that: 'Soviet headquarters have decided that they must disassociate themselves from the Warsaw adventure since they cannot assume either direct or indirect responsibility for it.'[153] In other words, since the Red Army could not subordinate the Home Army as a Soviet tool it would not help it. To that, Roosevelt and Churchill urgently issued this appeal: 'We are thinking of world opinion if the anti-Nazis in Warsaw are in effect abandoned. We believe that all three of us should do the utmost to save as many of the patriots there as possible. We hope you will drop immediate supplies and munitions to the patriot Poles of Warsaw or will you agree to help our planes in doing it very quickly?'[154] Stalin replied with an even harsher attack on the Home Army: 'Sooner or later the truth about the handful of power-seeking criminals who launched the Warsaw adventure will come out. Those elements, playing on the credulity of the inhabitants of Warsaw, exposed practically unarmed people to German guns, armour and aircraft. The result is . . . the Hitlerites . . . cruelly exterminating the civil population.'[155]

The Germans crushed organized Polish resistance by October, killing about 15,000 fighters and capturing around 15,000 more. Around 100,000 civilians died in the fighting and several hundred thousand fled. Warsaw was in ruins. Poland's Home Army was destroyed. Stalin gloated at instigating what became a decisive victory over two enemies.

Marshal Fyodor Tolbukin's Third Ukrainian Army Group and Marshal Rodion Malinovsky's Second Ukrainian Army Group overran Romania in August 1944. As they approached Bucharest, a faction of Romania's military overthrew pro-German dictator Marshal Ion Antonescu on 23 August, made King Michael the head of state and welcomed Soviet troops on 31 August. The Soviet conquest of Romania cost 69,000 casualties. The NKVD began infiltrating King Michael's government with communists.

After the Red Army overran Romania, Stalin targeted for conquest Bulgaria, its southern neighbour. Bulgarian King Boris had a quasi-alliance with Hitler. He supplied troops to help the Germans occupy Macedonia in Yugoslavian and let German troops transit his realm, but did not join the German invasion of the Soviet Union. After Boris died in 1943, a regency council ruled Bulgaria. Comintern agent Georgi Dimitrov spearheaded the Soviet effort to get the regency council to ally with Moscow. Stalin declared war against Bulgaria on 3 September and Zhukov led the Red Army's two-day overrun of the country and imposition of a communist regime in Sofia. The Soviet conquest of Bulgaria cost just a thousand casualties.

The Red Army then turned its guns westward against Yugoslavia. There Comintern agent Josef Broz Tito had established and headed the People's Liberation Army of Yugoslavia that fought a guerilla war against the German occupiers. The Red Army invaded Yugoslavia on 28 September and with Tito's partisans captured Belgrade on 24 October. As Tito established a communist government in Belgrade, the Soviets invaded Austria and Hungary northward. The Soviet conquest of Yugoslavia cost just 8,000 casualties.

Admiral Miklos Horthy was Hungary's fascist dictator and Hitler's ally. He had Hungary's army join the invasion of the Soviet Union and helped the Germans round up and dispatch 400,000 Jews to concentration camps. The Red Army fought its way into eastern Hungary in early October. Horthy sent a diplomatic team to Moscow to negotiate an armistice. Hitler responded by ordering Colonel Otto Skorzeny, his brilliant commando leader, to dispose of Horthy. Working with the fascist Arrow Cross Party, Skorzeny and his elite troops captured Horthy on 15 October and forced him to abdicate, with Arrow Cross leader Ferenc Szalasi being his replacement. The Red Army encircled Budapest on 24 December, but the German and Hungarian defenders held out.

***

Stalin finally got the 'second front' he had been demanding for three years.[156] On 6 June 1944, 150,000 troops from the American First and British Second Armies landed on five separate beaches on a 50-mile stretch of Normandy's coast. Over the next seven weeks, those armies fought their way slowly south and west while the Canadian First and American Third Armies squeezed in with them. Eisenhower was the commander of Montgomery's Twelfth Army Group of the Second British and First Canadian and General Omar Bradley's Twenty-First Army Group with the American First and Third Armies, with over 2,000,000 troops. The Germans slowly withdrew from one hedgerow and village to the next.

The Allied breakout came from 25 to 31 July, as General Courtney Hodges's First Army pushed the Germans aside and Patton's Third Army punched through a 10-mile-wide hinge in Normandy near the sea, with a corps dashing west to capture Brittany, a corps pushing south to the Loire River then east along it, a corps heading east and a corps cutting north to link up with the First Canadian Army pushing south. The Germans hastily withdrew, pursued by the Allies. Meanwhile, the Sixth American Army Group landed on southern France's Riviera on 15 August, swiftly captured Toulon and Marseilles, then advanced up the Rhone River Valley. A French division and an American division liberated Paris on 25 August. Units of the Third and Sixth Army greeted each other on 14 September. By mid-September, the Allied armies with nearly 3,000,000 troops extended along a 450-mile front from the Swiss border to the North Sea. But a lack of gasoline and German consolidation of their Siegfried Line of fortifications stalled the Allied advance for nearly six months. The Germans even launched a massive attack that smashed through a 40-mile-wide front in the Ardennes on 16 December, but the First and Third Armies managed to halt that advance and then eliminate the 'Bulge' over the next month.

***

Roosevelt and his military, economic and diplomatic advisors forged grand strategies first to win a global war then win a lasting global peace. As for post-war peace, they understood that the virtuous cycle of international trade, investments, cooperation, prosperity and peace were as inseparable as was the vicious cycle of international protectionism, animosities, poverty, depression and war. Secretary of State Cordell Hull succinctly explained that outlook: 'A world in economic chaos would be forever a breeding ground for trouble and war.'[157]

Roosevelt and his advisors were determined to avoid the tragic delusions and blunders of previous administrations. They had lived through the First World War, the Treaty of Versailles, the League of Nations, Germany's fate and America's policies toward each from 1914 to 1920. They deplored President Woodrow Wilson's acceptance of Versailles' tenets that scapegoated Germany as the war's aggressor and forced it to pay huge indemnities to the victors that destabilized its economy and nascent democratic political system. Atop that, Wilson failed to make compromises with Senate Republicans to ratify the Treaty of Versailles that pledged signatories to establish and join a League of Nations dedicated to resolving international conflicts and promoting international commerce. They also deplored the laissez faire policies of the three subsequent Republican administrations that let speculators bid the stock market up to fantastic heights unhinged from the economy until it imploded, plunging America into the Great Depression that Washington globalized with high tariffs that collapsed international trade. The mass joblessness, poverty and despair bolstered the existing fascist regimes in Italy and Japan and helped Hitler take power in Germany.

The key to realizing post-war prosperity and peace was establishing international organizations that promoted international commerce and security. The White House took that first crucial stride by inviting envoys from forty-four countries to meet at the Washington Hotel in Bretton Woods, New Hampshire, from 1 to 21 July 1944. There they agreed to set up the International Monetary Fund (IMF) and International Bank for Reconstruction and Development (IRBD) or World Bank to promote international investment, trade and economic development. Both were international banks for countries as members who contributed funds and could borrow money to develop their economies. The IMF established a fixed international currency system grounded on gold worth $34 an ounce; members suffering trade or payments deficits could borrow money at low interest rates to invest in ways that restored their dynamism.

With that done, Roosevelt sought to create the United Nations as an improved version of the League of Nations dedicated to 'collective security' or 'one for all, all for one' against potential aggressors while promoting economic development and political stability in all countries. The United States, Soviet Union, Britain and China – 'the Four Policemen' – would pursue policies that overlapped and paralleled the United Nation's principles. They would work together in the United Nations' Security Council to resolve common problems and act autonomously to resolve problems in their respective spheres of interest. Those spheres included Latin America for the United States, Eastern Europe for the Soviet Union, the Far East for China and, after granting its colonies independence, the Commonwealth for Britain.

What did Stalin think of these international organizations? He adamantly rejected the IMF and World Bank for strengthening the global economy and thus thwarting the likely post-war depression and chaos that he wanted for making communist revolutions more likely. On the other hand, he eagerly embraced Roosevelt's Four Policemen that gave him a free hand to impose communist regimes in Eastern Europe. As for the United Nations, American, Soviet, British and French diplomats negotiated the framework during the Dumbarton Oaks conference in Washington from 21 August to 7 October 1944. The United Nations Charter established a Secretariat or administration headed by a Secretary General, a General Assembly with an equal vote for each member that could only issue recommendations in the form of resolutions; and initially a ten-member (later expanded to fifteen) Security Council composed of Four Policemen – later expanded to five with France – as permanent members with each empowered to veto any measure, while the other six had two-year terms. Security Council resolutions were legally binding on all members. For the General Assembly, Stalin first demanded that the Soviet Union and its fifteen 'republics' be members but after Roosevelt and Churchill refused, they compromised on four members – Russia, Ukraine, Belorussia and Lithuania.

***

Relations between America and Britain on one hand and the Soviet Union on the other grew more strained and divisive during the war. Increasingly, the White House split over the nature of the Soviet Union and America's future relations with it, with appeasers versus Cassandras.

Appeasers included President Roosevelt himself, Vice President Henry Wallace, Treasury Secretary Henry Morgenthau, advisor Harry Hopkins and former ambassador to Moscow Joseph Davies. Each believed that they could sustain an amiable working relationship with Stalin that found compromises for issues that arose between them.

Indeed, Davies wrote a bestselling book, *Mission to Moscow*, published in 1941 and made into a Hollywood movie in 1943, that lauded Stalin and the Soviet Union.[158]

A growing group of Cassandras warned Roosevelt that Stalin was an untrustworthy mass murderer determined to conquer Eastern Europe and provoke communist revolutions there and elsewhere around the world. The most prominent eventually included Secretary of State Edward Stettinius, who had replaced an exhausted Cordel Hull on 1 December 1944, Averell Harriman, the ambassador to Moscow, former ambassador William Bullitt, Foreign Service Russian experts Charles Bohlen and George Kennan and General John Deane, who headed America's military mission in Moscow.

In a report to Army Chief of Staff George Marshall, Deane explained that communists 'simply cannot understand giving without taking and as a result even our giving is viewed with suspicion. Gratitude cannot be banked in the Soviet Union. Each transaction is complete in itself without regard to past favours. The party of the second part is either a shrewd trader to be admired or a sucker to be despised.'[159] Bullitt was America's ambassador in Moscow from December 1933 to May 1936. He arrived as someone curious about the communist experiment and soon recognized its genocidal depravity. In August 1943, he warned Roosevelt that: 'Hitler's aim was to spread the power of the Nazis to the ends of the earth. Stalin's aim is to spread the power of the communists to the ends of the earth. Stalin, like Hitler, will not stop. He can only be stopped.' To that Roosevelt lamely replied: 'I don't dispute your facts . . . I just have a hunch that Stalin is not that kind of man . . . I think that if we give him everything I possibly can and ask nothing in return . . . he won't try to annex anything and will work with me for a world of democracy and peace.'[160] Harriman warned Roosevelt the Allied leaders were unwittingly feeding a Soviet post-war threat: 'If the policy is accepted that the Soviet Union has a right to penetrate her immediate neighbours for security, penetration of the next immediate neighbours becomes at a certain time equally logical.'[161] That dynamic of communist expansion was later called the 'domino effect'. Kennan, the deputy ambassador in Moscow, wrote Bohlen at the State Department this bleak assessment of American policy failures with Stalin: 'We have consistently refused to make clear what our interests and our wishes were in eastern and central Europe. We have refused to name any limit for Russian expansion and Russian responsibilities, thereby confusing the Russians and causing them constantly to wonder whether they are asking too little or whether it is some kind of trap.'[162]

***

Meanwhile, Churchill was so alarmed by the Soviet imposition of one puppet regime after another across Eastern Europe that he flew to Moscow to try to cut a deal with Stalin on 10 October 1944. He jotted down for five countries ratios between British and Soviet influence with 10 per cent and 90 per cent for Romania, 90 per cent and 10 per cent for Greece, 50 per cent each for Yugoslavia and Hungary and 25 per cent and 75 per cent for Bulgaria.

Churchill then

> pushed this across to Stalin . . . There was a slight pause. Then he took his blue pencil and made a large tick across it and passed it back . . . It was all settled in less time than it takes to sit down . . . After this there was a long silence . . . I said, 'Might it not be thought rather cynical if it seemed we had disposed of these issues, so fateful to millions of people, in such an offhand manner? Let us burn the paper.' 'No, you keep it,' said Stalin.[163]

Throughout, Stalin kept his usual poker face but must have been amused, astonished and disdainful that such an experienced statesman could be so naïve. Troops, diplomats and spies on the ground would determine each country's fate. That piece of paper was meaningless to anyone but Churchill. So when Churchill asked him if he wanted the paper, Stalin replied that he could keep it.

***

Stalin and his high command prepared a knockout blow against the Nazi regime in early 1945. Over several preceding months, the Soviets massed 180 divisions with over 3,000,000 troops, 9,000 tanks, 9,000 warplanes and vast amounts of supplies along a 400-mile stretch of the Eastern Front from the Baltic east of Königsberg south-west through East Prussia into central Poland then south up the Vistula River valley to the Carpathian Mountains. From north to south, those troops were split among four 'Fronts' or 'Army Groups', with Marshal Ivan Chernyakhovsky's Third White Russian Front aimed at Königsberg, Marshal Konstantin Rokossovsky's Second White Russian Front at Danzig, Marshal Georgy Zhukov's First White Russian Front at Warsaw and Marshal Ivan Konev's First Ukrainian Front at Wroclaw. They faced 750,000 German troops in 80 divisions and 1,500 tanks, with General Heinz Guderian, that front's commander and also the Army Chief of Staff. South of the Carpathians, the Eastern Front stretched through eastern Czechoslovakia and Hungary, with the Germans still holding Prague and Budapest but the Red Army had overrun most of Bulgaria and Romania and had captured Belgrade along with much of eastern Yugoslavia. The Red Army's offensive on the Polish front erupted on 12 January 1945. In a double envelopment, Zhukov's troops advanced far beyond the Vistula and captured Warsaw in three days.

Stalin authorized the puppet Lublin communist regime to formally declare itself the Polish Provisional National Government on 3 January 1945. He informed Churchill that Moscow would recognize that government and urged him and Roosevelt to do the same. In a separate letter to Roosevelt, he detailed all the 'progressive' policies that the provisional government was pursuing in liberated Poland and hoped the president would embrace the new government.[164] On 9 February, the communist government moved to Warsaw's ruins and began asserting control over all of Poland cleared of Germans. The Polish communists worked with the Soviet Red Army to arrest and imprison any remnants of the Polish Home Army, eventually sending 30,000 to the Gulag after executing the leaders.

Everywhere the Red Army advanced, the troops looted, gang-raped and murdered, while political commissars imposed communist governments. The Soviets may have raped at least 2,000,000 German women, murdered tens of thousands of their victims, while thousands more committed suicide from utter despair.[165]

When communist Milovan Djilas complained about Red Army atrocities as they 'liberated' Yugoslavia, Stalin cut him short:

> Do you see what a complicated thing is man's soul, his psyche? Well, then imagine a man who has fought from Stalingrad to Belgrade – over thousands of kilometres of his own devastated land, across the dead bodies of his comrades and dearest ones? How can such a man react normally? And what is so awful in his having fun with a woman, after such horrors? You have imagined the Red Army to be ideal. And it is not ideal, nor can it be, even if it did not contain a certain percentage of criminals – we opened up our penitentiaries and stuck everyone in the army.[166]

To a Czech communist's protests, Stalin admitted in March 1945 that:

> The fact is that there are now 12 million people in the Red Army. They are far from being angels. They have been coarsened by war . . . On their way they have seen much sorrow and many terrible things. So do not be surprised if some of our people do not behave as they should in your country. We know that some of our soldiers with a low level of political consciousness are pestering and abusing girls and women . . . Let our

> Czechoslovak friends know that now, so that the attraction of our Red Army does not turn into disappointment.[167]

However, Stalin recognized that the more harshly his troops treated the people they conquered the harder it would be for communist regimes to establish power there. On 20 April, he issued this order to his Red Army commanders: 'You are to demand of the troops to change their behaviour toward the Germans, both POWs and the civilian population and treat them better. Harsh treatment of the Germans makes them fearful and forces them into resistance and not giving themselves up. The civilian population, fearing being swept away organizes itself into bands. Such a situation is not convenient to us.'[168]

***

Foreign Minister Molotov summoned Ambassador Harriman on 3 January 1945 and asked for America to give the Soviet Union a $6 billion loan with a 2 per cent interest rate for reconstruction. Harriman passed that request to the White House. Treasury Secretary Henry Morgenthau presented a plan to give Moscow a low-interest $5 billion loan to be repaid over 30 years to buy American-made products to help rebuild its war-devastated regions. Roosevelt and his advisors hoped that would also help alleviate any post-war economic depression by employing Americans who otherwise might be jobless. They split over whether to demand political concessions for the loan. Appeasers insisted that the loan be free of strings other than the interest rate. Secretary of State Stettinius led Cassandras in advocating tying the loan to the Soviets holding genuine free elections in Eastern Europe. Roosevelt wavered between the two sides. Finally, he decided to delay a decision until after an upcoming summit with Stalin at Yalta.

Before Yalta, Roosevelt, Churchill and the Combined Chiefs of Staff met at Malta from 30 January to 3 February. During that time, they tried to work out a common strategy to deal with Stalin on key issues. Roosevelt was at death's door and looked it, emaciated and feeble. He drifted in and out of focus through the discussions, socializing and dinners. At times, he mustered his natural conviviality but mostly deferred to others. With him as his aide was his son, Colonel Eliott Roosevelt.

During the Combined Chief of Staff meeting at Malta, British Chief of Staff Alan Brooke tried to gain approval for two of General Montgomery's demands, that he become the Western Front's ground commander and that his Twenty-First Army Group spearhead a single thrust toward Berlin while the American Twelfth and Sixth Army Groups stayed on the defensive. That would let Montgomery and the British enjoy all the glory while the Americans played a secondary role. Eisenhower informed Army Chief of Staff George Marshall that he opposed Montgomery's schemes and would resign if the Combined Chiefs approved either one. Marshall backed Eisenhower's attempts to stave off Montgomery's demands, promising him that, 'As long as I'm Chief of Staff I'll never let them saddle you with the burden of an overall ground commander.'[169] At Malta, Marshall denounced Montgomery's demands to be ground commander and lead a single thrust and warned that he would back Eisenhower's resignation as Supreme Commander if that did not happen. The Combined Chiefs rejected Montgomery's demands.

***

Roosevelt, Churchill and their entourages packed into separate planes at Malta's largest airfield after daylight on 3 February. Accompanied by squadrons of P-38 fighters, they flew to the airfield at Saki, Crimea. There Foreign Minister Vyacheslav Molotov greeted them and they crowded into a column of Jeeps and trucks escorted by Red Army troops for the six-hour journey on wretched roads south-east to the coast and then along it south-west to Yalta.[170]

The Soviets housed the American and British delegations in palaces half a dozen miles apart with themselves in the middle at the Yusopov Palace, with Roosevelt's team at the Livadia Palace, built for Tsar Nicholas II in 1911 and Churchill's team at the Vorontsov Palace. Security was tight. NKVD Chief Lavrenti Beria had previously ordered his troops to round up 189,000 mostly Crimean Tartars but also Greeks, Bulgarians and Armenians to be transported to Uzbekistan in May 1944; 17 per cent of them died within 18 months of their arrests. In the weeks preceding the conference, he had his troops investigate 74,000 'suspects,' of whom 835 were arrested on various charges and either executed or sent to the Gulag. Beria had the palace grounds surrounded by barbed wire and bunkers and deployed over 500 NKVD troops in the compounds and along the roads linking them. He had listening bugs planted in the palaces and grounds inhabited by Roosevelt, Churchill and their entourages. At least one Soviet spy was embedded in Roosevelt's team – Alger Hiss, one of Secretary of State Stettinius' aides.[171]

As he had at the Tehran summit, Roosevelt wanted to meet privately with Stalin to forge good feelings, trust and understanding.

He asked Stalin to meet him informally at his palace the next morning of 4 February before the conference convened. On meeting Stalin, Roosevelt expressed how appalled he was by the war destruction he had witnessed during his journey from Saki to Yalta, that he was now was 'more bloodthirsty in regard to the Germans' and hoped that Stalin would propose the same toast he had during their last summit for 'the execution of 50,000 officers of the German army'. Stalin replied that: 'We have all become more bloodthirsty. The Germans are savages.' They then talked about the campaigns on the Western and Eastern Fronts.[172]

That was the easy part for Roosevelt. Over the next week, Stalin would trounce him and Churchill on one issue after another, getting what he wanted in return for trifles. The Big Three and their advisors met later that day. As he had at Tehran, Stalin let Roosevelt preside at each session since he was the only head of state among them.

The first significant order of business was for Roosevelt, Churchill and Stalin to approve the European Advisory Commission's map of German and Austrian occupation zones. That was literally and figuratively a fatal decision for millions of Germans and Austrians who were trapped in Red Army zones.

Roosevelt asked Stalin for his impression of Charles de Gaulle, who had visited him in Moscow in December. Stalin said, 'I didn't find de Gaulle a very complicated person. But I feel he's unrealistic in the sense that France hasn't done very much fighting in this war and yet demands full rights with the Americans, British and Russians, who've carried the burden of the fighting.' Stalin asked Roosevelt if he thought France should have an occupation zone as de Gaulle insisted. Roosevelt made this puzzling reply: 'It's not a bad idea, only out of kindness.' Stalin diplomatically rejected the notion with these words: 'I think there might be complications in our work if we have a fourth member.' That prompted Churchill's passionate reply: 'This brings up the whole question of the future role of France in Europe. And I personally feel that France should play a very important role . . . We want to see their might grow, to help keep Germany down.' Stalin shrugged and said he did not object to Roosevelt and Churchill donating parts of their zones to the French, but certainly the Soviets would not contribute.[173]

During their previous summit at Tehran and in various foreign minister meetings, the Soviets had insisted that Germany pay reparations. The American and British position was that they would not take reparations for themselves but agreed that the Soviets deserved reparations for the vast destruction inflicted on their country by the German invasion and three years of war. Now Stalin had an aide present a specific amount – $20 billion, with the Soviets taking half and the other Allies splitting the rest. Churchill replied that imposing too onerous a reparations burden on Germany would likely promote political extremism as it had after the First World War.

The worst dispute was over Poland's fate. Roosevelt put America's position in writing with a letter to Stalin:

> In so far as the Polish Government is concerned, I am greatly disturbed that the three great powers do not have a meeting of minds about the political setup in Poland . . . I have had to make it clear to you that we cannot recognize the Lublin Government as now composed and the world would regard it as a lamentable outcome of our work here . . . It goes without saying that any interim government . . . would be pledged to the holding of free elections in Poland at the earliest possible date. I know this is completely consistent with your desire to see a new and democratic Poland emerge . . . from this war.[174]

Roosevelt's last line expressed not heavy, pointed irony, but instead naivete and ignorance about the inseparable essence of communism, Soviet imperialism and Stalin's tyranny.

Stalin was determined not just to impose a communist regime on Poland but move its frontiers 150 or so miles east. For that he was willing to make some gestures to appease Roosevelt and Churchill. He agreed to sign the Declaration on Liberated Europe with its set of democratic principles including civil rights and free elections that he had no intention of upholding. For the same reason he would sign a statement on Poland that included: 'The Provisional Government which is now functioning in Poland should . . . be reorganized on a broader democratic basis . . . This Polish Government of National Unity shall be pledged to the holding of free and unfettered elections.'[175] He would add a token London Pole or two to the communist government for the sake of political appearances.

To varying degrees, Roosevelt's advisors recognized that Stalin and the communists would systematically and ruthlessly violate the democratic principles of those two documents, but fatalistically accepted that as a reality the Western Allies were powerless to change. Only Roosevelt believed that Stalin would uphold those promises. Holding up the Poland declaration, Admiral William Leahy told Roosevelt, 'Mr. President, this is so elastic that the Russians can stretch it all the way from Yalta to Washington without ever technically breaking it.' Roosevelt replied 'I know it, Bill. But it's the best I can do for Poland at this time.'[176]

Meanwhile, Roosevelt and Churchill agreed to Stalin's demand that Poland cede to the Soviet Union a hundred or so miles on its eastern border to the Curzon Line, drawn by British Foreign Secretary George Curzon in 1919. Poland would be compensated by taking German territory westward all the way to the Oder-Neisse Rivers. That adjustment led to the displacement of 12 million Poles and Germans from their homes and livelihoods.

For America's Joint Chiefs of Staff, the crucial task was getting Stalin to fulfil his previous pledge to war against Japan within three months of Germany's defeat. Estimates were that the Americans would suffer at least 100,000 casualties in the invasion of Japan's island of Kyushu scheduled for September and at least 250,000 casualties for the invasion of the main island of Honshu in March 1946. Of course, those invasions would be unnecessary if the Manhattan Project successfully created atomic bombs to be dropped on Japanese cities. But the project might be nothing more than a $2 billion dud. If so, the invasions and several hundred thousand dead and maimed Americans were inescapable. And for that, massive Red Army attacks against Japanese forces in China and Korea might lead to a quicker victory.

With typical political finesse, Stalin played hard to get for a cherished opportunity. He was eager to conquer north-east Asia, take vital ports, railways and natural resources for the Soviet Union and aid communist revolutions in China and Korea. When asked, Stalin reassured the Western Allies that he was renewing his vows. The price he extracted was Sakhalin Island's southern half and most of the Kurile Island chain from Japan and rights to Manchuria's Southern Railway along with Darien and Port Arthur from China. For the China concessions he would sign a trade and friendship treaty with Generalissimo Chiang Kai-shek and promised to stop aiding Mao Zedong's Communist Party in the ongoing civil war between them. Of course, he would break that latter promise.

Stalin asked Roosevelt how long America would commit troops to occupy Europe. Ideally, Roosevelt would have said that American troops would stay in Europe as long as necessary to transform Germany from tyranny to democracy and rebuild its economy along with that of the other war shattered countries. Instead, he glibly replied: 'I can get the people and Congress to co-operate fully for peace but not to keep an army in Europe for a long time. Two years would be the limit.' Stalin managed to contain his exhilaration that the Americans would withdraw after two years, thus yielding a Europe split between the Soviet empire eastward and war-shattered unaligned countries westward where communist parties would metastasize amid a vicious cycle of poverty, hunger, homelessness, violence, corruption and political instability. Churchill understood the severity of Roosevelt's concession and gave the president a chance to walk it back by saying: 'I hope that would be according to circumstances.' But Roosevelt, with exhaustion compounding his naivety, could not fathom his remark's significance and so did not revise it.[177]

During the conference each leader hosted a formal banquet for his colleagues and selected guests. Stalin had at least two special guests at his banquet. Historian Simon Montefiore speculates why the tyrant insisted that Roosevelt's son Eliott join them: 'Stalin had specially invited him to the dinner. Perhaps he sensed the similarity with his scapegrace son, Vasily. Both were pilots, inadequate yet arrogant drunks who were intimidated and dominated by brilliant fathers. Both exploited the family name and embarrassed their fathers. Both failed in multiple marriages and abandoned their wives. Perhaps there is no sadder curse than the gift of a titanic father.'[178] NKVD Chief Beria was the other notable guest. Roosevelt noticed him seated at one of the tables and asked Stalin: 'Who's that in the pince-nez opposite Ambassador Gromyko?' 'Ah, that one, that's our Himmler. That's Beria.'[179] Roosevelt advisor Robert Sherwood vividly described Stalin as: 'an austere, rugged figure in boots that shone like mirrors, stout baggy trousers and snug-fitting blouse. He wore no ornament . . . He's built close to the ground, like a football coach's dream of a tackle.'[180]

Foreign Secretary Anthony Eden deplored the banquets, especially Roosevelt's: 'Dinner with Americans; a terrible party I thought. President vague and loose and ineffective. W[inston], understanding that business was flagging made desperate efforts and too long speeches to get things going again. Stalin's attitude to small countries struck me as grim, not to say sinister . . . I was greatly relieved when the whole business was over.'[181]

Through the summit, keen observers clearly saw that Stalin snookered Roosevelt and Churchill on every key issue. Foreign Undersecretary Alexander Cadogan wrote his wife that: 'Uncle Joe is in great form. The president flapped and the P.M. boomed, but Joe just sat taking it all in and being rather amused. When he did chip in, he never used a superfluous word and spoke very much to the point. He's obviously got a very good sense of humour – and a rather quick temper!'[182]

***

The Red Army and NKVD blatantly violated Stalin's Yalta pledges about democracy in Eastern Europe and his signature on the 'Declaration on Liberated Europe'. In each country, they ruthlessly imposed a communist regime in a series of carefully plotted steps over time.

After conquering Romania in August 1944, the Soviets let King Michael remain the government's figurehead as a source of stability. For the next half year, the Soviets purged any lingering sympathizers with the previous regime and developed a Romanian Communist Party that infiltrated the government, military, factories and mines and led a National Democratic Front of smaller socialist and agrarian parties. On 6 January 1945, the Red Army and NKVD rounded up around 70,000 ethnic Germans living mostly in Transylvania in northern Romania and neighbouring Hungary and deported them to Soviet slave labour camps. The Communist Party organized strikes and demonstrations in Bucharest and other cities to undermine the government, culminating with a hundred thousand protestors packing the square before the royal palace on 24 February.

The communist coup came the following day, 27 February. Andrei Vyshinsky was the Deputy Commissar for Foreign Affairs. Stalin wielded him as a roving 'ambassador', a troubleshooter who usually had 'troublemakers' shot. That day Vyshinsky strode into King Michael's office to demand that he oust all his pro-Western ministers, starting with Prime Minister Nicolae Radescu and replace them with communists. He warned the king that if he refused Romania would suffer the same fate as Transylvania's Germans and Poland where hundreds of thousands of enemies of the people were executed or exiled to Siberia. When he strode out, he slammed the door so hard behind him that it cracked the wall's plaster. Meanwhile Red Army units across the country surrounded Romanian units and demanded their surrender their weapons.

Terrified, King Michael complied. He dismissed Radescu and replaced him with Petru Groza, the head of the Ploughman's Party, and exchanged other pro-Western ministers for communists. Stalin then rewarded King Michael by detaching Hungary's Transylvanian region and adding it to Romania's. Churchill fumed at news of the coup but could not even protest because he had conceded a 90 per cent share of Romania to Stalin during his infamous October visit. The news also upset Roosevelt who briefly mulled protesting Stalin's glaring violation of his Yalta pledges but realized he was powerless.

In neighbouring Hungary, Budapest's defenders held out until 13 February 1945. The Red Army set up a provisional government dominated by communists. Hungary's conquest cost the Red Army around 160,000 casualties. The communist chokehold on Poland tightened. The NKVD rounded up 38,600 Polish 'enemies of the people' from January to April.[183] Among them were the Home Army's sixteen remaining leaders. The NKVD brought them to Moscow for trial and prison on 27 March. Soviet troops did to Austrians what they did to Germans – mass raped, robbed and murdered them. The Red Army captured Vienna on 13 April, but the atrocities persisted. The Red Army captured Prague on 8 May 1945, the last day of the war. Stalin had approved Zdeniek Fierlinger to be the prime minister of Czechoslovakia's provisional government in exile in Moscow on 4 April and he flew with his cabinet to take power in Prague on 10 May.

***

Along the Western Front, the Allied armies fought their way across the Rhine. The Germans destroyed all their Rhine bridges except at Remagen where the explosion was too weak. A division of Hodge's American First Army routed the defenders and captured the bridge. On 23 March, Patton's Third Army was next across along a thinly-defended stretch near Mainz; troops in amphibious vehicles landed on the eastern shore, secured it, then built pontoon bridges that division after division rumbled across. Montgomery and his staff had spent weeks planning and massing forces for the crossing of his Twenty-First Army Group on 24 March, including massive bombardments, artillery barrages, parachute drops and amphibious landings. Once across the armies raced eastward against disintegrating German opposition, taking hundreds of thousands of prisoners along the way.

Every general dreamed of leading his army to Berlin to capture Hitler's capital and perhaps the tyrant himself. Alas, that was a near impossible dream. Among the worst mistakes that Roosevelt and Churchill made during the war was agreeing to designate occupation zones for Germany before Allied armies overran it. They let the European Advisory Committee draw lines across a map in London that split Germany into roughly equal portions with Britain's zone in the north-west, America's in the south-west and the Soviet's in the east with Berlin in the centre. Although the allies agreed to split Berlin into three zones, the American and British occupiers would have to import all their supplies a hundred or so miles through Soviet East Germany.

As Nazi Germany's capital, Berlin was the greatest political and military prize. The ally whose army captured Berlin would reap high praise and the subsequent political benefits from dominating that centre of German power. Eisenhower staved off every request by a general to race to Berlin.[184] To Montgomery, he wrote that Berlin 'has become, so far as I am concerned, nothing but a geographical location and I have never been interested in these. My purpose is to destroy the enemy's forces and his power to resist.'[185] When Eisenhower informed Patton that Germany's capital was off limits, Patton angrily replied: 'Ike, I don't see how you figure that one. We had better take Berlin and quick and . . . on to the Oder' River where the Soviets then were stalled.[186]

Among the Big Three's minor decisions at Yalta was to let Eisenhower communicate directly with Stalin as the campaign unfolded, rather than via the Combined Chiefs, to respond more rapidly to any opportunities or conflicts that arose as the Western and Eastern Allied armies converged. Eisenhower sent Stalin a message on 28 March, in which he sought to share information on their approaching armies to avoid any problems between them: 'Before deciding firmly my plans, it is . . . most important that they should be coordinated as closely as possible with yours as to direction and timing. Could you . . . tell me your intentions . . . I am prepared to send officers to you for this purpose.' Eisenhower read Stalin's reply on 1 April: 'I agree . . . that the place for the joining up of . . . forces . . . should be the areas Erfurt, Leipzig and Dresden . . . Berlin has lost its former strategic importance. The Soviet high command therefore plans to allot secondary forces in the direction of Berlin.'[187]

Throughout the war, Churchill's 'soft underbelly of Europe' obsession clouded his strategic vision, but he was crystal clear when viewing Berlin. On 1 April, he powerfully demolished Eisenhower's assertions:

> I do not know why it would be an advantage not to cross the Elbe. If the enemy's resistance should weaken . . . why should we not cross the Elbe and advance as far east as possible? This has an important political bearing, as the Russian armies . . . seem certain to enter Vienna and overrun Austria. If we deliberately leave Berlin to them, even if it should be in our grasp, the double event may strengthen their conviction . . . that they have done everything. Further I do not consider myself that Berlin has yet lost its military and certainly not its political significance. The fall of Berlin would have a profound psychological effect on German resistance in every part of the Reich. While Berlin holds out great masses of Germans will feel it their duty to go down fighting . . . Therefore I . . . prefer persistence in the plan on which we crossed the Rhine . . . that Ninth U.S. Army should march with Twenty-First Army Group to the Elbe and beyond to Berlin.

Eisenhower lamely replied that if Germany collapsed 'we could rush forward and Lubeck and Berlin could be included in our important targets'.[188] Clearly, he hoped that would not happen.

Churchill fired off to Roosevelt a similar plea to do all possible to capture Berlin:

> Berlin remains of high strategic importance. Nothing will exert a psychological effect of despair upon all German forces of resistance equal to that of the fall of Berlin . . . The Russian armies will no doubt overrun all Austria and enter Vienna. If they also take Berlin will not their impression be they have been the overwhelming contributor to our common victory be unduly imprinted in their minds and may this not lead them into a mood which will raise grave and formidable difficulties in the future? I therefore consider that from a political standpoint we should march as far east into Germany as possible and that should Berlin be in our grasp we should certainly take it. This also appears sound on military grounds.[189]

General Alan Simpson's American Ninth Army reached the Elbe River on 12 April. Simpson excitedly informed Eisenhower that the road to Berlin was open and his troops could be there in 48 hours. Eisenhower ordered him not to advance. On 25 April, American and Soviet soldiers shook hands near Torgau beside the Elbe River.

***

Stalin believed that Eisenhower's cession of Berlin to the Red Army was an attempt to lull him into complacency while the Western armies raced forward and snatched it. On 2 April, he convened his top army group generals including Zhukov, Konev and Rokossovsky at the Kremlin and asked them: 'Well, who is going to take Berlin, us or the Allies?' Konev replied, 'We will capture Berlin. And we will take it before the Allies.'[190] They then worked out how to do that. The plan involved the Army Groups of Zhukov, Konev and Rokossovsky converging on Berlin with the combined forces of 2,500,000 troops, 7,500 warplanes, 6,250 tanks and 41,600 guns. The offensive opened on 16 April. As the three army groups converged on Berlin other Soviet forces raced to the Elbe to block any Western Allied forces advancing eastward. By 20 April, the Soviets had surrounded Berlin and began fighting their way to the centre.

Meanwhile, another race entangled the Americans and the Soviets. Under Operation Paperclip the Americans tried to capture as many cutting-edge German scientists, engineers, technologies, weapons and equipment as possible. General Leslie Groves, who commanded the

Manhattan Project, established a special army intelligence unit codenamed Alsos led by Boris Pash to search for German nuclear physicists, equipment and enriched uranium. They recovered 1,100 tons of uranium ore hidden in a salt mine near Stassfurt on 17 April. They captured most scientists who worked on Germany's nuclear bomb project, most vitally its director, the brilliant physicist Werner Heisenberg. Promises of high salaries and quality of life enticed most of them to move to the United States and work for America's nuclear programme. A different army unit tried to capture as many scientists and engineers who worked on Germany's V-1 and V-2 missile programme. They also succeeded in locating most of the personnel, including the director Wernher von Braun, and convincing them to immigrate to America and they found and shipped over missiles and tons of equipment. Stalin tasked the NKVD with creating a special unit to find their own nuclear and missile scientists, engineers and equipment.

Among Stalin's concerns was that the Western Allies would cut a separate peace with Germany. Report of contact in Berne between OSS Station Chief Allen Dulles and an envoy from General Albert Kesselring triggered his paranoia. He fired off a telegram to Roosevelt accusing him of violating understandings reached at Yalta.

That angered Roosevelt, who had bent over backward at Yalta to appease Stalin on one vital issue after another. On 5 April, he firmly replied:

> It is astonishing that a belief seems to have reached the Soviet Government that I have entered into an agreement with the enemy without first obtaining your full agreement . . . It would be one of the great tragedies of history if at the very moment of the victory now within our grasp, such distrust, such lack of faith should prejudice the entire undertaking after the colossal losses of life, material and treasure. Frankly I cannot avoid a feeling of bitter resentment toward your informers, whoever they are, for such vile misrepresentation of my actions or those of my trusted subordinates.

Stalin offered this contrite response: 'I have never doubted your integrity or trustworthiness, just as I have never questioned the integrity or trustworthiness of Mr. Churchill.'[191]

***

A brain haemorrhage killed Franklin Roosevelt, then 63 years old, on 12 April 1945. Stalin genuinely liked Roosevelt for his cheerful, confident geniality and willingness to compromise. Ambassador Harriman recalled that news of Roosevelt's death 'deeply distressed' Stalin, who tightly gripped his hand for 30 seconds when he told him.[192] Stalin later summarized the president's legacy: 'Roosevelt was a great statesman, a clever, educated, far-sighted and liberal leader who prolonged the life of capitalism.'[193] Churchill expressed to Stalin his feelings about Roosevelt death and hopes for continued good relations with the Soviet leader: 'I have been greatly distressed by the death of President Roosevelt with whom I had in the last five and a half years established very close ties of friendship. This sad event makes it all the more valuable that you and I are linked together by the many pleasant courtesies and memories even in the midst of all the perils and difficulties that we have surmounted.'[194]

Vice President Harry Truman became president.[195] He grew up on a farm in western Missouri, failed to enter West Point because of poor eyesight, captained an artillery company during the First World War and worked as a farmer, bookkeeper and store clerk before beginning a political career with Tom Pendergast's Democratic Party organization in Kansas City. He was elected to various district judgeships then in 1934, won an election to be a senator from Missouri. In the Senate, he had a distinguished decade with the highlight his formation and leadership of the Senate Special Committee to Investigate the National Defence Program that revealed vast waste and corruption through thirty-two reports and saved taxpayers billions of dollars. For the 1944 election, Roosevelt dropped his controversial leftist vice president Henry Wallace and made Truman his running mate. Yet Roosevelt did not include Truman in his inner policymaking circle or even inform him of key military, diplomatic and economic matters, including the top-secret Manhattan Project. Indeed, Secretary of War Henry Stimson did not brief him on the atomic bomb until 25 April, nearly two weeks after Truman took the presidential oath.

Fortunately, Truman was very bright, hardworking and soon understood those key issues. He was friendly, down-to-earth, pragmatic, hardworking and honest but was also quick fused with red tape, pedants, idealists and special interests. Many in the White House welcomed Truman's get the job done and move on attitude after a dozen years of Roosevelt's prevarications. Among them was Undersecretary of State Joseph Grew: 'When I saw him today, I had fourteen problems to take up with him and got through them in less than fifteen minutes with a clear directive for every one of them. You can imagine what a joy it is to deal with a man like that.'[196]

Truman had very mixed feelings toward the Soviet Union. When war broke out between the Nazi and Communist regimes in June 1941, he expressed this classic realist strategy: 'If we see that Germany is winning we ought to help Russia and if Russia is winning we ought to help Germany and that let them kill as many as possible, although I don't want to see Hitler victorious under any circumstances.'[197] After Pearl Harbor, he understood that allying with Moscow for the duration of the war was in America's interest.

As president, Truman got earfuls of conflicting advice from appeasers and Cassandras. He wanted to forge good relations with Stalin and his regime but only if grounded on mutual respect, compromise and fulfilment of promises. He was angry to learn that the Soviets were violating the Declaration on Liberated Europe that Stalin had signed at Yalta and confronted Molotov during his White House visit on 23 April. When Molotov insisted that the Soviets were realizing every understanding reached at Yalta, Truman interrupted, declared that wrong and demanded reciprocity. Molotov complained that 'I have never been talked to like that in my life.' Truman retorted, 'Carry out your agreements and you won't get talked to like that.'[198]

***

As the Soviets fought their way into central Berlin, Hitler and Eva Braun killed themselves in the command bunker on 30 April, her first by cyanide, then him by a pistol shot to his right temple. Aides carried the bodies outside to a crater, soaked them in gasoline, then tossed a match. The fire burned them to a crisp.

Nonetheless, the German defenders held out for another two days, surrendering on 2 May. The campaign that led to Berlin's capture initially pitted 2,300,000 Soviet troops, 6,250 tanks, 7,500 warplanes and 41,600 guns and mortars against 766,750 German troops, 1,159 tanks, 2,221 warplanes and 9,303 guns and mortars. The Germans had suffered 925,000 killed, wounded and captured along with thousands of captured or destroyed tanks, guns and warplanes while the Red Army suffered 361,317 casualties and the destruction of 1,997 tanks, 2,108 guns and 917 warplanes.[199]

Zhukov called Stalin to tell him of Berlin's capture and Hitler's death. Stalin was elated: 'So that's the end of the bastard. Too bad it was impossible to take him alive. Where is Hitler's body?' Zhukov replied that apparently Hitler's body was burned.[200] NKVD troops retrieved the charred remnants of Hitler and Eva and identified the Führer by comparing his dental records with his remaining teeth. They first buried the bodies in Magdeburg. Strangely, Stalin thereafter claimed that Hitler had escaped to Argentina, perhaps to divert attention away from Hitler's unmarked grave in the Soviet zone.

Hitler had turned over power to Admiral Karl Dönitz who with his staff on 2 May flew from Berlin to Flensburg near the Danish border. That night he radio-broadcasted the news that Hitler was dead, he was now Germany's leader and Germany would keep fighting to keep the Soviets from overrunning any more of the nation. He authorized generals facing Western Allied armies to surrender to them. On 6 May, he sent Geneal Alfred Jodl to Eisenhower's headquarters at Reims. Eisenhower rejected Jodl's plea that Germany surrender solely to the Western Allies. After getting Dönitz's permission, Jodl signed an unconditional surrender document to all the Allies on 7 May.

Without instructions liaison General Ivan Susloparov signed for the Soviet Union. Word of that enraged Stalin, who exclaimed: 'Who the hell is this famous Russian General? He will be punished harshly.'[201] Stalin phoned Zhukov to inform him:

> Today, in the town of Reims, the Germans signed an unconditional surrender document. It was the Soviet people who bore the brunt of the war, not the Allies . . . I . . . did not agree to the unconditional surrender being signed in a provincial . . . town and not in Berlin. We reached an agreement with the Allies that the surrender document signed at Reims should be considered the preliminary protocol of surrender. Tomorrow, representatives of the German High Command and the Supreme Command will arrive in Berlin.[202]

He designated Zhukov his representative and told him to find a suitable place for the signing. On 8 May, Zhukov, British General Arthur Tedder, American General Carl Spaatz and French General Jean de Tassigny signed with German General Wilhelm Keitel the unconditional surrender document at a mansion in Karlshorst, a relatively undamaged Berlin suburb.

The Reims and Karlshorst surrender documents differed in the dates they took effect, the former at midnight on 8 May, the later at midnight on 9 May. Ever since, the Western Allies and the Soviets have celebrated Victory in Europe Day (VE-Day) on those two different days.

***

Although the Allies had ended the war in Europe, war still raged across the western Pacific, China and Burma with no end in sight. On 1 April

1945, America's Tenth Army invaded Okinawa Island defended by 75,000 Japanese troops, who nearly all died fighting over the next three months. Hundreds of Kamikaze pilots flew their bomb-packed planes toward American warships and dozens evaded the barrage of anti-aircraft guns to crash into decks and kill and maim thousands of sailors.

Meanwhile, the Americans were trying to realize their vision of spreading democracy, free trade, prosperity and peace throughout the world. The United Nations Conference on International Organization convened with delegations from fifty countries at San Francisco from 25 April to 26 June 1945. Truman reacted angrily to messages that Molotov was making unreasonable demands. He first rejected Molotov's insistence that the conference chair rotate among the Big Four rather than remain the host's traditional seat, in this case American Secretary of State Edward Stettinius. He reluctantly agreed to Molotov's assertion that Soviet 'republics' Ukraine and Belorussian be admitted in the General Assembly but refused a seat for Poland's communist dominated government. Most importantly, he rejected Molotov's demand that the United States not interfere with Soviet relations with the Eastern European countries.

Truman stunned Stalin with two other policies. With the war in Europe won, Truman cancelled Lend-Lease for all recipients on 8 May. He also reduced the proposed low-interest loan to the Soviet Union from $5 billion to $1 billion with the prevailing market interest rate. Stalin and his advisors viewed those acts as designed to weaken the Soviet Union.

Ambassador Harriman remained an outspoken Cassandra. As the war in Europe ended, he warned: 'The Soviet programme in Eastern Europe is the establishment of totalitarianism, ending civil liberty and democracy as we know it.'[203] After Stalin had sixteen leaders of Poland's Home Army arrested and sentenced to ten-year prison terms, Truman asked Harriman why Stalin so blatantly violated his promises to uphold democracy for Poland. Harriman explained:

> I am afraid Stalin does not and never will fully understand our interest in a free Poland as a matter of principle. He is a realist . . . and it is hard for him to appreciate our faith in abstract principles. It is difficult for him to understand why we should want to interfere with a Soviet policy in a country like Poland, which he considers so important to Russia's security, unless we have some ulterior motive.[204]

William Donovan, the Office of Strategic Services chief, presented Truman a less daunting analysis. The 'Problems and Objectives of

United States Policy' concluded that for now American military and economic power far exceeded that of the Soviet Union, which the war had devastated. Although the Soviets would impose communist regimes across Eastern Europe they would not pose a military threat for at least a decade as they rebuilt their shattered country.[205]

***

The Big Three negotiated at the Cecilienhof Palace in Potsdam, a relatively undamaged Berlin suburb, from 15 July to 1 August 1945.[206] Initially the leaders included Truman, Stalin and Churchill. Churchill arrived at Potsdam under a dark political cloud. In Britain, a general election had been held on 5 July, the first since 1935, and he feared the results. The count would take a couple of weeks to complete as bags of ballots arrived in London from troops and sailors who voted on distant fronts around the world.

The initial impressions of Truman and Stalin of each other differed starkly. Truman went to Potsdam hoping to forge a friendly constructive relationship with Stalin like that of Roosevelt. Asked what he thought of the communist tyrant, Truman replied: 'I like Stalin! He is straightforward. Knows what he wants and will compromise when he can't get it.'[207] Stalin reminded Truman of Tom Pendergast, the Kansas City political boss who mentored his political career including his election to the Senate. Stalin masked with geniality his true feelings. When asked to compare the two American presidents, he replied 'They couldn't be compared. Truman was neither educated nor clever.'[208]

The key issues were reparations, the division of Germany's naval and merchant fleet, occupation zone problems in Germany and Berlin, the fate of democracy in Eastern Europe, Poland's borders, the creation of a Council of Foreign Ministers periodically to meet and resolve problems, Stalin's recognition of Chiang Kai-shek as China's head of state and how soon the Soviet Union could war against Japan. To varying degrees, they reached vague or specific 'understandings' on each issue. They agreed to concrete terms on four issues. Poland's borders would shift westward with the country extending between the Curzon Line and the Oder-Neisse River. They would implement a Council of Foreign Ministers. Stalin would sign a friendship treaty with Chiang in return for special Soviet privileges on Manchuria's Southern Railway and the ports of Darien and Port Arthur. The Red Army would attack Japan's army in north-east China and Korea on 8 August and would take from Japan the Kurile Islands and Sakhalin Island's southern half.

Amid the conference, Truman received word on 16 July that the atomic bomb test in New Mexico's desert had surpassed expectations in its destructive power.[209] He excitedly told Churchill and they rejoiced that they could swiftly end the war with Japan. Churchill immediately grasped how much America's atomic bomb could revolutionize geopolitics, if skilfully wielded first militarily then diplomatically:

> To quell the Japanese resistance man by man and conquer the country yard by yard might well require the loss of a million American lives and half that number of British . . . Now all this nightmare had vanished . . . Moreover, we should not need the Russians. The end of the Japanese war no longer depended on their armies for the final and perhaps prolonged slaughter . . . The array of European problems could therefore be faced on their merits and according to the broad principles of the United Nations.[210]

Yet they did not immediately request a meeting with Stalin to explain the just tested atomic bomb's incredible destructive power, that the Soviet Union need not war against Japan, indeed that the atomic bombs would win the war without the loss of another Allied life. Instead, Truman casually mentioned to Stalin that the United State had developed a new vastly destructive weapon. Churchill observed that Stalin looked delighted and said: 'A new bomb! Of extraordinary power! Probably decisive against the Japanese. What a bit of luck.'[211] Stalin already knew about the Manhattan Project from three spies imbedded in it, most notably physicist Klaus Fuchs.

Later Stalin discussed the atomic bomb's implications with Molotov and Gromyko: 'Our allies have told us the U.S.A. has a new weapon. I spoke with our physicist [Igor] Kurchatov as soon as Truman told me. The real question is should countries which have the bomb simply compete with one another or . . . should they seek a solution that would mean prohibition of its production and use?' He knew that the American and British 'are hoping we won't be able to develop the Bomb ourselves for some time' and 'want to force us to accept their plans. Well that's not going to happen.'[212]

Truman, Churchill and Chiang Kai-shek via an intermediary signed on 26 July, the Potsdam Declaration that called on Japan unconditionally to surrender or suffer 'prompt and utter destruction'. An Allied occupation government and troops would disarm and disband Japan's military, conduct war crimes trials, extract reparations for countries devastated by Japan's imperialism and construct a democratic government with full civil rights. Once the occupation government achieved those goals it would withdraw and Japan's new democratic government would enjoy full sovereignty over the country. The Potsdam Declaration was repeatedly broadcast to Japan while B-29s dropped tens of thousands of printed versions over the cities.

Japanese Prime Minister Kantaro Suzuki responded with one word, '*Mokusatsu*', which means to view something with utter loathing and contempt. Upon being told that response, Truman had Secretary of War Stimson implement a previously-decided plan. He had established an Interim Committee of military and scientific experts chaired by Stimson to determine how to use the atomic bomb. On 16 June the committee reported that the most effective way to use the bombs was to drop them without warning on cities until Japan's government surrendered. If the test bomb worked, two other bombs would be available by 1 August. The sooner the atomic bombs were dropped, the sooner the war would end and that would save millions of Japanese lives and hundreds of thousands of American lives. Otherwise, the American military would have to invade Japan itself which consisted of the main island of Honshu, the northern island of Hokkaido and the two southern islands of Kyushu and Shikoku defended by around 3,000,000 soldiers and tens of millions of Japanese militia composed of all able-bodied men and women 16 years and older. The Americans would invade Kyushu on 1 November 1945 and Honshu on 1 March 1946.

Churchill received the election results on 26 July. The Labour Party, led by Clement Atlee, trounced Churchill's Conservative Party and on 27 July, Atlee and Foreign Secretary Ernest Bevin replaced Churchill and Eden at Potsdam. The Big Three finished their conference and each departed for his capital on 1 August.

***

A B-29 dropped an atomic bomb on Hiroshima on 6 August; the explosion immediately killed around 60,000 people and radiation poisoning soon killed tens of thousands more. A B-29 dropped another on Nagasaki on 9 August; the explosion immediately killed around 35,000 people and radiation poisoning soon killed thousands more. That same day, the Red Army launched a massive offensive against Japanese forces in north-east China and Korea.

Despite these devastating blows, Japan's Imperial War Council split between three members determined to fight to the death no matter how many atomic bombs destroyed Japanese cities and three who wanted to surrender. Emperor Hirohito resolved the impasse by agreeing to surrender. On 14 August, he announced on the radio that Japan would surrender. A vast American fleet dropped anchor in Tokyo Bay on 2 September 1945. Aboard the battleship USS *Missouri*, General Douglas MacArthur led the American delegation as they watched the Japanese delegation sign the surrender document.

***

Japan's surrender officially ended the Second World War. The true number of people who died directly and indirectly will never be known. The general estimate is around 25 million military deaths and 50 million civilian deaths, including 27,000,000 Soviets, 20,000,000 Chinese, 7,400,000 Germans, 6,000,000 Poles, 3,100,000 Japanese, 600,000 French, 500,000 Italians, 450,000 British, 420,000 Americans and the rest from around fifty other countries and colonies. The cost of the destruction and lost economic potential is incalculable.[213]

Estimates of the number of Soviet war dead vary considerably depending on the methods and sources. Most experts agree that the Soviet Union suffered as many as 27,000,000 military and civilian deaths. Of the 35,000,000 people who served in the military, from 8,700,000 to 14,700,000 died and 19,700,000 were wounded. The Red Army lost 1,023,093 officers including 631,008 killed and 392,085 missing in action. In all, around 14 per cent of Soviets perished during the war.[214]

The Germans and their allies captured an astonishing number of Soviet troops, 5,700,000, including 3,300,000 in 1941, 1,339,00 in 1942, 487,000 in 1943, 203,000 in 1944 and 41,000 in 1945. Of those, 3,300,300 or 58 per cent died in captivity. That death rate compared to the 3.6 per cent death rate for 232,000 American and British prisoners. Eventually, 1,500,000 Soviet prisoners returned to the Soviet Union.[215] The Soviets captured 3,155,000 German soldiers of whom 1,186,000 or 38 per cent died.[216]

Stalin's paranoia about traitors and spies came true after Germany's invasion. As many as 1,500,000 Soviets served in the German army or administration during the war. Most were rear-echelon forces like truck drivers, stevedores, cooks and labourers but around 500,000 were combat troops recruited from prisoners of war and mostly deployed elsewhere in the Third Reich. The 45,000-man Russian Liberation Army fought on Soviet territory before its remnants withdrew westward. Anti-communists formed the Liberation of the Peoples of Russia movement. Atop that, the Germans forced 5,000,000 Soviets in their occupied territory to labour on various infrastructure projects. In Germany, they used 2,000,000 Soviet prisoners as labourers. Tragically, the Germans alienated far more Soviets than they liberated. Mobile SS killing units followed the German armies to round up and murder Jews and other 'undesirables'. The Germans slaughtered around 2,000,000 of the 5,000,000 Soviet Jews.[217]

Millions of Soviet deaths were self-inflicted in a second 'Great Terror'.[218] The Gulag system numbered 1,929,729 slave labourers on 1 January 1941 and when the war ended, the Gulag held 2,500,000 prisoners. During those years, around 930,000 prisoners perished in the camps and another 530,000 en route to them. As the Red Army pushed the Wehrmacht westward, the secret police rounded up 931,544 suspects in 1943 alone. Around 975,000 inmates were drafted into the military.[219] During 1941 and 1942, various Soviet authorities arrested 994,000 troops for desertion and other crimes, executed 157,000 of them and sent 420,000 to punitive units and 440,000 to prison. In contrast, the German military executed only around 15,000 servicemen for capital crimes. Viktor Abakumov ruthlessly commanded the Counterintelligence Directorate or Smersh. During the war, he presided over the arrests and executions of thousands of officers, including thirty-five generals on trumped-up treason charges. Beria issued this report to Stalin:

> In 1943, the troops of the NKVD who are responsible for security in the rear of the Active Red Army in the process of clearing the territory liberated from the enemy, arrested 931,549 people . . . Of these, 582,515 were servicemen and 349,034 were civilians. Of the total number, 80,296 have been unmasked and detained (as spies, traitors, members of punitive squads, deserters, bandits and similar criminal elements).[220]

The communists rounded up and deported to distant, harsh lands 2,600,000 people including ethnic Germans, Finns, Latvians, Lithuanians, Estonians, Greeks, Kurds, Georgian Muslims (Meshki), Armenian Muslims (Khemshchiny), Kalmyks, Chechens, Ingush, Karachai and Balbars.[221] The largest numbers included 1,500,000 Volga Germans, 520,000 Chechens and Ingushes and 300,000 Koreans. Disease, starvation and murder killed hundreds of thousands of the deportees on the way to or in their new settlements.[222]

Around 1,500,000 Soviet military and 2,500,000 civilian prisoners returned to the Soviet Union after the war. Stalin feared that the returnees were infected with liberal ideas that could undermine and even overthrow his regime. For precedent, he cited the Decembrist movement of Russian officers who had fought in western Europe during the Napoleonic Wars then conspired to transform Russia from an absolute into a constitutional monarchy. In 1825, Tsar Nicholas I had his secret police and soldiers round up the Decembrists for trials then execution for the leaders and Siberian penal colonies for the rest. For the Soviet military returnees, Stalin sent 10 per cent home, drafted 43 per cent into the army, sent 22 per cent to labour battalions and imprisoned 15 per cent in the Gulag.[223]

Stalin presided over a victory parade in Red Square on 24 June. To his rage, the white horse he was supposed to ride at the parade's head threw him during practice a few days before, although only his pride was seriously hurt. He reluctantly had Zhukov take his place and watched the parade from atop Lenin's Mausoleum with the other political and military leaders. The war in Europe was over, the war in the Far East would soon end, but a new war, a so-called Cold War would soon engulf the world.[224]

Chapter 8

COLD WAR

> 'This war is not as in the past; whoever occupies a territory also imposes on it his own social system. Everyone imposes his own system as far as his army has power to do so. It cannot be otherwise.' (Joseph Stalin)

> 'The Soviet programme in Eastern Europe is the establishment of totalitarianism, ending civil liberty and democracy as we know it.' (Ambassador Averell Harriman)

> 'Hitler's aim was to spread the power of the Nazis to the ends of the earth. Stalin's aim is to spread the power of the communists to the ends of the earth. Stalin, like Hitler, will not stop. He can only be stopped.' (Ambassador William Bullitt)

A cold war is a conflict in which each side wields every means except direct violence to undermine and, ideally, defeat the other. History's most crucial cold war – the Cold War – was between America and its allies versus the Soviet Union and its allies from 1947 to 1991.[1] From August 1945 to March 1947, the wartime alliance of America and Britain with the Soviet Union transformed into a Cold War that would last 44 years. A dynamic among three forces caused the Cold War, unreconcilable ideological and geopolitical conflicts exacerbated by the 'mirror image' each held of itself as personifying righteousness and of the other as personifying evil.

The Cold War's geopolitical and ideological causes were inseparable. Stalin asserted that the Second World War was historically unique as three ideologies struggled against each other, liberalism, fascism and communism. That offered unprecedented disasters for its losers and unprecedented spoils for its victors: 'This war is not as in the past; whoever occupies a territory also imposes on it his own social system. Everyone imposes his own system as far as his army can reach.'[2] He was exuberant after the Red Army overran half of Europe, imposing in its wake communist regimes beholden to Moscow in each country. He believed that history had reached a critical stage where the 'correlation of international forces' now favoured communism with revolutions mushrooming around the globe. He triumphantly declared: 'Our victory means above all that our social system has won . . . Our political system has won.'[3] Before leaving for the Potsdam summit with Truman and Churchill, Stalin shared this vision before an multinational conference of communists:

> The crisis of capitalism has manifested itself in the division of the capitalists into two factions – one fascist, the other democratic. The alliance between ourselves and the democratic faction of the capitalists came about because the latter had a stake in preventing Hitler's domination . . . We are currently allied with one faction against the other, but in the future we will be against the first faction of capitalists.[4]

A set of security dilemmas trapped both sides throughout the Cold War. Each side interpreted everything the other side did in the worst way, as an act of premeditated aggression, then responded with some 'get tough' act. Thus did initially questionable assumptions become hard persistent reality. The 'lesson' from 1930s British and French diplomacy toward the fascist powers was that appeasement invites and resistance deters aggression. The belief that the other side will view any concession as a sign of weakness deters oneself from making low- or no-cost gestures that might entice the other side to reciprocate, thus defusing rather than bolstering a crisis or chronic problem. Neither side wanted World War III and both sides believed that only military strength deterred an attack by the other. That drove each side to not just 'stand its ground' but expand its military power and allies. Each side pointed to the other's increases to justify its own. Thus did each side trap itself in a soaring arms and ally race.

Ideologically, liberalism and communism are diametrically opposed and committed to the other's destruction. The usual result is that most negotiations between liberals and communists become dialogues of the deaf. They may use the same expressions but with conflicting meanings. For liberals, free elections involve any citizen freely running for office alone or in a political party of his choice and voters freely choosing among candidates with each vote counted equally. For communists, the Communist Party choses candidates and parties to run and win, manipulating votes accordingly. So when Roosevelt and Churchill insisted that Stalin promise to hold free elections in Eastern

European countries, they naturally expected the liberal version and Stalin naturally delivered the communist version.

Compounding that dilemma is a fundamental difference over the nature of truth. For liberals, truth is based on facts which are provable; anything else is either an idea, delusion or lie. Of course, they recognize that at times leaders will conceal the truth or even tell mistruths but rarely and only to protect vital security interests including sources and methods of intelligence gathering. To Stalin at the 1943 Tehran conference, Churchill famously remarked that 'In wartime truth is so precious that she must always be protected by a bodyguard of lies'.[5] For communists, 'truth' is always relative aside from the historical truth of class conflict. Communists lie with impunity to advance their interests. Of course, communists lose credibility the more they lie and the more easily their lies are exposed, the 'little boy who cried wolf' syndrome. But communists understand that most people prefer simple myths or lies that reflect their beliefs, hopes, prejudices and fears rather than the often complex and paradoxical hard truths that challenge them.

***

Geopolitically, Soviet imperialism was most blatant before the eyes of Western military and diplomatic officials in West Germany and Berlin.[6] The Soviets got around 40 per cent of Germany's territory, 36 per cent of its population and 33 per cent of its industry. In Berlin, they got eight boroughs while the British and Americans each got six boroughs. The British later gave the French two of their Berlin boroughs while the Americans gave the French a zone in south-west Germany.[7]

The Allies were supposed to govern Berlin and Germany through an Allied Command Council. That soon became an acrimonious snake-pit of accusations of unfulfilled promises and deliberate obstructionism among the representatives. Around 2,200,000 people lived in the three western Berlin sectors. The Soviets played every trick they could to impede the Western Allies from assuming control over those zones. They refused to send any food, fuel and other vital supplies to the western zones so the Allies had to ship everything from West Germany through the East German zone to their Berlin sectors. Meanwhile, around 5,000,000 refugees fled communism to America's German zone and virtually all of them had to be fed and housed with the adults productively employed and the children schooled as soon as possible. The cost of feeding those refugees was $1.5 billion in 1945 alone.[8]

The Soviet Military Government systematically stripped not just East Germany but the western zones of factories, equipment, vehicles, natural resources, consumer goods, household furnishings and anything else of economic value. Stalin had Malenkov and Beria oversee the transfer of much of East Germany's industry to the Soviet Union. In all, they supervised East Germany's loss and the Soviet Union's gain of 'some 1,500 plants and factories, 1,115,000 pieces of equipment and 2,000,000 million jobs'.[9] The official Soviet count for loot up to 8 July 1945, was $1.5 billion with

> 400,000 railway wagons of war booty . . . dispatched from Germany to Russia, containing, among other things, 60,149 pianos, 45,8612 radios, 188,071 carpets, 941,605 pieces of furniture, 3,338,348 pairs of shoes and 1,005,503 hats. Interspersed with those household items were 24 railway wagons of museum pieces, 154 wagons of furs and valuable glassware, more than 2 million tons of grain and 20 million litres of alcohol. A total of 2,885 German factories were slated to be dismantled and shipped to Russia by 1946.[10]

Having conquered Eastern Europe, the Soviets changed the rail gauge throughout the region to the wider Russian version. That effectively severed easy rail access to western Europe. Politically, the Soviet Military Government forced the German Social Democratic Party (SDP) led by Otto Grotewohl to unite with the German Communist Party (KPD) led by Wilhelm Peck to form a Social Unity Party (SED).

The one issue that united the Soviets, Americans and British was denazification or purging Nazis from public posts in their respective zones and prosecuting war criminals. The war crimes trial at Nuremberg was denazification's showcase. The trial lasted from 20 November 1945 to 1 October 1946 with four judges and four prosecutors, one each from the United States, Soviet Union, Britain and France. Initially the Office of Chief Counsel for War Crimes indicted twenty-four defendants on charges of war crimes and crimes against humanity and peace. Two had evaded capture so twenty-two stood trial with Hermann Göring the highest ranking Nazi. The judges found nineteen guilty, sentenced twelve for death by hanging and seven to prison and acquitted three; Göring cheated the hangman by committing suicide. The Counsel for War Crimes identified at least 2,500 other suspects, but only brought 177 to trial, of which 112 were found guilty and 25 executed and the rest imprisoned.[11]

***

The first post-war crisis was over petroleum-rich Iran. After Germany invaded the Soviet Union on 22 June 1941, Iran's Reza Shah Pahlavi expressed sympathy for Nazi Germany. To prevent him from allying with Berlin, Churchill and Stalin agreed jointly to occupy Iran with their forces respectively in the south and north of the country in August 1941, to be withdrawn within six months of the end of the war. They forced Reza to abdicate in favour of his pliable son Mohammed Reza Pahlavi on 16 September. Roosevelt dispatched a small token force to Tehran, the capital. When the war ended, the Americans and British withdrew their contingents. Stalin not only kept Soviet troops in northern Iran but demanded petroleum concessions and announced the establishment of the autonomous communist-controlled Azerbaijan Republic in north-western Iran across the border from the Soviet Union's Azerbaijan Republic.

Truman protested those violations and encouraged the Iranians to issue a formal complaint to the United Nations Security Council on 19 January 1946. The Soviets threatened to veto any Security Council resolution against them. On 5 March, the same day as Churchill's Iron Curtain speech, Truman issued Stalin a formal demand to withdraw from Iran. Stalin and Shah Mohammed agreed that the Soviet Union would withdraw its troops from Iran and its recognition of the communist controlled Azerbaijan Republic in north-western Iran. The Iranian army restored control over that region and destroyed Stalin's puppet state.

***

In China, the civil war resumed between Chiang Kai-shek's Nationalist Party with its capital at Chunking and Mao Zedong's Communist Party with its capital at Yenan.[12] Stalin's policy toward China was typically Janus-faced. In the Treaty of Friendship and Alliance signed on 14 August 1945, the Soviets recognized Chiang's regime, promised to stop aiding the Communist Party and withdraw Soviet troops from China, in return for which Chiang recognized the independence of Outer Mongolia, a communist country allied with Moscow and agreed to joint administration of Manchuria's rail network. Meanwhile, Stalin turned over captured military supplies to Mao's Red Army.

Truman dispatched 50,000 troops to China's coastal cities to disarm Japan's military and keep order while Nationalist military units arrived to take over. He sent what became billions of dollars of economic and military aid to Chiang's regime, but most of it was looted and squandered. In December 1945, Truman dispatched General George

Marshall to China to forge a ceasefire between the Nationalists and Communists as the first step toward a coalition government between them. The belligerents agreed to a ceasefire in February 1946 but soon resumed fighting. Chiang and Mao each confidently expected to win the civil war. One of them was prescient.

***

Soviet imperialism had its limits. One vital constraint was economic. Stalin faced a worsening economic crisis after Truman ended Lend-Lease. The war had destroyed about 30 per cent of the Soviet economy. Farm production in 1945 was 80 per cent of the 1914 level. The official Soviet count

> included the total or partial destruction of 1,700 towns, 70,000 villages, 6,000,000 buildings, 84,000 schools, 43,000 libraries, 31,000 factories and 1,300 bridges. Also demolished were 98,000 kolkhozes [collective farms] and 1,876 sovkhozes [agricultural factories]. The Soviet economy lost 137,000 tractors and 79,000 combine-harvesters as well as 7,000,000 horses, 17,000,000 head of cattle, 20,000,000 hogs and 27,000,000 sheep and goats.[13]

As with the population, much economic destruction was self-inflicted. The Kremlin's scorched earth strategy as the Red Army retreated in 1941, combat over three years and the Germans' scorched earth strategy as they withdrew rendered most of the western Soviet Union a wasteland of destroyed cities, towns and collective farms. Around 26,000,000 people fled the fighting and returned to find their homes and jobs in rubble. Around a million orphans were among the homeless. Somehow the state had to find shelter, food and jobs for all those desperate people.

Stalin and his regime had to rebuild the Soviet Union, but their communist ideology straitjacketed that effort. Using markets to determine prices and profits to entice enterprise was, of course, anathema. All they could do was impose the latest Five-Year Plan with countless contrived production allocations, prices and quotas.

As a result, mass death did not end with the war. A bad harvest and famine in 1946 exacerbated by chronic collectivization malnourished 100,000,000 Soviets and killed 1,000,000 of them from starvation and disease.[14] Stalin's mass enslavements and murders persisted into the post-war years. Interior Minister Sergei Kruglov reported to Stalin that Gulag prisoners increased from 2,199,535 in 1948 to 2,550,275, with 366,489 serving terms of more than ten years in 1950, along with twenty-seven new camps built.[15]

Treating people as 'enemies of the people' became self-fulfilling. Not everyone went meekly to prison or death. Groups of desperate people preferred to die on their feet rather than submit on their knees to the communist regime. Several hundred 'bandit groups' in Estonia, Latvia and Lithuania committed over 8,000 'counterrevolutionary' attacks against Stalinism from 1944 to 1946, during which over 13,000 civilian and military personnel were killed. There were 14,400 'terrorist raids' in Ukraine from July 1944 to March 1953. Just in Lithuania, the Red Army and NKVD killed over 25,000 guerrillas in 1947 and 1948. Most resistance was non-violent. Workers went on strike for eight-hour days, higher wages and more benefits.[16]

Despite all the disruptions, the Soviet economy gradually recovered and food shortages diminished. Demobilizing most of the Red Army and deploying those able-bodied men and women to factories, fields, mines and construction sites was critical for reconstruction. From 1945 to 1948, the Red Army fell from 11,365,000 to 2,874,000 troops.[17] The Soviet Union slowly recovered from the war's devastation. The Soviet population was 194,000,000 in 1940 and 178,500,000 in 1950, even after a post-war baby boom.[18]

***

Stalin gave the Soviet spy agencies their latest names, with the Committee of Intelligence to oversee the First Directorate of State Security (MGB) and the Main Intelligence Directorate (GRU). He instructed ambassadors to prioritize supervising intelligence gathering and other covert operations. Stalin hated the paradox that his foreign policies vitally depended on intelligence gathered and analysed from people he distrusted. Molotov expressed that suspicion: 'I believe that one cannot rely upon the intelligence officers. One should listen to them, but it is necessary to check up on them. The intelligence officers can lead you to a very dangerous position . . . There are many provocateurs here, there and everywhere.'[19]

Post-war Soviet intelligence suffered handicaps. Stalin had wiped out most of the intelligence community during the 1930s purges. A new generation of spies took their place but were inhibited by inexperience and terror that they might be recalled if they took any initiative. Nonetheless, Soviet espionage scored some brilliant victories.[20]

During the early 1930s, NKVD Officer Yuri Modin recruited what became known as the 'Cambridge Five' for their ties to the university and at least another half-dozen other traitors may have been in the spy ring. Of the Five, Harold 'Kim' Philby and Guy Burgess became senior British Secret Intelligence Service (MI6, like CIA) officials, Donald Maclean a MI5 (like FBI) official and Anthony Blunt and John Cairncross Foreign Office officials. Philby and Maclean eventually defected to the Soviet Union and the other three escaped prosecution. Together they passed critical intelligence to Moscow.[21]

Naturally, the United States was the number one target country. In America, no matter what the name of the organization they worked for, Soviet agents never stopped recruiting spies and sponsoring front organizations to undermine American democracy. Among the most influential American traitors who spied for Moscow were Alger Hiss of the State Department and Dexter White of the Treasury Department. Hiss became president of the Carnegie Endowment for International Peace in 1946. White became an IMF board member in 1947. Hiss was eventually convicted of perjury but not espionage.

The spies who passed nuclear weapons secrets to Moscow inflicted the worst damage to American national security. They either worked in the nuclear complex or acted as conduits to NKVD agents. The first post-war spy scandal erupted on 26 February 1946, when Canada's government announced that it had arrested and charged with espionage twenty-two people in a plot to steal and give nuclear arms secrets to Moscow. Other Soviet spies later uncovered included Klaus Fuchs, Harry Gold, David Greenglass, Theodore Hall, George Koval and Julius and Ethel Rosenberg; the Rosenbergs were found guilty of espionage and executed on 19 June 1953.[22]

In America alone, there were scores of communist front organizations and tens of thousands of communist sympathizers, many as much from as an affected far-left fashion sense as from conviction, especially among academics and bohemians.[23] Among the most prominent fronts was the National Citizens Political Action Committee founded by radical labour activist Eliner Gimbel in 1944 and renamed the Progressive Citizens of America (PCA) during a congress at New York in December 1946. Within a year, the organization boasted 25,000 members. The best-known PAC member was Henry Wallace, an ill-disguised communist sympathizer who President Franklin Roosevelt appointed Agriculture Secretary from 1933 to 1940, Vice President from 1941 to 1945 and Commerce Secretary from 1945 to 1946 until President Harry Truman fired him. Wallace contested and lost against Truman for the 1948 Democratic Party's presidential nominee. Whether Wallace ever passed secrets to Moscow has not been verified.

In Congress, the House Committee on Un-American Activities (HUAC) investigated allegations of communist spies and sympathizers infiltrating American government, labour unions and Hollywood. Former communists turned informants Whittaker Chambers, Elizabeth Bentley and Louis Budenz testified on how pervasive the infiltration was.

Scores of genuine American traitors worked for the Soviet Union, but there were legions of imagined spies and subversives. The paranoia seeping through America provoked the worst in many people. On 9 February 1950, Senator Joseph McCarthy of Wisconsin falsely claimed to have a list of 205 spies in the State Department alone and insisted that communists riddled all federal departments and agencies including the Defence Department and CIA. That inaugurated what became known as McCarthyism, when the senator and other far right politicians and pundits made hundreds of false accusations against people that destroyed their careers and sometimes their lives from suicide.[24] In Moscow, Stalin and his coterie gloated as Americans turned viciously against each other and their democratic political system.

A number of left-leaning American intellectuals squared off with communism. Arthur Schlesinger and theologian Reinhold Niebuhr founded the Americans for Democratic Action (ADC) in January 1947. *Partisan Review*'s editors – Sidney Hook, William Philips and Philip Rahv – were the boldest to square-off with Stalinists and other variants of communism. They devoted four bimonthly 1947 issues to essays exploring and debating 'The Future of Socialism'. An array of liberal and socialist intellectuals, including Melvin Lasky, Sidney Hook, James Burnham, Alfred Kazin and Arthur Koestler, founded the Congress for Cultural Freedom on 25 June 1950. The site, West Berlin, could not have been more appropriate.[25]

Three left-leaning writers had no delusions about the totalitarian nature of Stalin, the Soviet Union and communism. Their brilliant novels that revealed Stalinism's pathologies were Aldous Huxley's *Brave New World* (1932), Arthur Koestler's *Darkness at Noon* (1940) and George Orwell's *Nineteen Eighty-Four* (1948). Orwell captured the mindset of apologists and dupes for Stalin in his essay, 'Politics and the English Language'. He wrote:

> Consider, for instance, some comfortable English professor defending Russian totalitarianism. He cannot say outright, 'I believe in killing off your opponents when you say you can get good results by doing so.' Probably . . . he will say something like this: 'While freely conceding that the Soviet regime exhibits certain features which the humanitarian may be inclined to deplore, we must, I think, agree, that a certain curtailment of the right to

> political opposition is an inevitable concomitant of transitional periods and the rigors of which the Russian people have been called upon to undergo have been amply justified in the sphere of concrete achievement.'[26]

***

President Truman welcomed Winston Churchill to the White House during his visit to the United States in February and March 1945. Churchill agreed to Truman's request that he give the commencement address at Westminster College in Fulton, Missouri. With Truman beside him, he delivered what was soon dubbed his 'Iron Curtain Speech' on 5 March 1946.[27]

Churchill warned Americans and the rest of the free world that:

> A shadow has fallen upon the scenes so lately lighted by the Allied victory . . . Nobody knows what Soviet Russia and its Communist international organization intends to do in the immediate future or what are the limits, if any, to their expansive and proselytizing tendencies . . . From Stettin in the Baltic to Trieste in the Adriatic, an Iron Curtain has descended across the continent. Behind that line lie the capitals of the ancient states of central and Eastern Europe. Warsaw, Berlin, Prague, Vienna, Budapest and Sofia, all the famous cities and the populations around them lie in what I must call the Soviet sphere and all are subject . . . to a very high and increasing measure of control by Moscow.[28]

Despite Churchill's warning, Truman hesitated to declare Cold War against the Soviet Union. Indeed, he and his advisors debated what to do with the atomic bomb power in their hands.[29] Cassandras argued that nuclear power was America's political and military ace in the hole that deterred a Soviet attack on western Europe and might be wielded in crises to resolve them favourably for America. Appeasers argued that nuclear weapons were so devastating that they should never again be used in war and instead the technology should be given to the United Nations for safe-keeping. Churchill succinctly explained what America could have done with the bomb and why it failed to do so: 'For a time when the United States was the sole effective possessor of nuclear weapons, there had been a chance of a general and permanent settlement with the Soviet Union. But it is not the nature of democracies to use their advantages in threatening or dictatorial ways.'[30]

Truman opted for a middle position, keeping nuclear power but not threatening to use it if Stalin did not agree to American demands. He explained America's nuclear bomb policy during a speech on 27 October 1945:

> In our possession of this weapon . . . there is no threat to any nation. The world, which has seen the United States in two recent wars, knows that full well. The possession in our hands of this new power of destruction we regard as a sacred trust. Because of our love of peace, the thoughtful people of the world know that that trust will not be violated, that it will be faithfully executed.[31]

Truman reconsidered that policy after listening to Vannevar Bush, who headed the wartime Office of Scientific Research and Development that managed the Manhattan Project. Bush argued that the Soviets would eventually develop nuclear weapons, but the United States might prevent that with a treaty whereby both sides gave up their existing technologies and opened their laboratories to the United Nations which would form the Atomic Energy Commission for that oversight. Truman embraced that policy on 7 November 1945 and named Bernard Baruch to be America's representative to the UN's Atomic Energy Commission.

Baruch was a self-made millionaire financier, generous Democratic Party donor and advisor to Roosevelt and Truman. On 14 June 1946, he presented what was soon dubbed the Baruch Plan whereby the Soviet Union would renounce its development of nuclear weapons and open all its nuclear facilities to AEC inspection in return for which the United States would transfer its nuclear weapons to the AEC but retain nuclear bomb grade uranium and plutonium. Soviet Ambassador Andrei Gromyko replied on 19 June that first the United States must surrender its nuclear arsenal to the AEC after which the Soviet Union would accept AEC inspections. The Truman White House insisted on the Baruch Plan. On 29 October, Foreign Minister Molotov denounced the Baruch Plan for maintaining America's nuclear monopoly. The Atomic Energy Commission voted ten to two, with the Soviet Union and Poland abstaining, for the Baruch Plan on 30 December 1946, but the next day when the resolution appeared before the Security Council, the Soviets vetoed it.

***

Soviet aggression in one country after another around the world and their diplomats' bad manners and wild accusations confounded Secretary of State James Byrnes. He asked George Kennan, the deputy ambassador in Moscow, to explain Soviet behaviour, capabilities and intentions.[32] Arguably, Kennan was the most influential State Department official who never became Secretary of State. After getting an undergraduate degree in history from Princeton University, he entered the foreign service and served in Geneva and Riga, got an advanced degree in Russian studies from the University of Berlin, then served in Moscow under Ambassador William Bullitt alongside colleague Charles Bohlen. When Joseph Davies, a Stalin apologist, became ambassador, Kennan transferred to Lisbon and then London. When Averell Harriman became ambassador in Moscow, he asked for Kennan to be his deputy.

During his second stint in Moscow, Kennan fathered the containment strategy. He responded to Byrnes' query with an 8,000-word 'Long Telegram' that he sent on 22 February 1946 and publicly expanded his analysis with his 'Mr. X' article 'The Sources of Soviet Conduct' in the July 1947 edition of the journal *Foreign Affairs* and in his *Memoirs*.[33] In those essays Kennan elaborated Winston Churchill's famed explanation of the Soviet Union: 'I cannot forecast to you the action of Russia. It is a riddle wrapped in a mystery inside an enigma; but perhaps there is a key. That key is Russian national interests.'[34]

In full accord, Kennan explained some of the paradoxes:

> We are incapable of understanding the role of contradiction in Russian life. The Anglo-Saxon instinct is to attempt to smooth away contradictions, to reconcile opposing elements, to achieve something in the nature of an acceptable common ground as the basis for life. The Russian tends to deal only in extremes and he is not particularly concerned to reconcile them. To him contradiction is a familiar thing. It is the essence of Russia . . . [P]rolonged sloth and sudden feats of energy, exaggerated cruelty and exaggerated kindness, ostentatious wealth and dismal squalor, violent xenophobia and uncontrollable yearning for contact with the foreign world, vast power and the most abject slavery . . . these are only some of the contractions which dominate the life of the Russian people.[35]

Thus were Russians culturally predisposed to embrace communism's contradictions, absurdities, repression, exploitation and violence. The Soviet Union was a totalitarian version of autocratic Russia and Soviet foreign policy was a communist version of traditional Russian foreign policy. Over 1,200 years, Russian leaders sought security by expanding their empire ever further outward ideally to easily defended rivers, seas, mountains and deserts. Communism ideologically justified Moscow's promotion of communist revolutions around the world. Stalin's 'socialism in one country' policy was a reaction to the failure of those efforts.

Communists claim to be internationalists who understand what they insist is history's core dynamic – class struggle. In reality, their ideology's simple-minded shibboleths straitjacket and blind them to history's complexities along with fundamental human decencies, thus rendering them ignorant, parochial, paranoid and dogmatic. And that poses a dilemma for Western statesmen and diplomats who must negotiate with them. Kennan explained:

> These prominent Soviet leaders know little of the outside world. They have no personal knowledge of foreign statesmen. To them the vast pattern of international life, political and economic, can provide no associations, can hold no significance, except in the way they conceive to be its bearing on the problems of Russian security and Russian internal life. It is possible that the conceptions of these men might occasionally achieve a rough approximation to reality and their judgments a similar approximation to fairness; but it is unlikely.[36]

Soviet foreign policy was opportunistic, not programmed, adaptive, not rigid. They would probe for weaknesses and seize any they found but would withdraw before determined opposition. They behaved like thieves in a hotel corridor at night, trying each door until they found one that was open, but even then would likely retreat hastily if the occupant resisted. In diplomacy, the Soviets were often rude, boastful, insulting and threatening. Western diplomats should stay firm, calm and patient, acting like mature adults toward petulant children and should make concessions only if the Soviets reciprocated with their own.

The Soviet post-war threat was political, not military. Communist Parties would politically fatten off the mass poverty, joblessness, homelessness and despair of people in the war-devastated countries of Europe and Asia. If they won power through democratic elections they would eventually establish dictatorships allied with the Soviet Union. Militarily, the Red Army was impressive on paper with over five million personnel. Yet, Lend Lease's cancellation made supplying all those troops increasingly burdensome. Stalin would have to rapidly reduce the military's size to free able-bodied men and women to rebuild the Soviet Union's shattered cities, industries and infrastructure.

The United States could thwart or 'contain' the Soviet Union's political threat by extending first humanitarian aid that alleviated immediate problems of famine, sickness and homelessness and then long-term development aid that rebuilt cities, industries and infrastructure. The existing International Monetary Fund (IMF) and International Bank for Reconstruction and Development (IRBD, World Bank) would supplement American economic aid with their own low interest loans to needy countries. The IMF's fixed currency system based on a gold standard worth $32 an ounce was critical to stabilizing and promoting global commerce. A future World Trade Organization that required members to dismantle their trade and investment barriers would further expand the global economy by stimulating international commerce. Here too the United States would lead by opening its own markets to foreign trade and investment. Transforming mass poverty into mass prosperity would eliminate communism's political appeal and thus its threat. As for military power, eventually the Soviets would rebuild their army but would wield it mostly to crush rebellions within their empire. The United States, western European countries and Japan should have militaries powerful enough to deter Soviet aggression and stimulate rather than burden their economies.

So the 'containment strategy' would be 'selective' in two ways, by emphasizing economic means and concentrating its programmes on western Europe and Japan.[37] Once those industrialized countries revived and integrated their trade and investments with the United States, the entire global economy would prosper and peace would prevail.

Communist takeovers of poor, pre-industrial countries like China or Yugoslavia did not pose any threat. Most revolutionaries in poor countries were stronger nationalists than communists. Washington should try to co-opt rather than resist communist revolutions in Latin America, Africa and Asia. Sooner or later the communist regime would have to open the country to international trade and investment to survive and develop. And that eventually would wean them from communism and ties with Moscow. Likewise, the European overseas empires were doomed to extinction as their myriad peoples sought to govern themselves. The Americans should encourage the British, French and other imperial Europeans gracefully to nurture their colonies to independence; trying to crush independence movements would only make them more radical, violent, vengeful and more likely to turn to Moscow for help. Kennan predicted that if Washington followed this selective containment strategy, communism would disappear within two or three generations. And his prediction came true.

***

Kennan's analysis reached the White House just as a crisis flared with Stalin. The Soviets threatened Greece and Turkey in what had been Britain's sphere of influence in the eastern Mediterranean.[38] A civil war raged in Greece between the non-communist government and communist rebels. Stalin secretly aided the communists while denying to London and Washington that he was doing so. On 7 June 1945, Stalin had Molotov issue Turkey the first of a series of demands to transfer the former Russian provinces of Kars and Ardagan in eastern Turkey to the Soviet Union and let the Soviets construct a naval base within and warships transit the straits between the Black and Mediterranean Seas. In 1922, Lenin had ceded those provinces to Turkey in return for a peace treaty. The 1936 Montreux Convention, which Stalin did not sign, prevented any warships other than Turkey's from navigating the Straits, thus bottling up the Soviet's Black Sea fleet. Stalin was determined to cancel those humiliating concessions and restrictions. The British sent military and economic aid to both beleaguered countries, but financial constraints prevented any more after 31 March 1947. Prime Minister Clement Atlee informed Washington, Athens and Ankara of that deadline and asked Truman for the United States to fill that void.

That provoked a debate among Truman and his advisors over what to do. Eventually they embraced Kennan's analysis and advice. Truman called a joint session of Congress for 12 March 1947, during which he explained the global problem America and the free world faced and how to overcome it:

> At the present time in world history nearly every nation must choose between alternative ways of life. The choice too often is not a free one. One way of life is based upon the will of the majority and is distinguished by free institutions, representative government, free elections, guarantee of individual liberty, freedom of speech and religion and freedom from political oppression. The second way of life is based on the will of a minority forcibly imposed upon the majority. It relies upon terror and oppression, a controlled press and radio, fixed elections and the suppression of personal freedom. I believe it must be the policy of the United States to support free peoples who are resisting attempted subjugation by armed minorities or by outside pressures.[39]

Congress approved the $400 million Greek-Turkish aid bill with a Senate vote of 67 to 23 and House vote of 287 to 107.

The Truman administration followed that up with a momentous announcement by Secretary of State George Marshall during his commencement address at Harvard University on 5 June.[40] Under the European Recovery Program, soon dubbed the Marshall Plan, the United States would provide what eventually became $17 billion to reconstruct its war-shattered economies and restore the continent to prosperity. Washington called on recipients to form the Organization for European Economic Cooperation (OEEC) to receive and distribute the aid. In doing so, America fathered what eventually became the European Union.

Congress passed the European Economic Recovery Act with the initial $5 billion tranche by a House vote of 329 to 74 and a Senate vote of 69 to 17. Meanwhile Congress passed a series of foreign aid bills for Japan that eventually amounted to $2.2 billion. The State Department formed the Economic Cooperation Administration to supervise the aid distribution to and implementation by recipients. Much of the aid was tied to purchases of American goods and services to stimulate trans-Atlantic trade and prosperity.

Marshall Plan aid was available to any country that requested it, including the Soviet Union and its Eastern European puppet regimes. Sixteen western European countries initially formed and joined the OEEC on 12 July. That posed a dilemma for Stalin. The Soviet bloc desperately needed economic aid but taking it might undermine the Kremlin's rule by pulling those captive countries westward into the OEEC. He had Molotov denounce the Marshall Plan.

Truman and Congressional internationalists worked together to devise and pass the National Security Act, which he signed on 26 July 1947. The bill gave the United State the policymaking, military and intelligence organizations vital to fighting the Cold War against the Soviet Union and its allies. The War and Navy Departments were dissolved into a Defense Department headed by a Defense Secretary and overseen by the Joint Chief of Staff that included a Chair, Vice Chair and the secretaries of the army, navy, air force and marines. A Central Intelligence Agency (CIA) was created to gather and analyse intelligence and perform covert actions designed to favourably shape politics in foreign countries in America's favour. CIA had a directorate for administration, recruitment and training; an operations division that gathered intelligence and conducted covert actions overseas; an analytical division that interpreted the intelligence; and a science and technology division that provided needed services. The CIA director had two duties, one to manage his own organization and the other to coordinate intelligence gathering and analysis with other government agencies. A National Security Council (NSC) was created, made up of the president, vice president and other key department heads and the CIA director and was headed by a National Security Advisor (NSA) to complement the State Department. While the State Department dealt with long-term relations with foreign countries and international organizations, the NSC would focus on managing crises and other immediate threats to American security. The NSC was organized like a mini-State Department with regional and functional sections but numbered a couple of hundred experts compared to thousands of State Department employees.

The Truman administration organized a conference at Rio de Janeiro of diplomats from the countries of the Western Hemisphere. On 2 September 1947, they signed the Rio Pact Inter-American Treaty of Reciprocal Assistance. In doing so, the United States formally realized President Roosevelt's vision of America acting as the Hemisphere's 'policeman.' That was the first major American effort to promote pro-western regional organizations in poor parts of the world.

***

The Middle East was increasingly a disputed Cold War region. After the First World War, the British and French had split the Ottoman Empire's Middle Eastern provinces between them as League of Nations mandates eventually to be nurtured into independent countries. The French got Lebanon and Syria and the British got Palestine, Jordan and the three provinces of Basra, Baghdad and Mosul which they combined to create Iraq. In the 1890s, the Zionist movement arose to establish a Jewish state in Palestine. Foreign Secretary Arthur Balfour had promised Lionel Rothschild, who headed Britain's Zionists, that Britain was committed to obtaining a 'national homeland' for Jews after the war. Although Jewish communities lived in Palestine, most people were Arab Muslims. During the 1920s and 1930, ever more Jews migrated to Palestine. Tensions worsened among Jews, Muslims and British until a three-way war erupted among them amid the Second World War and persisted through 1946 and 1947 as Jewish survivors of concentration camps tried to immigrate to Palestine. The British gave up their mandate to the United Nations. General Assembly Resolution 181 would split Palestine into a mostly Muslim state and a mostly Jewish state six months after passage. On 29 November 1947, the General Assembly passed Resolution 181 by 33 in favour, 13 opposed and 10 abstentions.

The two-state solution for the Palestine war was a rare example of accord between Washington and Moscow. President Truman believed that both peoples, but especially the Jews, deserved their own countries despite being advised by the State Department that doing so might jeopardize American relations with Arab states. Stalin intended to forge strong relations with both countries and broker any disputes between them. He hoped eventually to transform both countries into communist client states.

The Arab states opposed partition, prevented the Palestinians from forming an independent state and went to war against Israel when it declared independence on 14 May 1948. The Israelis eventually defeated the Arabs and negotiated armistices with each but the Arabs did not recognize Israel's right to exist.

***

Britain, France, Belgium, the Netherlands and Luxembourg signed a treaty that formed the Brussels Pact or Western European Union military alliance on 17 March 1948. Stalin retaliated on 1 April, by having East German troops and police inspect all travellers passing between the western German zones and Berlin through the Soviet zone on trains and highways. That led to long delays.[41]

General Lucius Clay, who commanded occupation troops in America's sector in Germany and Berlin, warned the Truman White House that if: 'We retreat from Berlin . . . Berlin falls' and 'Western Germany will be next. If we mean to hold Europe against Communism, we must not budge . . . I believe the future of democracy requires us to stay.'[42] Clay began an airlift to supplement supplies delayed by the inspections. On 5 April, a Soviet fighter plane harassing a British transport plane collided with it and that pilot and fourteen people, including two Americans, aboard the transport died in the crash. After consulting each other Truman and Atlee authorized American and British fighters to escort their transports.

American and western European diplomats met for the London Conference on Germany and on 7 June announced their London Recommendations to unify their three German zones in a federal republic with a democratic constitution and their three Berlin zones, with the deutschmark replacing the reichsmark as the currency for both West Germany and Berlin.

The Soviets imposed a total blockade of road and railway routes to Berlin on 20 June. West Berlin's 2,400,000 inhabitants faced crippling and potentially deadly shortages of food, fuel and other essential goods. Truman responded by expanding the Berlin Airlift to transport all those vital goods. Prime Minister Altee retaliated against Moscow by cutting off monthly shipments of a million tons of coal and 30 million tons of steel as reparations from the Ruhr valley to the Soviet Union.

The Berlin Airlift would last 324 days. West Berlin had two small airports, Tempelhof and Gatow. Initially, fifty-two C-54s and eighty C-47s made two daily round-trip flights or around 250 trips; for the winter, seventy-five more C-47s carried coal to keep West Berlin's power plants and home stoves fuelled. In all there were over 200,000 flights which carried an average 4,500lbs of supplies. The stress on pilots was gruelling with the short landing strips, tight schedule and often foul weather. Forty-eight pilots died altogether in seventeen American and seven British crashes.[43]

Throughout the Berlin crisis, the Western Allies and Red Army troops were on high alert. An exchange of gunfire between opposing guards at a checkpoint might trigger World War III if each side escalated its military response. To deter a Soviet attack, Truman ordered sixty B-29 bombers to fly from the United States to British bases. The message was clear that the United States could rain destruction, including nuclear bombs, on the Soviet Union if war erupted. The Americans then had around fifty nuclear bombs and around thirty B-29s specially fitted to carry them.[44]

A potential aggressor can be deterred if he believes the other side has both the military capacity and will to assert it that will inflict unacceptable losses on the aggressor. Stalin understood that America had both a large and growing nuclear arsenal and had used it to end the war with Japan. He was careful not to be too aggressive in Berlin and other disputed places around the world.

Publicly, Truman asserted that the United States and its allies would defend West Berlin and West Germany. Privately, he wrestled with the moral dilemma posed by nuclear weapons. He claimed that he never lost a minute's sleep thinking about the atomic bombing of Hiroshima and Nagasaki because Japan's imperial government surrendered just days later. Thus by killing several hundred thousand did the bombings save perhaps millions of lives in a prolonged war with American invasions of the Japanese islands. But Truman became angry at the insistence of Defence Secretary James Forrestal and other advisors that nuclear bombs were solely a deadlier form of military power and should be readily wielded. Truman replied: 'You have got to understand that this isn't a military weapon. It is used to wipe out women and children and unarmed people . . . You have got to understand that I have got to think about the effect of such a thing on international relations. This is no time to be juggling an atomic bomb around.'[45]

Truman sought a diplomatic solution to the crisis in late July. He sent Charles Bohlen to London to forge a common diplomatic strategy with British and French diplomats, then request talks via American Ambassador Walter Bedell Smith to Foreign Minister Molotov in Moscow. Stalin agreed. Smith along with British ambassador Frank Roberts and French ambassador Yves Chataigneau met with Molotov for several sessions before Stalin joined them on 2 August. Stalin offered to end the blockade if the Western Allies cancelled their plans to unite their zones into West Germany and agreed to replace the deutschmark with the Soviet mark in West Berlin. That led to discussions among Washington, London and Paris over whether to accept Stalin's offer and what, if anything, to counter-offer. Talks among themselves and with the Soviets continued through August. Berlin's four military governors met on 31 August, but could not agree on any serious issue. On 22 September, the Western Allies sent Stalin an offer to open general negotiations on any array of Berlin and German issues if he lifted the blockade. Stalin refused.

Truman and other Western leaders agreed that a formal military alliance among them was essential to deter Soviet aggression. In Washington, envoys of the United States, Britain, France, Canada, Italy, Belgium, Denmark, Iceland, the Netherlands, Norway, Portugal and Luxembourg signed a treaty establishing the North Atlantic Treaty Organization (NATO) on 4 April 1949.[46] The key tenet of NATO's charter was Article 5 whereby:

> an armed attack against one or more of them . . . should be considered an attack against them all and . . . each of them . . . will assist the party or parties so attacked by taking . . . individually and in concert with the parties such action as it seems necessary including the use of armed force to restore and maintain the security of the North Atlantic area.

West Germany's unification followed. On 9 May, the Parliamentary Council unveiled a constitution, called the Basic Law, for the Federal Republic of West Germany with its capital at Bonn, on the west bank of the Rhine.

Stalin authorized a statement on 12 May that the blockade would end. Truman issued Stalin a formal invitation for a summit in Washington in February 1949. Stalin's reply was surprisingly cordial: 'I am grateful for President Truman for his invitation to Washington. A trip to Washington has long been my desire, which I mentioned to President Roosevelt in Yalta and to President Truman in Potsdam. Unfortunately, I am at present unable to fulfil my desire to travel any significant distance, especially by ship or air, as the physicians strictly forbid it.'[47]

***

Stalin fumed that without nuclear weapons he had to back down on that and other military confrontations with the West. The rapid succession of Hiroshima, Nagasaki and Japan's surrender stunned Stalin and his inner circle. Until then, Molotov had presided over the

Soviet bomb project but had made little progress. Stalin turned the bomb project over to Beria and authorized him to mobilize whatever human, industrial and technological resources were vital to realizing it.[48] Beria's ruthlessness was not enough to accelerate the project because he knew nothing about science. For that Stalin appointed Igor Kurchatov, a brilliant physicist, to head the project on 25 January 1946. Soviet espionage bolstered the Soviet programme with pilfered designs of bombs, reactors and other key equipment. The Soviets first successful tested an atomic bomb on 29 August 1949.

Stalin was a Soviet nationalist first and communist internationalist second. He always put Soviet interests ahead of all other concerns, including communist revolutions around the world. He gleefully imposed puppet communist regimes on the countries his Red Army conquered but was leery of communist movements and takeovers elsewhere around the world that he could not manipulate to advance Soviet interests. Yugoslav communist Milovan Djilas explained: 'He felt instinctively that the creation of revolutionary centres outside of Moscow could endanger its supremacy in world Communism and of course that is exactly what happened. That is why he helped revolutions only up to a certain point – up to where he could control them – but he was always ready to leave them in the lurch whenever they slipped out of his grasp.'[49]

The Soviets completed Czechoslovakia's Stalinization in 1948. A 1946 election in which the Communist Party won most seats forced President Eduard Beneš to pack his cabinet with communists including Klement Gottwald as prime minister and Vaclav Nosek as interior minister. When Nosek purged the police hierarchy and replaced it with communists, twelve non-communist ministers resigned. Foreign Minister Jan Masaryk remained the only non-communist. On 10 March 1948, Masaryk was found dead on the pavement below his apartment building, most likely after being thrown from a window. Gottwald filled his seat and the other twelve empty seats with communists.

Stalin established the Information Bureau of the Communist and Workers' Parties (Cominform) as the Communist International's (Comintern) successor on 17 April 1948. The purpose was identical – for the Kremlin to nurture and coordinate Communist Parties in their revolutionary struggles around the world. He formed the Council for Mutual Economic Assistance (COMECON) among the Soviet Union and its eastern bloc countries on 8 January 1949.

Josef Broz Tito, Yugoslavia's leader, refused to conform to the Kremlin's commands.[50] Tito and Georgi Dimitrov, Bulgaria's premier, negotiated a Treaty of Friendship, Cooperation and Mutual Assistance on 1 August 1947. That treaty preceded a similar treaty being negotiated between Moscow and Sofia that was signed on 1 September. Stalin condemned any relations among communist states that did not run through the Kremlin's hub. On 10 February 1948, he castigated the 'reckless and independent actions' of Tito and Dimitrov and demanded that they renounce the treaty. Dimitrov did but Tito insisted that Yugoslavia would conduct its own foreign policy to serve its own interests. Stalin retaliated by expelling Yugoslavia from Cominform in 1948. He infamously boasted and warned: 'I will shake my little finger – and there will be no more Tito.'[51] He sent in hit squads to fulfil that threat and replace Tito with a compliant communist. All failed.

After Stalin excommunicated his regime, Tito issued this public response:

> We do not ask of the Soviet government that it should have a liking for the way we are building socialism. We have no liking for their unsocialist methods which . . . compromise the idea of socialism . . . But what we demand from the Soviet government is this: that they should behave with due respect for the independence of the peoples of Yugoslavia and their desire to work in peace and without threatening anyone.

He condemned the 'leaders of a country where an unheard of crime of genocide has been committed, where whole nations have been annihilated'.[52] At some point, Tito sent Stalin a letter that read: 'Comrade Stalin, I request that you stop sending terrorists to Yugoslavia to kill me. We have already caught seven men, one with a revolver, another with a grenade, the third with a bomb, etc. If this does not stop, I will send one man to Moscow and there will be no need to send another.' The letter was found in Stalin's desk after he died.[53]

Tito developed Yugoslavia with his version of Lenin's New Economic Policy. He nationalized the banks, industries, mines, transportation and communication networks and large-scale farms but let Yugoslavs run small businesses and farms and migrate to work in Western Europe and send back money to their families. He also encouraged tourists to visit Yugoslavia's lovely cities and Adriatic Sea beaches. Under 'Titoism', Yugoslavia's economy diversified and grew rapidly, although most Yugoslavs remained poor.

***

China would emerge to pose the greatest threat to displace the Soviet Union as the head of global communism. At Beijing on 1 October

1949, General Secretary Mao Zedong declared that the Communist Party (CCP) had liberated China's mainland and would soon takeover Taiwan where the remnants of Chiang Kai-shek's Nationalist Party (KMT) had retreated.[54] That ended a civil war that began 23 years earlier in 1927 when Chiang ordered KMT troops to destroy the CCP that he had allied with in 1923 to unify China. The KMT routed the CCP from most eastern cities and the remnants gathered in Jiangxi Province in the south-east. The KMT launched an offensive in 1934 that threatened to encircle and destroy the CCP's remnants. Mao Zedong was among the CCP's leaders who organized what was known as the Long March. The CCP army and its followers numbered around 65,000 when they headed west on 16 October 1934 and a year later there were only 8,000 left when they reached safety at Yenan in northern China.

Mao now was the CCP's General Secretary. He developed the region around Yenan into an impregnable military and political fortress. His peasant-based communist revolution involved confiscating property from land and large business owners, tolerating family businesses, imposing equitable taxes, distributing land to the tillers in village cooperatives, providing each village or town district with a health clinic and school, planting cadres in all groups, tolerating no dissent and building a People's Red Army to fight the Nationalist Chinese regime and Japanese invaders. To promote revolution across China, the Communist Party had a military wing to destroy its enemies and a political wing to build a communist system in the ruins.

Against both the Nationalists and Japanese, the Red Army steadily expanded in numbers and territory with a three-stage strategy, with the first two unfolding from 1935 to 1945 and the last from 1946 to 1949.[55] First was 'hit and run' as small bands of guerillas hiding among the people attacked isolated military posts and tried to provoke the government into launching retaliatory attacks that mostly killed civilians, thus pushing ever more enraged people into communist ranks. As the strength of the military and political wings rose, the Red Army would then 'take and hold' swaths of the countryside and cities and defeat any military offensives. The final stage was 'circle and destroy' as Red Armies fought a conventional war that routed enemy forces and overran evermore of the country.

Mao believed that mind or soft power far exceeded physical or hard power. The key for communists was to understand the course of history and commit themselves to doing whatever was possible to accelerate its progress toward communism. As Mao put it: 'The most important factors in the making of history were how men thought and their willingness to engage in revolutionary action.'[56] Mao recognized that in a revolutionary struggle, the side that better mobilized 'hearts and minds' would likely win. Chiang and his Nationalist Party had alienated the masses of Chinese people because they were corrupt, inept and brutal. After Stalin died, Mao would promote himself and his Maoist version of communism as the leader of global communism.[57]

Stalin pursued a two-level policy toward China. He fulfilled his wartime promise to America and Britain to recognize Chiang's KMT as the legitimate government while he secretly aided the CCP. After the Soviet Red Army attacked and overran the Japanese army in north-eastern China in August 1945, the Soviets turned over vast amounts of weapons, munitions and other supplies to Mao's Red Army. Stalin withdrew his army from China three months after his invasion.

Despite the CCP's advantages in hard and soft power, it still took four years of hard fighting before Mao could claim victory. During that time, the Truman administration first tried to broker a coalition government between the KMT and CCP, but when that failed, the United States extended massive military and economic aid to the KMT. The KMT squandered most of that aid and even sold some of it to the CCP.

In neighbouring Korea, Washington and Moscow had agreed jointly to occupy the peninsula with Soviet troops north and American troops south of the 38th Parallel, to be withdrawn six months later. Each set up a provisional government with a dictator heading it, with the Soviet-backed Kim Il-sung in power at Pyongyang and the American-backed Syngman Rhee in Seoul. Washington and Moscow extended military and economic aid and advisors to their respective regimes. Rhee and Kim each built an army and threatened to unify Korea through war. Firefights flared along the frontier and South Korean troops and police hunted communist guerrillas.

The Truman administration treated Korea as they had Germany, accepting its division as a sensible compromise. The president got the United Nations to supervise elections for South Korea in May 1948 and recognize the Republic of South Korea in December 1949. Congress approved a military and economic aid programme for South Korea to expand its army to 100,000 troops.

***

A communist revolution was unfolding in Indochina, but Stalin was indifferent to it. France conquered the independent kingdoms of Vietnam, Cambodia and Laos, collectively called Indochina, in the late nineteenth century. Communist movements arose in each country but French authorities eventually suppressed them. The communist leaders went into exile in neighbouring China or faraway Europe, where they tried to rebuild their parties to infiltrate their homelands. Nationalism was important to each Communist Party. Germany's conquest of France in 1940 and Japan's takeover of Indochina gave those nascent Communist movements the opportunity their adherents had long awaited.

Ho Chi Minh was as critical for a successful revolution in Vietnam as Lenin was for Russia and Mao for China. Originally named Nuyen Ai Quoc, Ho left China as a young man to live first briefly in the United States then for several years in France. American democracy and prosperity through private property and free markets greatly inspired him but he knew that was inappropriate for Vietnam. In France, he joined the Communist Party and formed the Vietnam Communist Party in 1922. He trained in Moscow for several years then as a Comintern agent journeyed to Kunming, China where he established the Vietnamese Communist Party under several guises including the Vietnam Workers Party, Indochina Communist Party and Viet Minh.

Ho established the Viet Minh in 1941, with the Vietnamese Communist Party the core of an alliance with an array of other nationalist, socialist and religious groups dedicated to liberating Vietnam from the Japanese occupiers and their French puppet regime. In 1945, American Office of Strategic Services (OSS) officers reached Ho's headquarters, now in the remote jungle of northern Vietnam, and provided the Viet Minh with arms and advisors and stood beside him as he publicly declared Vietnam's independence in Hanoi, Vietnam's capital, on 2 September 1945.

The French were determined to reconquer Indochina after Japan's surrender. Fighting erupted between the swelling French and Viet Minh armies and persisted. Ho emulated Mao's peasant-based revolution and three-stage war to fight the French and the Viet Minh steadily expanded their territory. Stalin and Mao recognized Ho's Democratic People's Republic of Vietnam in January 1950.

***

The Truman administration had no choice but bitterly accept what they had failed to prevent, the communist conquest of China. On 5 January 1950, Truman declared that the United States would not interfere in China's takeover of Taiwan. On 12 January, Secretary of State Dean Acheson pointedly did not include South Korea or Taiwan in an American security zone for the western Pacific that did include Japan and the Philippines.[58]

Nonetheless, the Truman White House viewed with increasing alarm the series of communist challenges or victories around the world, especially the Berlin crisis, the Soviet detonation of an atomic bomb and the communist conquest of China. Conservatives argued that Kennan's selective containment strategy that emphasized political and economic development in Europe and Japan had failed to stem Soviet aggression and communism's expansion.

Secretary of State Dean Acheson authorized Paul Nitze, who replaced George Kennan as the Policy Planning chief, to propose an alternative strategy. On 7 April 1950, Nitze issued NSC-68 to President Truman.[59] NSC-68's key assertion was that the Soviet and communist threat was global and military. After communists conquered a country, they made it a base of operations to subvert neighbouring countries, a process soon dubbed the 'domino effect'. The United States could only counter that threat with a massive conventional and nuclear arms build-up to assert overwhelming military power in every threatened region or country around the world no matter how remote, poor or small in population it might be. Defence budgets should skyrocket from the current $13 billion to $50 billion. Washington also had to develop military alliances in every region around the world to crush communist revolutionaries. Communists could never be trusted to tell the truth or keep their word so talks and deals were fruitless with them. Washington must mobilize all potential American sources of political, economic, social and cultural power to wage this global struggle. In the Kremlin, Stalin orchestrated the global communist movement so America's president had to orchestrate the global anti-communist movement.

***

Indeed, as Nitze devised NSC-68, Stalin hosted two communist national leaders. Mao Zedong was the first to arrive in Moscow on 16 December 1949 and he lingered until late February 1950. Stalin snubbed him most of his sojourn. He knew well that Mao offered a rival, peasant-based revolutionary strategy and as the leader of the world's most populous, if poverty-stricken, country, had enormous potential future power. Stalin made it clear that he considered Mao a subordinate party and national chief. During their infrequent meetings, official communiques later described Stalin as 'receiving' Mao that implied having an audience with a lesser rather than the equalitarian phrase 'meet with' and 'receive visits from' that described summits with Winston Churchill and Franklin Roosevelt.[60]

Mao's sophisticated deputy Chou Enlai broke the impasse not long after he reached Moscow on 22 January 1950. Chou and Molotov negotiated what became the Treaty of Friendship, Alliance and Mutual Aid signed on 14 February 1950. That done, Mao, Chou and their entourage returned to Beijing.

Kim Il-sung journeyed to Moscow with one goal, to get Stalin's support for North Korea's conquest of South Korea.[61] On 7 March, Stalin rebuffed Kim's request, citing the weakness of North Korea's army and economy and seeming strength of South Korea's army and economy. Kim persisted and sometime in April Stalin agreed as long as he got Mao's support. Meanwhile, Stalin would send weapons and munitions to North Korea. Kim journeyed to Beijing for a summit with Mao from 13 to 16 May. During that time, they reached an understanding on a North Korean attack on South Korea and informed Stalin on 14 May. Stalin approved their understanding. Mao agreed to send weapons, munitions and other war supplies to North Korea.

***

Kim launched 135,000 troops, 1,400 guns, 126 tanks and 110 warplanes against South Korea's 100,000 defenders on 25 June 1950, in concert with 6,000 guerrillas who had previously infiltrated.[62] The Red Army routed the South Koreans and captured Seoul on 28 June. Rhee, his government and the remnants of his army fled to the port of Pusan in south-east Korea for a last stand.

Upon learning of the invasion, Truman gathered his advisors to debate the attack's significance and what to do about it. They concluded that Stalin had coordinated the invasion to divert American attention to Korea while he provoked another crisis in Berlin. They abandoned Kennan's selective containment and embraced Nitze's global containment strategy. They agreed that they had to militarily aid South Korea or else Stalin would be encouraged to invade Berlin. On 27 June, the Americans got the United Nations Security Council to pass a resolution that condemned North Korea's invasion of South Korea and authorized the United States to form and lead an alliance that drove the North Korean army back across the 38th Parallel.

Truman could get the Security Council to pass that resolution because the Soviet ambassador was not present to veto it. The North Korean invasion's timing surprised Stalin. He had withdrawn the Soviet ambassador from the Security Council to protest that China's seat was occupied by an ambassador from Taipei rather than Beijing. Unfortunately, no one in the Truman White House understood what that absence meant. It belied their narrative that Stalin was the global communist puppet-master who determined all revolutionary strategies. Surely Stalin would have had his ambassador in place to veto any American resolutions if he had planned the invasion.

Truman authorized General Douglas MacArthur, who headed America's occupation of Japan, to command the ground, air and naval forces in Korea. He transferred troops to reinforce those already based in the region. He ordered the 7th Fleet to the straits between Taiwan and China's mainland to shield Chiang's Nationalist regime from a communist Chinese invasion. He sent military aid to the French fighting communists in Indochina. He got Congress to appropriate money for all these actions. Although eventually sixteen countries joined the alliance against North Korea, the United States provided 50 per cent of the ground, 86 per cent of the sea and 93 per cent of the air power.[63]

MacArthur sent American troops to bolster the defence perimeter the South Korean army had established to protect Pusan. On 15 September, the Eighth American Army led by General Walton Walker landed at Inchon, the port for Seoul, swiftly captured it and the capital, then fought its way east through the North Korean army's rear. That forced the North Koreans to rapidly withdraw from South Korea.

MacArthur ordered his army to pursue but then committed four blunders. He ignored a Chinese warning on 2 October that they would retaliate if American forces crossed the 38th Parallel but did not mention the South Korean army. He split his army into separate forces that could not easily support each other because of intervening mountain ranges. He disregarded CIA reports that Mao had sent a Chinese army across the Yalu River frontier into North Korea. And he did not order winter clothing or other equipment for his troops.

The communists attacked with 200,000 Chinese and 50,000 North Korean troops on 26 November and routed the Americans and their allies. General Walker died in a jeep accident on 23 December and Truman replaced him with General Matthew Ridgway. The relentless communist advance continued and captured Seoul on 7 January 1951. Ridgway's American and allied troops finally halted the enemy's offensive on 24 January and began a counteroffensive the next day that recaptured Seoul on 14 March. Truman fired MacArthur as the theatre commander on 11 April 1951, after he publicly criticized the White House's strategy and called for bombing Chinese cities, and appointed General Ridgway to take his place. The allies fought their way north to a meandering line midway across the peninsula. And there the war stalemated for the next two and a half years. The Chinese and North

Koreans had deployed so many troops on such a heavily-fortified line that they could repel any assault.

Stalin saw the Korean War as a brilliant opportunity to drain American power. He sent massive amounts of war supplies to the Chinese and North Korean armies. He also let Soviet pilots man the MiG-15 jet fighters that had North Korean insignia. He could gloat that the MiG-15 was a superior jet fighter plane to America's F-86 Sabre. From November 1950 to December 1951, Soviet pilots shot down 569 American warplanes while losing only 63.[64] Washington and Moscow kept their air war secret. They feared that publicity might pressure either of them to escalate the war by bombing supply sites in China or Japan. And that might pressure each side to escalate to a nuclear war that both sides wanted to avoid at all costs. They tacitly agreed to contain the war to the Korean Peninsula.

***

If American foreign policy failed catastrophically in Korea, George Kennan's original selective containment strategy brilliantly succeeded in West Europe and Japan whose economies fully recovered from their wartime devastation and democratic political systems became well established. European unification took its latest major step when envoys of France, West Germany, Italy, the Netherlands, Belgium and Luxembourg on 18 April 1951, signed the Treaty of Paris that created the European Coal and Steel Community (ECSC).

Meanwhile, Washington successfully transformed Japan from a war-devastated, poverty-stricken country into a prosperous country and from a fascist state into a liberal democratic political system.[65] MacArthur headed Japan's military occupation and the political, economic and social reforms imposed by foreign-service officials. The Americans guided Japan's demilitarization, democratization, land reforms that morphed poor peasants into well-to-do farmers, transformation of the emperor from a demigod into a constitutional monarch, toleration of trade and investment barriers that forced foreign businesses to license their technologies to their Japanese rivals and integration of Japan into the global economy. By 1951 when America's occupation ended, Japan was an economically dynamic, democratic country. All along the Americans staved off Soviet demands for more than token representation in the occupation while Japan's Communist Party rarely garnered more than in one in ten votes during elections.

***

Joseph Stalin was in his last years. Biographer Adam Ulam vividly describes Stalin as an aging tyrant: 'He could seldom sit still. People summoned for conferences recall how he would walk around the room while questioning them, how the stated business of the meeting would often be changed or terminated by a sudden question or gesture. At his less and less frequent public appearances, the audience's dutiful applause would be cut short with an impatient wave of his hands.'[66] Alexander Solzhenitsyn offered this vivid portrait:

> Although he was afraid to admit it, he had noticed that his health was getting worse every month. He was suffering from lapses of memory and attacks of nausea . . . He lost track of his train of thought and starred with blurred gaze around the room . . . He was an old man without any friends. Nobody loved him . . . Loneliness crept over him like a paralysis.[67]

Stalin at once desperately sought and detested companionship, a contradiction that worsened with his years. Nikita Khrushchev recalled:

> He suffered terrible from loneliness. He needed people around him all the time. When he woke up in the morning, he would immediately summon us . . . It's true that sometimes State and Party questions were decided, but we spent only a fraction of our time on those. The main thing was to occupy Stalin's time so he wouldn't suffer from loneliness. He was depressed by loneliness and feared it.[68]

One reason to shun solitude is to mask with conviviality all the guilty thoughts and memories that crowd it. Did the ghosts of all the former comrades and even friends that Stalin had murdered haunt him? Stalin harboured a pathologically dwarfed conscience but even that might pose painful accusations when he was by himself. He diluted those voices by immersing himself with sycophants who constantly told him how great and infallible he was.

The tyrant surprised his inner circle one day with this notion:

> In 1952, Stalin called us together and suggested that we should convene a Party Congress. He didn't need to persuade us. We all considered it incredible that there hadn't been a Party Congress for thirteen years. Nor had there been a Central Committee plenum for some time. The Central Committee had not met in either its policy-making or its consultative capacity for years. In short, the Party at large and the Central Committee in particular had been taking no part whatever in the collective leadership. Stalin did everything himself, bypassing the Central

> Committee and using the Politburo as little more than a rubber stamp. Stalin rarely bothered to ask the opinion of Politburo members about a given measure. He would just make a decision and issue a decree.[69]

During the Nineteenth Party Congress from 4 to 14 October 1952, Stalin had the delegates approve some minor administrative changes. The Politburo was renamed the Presidium and its members expanded from eleven to twenty-five. The Orgburo was abolished and the Secretariat assumed its duties with an executive of ten members with the General Secretary. The Central Committee was expanded to 133 members.

The biggest change was Stalin asking to be relieved as General Secretary because of his health and age, with the post bequeathed to Georgi Malenkov. Malenkov was very bright, having graduated summa cum laude from high school. Rather than go to college he joined the Communist Party and first achieved acclaim as the chief propagandist aboard a Red Army armoured train during the civil war. He attended the Advanced Technological School in Moscow from 1923 to 1925, then served as a staff member for the Central Committee's Organizational Bureau (Orgburo). His diligence and loyalty attracted Stalin who made him a key investigator during the purges of the late 1930. Stalin named Malenkov head of the Communist Party's Cadre Directorate in 1939 and during the Second World War, elevated him to the State Defence Committee along with himself as chair and Beria, Voroshilov and Molotov. He also named Malenkov deputy premier from May 1944 to March 1946 and from August 1946 to March 1953.

***

A brain haemorrhage killed Joseph Stalin at age 74 on 5 March 1953.[70] His death followed a typical prolonged drunken night with his henchmen Molotov, Beria, Malenkov and Khrushchev. The official state announcement came two days later along with the warning for people to avoid 'disorder and panic'. The authorities displayed his embalmed body in its casket in the Kremlin's Hall of Columns from 6 to 9 March. At noon on 9 March, the Presidium's eight highest members shouldered his casket, carried it to the mausoleum and laid it beside Lenin's casket. There was one minute of silence at noon then a 21-gun salute. From atop the mausoleum, the last people who saw him alive – Molotov, Beria, Malenkov and Khrushchev – gave eulogies.

Most Soviets genuinely and deeply grieved the loss of the leader that for decades the communist system socialized them to adore. Hundreds of thousands of mourners packed Moscow's streets; a panic in Trubnaya Square trampled at least 109 people to death and perhaps as many as a thousand. Among the mourners was Chou Enlai, China's foreign minister. Mao Zedong chose not to attend. He would soon assert himself as communism's global leader with a revolutionary strategy appropriate for the Third World's peasant-based societies.

Soviet writers unleashed their latest flood of panegyrics, now glorifying Stalin in death as they previously had for his life. This one by poet Alexi Surkov was typical: 'Death closed those eyes that looked so far into the future.'[71]

Chapter 9

AFTERLIFE

> 'Because the regime is captive to its own lies, it must falsify everything.' (Vaclav Havel)

> 'It is sometimes said that Stalin did not know about many of the instances of lawlessness. Documents at our disposal show that this is not so. The guilt of Stalin and his immediate entourage before the party and the people for the wholesale repressive measures and acts of lawlessness is enormous and unforgiveable. This is a lesson for all generations.' (Mikhail Gorbachev)

> 'Acting on the will of the people of Russia, I am inviting you, the people of the United States, to join us in partnership in the name of a worldwide triumph of democracy, in the name of liberty and justice.' (Boris Yeltsin)

Joseph Stalin was dead but his system and spirit lingered for decades in the Soviet Union, in the Eastern European empire and in communist regimes and movements elsewhere around the globe.[1]

Georgi Malenkov was already General Secretary and became prime minister of the council of ministers on 5 March 1953, when Stalin died. But he lacked Stalin's implacable will, ambition, deviousness and ruthlessness to purge his rivals and become a tyrant. Instead, Malenkov initially was the first among an inner three with Beria, the Interior Minister and State Security Minister and Molotov, the Foreign Minister.

The new rulers took a major step in de-Stalinization when they agreed to steadily dismantle the Gulag slave labour system. For this, Beria led. On 24 March 1953, just three weeks after Stalin's death, he wrote to the Presidium that of 2,526,402 current prisoners only 224,435 were dangerous and the rest should be amnestied. By July 1954 over 1,200,000 had been released.[2] That was an astonishing policy backflip for the man who had ordered millions of people rounded up for concentration camps and tens of thousands of them executed before they got there.

Fear and loathing of Beria united Malenkov and Molotov who brought Nikita Khrushchev into their cabal. They plotted a coup set for 23 June 1953, when they invited him to join them at the Kremlin, then had him arrested, imprisoned and harshly interrogated. He confessed to all charges lodged against him. Beria and six of his cohorts went on trial on 18 December and were found guilty and executed on 23 December 1952. Meanwhile, the cabal agreed to make Khrushchev the Communist Party's General Secretary on 7 September 1953.

***

As for the Cold War, Malenkov issued these reassuring words to the world from a speech he made before the Supreme Soviet: 'At the present time there is no disputed or unresolved question that cannot be settled peacefully by mutual agreement of all the interested countries. This applies to all states including the United States of America.'[3]

Newly-elected President Dwight Eisenhower viewed that message with mingled hope and caution. He knew how intractable and untrustworthy communists were. He worried that each side was now so suspicious of the other that even minor understandings were unreachable, that any concession would be viewed as a sign of weakness to be exploited. He expressed his doubts to Churchill:

> We have come to the point when every additional backward step must be deemed a defeat for the Western world. In fact, it is a triple defeat. First, we lose a particular ally. Next, we give to an implacable enemy another recruit. Beyond this every such retreat creates in the minds of neutrals the fear that we do mean what we say when we pledge our support to people who want to be free.[4]

That mentality was central to the 'Global Containment Strategy' devised by Paul Nitze and adapted by the Truman administration after North Korea invaded South Korea on 25 June 1950. Global containers viewed every Cold War conflict as resulting either in a victory or defeat and never a mutual win or mutual loss.

Nonetheless, Eisenhower's priority after taking the presidential oath on 20 January 1953 was to cut America's losses on the Korean Peninsula with an indefinite truce in place. After months of negotiations, the Americans and communists signed an armistice on

27 July 1953. The major obstacle was the communist insistence that all their captured troops be returned, including those who preferred to stay as refugees. The North Koreans finally agreed to let them go. In the subsequent exchange, the Americans sent 70,000 North Koreans and 5,600 Chinese north while the communists released 12,700 Allied troops including 7,500 South Koreans and 3,600 Americans. Around 23,000 North Koreans and Chinese and 350 allied troops preferred to stay.[5]

Stalin did not live to see the Korean War's end, but until his death he could gloat over how much American blood and treasure it drained. The Americans suffered 54,246 dead, including 33,652 from combat and 103,284 wounded; the South Koreans 227,800 dead and 717,100 wounded; and the other fourteen allies several thousand dead and wounded. The Chinese and North Korean together suffered 1,800,000 casualties or around 900,000 dead, wounded and missing each. Around 3,000,000 Korean civilians died during the war from combat, execution, disease and starvation.

The war cost the United States $30 billion then or $341 billion in 2011 dollars. American military personnel rose from 1,400,000 in 1950 to 2,500,000 in 1951 to 3,300,000 in 1954 then dropped to 2,900,000 in 1955. American defence spending rose from $144.2 billion in 1950 to $224.3 billion in 1951, $402.1 billion in 1952 and $442.3 billion in 1953 before falling slightly to $420.9 billion in 1954.[6] Eisenhower understood how debilitating and self-defeating those costs were: 'Every gun that is made, every warship launched, every rocket fired signifies, in the final sense, a theft from those who hunger and are not fed, those who are cold and are not clothed . . . The cost of one modern heavy bomber is this: a modern brick school in more than 30 cities.'[7] Of course, those trade-offs were even worse for the Soviet Union and other communist regimes whose economies were a fraction that of America's and whose populations were wretchedly poor and exploited rather than prosperous.

The Americans had fought their first indecisive war that ended in stalemate at a vast cost. General Matthew Ridgway explained a key Korean War lesson: 'Before Korea, all our military planning envisioned a war that would involve the world and in which the defence of a distant and indefensible peninsula would be folly. But Korea taught us that all warfare from this time forth must be limited. It could no longer be a question of whether to fight a limited war, but of how to avoid fighting any other kind.'[8] Ridgway was partly right. Certainly, both sides needed to avoid wars that might escalate into a nuclear holocaust. But another vital lesson was to avoid unwinnable wars that ended in stalemate or, far worse, outright catastrophic defeats as the Americans suffered in Indochina and the Soviets in Afghanistan.

***

Moscow's official view of Joseph Stalin persisted after his death. Publicly, his successors continued to treat him as the Soviet Union's demigod, second only to Lenin in the communist pantheon. The Kremlin would have upheld Stalin's personality cult indefinitely had one man lacked the courage and will to dispute that.

For decades, Nikita Khrushchev was among the countless devout members of the Stalin cult. Even after Stalin died, he needed three years to deprogram himself from that cult's iron grip and see Stalin as he really was. He explained that evolution in his memoirs that he wrote in the late 1960s, after Leonid Brezhnev ousted and exiled him in 1964. It was nearly impossible to de-Stalinize himself as forbidden questions and thoughts increasingly assailed him:

> I still mourned Stalin as an extraordinarily powerful leader. I knew that his power had been exerted arbitrarily . . . Stalin may have used methods which were . . . improper or even barbaric . . . I hadn't yet begun to challenge the very basis of Stalin's claim to a place of special honour in history. However, questions were beginning to arise for which I had no ready answer. Like others, I was beginning to wonder why of all those imprisoned no one had ever been released. I was beginning to doubt whether all the arrests and convictions had been justified . . . But then Stalin had been Stalin. Even in death he commanded almost unassailable authority and it still hadn't occurred to me that he had been capable of abusing his powers.[9]

Khrushchev contrasted the Revolution's austere but idealistic first three decades with more recent less poverty-stricken but more cynical post-Stalin times:

> In those days, in order to be a Communist, you couldn't expect to be rewarded for your sacrifices with eventual blessings. It is not like that nowadays. Of course, there are still people of principle among Communists, but there are also many people of without principle, lickspittle functionaries and petty careerists. Nowadays a Party card all too often represents nothing more than its bearer's hope of finding a comfortable niche for himself in our Socialist society. Shrewd people these days manage to get much more out of our society than they put into it . . . I don't mean to say that there wasn't a certain amount of

opportunism among would-be Communists in the first years of the Revolution.[10]

Yet to varying degrees, Khrushchev and his colleges, Molotov, Malenkov and Kaganovich along with other top Communist Party officials, believed that they had to demystify Stalin's lingering personality cult and the powers that might enable someone else to become an unchallenged tyrant. Khrushchev explained those tentative first steps: 'After Stalin's death, the Central Committee began to implement a policy of explaining concisely and consistently that it is impermissible and foreign to the spirit of Marxism-Leninism to elevate one person, to transform him into a superhuman possessing supernatural characteristics akin to those of a god. Such a man supposedly knows everything, sees everything, thinks for everyone, can do anything, is infallible in his behaviour.'[11]

Like Stalin before him, Khrushchev used his position as General Secretary to pack the Communist Party with his followers. On 8 February 1955, he got the Central Committee to demote Malenkov from prime minister to deputy prime minister and replace him with his ally Nikolai Bulganin. Even with that dominant position within the Soviet Union, Khrushchev needed another year before he had garnered enough support to dethrone the communist world's demigod.

Khrushchev took de-Stalinization's decisive step during the Twentieth Party Congress in Moscow from 14 to 25 February 1956. He denounced Stalin's tyranny and genocide in a long report that detailed his worst crimes. He condemned 'Stalin who absolutely did not tolerate collegiality in leadership and in work and who practiced brutal violence, not only toward everything which opposed him, but also toward that which seemed to his capricious and despotic character, contrary to his concepts'. He compared Lenin and Stalin as leaders:

> Lenin's traits – patient work with people; stubborn and painstaking education of them; the ability to induce people to follow him without using compulsion, but rather through the ideological influence on them of the whole collective – very entirely foreign to Stalin. He [Stalin] discarded the Leninist method of convincing and educating . . . for that of administrative violence, mass repressions and terror. He acted on an increasingly larger scale . . . violating all existing norms of morality and of Soviet laws. Arbitrary behaviour by one person encouraged and permitted arbitrary behaviour in others. Mass arrests and deportations . . . executions without trial and without normal investigation created conditions of insecurity, fear and even desperation.[12]

Khrushchev's revelations provoked an uproar as most communists remained firmly committed to the Stalin cult and denied any implication that communism itself was inherently totalitarian and genocidal. Instead, they condemned the whistle-blower. Khrushchev recalled the accusations:

> What's the matter with you? How can you talk like that? . . . You think you can bring all this out at the Congress and get away with it? How do you think it will reflect on the prestige of our Party and our country? You won't be able to keep what you say secret. Word will get out about what happened under Stalin and then the finger will be pointed straight at us. What will we be able to say about our own roles under Stalin?[13]

The Twentieth Congress did not debate, let alone resolve what to do with, Khrushchev's revelations. Most delegates and leaders remained diehard Stalin devotees. Indeed, it took Khrushchev another five years before he got the Twenty-Second Congress to approve the symbolic removal of Statin's body from its place beside Lenin within the mausoleum and buried outside at the base of the Kremlin wall on 30 October 1961.

Polish Premier Wladyslaw Gomulka was the only other communist regime leader to echo Khruschev's denunciation of Stalin, Stalinism and personality cults. In a speech before the Polish Communist Party's Eight Plenum on 20 October 1956, he boldly declared that:

> The cult of personality cannot be reduced merely to the person of Stalin. This cult of personality is a certain system which prevailed in the Soviet Union and which was transported to probably all the Communist parties . . . In the bloc of socialist states it was Stalin who stood at the top of the hierarchic ladder. All those who stood on lower rungs bowed their heads to him . . . They in turn donned the robes of infallibility and wisdom . . . The chief figure in a cult of personality understood everything, knew everything, decided everything and directed everything . . . The system of the cult of personality shaped the minds, shaped the mode of thinking of party leaders and members . . . It followed that everything that did not correspond to his ideas and orders was harmful . . . Under this system the characters and consciences of men were broken, people were trampled underfoot and their honour was besmirched . . . Terror and demoralization were spread far and wide.[14]

Italian Communist Party chief Palmiro Togliatti dismissed Stalin and Stalinism as a deviation from communism's utopian vision. He condemned both Stalin's sycophants and critics:

> First, all that was good was attributed to the superhuman positive qualities of one man: now all that is evil is attributed to his equally exceptional and even astonishing faults . . . The true problems are evaded, which are why and how Soviet society could reach and did reach certain forms alien to the democratic way and the legality that it set for itself, even to the point of degenerating.[15]

The debate between Stalinism's apologists and critics was especially virulent in France.[16] The French Communist Party was Moscow's most devout and doctrinaire foreign party and much of France's intelligentsia were card-carrying members. Jean-Paul Sartre was the most influential communist spokesperson with his journal *Le Temps Moderne* and numerous essays. Other prominent Stalinists were Simone de Beauvoir, Maurice Merleau-Ponty and Francis Jeanson. Bernard-Henri Levy, Raymond Aaron, Jean-Francois Revel and Albert Camus were humanist scholars who condemned Stalinism and other totalitarian communist regimes.

Aaron was France's most profound and prolific scholar on the nature of communism, liberalism and the modern world with books like *L'Homme Contre Les Tyrans* (1944), *Le Grand Schisme* (1948), *Les Guerres en Chaine* (1952), *L'Opium des Intellectuals* (1957) and *Democratie et Totalitarianisme* (1965). Aaron captured the mindset of France's leftists who were and remain obsessed with appearing in vogue rather than pursuing truth: 'The fashionable philosophies of in France are Marxism and existentialism. The intellectuals of the Left who give their reserved and uneasy support to the Moscow cause without being members of the Communist Party use concepts taken from Hegel, Husserl or Kierkegaard to justify their semi-acceptance of it.' He revealed how seemingly opposed ideological extremists morph into each other: 'In its identification of the party with the state . . . in its transformation of minority doctrine into a national orthodoxy, in the violence of its methods and the unlimited powers of the police, the Hitlerite regime surely has more in common with Bolshevik Russia . . . Right and Left or Fascist pseudo-Right and Communist pseudo-Left can be said to meet each other in totalitarianism.'[17]

Two quotes illustrate the unbridgeable chasm between apologists and critics. Sartre echoed the party line that: 'To keep hope alive one must, in spite of all mistakes, horrors and crimes, recognize the obvious superiority of the socialist camp . . . the USSR is . . . located on the side of those who are struggling against the forms of exploitation.' Levy scorned the twisted logic, amorality and delusions by which Sartre and his comrades justified totalitarianism, mass murder and mass slave labour: 'You know, the intellectual as prophet, the intellectual announcing the course of history has done terrible damage: in his name, all the totalitarian systems of the twentieth century have been justified.'[18]

In America, Stalin and Stalinism had no prominent defenders, only legions of scholarly and popular critics. With the shadowing imperative 'know your enemy', the Cold War prompted the rise of 'Sovietology' in America's academic world, often with generous grants from the federal government and foundations like Ford, Rockefeller and Carnegie. Harvard, Columbia and the University of California at Berkely developed the largest Russian studies departments. Scholars delved deep into the Soviet Union and other communist countries along with the nature of revolutions, authoritarianism and totalitarianism. First-generation landmark books included Isaac Deutscher's *Stalin: A Political Biography* (1949), Richard Crossman's *The God That Failed* (1949), Barrington Moore's *Soviet Politics* (1950), Merle Fainsod's *How Russia Is Ruled* (1953), Carl Friedrich's *Totalitarianism* (1954), Barrington Moore's *Terror and Progress USSR* (1954), Carl Friedrich and Zbigniew Brzezinski's *Totalitarian Dictatorship and Autocracy* (1956), Raymond Bauer, Alex Inkles and Clyde Kluckhohn's *How the Soviet System Works* (1956), Zbigniew Brzezinski's *The Permanent Purge: Politics in Soviet Totalitarianism* (1956) and William Ebenstein's *Today's Isms* (1958).

***

Meanwhile around the world, Maoism vied with Stalinism as communism's leading version. Mao Zedong brilliantly led a peasant-based communist revolution for China that provided a model for communist revolutions in other predominantly peasant countries elsewhere. After Stalin died, Mao aspired to succeed him as the globe's communist leader. His efforts to do so broke down relations between Beijing and Moscow. Khrushchev withdrew Soviet advisors and aid from China in 1959. The two countries fought a short border war in the Ussuri River valley in 1969. Meanwhile, in practice, Maoism was as catastrophic for China as Stalinism was for the Soviet Union. Mao's insistence on swiftly realizing pure communism inflicted mass death on China. Perhaps 20 million or more people died from starvation, disease and murder during his Great Leap Forward of 1958 to 1959 and millions more perished during his Cultural Revolution from 1966 to 1970.

The debate over whether Stalin's or Mao's version of communism killed more people will never be definitively resolved. What is clear is that the only significant difference between the regimes was theoretical, their respective emphases on the proletariat or peasants as the revolution's foundation. Structurally, Mao's regime was nearly identical to Stalin's and all other communist systems.

Of course, no Stalinist regime including Stalin's ever achieved 'total' power, but each came close. There was always a black market with prices determined by supply and demand. Political scientists Carl Friedrich and Zbigniew Brzezinski observed that:

> even with the grip of the total demand for identification with a totalitarian regime, some persons and even groups . . . manage to maintain themselves aloof, to live in accordance with their personal convictions and perhaps to organize some minor opposition to the regime . . . Yet such islands of separateness are not only eloquent testimonials to the strength of human character and to the unquenchable thirst for freedom, they are also helpful in preserving some human beings for a better day.

Yet, those free spirits are extremely rare because the regime is so effective at brainwashing nearly everyone to believe and conform to its ideology: Friedrich and Brzezinski call that the 'internalized totalitarianism' of individuals and groups because 'the controls remain all-permeating and the dictator continues to have the last word, it remains a system of total power'.[19]

Most importantly, nearly every Stalinist regime, including that of the Soviet Union, could not sustain itself. Ironically, communism, the justification for the totalitarian system, ultimately corroded it. Communism is the most effective system ever devised for a tiny elite – the Dictatorship of the Proletariat – to repress and exploit a population, but disastrous for developing the economy over decades. By controlling everything and everyone, communism destroys the incentive and ability for creative people to innovate and natural prices for products shaped by supply and demand. Communist regimes fell further behind countries with democratic governments, free populations and markets, private property and profits. So, gradually and grudgingly, the communist regimes had to diminish their control over people and production to reap benefits from human creativity and enterprise.

The result was the transformation of most totalitarianism systems into post- or quasi-totalitarian systems. The secret police and slave labour camps persisted but the Communist Party wielded them less and less. Regimes still commanded the nationalized economies through five-year plans, but tolerated local black markets for goods produced beyond the quotas imposed on the factories, mines and collective plantations. Rather than murder those who dared criticize the 'workers' paradise', the communists instead locked them up, sometimes in insane asylums, and ignored those who escaped to foreign exile. Authorities increasingly shrugged at the 'samizdat' or dissident literature secretly printed or smuggled and furtively exchanged. Nonetheless, the Soviets did crush communist governments that implemented some liberal reforms in East Germany and Poland in 1951, Hungary in 1956, Czechoslovakia in 1968 and Poland in 1981.

***

Humour was the most constructive way people dealt with the communist regime's repression, exploitation, lies and absurdities. 'The Seven Wonders of Soviet Power' included:

> 1. There is no unemployment, but no one works; 2. No one works, but the plan is fulfilled; 3. The plan is fulfilled, but there is nothing in the shops; 4. There's nothing to buy, but there are queues everywhere; 5. There are queues everywhere, but we are on the threshold of plenty; 6. We are on the threshold of plenty, but everyone is dissatisfied; 7. Everyone is dissatisfied, but everyone votes yes.[20]

And there was the succinct: 'The state pretends to pay us and we pretend to work.'

Vaclav Havel was a brilliant Czech playwright, poet and essayist who revealed how communist regimes stunt and warp the minds of their populations. His best plays that explored that theme were *The Garden Party* (1963), *The Memorandum* (1965) and *Conspirators* (1971). On 6 January 1977, Havel helped draft and was among 242 writers, artists, intellectuals and other free-loving individuals who initially signed and joined the Charter 77 Group to pressure the government to uphold the civil and human rights guaranteed by the 1960 Constitution and the Final Act or Helsinki Accords of the Conference on Security and Cooperation for Europe (CSCE) signed by Czechoslovakia and thirty-four other democratic and communist states on 1 August 1975.

Havel exposed the bundle of Orwellian pathologies that pervade communist societies:

> Ideology, in creating a bridge of excuses between the system and the individual, spans the abyss between the aims of the system and the aims of life . . . It is a world of appearances trying to pass for reality . . . That is why life in the system is so permeated with hypocrisy and

> lies: government by bureaucracy is called popular government; the working class is enslaved in the name of the working class; the complete degradation of the individual is presented as his or her ultimate liberation; depriving people of information is called making it available; the use of power to manipulate people is called public control of power and the arbitrary abuse of power is called observing the legal code; the repression of culture is called its development; the expansion of imperial influences is presented as support for the oppressed; the lack of freedom of expression becomes the highest form of freedom; farcical elections become the highest form of democracy; banning independent thought becomes the most scientific of world views; military occupation becomes fraternal assistance. Because the regime is captive to its own lies, it must falsify everything.[21]

***

The Cold War resulted in the complete victory of the United States and its allies. Stalinism as a system persisted for two more generations before the Soviet empire and communism imploded from 1989 to 1991 and was replaced with liberal political and economic systems. Two long-term forces – America's selective containment policies and communism's self-destructive contradictions – and two-short term forces – Mikhail Gorbachev and Boris Yeltsin – caused that liberal triumph over communist tyranny.

George Kennan's selective containment strategy saved western Europe and Japan from communism by transforming the mass poverty and despair of those war-ravaged peoples into mass prosperity. As most people's living standards and quality of life improved, communism's appeal withered. Massive American humanitarian aid to the Europeans and Japanese alleviated immediate post-war problems of hunger, homelessness and disease while long term development aid rebuilt shattered infrastructure and industries. Meanwhile, the Americans worked with their counterparts to strengthen each country's democratic political system.

International commerce, prosperity and peace were inseparable. In 1944, Washington convened the Bretton Woods Conference of forty-four nations that established two international banks crucial for reviving global trade. The International Monetary Fund (IMF) created a gold-based currency exchange system with low interest loans for member countries with payment deficits. The International Bank for Reconstruction and Development (IRBD, World Bank) gave low-interest loans for large-scale projects that reconstructed and developed a member's economy. In 1947, the Truman administration invited envoys from twenty-three countries to meet at Geneva and establish the General Agreement on Trade and Tariffs (GATT) based on Most Favoured Nation (MFN) or for each member to give to all the same trade advantages it gave to some while periodically the members would convene to cut tariff and non-tariff trade and investment barriers. America's European Recovery Act, better known as the Marshall Plan, eventually distributed over $17 billion in development aid to European countries but only through the Organization of European Economic Cooperation (OEEC). Washington also encouraged France, West Germany, Italy, Belgium, the Netherlands and Luxembourg to negotiate and sign the 1951 Treaty of Paris that established the European Coal and Steel Community (ECSC), the first step in a series of ever greater economic and political union among ever more states resulting in the European Union. All along, the United States kept limited import barriers while tolerating larger trade and investment barriers in Europe and Japan. Finally, the United State provided military security for those countries with NATO and bilateral American-Japanese defence alliance. By bearing much of the defence burden, Washington freed those countries to invest in often more lucrative industries and technologies that better developed their economies.

Communism's internal contradictions made the self-destruction of Stalinist regimes likelier if not certain over time. Communism is the best system ever devised for repressing and exploiting masses of people, but is incapable of developing a diversified, dynamic, productive, prosperous economy. Communists abolish private property and free markets and try to control all production and prices by command through Five Year Plans. The result is to destroy the human incentives for self-expression and creativity that leads to the investments, innovations and inventions that produce and distribute wealth. Five Year Plans churn out masses of goods with usually dismal quality. The Soviets did establish a few viable industries like nuclear arms and missiles by gathering the best scientific and engineering minds and forcing them to produce. Compounding those problems was the elitism, corruption and incompetence that pervades any communist country. Around five per cent of each Stalinist country's population were in the Communist Party, an exclusive club whose members enjoyed what little wealth and benefits the system could produce. Meanwhile, the other nineteen of twenty people lived wretched existences of joyless poverty, shortages and toil; countless people escaped the tedium and exploitation through addiction to vodka. Communist regimes swiftly silenced anyone who dared to criticize the 'workers' paradise'.

Overall the gap between command and free economies widened steadily. The subject peoples of the Stalinist regimes were aware that most West Europeans and North Americans enjoyed prosperous, self-expressive lives. Countless people tried to escape to those promised lands, with a lucky few making it but most arrested and imprisoned.

Moscow exacerbated communism's inherent flaws with massive military spending that may have reached a quarter of the economy. The invasion of Afghanistan in December 1979 led to a decade of a debilitating war that the Soviets eventually lost. The Red Army was thoroughly demoralized. Russians composed 80 per cent of the officers and 95 per cent of the high command. Ethnic and religious tensions permeated the ranks and troops joined gangs for protection. Hazing of draftees resulted in as many as 10,000 murders and suicides from 1986 to 1989. Around 360,000 draftees did not appear for duty or deserted in 1991. Food, housing, health care and recreation were wretched on most bases.[22]

Atop that was the Politburo's increasingly aged and sickly leadership headed by Nikita Khrushchev from 1956 to 1964, Leonid Brezhnev from 1964 to 1981, Yuri Andropov from 1981 to 1983 and Konstantin Chernenko from 1983 to 1985. That gerontocracy was incapable of understanding the worsening problems afflicting their regime let alone taking decisive measures to alleviate them. They could only rigidly adhere to communist dogma and mutter ideologically correct shibboleths as the Soviet Union and its Eastern European puppets fell further behind the West. The only significant change to Stalinism was how the regimes treated 'enemies of the people'. Referring to Boris Yeltsin, Historian Daniel Diller writes: 'Under Stalin a maverick such as Yeltsin would have been shot; under Khrushchev he would have been jailed; under Brezhnev he would have been sent to an insane asylum.'[23]

***

China's communist regime alleviated that array of related pathologies by giving up communism. Mao Zedong's death in 1976 led to a three year struggle between hardliners and reformers led by Deng Xiaoping. Deng and his faction managed to overthrow the hardliners by 1978 and began a series of reforms that revolutionized China's economy. They still imposed quotas on collective farms but let them sell their excess production in local markets with prices determined by supply and demand. Each peasant family was allocated a garden in which to grow and eat or sell whatever they liked. People could start private businesses and hire up to ten employees without being arrested and imprisoned or executed for 'exploiting labour'.

Beijing targeted an increasingly sophisticated spectrum of industries and technologies for development including textiles, toys, steel, chemicals, machine tools, automobiles, microelectronics and aerospace, to name the most prominent. State enterprises that sold shares in themselves were established for each of these industries. Deng opened China to foreign investors to partner with Chinese state owned companies who would own at least 51 per cent of the enterprise. The Chinese yuan was undervalued to give Chinese products an advantage in foreign markets. Chinese state and private corporations often 'dumped' or sold below production costs their products in foreign markets to bankrupt their foreign rivals and capture their markets. The Chinese blatantly stole rather than licensed cutting-edge foreign technologies. The regime encouraged and subsidized hundreds of thousands of young people to study abroad in the best universities then bring their knowledge and skills back home. China's economy grew around 10 per cent annually after Deng began initiating all these reforms and strategies.

All along, the Communist Party mobilized political power and crushed any dissent, most brutally the thousands of young people calling for democracy in Tiananmen Square, Beijing in June 1989. Nonetheless, the Communist Party achieved legitimacy in the eyes of most Chinese whose lives steadily improved. China retained a Stalinist political structure while adapting an increasingly mixed and dynamic economy of state and private enterprises.

***

Mikhail Gorbachev became the Soviet Communist Party's General Secretary on 11 March 1985. He was a committed communist determined to initiate reforms that revived communism.[24] He was born into a peasant family on a collective farm near Stavropol. He was very bright and earned admission to Moscow State University from which he graduated with a law degree in 1958. His career began in Stavropol where first he was a secretary for Komsomol then worked his way up the regional Communist Party's ranks to become its secretary. In 1971, he transferred to Moscow where he was elected to the Central Committee, became a Politburo candidate member in 1978 and full member in 1979. He acquired an in-depth understanding of the Soviet Union's problems as head of the Legislative Proposals Committee from 1979 to 1984. He owed his rapid rise to powerful communist officials who welcomed his intelligence, geniality, loyalty and hard work. Further enhancing his career was his wife Raisa, who was elegant, charming and bright and, unlike most Soviet wives, appeared in public with him. When Chernenko died on 10 March 1985, the Central Committee elected Gorbachev the Communist Party's General Secretary and thus the Soviet Union's leader.

Gorbachev unleashed a bundle of reforms designed to revive communism but ended up destroying it. *Glasnost* or 'openness' required policymakers to openly investigate and debate all problems then to devise policies that alleviated or eliminated them. Previously, the Communist Party denied and hid problems which caused them to fester. From now, Party members, government officials, newspapers and television news programmes must expose truths rather than obscure them with lies. *Perestroika* or restructuring were the practical measures implemented to overcome problems. *Demokratizatsiya* or democratization meant that the Communist Party no longer selected one candidate for each elected position that voters either approved or rejected. Now two or more Communist Party members could openly compete for each position. The Central Committee approved all of Gorbachev's proposals. Meanwhile he fired corrupt, inept bureaucrats and replaced them with honest, hardworking cadres. By January 1986, he 'had replaced 45 of 159 regional party first secretaries and 4 of 15 first secretaries of republics. In addition, 19 of 59 government ministers were replaced, while 37 of 113 seats on the Council of Ministers changed hands.'[25]

Détente or lessened tensions and mutually advantageous deals with the United States and other countries was critical to Gorbachev's reforms. He sought to cut the Soviet Union's defence burden through arms control agreements. To that end, he conducted several summits with American President Ronald Reagan and they forged a friendly, trusting relationship. On 8 December 1987, they signed the Intermediate Nuclear Forces (INF) Treaty whereby each side withdrew all its medium-range nuclear missiles from Europe and dismantled them before bi-national teams of inspectors. Gorbachev then made some dramatic and substantive concessions. He announced on 7 December 1988 that he would reduce the Red Army by 500,000 troops and on 1 July 1990 that he was abolishing the Warsaw Pact military alliance of the Soviet Union with its east European regimes.

Finally, Gorbachev fought the Neo-Stalinism, nostalgia and coverups for the tyrant and his crimes against humanity. He explained that: 'It is sometimes said that Stalin did not know about . . . the instances of lawlessness. Documents at our disposal show that this is not so. The guilt of Stalin and his immediate entourage before the party and the people for the wholesale repressive measures and acts of lawlessness is enormous and unforgiveable. This is a lesson for all generations.'[26]

***

Gorbachev liberated the Soviet empire's subject states in Eastern Europe. In what Foreign Ministry spokesman Gennadi Gerasimov dubbed the 'my way' policy after Frank Sinatra's famed song with that name, Gorbachev repeatedly declared that the Soviet Red Army would not crush liberal reformers in its Eastern European empire; each communist regime was free to follow policies that it believed were best.

Liberal movements arose in every Eastern European country and every Soviet republic. One by one, mass democracy movements forced every communist regime to give up power. The first liberal revolution was in Poland led by the Solidarity labour movement and the Catholic Church with its Polish Pope John Paul II that brought Tadeusz Mazowieki to power in August 1989, followed by other liberal revolutions in East Germany, Czechoslovakia, Bulgaria and Romania by the end of the year.

The most dramatic change was in East Germany. Premier Egon Krenz announced that he would demilitarize and open the Berlin Wall on 9 November 1989. That night tens of thousands of people armed with sledgehammers and champagne swarmed alongside and atop the Berlin Wall and joyfully began demolishing that symbol of communist oppression. Krenz resigned and a coalition government of liberal and socialist groups took power. East Germany replaced its worthless currency with West Germany's deutschmark on 2 July 1990 and dissolved itself into West Germany on 3 October 1990 under Chancellor Helmut Kohl.

The only violence was in Romania where Communist Premier Nicolae Ceausescu ordered his security forces to fire on demonstrators, killing perhaps a thousand. Eventually, the army overthrew the regime and executed Ceausescu and his wife Elena on 25 December 1989.

***

Gorbachev's reforms ended up not saving but destroying communism. He failed to study let alone emulate Deng's strategy of retaining iron political control while slowly, steadily freeing the economy that let people enjoy higher living standards and quality of life. Gorbachev did the opposite. He liberalized politics while retaining the Stalinist economic system. That led to an explosion of pent-up rage of the long exploited Soviet masses against the communist system without any economic means of alleviating their miserable plight.

Gorbachev wanted the Soviet Union to have a genuine working parliament. He first got the Politburo then the Central Committee to approve the creation of a popularly-elected 2,250-member Congress of People's Deputies with two wings, the Soviet of the Union and the Soviet of Nationalities that met twice yearly. Congress would elect a Supreme Soviet or working parliament that would stay in session much of the year. For both bodies one could run either as a Communist Party member or an independent; other political parties were outlawed. The Congressional election and runoffs were held from March to May 1989, with 1,500 seats from single-member territorial districts and 750 seats from public organizations including 100 from the Communist Party, 100 from the Trade Union Council, 75 from the Komsomol, 75 from the Committee of Soviet Women and 325 from other groups. Communists won 1,931 seats or 87.6 per cent and mostly liberals 319 seats. Once convened, Congress elected a 542 member Supreme Soviet with 475 Communist and 67 independent seats and Gorbachev its chair.[27]

Meanwhile, each Soviet republic elected its own Congress and Supreme Soviet. In March 1990, Russia's 1,068-seat Supreme Soviet was elected with Communist Party members winning 920 of the seats. Once convened, the Russian Supreme Soviet's first task was to elect a chair. Boris Yeltsin won most votes despite Gorbachev's pleas that they pick someone else.

Boris Yeltsin was critical to the extraordinary democratic and geopolitical revolutions from 1989 to 1991.[28] He received a degree in construction engineering from Kirov Polytechnique University in 1955 and from then to 1968 managed a series of projects in the region around Sverdlovsk, his hometown. He was thirty when he joined the Communist Party in 1961, but did so to advance his career. He criticized the Communist Party's corruption, incompetence, waste and exploitation of the people and demanded reforms. He was elected secretary of the Sverdlovsk Central Committee in 1976 and thereafter struggled to alleviate the communist pathologies. Learning of his courageous efforts, Gorbachev appointed Yeltsin secretary of Moscow's Communist Party in 1985 and made him a Politburo candidate member in 1986. During his speech at the 1986 Twenty-Seventh Party Congress, Yeltsin blasted the Communist Party for a litany of failings. For that most Communist Party members hated Yeltsin and most Muscovites adored him. In 1989, he was elected to the Congress of People's Deputies where he forged and led the Interregional Group of over

200 reformers and the Democratic Platform. He then won elections to Russia's Supreme Soviet in March and was elected the Chair in May.

The Communist Party held its Twenty-Eighth Congress in July 1990. Gorbachev was re-elected General Secretary by 3,411 to 1,116 votes for other candidates on 10 July. During his speech on 12 July, Yeltsin turned in his Communist Party membership card while declaring, 'I can only subordinate myself to the will of the people and its elected representatives'.[29] He then walked out as many delegates jeered him.

Gorbachev had a referendum held on 17 March 1991, in which voters checked 'yes' or 'no' on whether to change the country's name to the Soviet Union of Sovereign States. Six of the fifteen republics – Lithuania, Latvia, Estonia, Georgia, Armenia and Moldavia – refused to participate because they sought complete independence. Among the nine participating republics, three out of four voters or 76.2 per cent approved replacing 'Socialist' with 'Sovereign' in the country's name. A treaty was drafted to change the Soviet Union's name to 'of Sovereign States.' On 23 April, Gorbachev signed that treaty with the presidents of the other nine republics. Eight of the nine ratified the treaty, but Ukraine balked at doing so. The treaty was scheduled to be ratified in Moscow on 20 August.[30]

In Russia the referendum also included a question on whether there should be a popularly-elected president; 69.85 per cent voted yes. Russia held its presidential election on 21 June 1991 and Yeltsin won with 57.30 per cent of the vote and the rest spread among five other candidates.[31] Yeltsin issued a decree on 20 July that banned official Communist Party positions in government and he proposed a law banning them in the military.

The Politburo's hardline members were dead set to halt and reverse the revolutionary changes initiated by Gorbachev, Yeltsin and other reformers. Vice President Gennady Yanaev, Prime Minister Valentin Pavlov, KGB Minister Vladimir Kruchkov and Defence Minister Dmitry Yazov called themselves the State Committee of State Emergency. Gorbachev left Moscow on 4 August for a two-week vacation at his dacha at Foros, Yalta. On 18 August, the coterie appeared at Gorbachev's dacha to pressure him to repudiate the treaty and other reforms. When he refused, they informed him that he was under arrest and that Yanaev would become the Soviet president.

News of the coup provoked mass demonstrations in Moscow and other cities across Russia and the other Soviets. Russia's parliament and presidency was in a twenty-storey white building dubbed the 'White House.' A hundred-thousand or so demonstrators packed the square before the White House. Russian President Yeltsin appeared among them, climbed atop a tank and with a loudspeaker called on the coup leaders to release Gorbachev and surrender to the authorities. That day and the next nearly all top military leaders joined Yeltsin, most vitally Army Chief of Staff Mikhail Moiseyev who halted troops moving toward Moscow that the coup leaders had ordered. The coup leaders gave up and were arrested on 21 August.

Gorbachev flew back to Moscow. Yeltsin had Gorbachev appear with him before Russia's assembly on 23 August. Yeltsin announced that he was issuing a decree that suspended the Communist Party in Russia as investigators determined its role in the coup. As he signed it, a stunned Gorbachev sputtered in protest.

Russia's Congress granted Yeltsin the power to issue economic reform decrees without parliamentary approval for a year starting on 2 November. Yeltsin issued decrees making himself prime minster and head of all military forces within Russia and outlawing the Communist Party in Russia on 6 November. Congress reduced the Supreme Soviet to 386 members, 238 voting and 138 non-voting.

Before the coup, only Lithuania had officially declared independence. Thereafter every Soviet republic one by one asserted its own independence. Ukraine's parliament voted on 1 December, to dissolve the Soviet Union with each republic to become an independent country. On 8 December, the presidents of Russia, Ukraine and Belorussia declared the creation of the Commonwealth of Independent States (CIS), which eight other republics joined by 21 December; Estonia, Latvia, Lithuania and Georgia wanted to maintain full independence. Gorbachev gave the world its greatest Christmas gift when on 25 December 1991 he resigned as the Soviet president and signed a decree abolishing the Soviet Union.

***

The Eastern European countries have flourished as liberal democracies and economies since they escaped the Soviet empire and communism. Those that joined the European Union (EU) included Poland, Hungary, the Czech Republic, Estonia, Latvia, Lithuania, Slovakia and Slovenia in 2004; Bulgaria and Romania in 2007; and Croatia in 2013. Those that joined the North Atlantic Treaty Organization (NATO) included Hungary, Poland and the Czech Republic in 1999; Romania, Bulgaria, Estonia, Lithuania, Lativa, Slovakia and Slovenia in 2004; Croatia and Albania in 2009; Montenegro in 2017 and North Macedonia in 2020.

Russia was the key failure of the liberal revolutions. Boris Yeltsin remained Russia's president until New Year's Eve 1999, when he announced his retirement. During his decade in power he struggled to transform Russia from a communist dictatorship into a liberal democracy and a command economy into a market economy. He addressed America's Congress on 17 June 1992 and declared: 'Acting on the will of the people of Russia, I am inviting you, the people of the United States, to join us in partnership in the name of a worldwide triumph of democracy, in the name of liberty and justice.'[32]

Yeltsin's words were ironic since Russia's Congress had essentially given him dictatorial powers of decree. On 21 September 1993, Yeltsin decreed the abolition of Russia's Congress and Supreme Soviet to be replaced with a bicameral legislature with an appointed upper Council and a popularly elected lower Assembly or Duma, with 225 single member districts and 225 seats distributed among political parties according to their share of votes with 5 per cent the threshold. He established a Constitutional Assembly to draft a constitution for this new legislation along with the executive and judicial branches and the rights and duties of citizenship.

Russia's authoritarian political culture is deeply entrenched. The first election was on 12 December 1993 and the results have varied little in elections since then. Liberal candidates and parties win around 10 per cent of the votes while conservative and authoritarian candidates and parties win around 90 per cent.

Meanwhile, Yeltsin abolished the detested Committee for State Security (KGB) and split it into five separate autonomous agencies on 3 December 1991. He recombined those intelligence agencies into the Federal Security Service (FSB) including the Foreign Intelligence Service (SVR) and Main Directorate of Special Programs (GUSP) on 3 April 1995.

Yeltsin scored some key foreign policy successes. He signed with President George Bush the Strategic Arms Reduction Treaty (START I) on 31 July 1991 and START II on 3 January1993, that sharply reduced the Russian and American nuclear arsenals. The Group of Seven Countries invited Yeltsin to join their 1992 summit during which on 1 April Bush announced that they would extend Russia a $24 billion low interest loan to aid its economic development. Russia and most other former Soviet republics became IMF and World Bank members on 27 April 1992.

Russia auctioned off its over 200,000 state economic corporations in a series with the first of 2,500 enterprises on 15 March 1992. Privatization led to the control of Russia's economy by monopolies and oligopolies. The Russian 'mafia' are crime organizations that shake down corporations and businesses for protection money and investment shares, traffic in prostitution, weapons and illegal drugs, bribe or blackmail bureaucrats and politicians to grant them favours and murder their enemies. Corruption permeates the political and administrative system. Dominating Russia's government and economy is the Security Elite (*Siloviki*) and an alliance among oligarch, intelligence, defence and mafia leaders. Yeltsin not only presided over all this but enriched himself, his family, his friends and his political allies from it.

Russia's economy had all but collapsed by 1999. Oligopolies and monopolies straightjacketed the economy with insider trading, sky-high prices and profits, shoddy goods and services. Hyper-inflation diminished everyone's income, especially retirees on fixed incomes. The government's budget deficits, foreign debt and national debt reached their latest record levels. Far more money was fleeing abroad to tax havens than was invested in Russia. The ruble's value reached its latest record low.

Boris Yeltsin was ready to retire but wanted to leave Russia in the hands of a cool-headed technocrat. On New Year's Eve 1999, he announced his resignation and appointment of Vladimir Putin as interim president before an election scheduled for March 2000. That was a remarkable and fateful choice.

Vladimir Putin rose from rags to heights of super wealth and power.[33] Like virtually all Soviets, he grew up in poverty, in his case the only child of hardworking parents in a cramped Leningrad apartment with a communal toilet and kitchen. He was bright and got a legal degree from Leningrad University. The KGB accepted him and after training dispatched him to Dresden where he worked with local East German officials to crush any threats to communist rule. He felt helpless and disillusioned as mass democratic protesters forced East Germany's communist regime to hand over power like their comrades elsewhere in Eastern Europe. He returned to Leningrad where he eventually became Mayor Anatoly Sobchak's top advisor. He became a billionaire and part of the oligarchy and *Siloviki* supervising the privatization of regional state corporations. Learning of his administrative skills and oligarchic ties, Yeltsin summoned him to Moscow for a series of increasingly powerful positions.

Putin won the 2000 presidential election with 53.0 per cent and re-election in 2004 with 71.3 per cent, 2012 with 63.6 per cent, 2018 with 77.8 per cent and 2024 with a resounding 88.5 per cent. Because the constitution then had term limits of two, he served as prime minister while his ally Dmitri Medvedev won the presidency with 71.2 per cent. Putin got the Duma to amend the constitution to eliminate any presidential term limit.

Putin is a fervent Russian nationalist, authoritarian and imperialist. He sees himself as an enlightened tsar dedicated to making Russia great again. He viewed the Soviet Union's collapse as 'the greatest political catastrophe of the twentieth century'.[34] He longed to revive the Russian empire but not the system that controlled it for seventy-four years. Having lived most of his life under communism, he knew well its pathologies that warped and stunted any country's development and the well-being of virtually any one not in the party. After becoming president, he offered these reassuring words: 'I am against the restoration of an official state ideology in Russia in any form.' Instead, 'Patriotism, our history and religion can and, of course, should become such basis values'. He defined patriotism as 'a feeling of pride in one's country, its history and accomplishments [and] the striving to make one's country better, richer, stronger and happier'.[35] Yet Russia is an exceptional country with Moscow the 'third Rome' for Orthodox Christianity and its mission to unite and lead the Slavic peoples against their enemies.

Like most Russians, Putin is an unabashed Stalin fan. Putin admires Stalin's cool-headed ruthlessness and nationalism. Putin is anti-American and anti-Western. He wants NATO and the EU to break up and the Europeans to abandon 'Atlanticism' under America's leadership for 'Euroasianism' with Russia's leadership. Nonetheless, for his first 14 years in power, he did cooperate with the West when it served Russian interests, especially the American-led global war against al Qaeda and other Islamist revolutionary movements.

He first defied the West in April 2008, when the Russian army invaded Georgia to 'liberate' two provinces, Abkhazia and South Ossetia, as 'independent' people's republics. He defied the West again in February 2014, when the Russian army invaded Crimea and eastern Ukraine to 'liberate' the Russian-speaking peoples there. The West's muted condemnations and sanctions encouraged him to make an all-out effort to conquer Ukraine in February 2022. Here he and his advisors miscalculated, believing a Russian blitzkrieg would quickly overrun the country and western protests would be limited. Instead, the Ukrainians blunted the Russian onslaught, bolstered by eventually over a hundred billion dollars in American-led Western military aid and NATO logistical, training and intelligence backing. Nonetheless, Putin announced Russia's annexation of the eastern Ukrainian provinces Donetsk, Luhansk, Kherson and Zaporizhzhia in September 2022.

Putin did not confine his aggression to restoring parts of the Russian empire. In America's 2016 election, the Kremlin orchestrated a massive internet disinformation campaign to promote Republican Party candidate Donald Trump and denigrate Democratic Party candidate Hilary Clinton along with America's democratic political system. How much Russia's efforts contributed to Trump's victory is impossible to determine but they may have been decisive. As president, Trump literally embraced Putin and his policies along with Kim Jong-un, North Korea's Stalinist tyrant, while condemning NATO, the anti-global warming agreement and the agreement that forced Iran to give up its nuclear weapons programme. In 2016, the Kremlin also orchestrated a massive disinformation campaign to promote Britain's exit from the European Union ('Brexit'). Here again how much that effort led to the 54 per cent to 46 per cent vote favouring Britain's withdrawal cannot be precisely determined but may have been decisive.

Putin's efforts to rebuild the Russian empire persisted. He forged close military and economic relations with China, North Korea and Iran. Despite Russia having suffered half a million casualties in his war against Ukraine, Putin mobilized and dispatched ever more troops, weapons and supplies there. The Kremlin again allied with Donald Trump for his 2024 bid for re-election with another disinformation campaign. Trump won a second term as president.

Joseph Stalin lives on in Putin's Russia as an adored cultural icon but not as a totalitarian political system let alone the systemic genocide of imagined 'enemies of the people'. Putin's regime is authoritarian not totalitarian. He continues to win re-elections in an only slightly rigged system because he is genuinely popular. He won 88.5 per cent of the vote in the 2024 presidential election, up from 77.8 per cent in the 2018 election. In the 2021 Duma election, his party United Russia won half the votes or 50.9 per cent.[36]

Likewise, Russian power is a fraction of Soviet power. The Russian empire renamed the Soviet Union peaked under Stalin with Eastern Europe's conquest and conversion to communism. The loss of not just Eastern Europe to the EU and NATO, but the breakup of the Soviet Union itself has rendered Russia a shadow of its former power. Russia's only unquestionable source of power are nuclear weapons with a roughly equal number to America's nuclear arsenal.

By all other hard power indicators, Russian power is a fraction of the West's. In 2024, Russia's population was 140,820,810, with a net loss of nearly 8 million from 145,689,000 in 1991 from migration to foreign lands with greater opportunities, a low birth rate and a high death rate from alcoholism, disease and suicide. The economy was valued at $4.027 trillion and per capital income at $27,500. In stark contrast, America had 341,963,408 people, a $21.538 trillion economy and a $65,600 per capita income; the European Union's 27 countries had 451,815,312 people, a $20,579 trillion economy and a $46,000 per capita; and Britain had 68,459,055 people, a $3.187 trillion economy and a $47,600 per capita income.[37]

Putin has enhanced Russian power by forging closer economic and military ties with China's Premier Xi Jinping, North Korea's Kim Jong-un and Iran's Ayatollah Ali Khamenei. Of the four regimes, only Kim's regime is a Stalinist tyranny; the others are authoritarian dictatorships over mixed economies of large state enterprises and oligopolies along with small and medium sized private businesses and farms. To varying degrees each leader emulates Joseph Stalin's ruthless yet sophisticated political skills that eliminate rivals, promote loyalty and bolster his power.

Chapter 10

APPRAISALS

'Every crime was possible to Stalin, for there was not one he had not committed . . . For in him was joined the criminal senselessness of a Caligula with the refinement of a Borgia and the brutality of a Tsar Ivan the Terrible.' (Milovan Djilas)

'You come to Stalin's table as a friend, but you never know if you'll go home by yourself or if you'll be given a ride – to prison.' (Nikolai Bulganin)

'What good things were associated with the name of Stalin in those years for us, and for me in particular? Very much, practically everything, if only because at that time in our imaginations almost everything came from him and was shrouded in his name.' (Konstantin Simonov)

Joseph Stalin may be history's greatest tyrant as someone with unrestrained power over others. Nikita Khrushchev described how: 'When Stalin proposed something, there were no questions, no comments. A "proposal" from Stalin was a God-given command and you don't haggle about what God tells you to do – you just offer thanks and obey.'[1]

Stalin was not born a tyrant; he made himself one through hard, perilous struggle over four decades. He was born into poverty, a broken family and a cruel father. At 19 years old, he dedicated himself to overthrowing Russia's tsarist government with a communist revolution. He was caught, convicted, sent to exile in Siberia, then escaped and was recaught half a dozen more times. He received a government amnesty in time to join the Communists in Petrograd in the months before they destroyed that government. He entered Communist Party leader Vladimir Lenin's inner circle and helped Lenin spearhead the coup d'etat, impose a dictatorship, nationalize the major industries and largest farms, defeat counterrevolutionary armies in a civil war and transform Russia into the Union of Soviet Socialist Republics. After Lenin died in 1924, Stalin systematically eliminated any rivals to head the Soviet Union by 1929. He then imposed 'total' communism with the Party elite controlling and determining all political, economic, social and cultural relations. At least 11 million people died from starvation, disease, execution and being worked to death as Stalin achieved communism over the next decade. Germany and its allies invaded the Soviet Union in June 1941. As Soviet commander-in-chief, Stalin eventually led the nation to victory after nearly four years of a titanic struggle in which 27 million Soviets perished. During the war, he forged an alliance with America and Britain from which he received over $11 billion in military and economic aid. As the Red Army drove the German army westward, it imposed communist dictatorships in every Eastern European country it overran. He cut a deal with Roosevelt and Churchill to split Germany equally among them and for the Soviet Union to extract billions of dollars' worth of reparations. Animosities between the Soviet Union and the American-led western countries worsened into the Cold War, in which each side did anything it could to undermine the other short of directly warring against it. The Soviet Union's successful test of an atomic bomb in 1949 let Moscow eventually develop a nuclear arsenal that offset that of the United States that dated from 1945. China's Communist Party took power in 1949, although Stalin did little to assist that. Communist North Korea invaded non-communist South Korea in 1950. The Americans intervened, then the Chinese in a stalemated war that an armistice finally ended in 1953. Stalin retained totalitarian power over the Soviet Union, its empire and its several hundred million subjects until a brain haemorrhage killed him on 5 March 1953.

How did Stalin achieve all that? A dynamic mix of character, choices and chance explains Joseph Stalin's extraordinary life. His character's crucial traits were keen intelligence, patience, ambition, ruthlessness, self-control, amorality and brilliant political skills. From a young age, he mastered and channelled his volatile emotions. Khrushchev explained: 'Both Stalin's temper and his self-control were developed to an advanced degree. He was, in short, an overpowering personality.'[2] US Ambassador Averell Harriman gave this balanced assessment of Stalin's character: 'It is hard for me to reconcile the courtesy and consideration that he showed me personally with the ghastly cruelty of his wholesale liquidations. Others, who did not know him personally, see only the tyrant in Stalin. I saw the other side as well – his high intelligence, that fantastic grasp of detail, his shrewdness and the surprising human sensitivity that he was capable of showing.'[3]

Pathological means an abnormal, excessive, destructive trait. By that, Stalin was a pathological paranoic, murderer, bully and liar. Yet, somehow, he kept outwardly calm under even the most stressful circumstances. At times he erupted in rage but soon regained self-control. He harboured hatreds and lusts for vengeance that often took years of strained patience to fulfil.

***

Stalin developed brilliant political skills. Among them was encouraging his rivals to underestimate him as a threat by keeping a low political profile until he mustered enough powerful allies to prevail. In that he was like a crocodile on a bank, patiently waiting and eyeing prey until it got within striking distance. For instance, Trotsky may have exceeded Stalin in intellect, but Stalin persistently outfoxed him politically. Trotsky scorned Stalin as intellectually inferior while Stalin systematically turned the Communist Party against him, denounced him for a litany of 'crimes', stripped him of power, expelled him from the Soviet Union and eventually had him murdered in Mexico City in 1940. Stalin excelled at political judo, at adeptly sidestepping and seizing a rival's attack and wielding it against him. For example, he transformed German revelations of the Soviet massacre of 22,000 Poles in the Katyn Forest into an excuse to disavow the exiled democratic Polish government in London that called for an independent international investigation. Thereafter he shunned the London Poles as he placed a communist Polish government in power.

Stalin was a wily statesman.[4] Ambassador Harriman made this comparison: 'I found him better informed than Roosevelt, more realistic than Churchill, in some ways the most effective of the war leaders. At the same time he was, of course, a murderous tyrant. I must confess that for me Stalin remains the most inscrutable and contradictory character I have known.'[5]

Stalin mastered the assertion of both 'hard' or physical power and 'soft' or psychological power and the dynamic relationship between them. Steadily over years, he packed government and party institutions with devoted followers so that his commands were immediately implemented. He had millions of mostly imagined enemies rounded up and either murdered or sent to slave labour camps. Those acts personify hard power. Yet, he also understood that his tyranny would best endure if he were loved nearly as much as he was feared, willingly followed rather than coerced. To that end, Stalin had his sycophants create a personality cult around him.

Stalin's personality cult worked brilliantly. Most Soviets adored him as a wise, just, heroic, infallible, all-knowing father-figure, who sternly loved and protected them. Neary all angrily rejected any evidence that Stalin was a mass murderer who viewed them as pawns in his quest for total power and communism.

Historian Roy Medvedev explained the tyrant's popularity:

> Stalin was supported by the majority of the Soviet people both because he was clever enough to deceive them and because they were backward enough to be deceived. Not only Stalin's craftiness as a demagogue contributed to this but also the people's inadequate historical experience, their low level of culture and education and the weakness of democratic traditions. Russia's previous development prepared it for revolution but also for the possibility that the revolution would evolve into a totalitarian system of despotic barracks-style socialism – that is, Stalinism.[6]

Looking back, Konstantin Simonov's adoring view of Stalin mirrored those of nearly all other Soviets: 'What good things were associated with the name of Stalin in those years for us and for me in particular? Very much, practically everything, if only because at that time in our imaginations almost everything came from him and was shrouded in his name.'[7]

No one better understood Stalin's tyranny and personality cult than his daughter Svetlana. She described how power and his cult dehumanized him as it elevated a hundred million or so devoted believers:

> For twenty-seven years I was witness to . . . day after day how everything human in him left him and how gradually he turned into a grim monument to his own self . . . But my generation was trained to think that this monument was the embodiment of all that was most beautiful in the ideals of Communism, its living personification . . . Lenin was our icon, Marx and Engels were our apostles – their every word Gospel truth. And my father's every word, either spoken or written, was accepted as a revelation from on High.

She explained how communism and the cult bolstered each other: 'To me, in my early years, Communism was an unshakeable stronghold. Unshakeable remained my father's authority and the belief that he was right in everything without exception.' But then, gradually, she questioned the 'truths' propounded by the Communist Party and her father: 'I became more and more convinced of his senseless cruelty. The theories and dogmas of Marxism-Leninism began to wither away . . . Little by little, it became more than obvious not only that my father had been a despot and had brought about a bloody terror, destroying millions of innocent people, but the whole system which had made that possible was profoundly corrupt.'[8] She no longer believed in the God and the religion that made him possible. Yet, her experience was exceptional. True believers angrily reject any evidence that repudiates their beliefs.

***

Stalin asserted supreme command of the Red Army during the Second World War. He was central to all major planning and made all the major decisions. How did he do?[9] Marshal Grigory Zhukov observed Stalin improve with time:

> Until the defeat of German forces at Stalingrad he had a superficial understanding of combined arms operations. Not having a strong grasp of the complexities, methods and potential of modern army group level operations . . . Stalin frequently demanded patently unrealistic periods of time for the preparation and carrying out of operations . . . in the second half of the war . . . Stalin showed definite flashes of insight into modern war.[10]

Historian Dmitri Volkogonov offered this balanced assessment:

> If by 'military leader,' we mean someone whose talents include creative thinking, profound strategic thought, war experience and ability, intuition and will, then Stalin did not fit the bill. He was, however, a political leader, harsh, strong-willed, determined and power-hungry, who was compelled by historic circumstances to deal with military matters. As Supreme Commander-in-Chief, his strength lay in his absolute power. But it was not this alone that raised him above the other military leaders. Unlike them, he could see the profound dependence of the armed struggle on an entire spectrum of other non-military factors: economic, social, technical, diplomatic, ideological and national.[11]

A psychological trap for any leader is believing his own propaganda. Tyrants are most susceptible with the incessant extolling of their 'genius' and 'greatness' by fawning sycophants, mass-media messages and adoring crowds. Khrushchev revealed how Soviet propaganda unwittingly aided the 1941 German onslaught: 'Stalin very much overestimated the preparedness of our army. Like so many others, he was under the spell of films showing our parades and troop manoeuvres. He didn't see things as they really were in real life. He rarely left Moscow. In fact, he rarely left the Kremlin except to go to his dacha or his vacation retreat in Sochi.' Khrushchev then added: 'The weakness of the military command are well known. Our best commanders were eliminated as enemies of the people.' Stalin then compounded the disasters and chaos by 'interfering with operations and issuing orders which did not take into consideration the real situation at a given section of the front and which could not help but result in large personal losses'.[12] To those criticisms can be added Stalin's decimation of the military's commanders by purging several hundred thousand officers during the late 1930s.

***

The popular dichotomy between democracies and dictatorships is terribly misleading. The differences between them are relative rather than absolute, fifty shades of grey rather than black and white. Any country's political system can be identified on a spectrum with anarchy or no government at one end and totalitarianism or complete government control at the other. Over time governments inevitably shift along that spectrum, mostly subtly through reforms or repressions and occasionally dramatically through coups or even revolutions.

Stalin fathered the modern totalitarian state with 'total' control and manipulation of all key political, economic, social, cultural and religious relationships. He achieved that by realizing an ideology – communism – that called for a totalitarian system and mastering recent revolutionary technologies for surveillance, communications and transportation.

Communism is the most extreme ideology. Tyranny – the Dictatorship of the Proletariat – is communism's core moral and thus organizing principle. Dictatorship is morally justified because only the Communist elite have the knowledge, courage and ruthlessness to transform the ignorant, fearful, exploited masses into a revolutionary steamroller. Communism is a secular religion with a harsh theology and grim fate for any heretics. Communism at once scorned supernatural divinity and celebrated semi-divine prophets like Marx and Engels and enlightened rulers like Lenin and Stalin.

Communism is so contrary to human nature that it can only be imposed by the Communist Party's elite, the Dictatorship of the Proletariat, at gunpoint and through terror.[13] Communism's totalitarian system at once reflected and warped the zealots who served it. True communists must transcend sophism, irony, self-awareness, morality and objective reality to unquestionably believe and act on all the revolutionary slogans. Svetlana, Stalin's daughter, vividly described how communism represses, exploits and dehumanizes all those trapped in the totalitarian system: 'My father was the instrument of this ideology . . . [H]e became its ideal embodiment, the most complete personification of power . . . built on the suppression of millions of human lives. And those who managed to survive physically were reduced to slavery, deprived of the right to think and create.'[14]

Totalitarianism and communism are inseparable; by definition one cannot exist without the other. Stalinism is shorthand for that dynamic. A Stalinist regime has a tyrant atop a suppressive and exploitive system that eliminates all political rivals, abolishes private property and markets, controls and determines all production and prices and indoctrinates all people to submit willingly or die through the mass media, schools, military and workplaces. Carl Friedrich and Zbigniew Brzezinski explained the mentality: 'It is precisely this attempt to impose on society a rationality or rather pseudo-rationality, conceived pattern of distinctly novel forms of social organization that leads to totalitarian oppression. Since, furthermore, this oppression is justified in terms of the ideology, the ideology is totalitarian.'[15]

Totalitarianism is a secular religion that insists that either every subject completely believes and upholds all of the ideology's tenets or is condemned and prosecuted for heresy. Historian Simon Tormey explained that:

> Totalitarian regimes are never happy merely with securing obedience or compliance: simply carrying out the commands of the authorities is never enough to guarantee a person's safety as it would be in most other forms of dictatorship. What the regime demands is a change in the entire outlook on life, the opinions, the beliefs, values and aspirations of ordinary people. The corollary of such a demand is thus that individuals must give up their autonomy, their independence. The must conform rigidly and absolutely with the role defined by the regime. Freedom as the ability of individuals to set their own goals is entirely anathema to the totalitarian outlook. It is in essence a threat to the order and regimentation of life that they require . . . Totalitarianism works by making people think they are free where in reality they are merely pawns in the regime's schemes.[16]

Stalin's regime, like every communist tyranny, was essentially a Potemkin village on a vast national scale. Each regime had an unbridgeable chasm between the utopian workers' paradise that the communists insisted was achievable and the harsh realities. The Soviet Constitutions of 1924, 1936 and 1977 were all Potemkins with their promises of an array of rights for the people which were harshly denied in practice. Communism was built on pyramid schemes of lies. Historian Leszek Kolakowski escaped and later explained communism's collective pathology and elite exploitation of masses of cowed, brainwashed people:

> Half-starved people, lacking the bare necessities of life, attended meetings at which they repeated the government's lies about how well off they were and in a bizarre way they have believed what they were saying . . . Truth they knew was a party matter and therefore lies became true even if they contradicted the plain facts of existence. The condition of their living in two separate worlds at once was one of the most remarkable achievement of the Soviet system.[17]

Many, perhaps most people, suspect that most or all of the regime's propaganda is nonsense, but outwardly they conform or 'live the lie' to avoid prison or execution.

As a tyrant, Stalin sought to provoke as much fear as love in his subjects. He terrified the Soviet people from his inner circle of sycophants to the lowest workers on factory floors, collective farms and office buildings. The stress was worse among those who worked with him. Nikolai Bulganin vividly described the paranoia: 'You come to Stalin's table as a friend, but you never know if you'll go home by yourself or if you'll be given a ride – to prison.' Khruschev elaborated: 'All of us around Stalin were temporary people. As long as he trusted us to a certain degree, we were allowed to go on living and working. But the moment he stopped trusting you, Stalin would start to scrutinize you until the cup of his distrust overflowed. Then it would be your turn to follow those who were no longer among the living.'[18]

The most paranoid Soviets were those literally in Stalin's shadow. Blind obedience and snivelling sycophancy was essential to being in Stalin's inner circle. That minimized but surely did not prevent the chance of being arrested, tried and executed for trumped-up 'crimes against the people'. As for Stalin's personality cult, Khrushchev offers this insight: 'I used to think this urge to glorify himself was a weakness unique to Stalin, but apparently men like Stalin and Mao are very similar in this respect: to stay in power, they consider it indispensable for their authority to be held on high, not only to make the people obedient to them, but to make the people afraid of them as well.'[19]

***

Among countless other people, Stalin at once fascinated, appalled and puzzled Yugoslav communist Milovan Djilas:

> Every crime was possible to Stalin, for there was not one he had not committed . . . For in him was joined the criminal senselessness of a Caligula with the refinement of a Borgia and the brutality of a Tsar Ivan the Terrible. I was . . . interested . . . in how such a dark, cunning and cruel individual could ever have led one of the greatest and most powerful states, not just for a day or a year, but for thirty years![20]

Just what were those crimes?

Joseph Stalin wins the world historical record for mass murder and imprisonment. At least 11,000,000 people died directly or indirectly from his policies while he enslaved another 18,000,000 in labour camps. Only one other tyrant, Mao Zedong, had nearly as many people murdered or enslaved, with Adolf Hitler and Pol Pot runners up for title of history's most murderous tyrant.

Survivors suffered an array of emotional wounds. Khrushchev observed: 'Our Party is still scarred by the damage done during the purges. The attitudes which Stalin uncalculated in the minds of many Party members left a kind of encrustation on the consciousness . . . especially dull, limited people. Even today you'll find those who think that Stalin's way was the only right way to build Socialism and get things done in our country.'[21]

Stalin justified his mass arrests, torture, imprisonment and murder with Communist bromides about achieving a workers' paradise was impossible without first eliminating all 'enemies of the people'. He liked to compare himself to his role model, Tsar Ivan the Terrible who massacred the boyar or merchant class that he feared threatened his rule. He often declared: '"Who's going to remember all this riffraff in ten or twenty years' time? No one. Who remembers the names now of the boyars Ivan the Terrible got rid of? No one . . ." The people had to know he was getting rid of all his enemies. In the end, they got what they deserved.'[22]

Emotionally Stalin could commit mass murder because he lacked a conscience and believed his own cult of semi-divine worship in which he could do no wrong. Yugoslav Communist Milovan Djilas observed that

> The deification of Stalin or the 'cult' of the personality . . . was at least as much the work of Stalin's inner circle and the bureaucracy, who required such a leader, as it was his own doing . . . Turned into a deity, Stalin became so powerful that in time he ceased to pay attention to the changing needs and desires of those who had exalted him . . . He knew

> he was one of the cruellest, most despotic personalities in human history. But this did not worry him one bit, for he was convinced that he was executing the judgment of history. His conscience was troubled by nothing, despite the millions who had been destroyed in his name and by his order, despite the thousands of his closet collaborators whom he had murdered as traitors because they doubted that he was leading the country and people into happiness, equality and liberty.[23]

Questioning a mass murderer's mental state could not be more appropriate. The trouble is that despite twelve decades of steady development, psychology remains as much an art as a science. The popular notion of sane or insane is white versus black when fifty shades of grey from the near white of sainthood to the near black of pure evil reflects reality. Scientists have yet to devise an accurate scale with a similar degree of subtlety probably because individual minds are too complex, shifting and paradoxical to precisely map.

Nonetheless, how can one argue against this condemnation by Charles Bohlen, a Russian expert who served in Moscow during the 1930s and was a key Roosevelt advisor. In his memoir, he issued this condemnation: 'Historians will argue whether Stalin was simply a realist with no moral values or a monster whose paranoia led him into senseless crimes. Judged by his actions, I believe he runs high on the list of the world's monsters.'[24] Clearly, but Stalin was as much a realist as a monster.

Biographer Adam Ulam ponders this key question about the tyrant during his years of ordering mass murder and enslavement:

> We must now pose the question whether . . . Stalin . . . was insane, whether his pathological fear of betrayal and the extraordinary courage he displayed on occasion . . . were the workings of a sick mind. If our definition of insanity includes utter lack of moral sensitivity, then Stalin in his fifties might be so adjudged. If it does not, we cannot hold Stalin in this period to have been insane . . . The pathological elements of his nature reinforced and exaggerated those of the system in which he lived, whether as conspirator, high official or dictator . . . Stalin's mentality made him peculiarly suitable for operating with the context of Soviet reality.[25]

For biographer Robert McNeal, Stalin inspired and engineered a collective delusion and madness in most Soviets:

> If Stalin was mad, he possessed the genius of projecting his own reality into large numbers of normal people. They were ready, for the most part, to believe that large numbers of their erstwhile comrades were traitors.

> They were ready to renounce, to turn away from the incriminated and from their spouses and children. Here Stalin's success is in implanting in the minds of many party members his own heroic image . . . The atmosphere of devotion to the leader and alienation from suspect 'comrades' led to the atomization of members of the Soviet elite. Normal human relationships . . . dissolved . . . And so terror, rationality and insanity appear as intertwined in Soviet society under Stalin.[26]

***

Comparing Joseph Stalin and Adolf Hitler along with their regimes reveals fascinating parallels and profound differences.[27]

They had similar childhoods. Both grew up in poor, marginalized families with domineering, punishing fathers and doting, if strict mothers. Both had physical defects that shamed them, Stalin short statue, pockmarked face and body and withered left arm; Hitler apparently a missing testicle. From their boyhoods, they wanted to be heroes. Both believed they were survivors destined for greatness. Stalin's mother often reminded him that his two older brothers had died as babies and he was lucky to survive to live a good and productive life, ideally as a priest. Hitler survived numerous near-death experiences in the trenches of the First World War, none closer than when his captain gave him a message to carry to headquarters and as he dashed away a shell burst behind him and killed his captain and others in that bunker.

As for character, Stalin and Hitler both were deeply insecure narcissists who overcompensated for their inferiority complexes by struggling to become great leaders with immense power. Both resented those more intelligent, knowledgeable, cultured, sophisticated and attractive than themselves. Both sought vengeance for real and imagined injustices they suffered. Both were paranoid and saw enemies everywhere. Each martyrized himself and projected his own vilest traits on hated others, for Stalin kulaks and other class and ethnic enemies, for Hitler Jews, Slavs and gays.

Both hated and persecuted modern artists and writers, but they enjoyed traditional painting, literature, classical music and theatre. Both aspired to be renowned for their creativity, Hitler as a painter and writer and Stalin as a writer, but were panned by critics, at least before they became tyrants. As a young man Hitler struggled to succeed as a painter in Vienna but was rejected by fellow artists, art academies and potential patrons. Later his book *Mein Kampf* (1925) that expressed his Nazi philosophy and plans became a best seller. Stalin wanted to be considered a great communist theorist. Although his essays and booklets were leaden in prose and analysis, his personality cult celebrated their 'profundity'.

Both took a radical political philosophy and developed its most extreme version, Hitler fascism into Nazism and Stalin Leninism into Stalinism. Both initially failed as revolutionaries, were arrested and served prison terms. They tended to favour practical over ideological interests. Ideologically Communists and Nazis were mortal enemies but that did not stop Stalin and Hitler from allying their countries. Both had political role models, Lenin for Stalin and Mussolini and Stalin for Hitler. Both mastered political symbolism and propaganda and created personality cults of themselves as brilliant leaders to be adored and obeyed by all. Each had a one-party state with auxiliary organizations that mobilized women, youths and professional groups.

Each had a feared secret police that arrested and prosecuted all 'enemies of the people', and a concentration camp system either to exploit them as slave labour or to exterminate them. Stalin developed an existing prison system founded by Lenin. Hitler began his system. Stalin's system was deadlier with 11 million deaths from murder, starvation, disease, suicide or being worked to death compared to six million people in Hitler's system.[28] Likewise, Stalin uncovered hundreds of thousands of 'traitors' within the Communist Party, while Hitler only purged hundreds of Nazis.

In some ways, Stalin and Hitler differed greatly. During the First World War, Hitler was a genuine war hero who served four years in the trenches, was wounded three times and won two Iron Crosses for exemplary courage. During Russia's civil war, Stalin was a political commissar who served far from the front lines. Their management skills differed. Stalin micromanaged; Hitler delegated. Stalin put in 12-hour days, Hitler half that. Stalin preferred listening to talking and when he did talk was parsimonious with his words; Hitler loved lecturing others at dismaying lengths. Both could speak crudely and erupt in rages, but Stalin controlled himself much better. Neither was naturally charismatic, but each developed a charismatic persona as a key political skill. Hitler's charisma was flamboyant in gestures, expressions and rhetoric. Stalin's charisma exuded a calm, calculating, powerful presence, at once reassuring and disquieting.

As for their sex lives, Stalin was twice married and had one child with his first wife, two with the second and may have fathered one out of wedlock; he occasionally had other affairs. Hitler's sex drive apparently was low. He enjoyed being near beautiful women but was bashful with them. He fathered no known children and had only two significant relationships, of which he married the second, Eva Braun, days before they committed suicide to evade capture by the Red Army. Both had partners who committed suicide, Stalin's wife Nadya and Hitler's girlfriend and niece Geli Rabaul, in addition to Eva Braun.

Hitler surpassed Stalin as an imperialist by starting every war fought during his regime, including against the Great Powers, Britain, France and the Soviet Union. Stalin's imperialism was confined to much weaker countries like his war with Germany against Poland, his unilateral war against Finland, his conquests of Bulgaria, Romania, Czechoslovakia, Hungary, his second war against Poland and his unopposed takeovers of Estonia, Latvia and Lithuania. Stalin ultimately won all his wars while Hitler ultimately lost his war against the Soviet Union, Britain and America.

Stalin took over an existing highly authoritarian quasi-communist regime and made it a totalitarian communist regime, while Hitler took over a liberal democracy and made it highly authoritarian. They seized power by different means. Stalin worked his way up the Bolshevik/Communist Party's ranks through a revolution that established a dictatorship, civil war and then struggle within the elite that unfolded over two decades; by 1929, Stalin had eliminated his rivals to become the great Soviet *Vozhd* or Leader. Hitler took over the Nazi Party shortly after it was founded, led it through a series of elections during the 1920s in which the Nazis only won a few seats and then skyrocketed in popularity in the 1930, 1932 and 1933 elections in which they won a plurality of seats President Paul von Hindenburg named Hitler chancellor. Hitler then allied with another right-wing party for a majority of seats which he used to abolish the democracy and other political parties and establish a dictatorship as the *Führer* or Leader.

As for their dictatorships, Stalin's system was totalitarian, Hitler's was authoritarian. The Communist regime eliminated and nationalized all businesses and private property and determined all economic activity with Five-Year Plans. The Nazis guided and regulated the economy through indicative, not command, Four-Year Plans, especially the largest manufacturing, mining, transportation and communication industries to maximize production, but let people keep their businesses and homes; the Nazis did expropriate and sell the property of persecuted 'undesirables.' Most Germans were middle class homeowners; most Soviets endured poverty, repression and exploitation. Communism was strictly atheistic; Nazism espoused mystical ties with ancient Germans and other Aryans.

As for the fate of their respective tyrannies, Stalin's brilliantly succeeded while Hitler's catastrophically failed. Stalin died in his sleep, Hitler by putting a pistol to his right temple and squeezing the trigger as the Red Army fought its way toward his bunker in Berlin. Stalin's totalitarian regime endured after his death for 38 years while Hitler's died with him a mere dozen years after he founded it. Hubris explains those differences. As Germany's commander-in-chief, Hitler's plans led initially to stunning victories that warped him to believe he was indefatigable, with the worst delusion that he could vanquish the Soviet Union. Stalin never let his ambitions exceed his power to realize them.

***

Joseph Stalin consistently wins Russian polls for the most esteemed historical leader.[29] In 2019, 70 per cent of Russians polled believed that Stalin was 'positive' for Russia and in 2022 Stalin was the top figure in Russian history with 39 per cent followed by Vladimir Lenin with 30 per cent, Alexander Pushkin with 23 per cent, Peter the Great with 19 per cent and Vladimir Putin with 15 per cent.[30]

What explains Stalin's enduring popularity despite the overwhelming evidence that he was a tyrant and mass murderer? Stalin remains popular for several reasons. Countless people idealize and romanticize the past and they imagine their earlier years or some era before they lived was better than today. Stalin and his regime symbolizes order, purpose and identity for most Russians. Stalinism's enduring power is visceral. Countless people filled with low self-esteem, rage and fear worship and live vicariously through seemingly all-powerful tyrants like Stalin. Russian President Vladimir Putin feeds those feelings with frequent tributes to the tyrant.

Any book on Joseph Stalin best ends with these lines from poet Yevgeni Yevtushenko:

> 'And I turn to our government with a request:
> to double, treble the guard over that graveyard slab,
> so that Stalin should not rise and with Stalin – the past.'[31]

NOTES

Abbreviations

Stalin's Correspondence	Ministry of Foreign Affairs, *Correspondence between the Chairman of the Council of Ministers of the U.S.S.R and the Presidents of the U.S.A and the Prime Ministers of Great Britain during the Great Patriotic War of 1941-1945*, New York: Capricorn Books, 1965.
Stalin Works	Joseph Stalin, *The Works of Joseph Stalin*, vols 1–13, Moscow: Foreign Language Publication House, 1954.

Introduction

1 Isaac Deutscher, *Stalin: A Political Biography* (New York: Oxford University Press, 1949); Boris Souvarine, *Stalin* (Stanford, Calif.: Hoover Institute Press, 1964); Adam Ulam, *Stalin: The Man and his Era* (New York: Viking, 1973); Robert Tucker, *Stalin as Revolutionary, 1879-1929: A Study in History and Personality* (New York: W.W. Norton, 1973); Roy Medvedev, *On Stalin and Stalinism* (New York: Oxford University Press, 1979); Alan Ulam, *Stalin: The Man Behind the Myth* (New York: Viking, 1982); Robert McNeal, *Stalin: Man and Ruler* (New York: New York University Press, 1988); Robert Tucker, *Stalin in Power: The Revolution from Above, 1928-1941* (New York: W.W. Norton, 1990); Dmitri Volkogonov, *Stalin: Triumph and Tragedy* (New York: Grove Weidenfeld, 1991); Edvard Radzinsky, *Stalin* (New York: Anchor, 1996); Roman Brackman, *The Secret File of Joseph Stalin: A Hidden Life* (London: Frank Cass, 2001); Simon Montefiore, *Stalin: The Court of the Red Tsar* (New York: Alfred Knopf, 2004); Robert Service, *Stalin: A Biography* (London: Macmillan, 2004); Stephen Lee, *Stalin and the Soviet Union* (New York: Routledge, 2005); Hiroaki Kuromiya, *Stalin: Profiles in Power* (New York: Routledge, 2013); Stephen Kotkin, *Stalin: Volume 1, Paradoxes of Power, 1878-1928* (New York Penguin, 2015); Stephen Kotkin, *Stalin: Volume 2, Waiting for Hitler, 1929-1941* (New York: Penguin, 2018).

2 'Stalin Is More Popular Than Ever in Russia Survey Shows', *U.S. News and World Report*, 9 May 2019; 'Puttin Plummets, Stalin Stays on Top in Russians' Ranking of "Notable" Historic Figures—Poll', *Moscow Times*, 21 June 2021.

3 Ulam, *Stalin: The Man Behind the Myth*, 237.

4 Sergo Beria, *Beria, My Father: Inside Stalin's Kremlin* (London: Duckworth Publishers, 2001), 142.

5 Montefiore, *Stalin: Court of the Red Tsar*, 177.

6 Volkogonov, *Stalin*, 266.

7 Ulam, *Stalin: Man Behind the Myth*, 437.

8 Robert Conquest, *The Great Terror: A Reassessment* (New York: Oxford University Press, 1990), 56.

9 Roy Medvedev, *Let History Judge: The Origins and Consequences of Stalinism* (New York: Columbia University Press, 1989), 89.

10 Isaac Deutscher, 'The Leader and His Party', in Robert Daniels, ed., *The Stalin Revolution: Foundations of Soviet Totalitarianism* (Lexington, Mass.: D.C. Heath, 1972), 8.

11 Cordell Hull, *The Memoirs of Cordell Hull* (New York: Macmillan, 1948), 2:1311.

12 Milovan Djilas, *Conversations with Stalin* (New York: Harcourt, Brace and World, 1962), 62.

13 John Toland, *The Last 100 Days* (New York: Random House, 1966), 114.

14 Montefiore, *Stalin: Court of the Red Tsar*, 198.

15 'Khrushchev Secret Speech', Nikita Khrushchev, *Khrushchev Remembers* (Boston: Little, Brown and Company, 1970), 585.

16 Conquest, *Great Terror*, 59.

17 Leon Trotsky, *My Life: An Attempt at an Autobiography* (New York: Charles Scribners' Sons, 1930), 255.

18 Montefiore, *Stalin: Court of the Red Tsar*, 526–7.

19 Ibid., 437.

20 Khrushchev, *Remembers*, 257–8.

21 Ulam, *Stalin: Man Behind the Myth*, 408–09.

22 Volkogonov, *Stalin*, 234.

23 For communist theory, see: Peter Worsley, *Marx and Marxism* (New York: Routledge, 2002); Gregory Claeys, *Marx and Marxism* (New York: Bold Type Books, 2018). For histories of communism, see: David Priestfield, *The Red Flag: A History of Communism* (New York: Grove Press, 1999); Jean-Louis Panne et al, *The Black Book of Communism: Crimes, Terror, Repression* (Cambridge, Mass.: Harvard University Press, 1999); Richard

Pipes, *Communism: A History* (New York: Modern Library, 2003); Archie Brown, *The Rise and Fall of Communism* (New York: Random House, 2009); Robert Service, *Comrades: A History of Communism* (Cambridge, Mass.: Harvard University Press, 2010); Sean McMeekin, *To Overthrow the World: The Rise and Fall of Communism* (New York: Basic Books, 2024).

24 Souvarine, *Stalin*, 362–3.

25 Conquest, *Great Terror*, 292.

26 Ibid., 17.

27 Djilas, *Conversations*, 172.

28 For pioneering although dated explorations of totalitarianism, see: Friedrich von Hayek, *The Road to Serfdom* (Chicago: University of Chicago Press, 1944); Hannah Arendt, *The Origins of Totalitarianism* (1949) (New York: Harcourt, Brace and, Janovich, 1973). For more recent studies, see: Carl Friedrich and Zbigniew Brzezinski, *Totalitarian Dictatorship and Autocracy* (Cambridge, Mass.: Harvard University Press, 1956); Carl Friedrich, ed., *Totalitarianism in Perspective: Three Views* (New York: Praeger, 1969); Leonard Shapiro, *Totalitarianism* (New York: Praeger, 1972); Ernest Menze, ed., *Totalitarianism Reconsidered* (Port Washington, N.Y.: Kennikat, 1981); Simon Tormey, *Making Sense of Tyranny: Interpretations of Totalitarianism* (Manchester, U.K.: Manchester University Press, 1995); Abbott Gleason, *Totalitarianism: The Inner History of the Cold War* (New York: Oxford University Press, 2001); Philip Gray, *Totalitarianism: The Basics* (New York: Routledge, 2013); Timothy Synder, *On Tyranny: Twenty Lessons from the Twentieth Century* (New York: Crown, 2017); Paul O'Brien, *Total State: Totalitarianism and How We Can Resist It* (New York: Wordwell, 2023); Flagg Taylor, *The Great Lie: Classic and Recent Appraisals of Ideology and Totalitarianism* (New York: Regnery Gateway, 2023); Simona Forti, *Totalitarianism: A Borderline Idea* (Palo Alto, Calif.: Sanford University Press, 2024). For comparative studies, see: James Gregor, *Marxism, Fascism and Totalitarianism: Chapters in the Intellectual History of the Twentieth Century* (Palo Alto, Calif.: Stanford University Press, 2008); Michael Geyer and Sheila Fitzpatrick, eds, *Beyond Totalitarianism: Stalinism and Nazism Compared* (New York: Cambridge University Press, 2008); Bruce Pauley, *Hitler, Stalin and Mussolini: Totalitarianism in the Twentieth Century* (New York: Wiley Blackwell, 2014).

29 Ralph Abramovitch, *The Soviet Revolution, 1917-1939* (New York: International Universities Press, 1962), 415; Leonard Shapiro, *The Communist Party of the Soviet Union* (New York: Random House, 1970), 381.

30 Conquest, *Great Terror*, 310.

31 Ibid., 310–11, 275.

32 Arendt, *The Origins of Totalitarianism*, xxiv.

Chapter 1: Radicalization

1 Simon Montefiore, *Young Stalin* (New York: Vintage, 2009).

2 Daniel Rancour-Laferreriere, *The Mind of Stalin* (New York: Ardis, 1988); James Greensmith, *In the Mind of Stalin* (London: Pen and Sword, 2023).

3 Montefiore, *Young Stalin*, 181.

4 Ibid., 182.

5 Isaac Deutscher, 'Marxism and Primitive Magic', in Tariq Ali, ed., *The Stalinist Legacy: Its Impact on Twentieth Century World Politics* (Boulder, Colo.: Lynne Rienner, 1984), 114.

6 Montefiore, *Young Stalin*, 564.

7 Tucker, *Stalin as Revolutionary*, 4.

8 Gregory Freeze, *Russia: A History* (New York: Oxford University Press, 2009); Geoffrey Hoskins, *Russia and the Russians* (Cambridge, Mass.: Belnap Press, 2011); Paul Bushkovitch, *A Concise History of Russia* (New York: Cambridge University Press, 2011); Orlando Figes, *The Story of Russia* (New York: Metropolitan Books, 2023).

9 Maureen Perrie, *The Cult of Ivan the Terrible in Stalin's Russia* (New York: Palgrave Macmillan, 2001).

10 For the best overview of Russian culture, see: Orlando Figes, *Natasha's Dance: A Cultural History of Russia* (New York: Henry Holt, 2002). See also: James Billington, *The Icon and the Axe: An Interpretive History of Russian Culture* (New York: Vintage, 1970); Catherine Merridale, *Night of Stone: Death and Memory in Russia* (New York: Viking, 2001); Alexander Schmeman, *The Foundations of Russian Culture* (New York: Holy Trinity Seminary Press, 2024).

11 Orlando Figes, *Revolutionary Russia, 1891-1991* (New York: Henry Holt, 2014), 13.

12 Montefiore, *Young Stalin*, 26–7.

13 McNeal, *Stalin*, 4.

14 Svetlana Alliluyeva, *Only One Year: A Memoir* (New York: Harper and Row, 1969), 361, 362, 377.

15 Franco Venturi, *The Roots of Revolution: A History of the Populist and Socialist Movements in Nineteen Century Russia* (New York: Legare Street Press, 2023).

16 Medvedev, *Let History Judge*, 597.

17 McNeal, *Stalin*, 12.

18 Volkogonov, *Stalin*, 201.

19 Medvedev, *Let History Judge*, 32.

20 Ibid., 589–90.

21 Louis Fisher, *The Life of Lenin* (New York: Harper and Row, 1964); Robert Service, *Lenin: A Political Life*, 3 vols (Bloomington: University of Indiana Press, 1985, 1991, 1995); Robert Service, *Lenin: A Biography* (Cambridge, Mass.: Harvard University Press, 2000); Tomas Kreusz, *Revolutionary Lenin: An Intellectual Biography* (New York: Monthly Review Press, 2018); Victor Sebestyn, *Lenin: The Man, Dictator and the Master of Terror* (New York: Vintage, 2018).

22 Medvedev, *Let History Judge*, 94.

23 Service, *Lenin: A Biography*, 29.

24 Alan Bullock, *Hitler and Stalin: Parallel Lives* (New York: Vintage, 1993), 77.

25 Harrison Salisbury, *Black Nights, White Snow: Russia's Revolutions, 1905-1917* (New York: Da Capo, 1981); Abraham Ascher, *The Revolution of 1905: Russia in Disarray* (Stanford, Calif.: Stanford University Press, 1988); Jon Smele and Anthony Heywood, *The Russian Revolution of 1905: Centenary Perspectives* (New York: Routledge, 2005).

26 Walter Sablinsky, *The Road to Bloody Sunday: Father Gapon and the St. Petersburg Massacre of 1905* (Princeton, N.J.: Princeton University Press, 1976).

27 Ibid., 344.

28 Figes, *Revolutionary Russia*, 29–30.

29 Ibid., 49.

30 Montefiore, *Young Stalin*, 30.

Chapter 2: Revolution

1 Jack Goldstone, ed., *Revolutions: Theoretical, Comparative and Historical Studies* (New York: Centage, 2002); Stephen Sanderson, *Revolutions: A Worldwide Introduction to Social and Political Contention* (New York: Routledge, 2010); Theda Skocpol, *States and Social Revolutions* (New York: Cambridge University Press, 2015); Jack Goldstone, Leonid Grinin and Andrey Korotayev, eds, *The Handbook of Revolutions in the 21st Century* (New York: Springer, 2022).

2 For overviews, see: Edward Hallett Carr, *The Bolshevik Revolution, 1917-1923*, 3 vols (London: Macmillan, 1950–2); Richard Pipes, *The Formation of the Soviet Union: Communism and Nationalism, 1917-1923* (Cambridge, Mass.: Harvard University Press, 1964); Ralph Abramovitch, *The Soviet Revolution, 1917-1939* (New York: International Universities Press, 1962); Robert Service, *The Bolshevik Party in Revolution: A Study in Organizational Change, 1917-1923* (London: Macmillan, 1979); Orlando Figes, *A People's Tragedy: The Russian Revolution, 1891-1924* (New York: Penguin, 1998); Orlando Figes, *Revolutionary Russia, 1891-1991* (New York: Henry Holt, 2014); Mark Steinberg, *The Russian Revolution, 1905-1921* (New York: Oxford University Press, 2017); Sheila Fitzpatrick, *The Russian*

Revolution, 1917-1921 (New York: Oxford University Press, 2017); Laura Engelstein, *Russia in Flames: War, Revolution and Civil War, 1914-1921* (New York: Oxford University Press, 2017); Anthony Beevor, *Russia: Revolution and Civil War, 1917-1921* (New York: Viking, 2022). For an excellent comparative study, see: Arno Mayer, *The Furies: Violence and Terror in the French and Russian Revolutions* (Princeton, N.J.: Princeton University Press, 2000). For the events of 1917, see: Robert Slusser, *Stalin in October: The Man Who Missed the Revolution* (Baltimore: Johns Hopkins Press, 1987); Alexander Rabinovitch, *The Bolsheviks Come to Power: The Revolution of 1917 in Petrograd* (New York: Haymarket Books, 2017).

3 Robert Service, *The Last of the Tsars: Nicholas II and the Russian Revolution* (New York: Macmillan, 2017).

4 Niall Ferguson, *The Pity of War: Explaining World War I* (New York: Basic Books, 1999); G.J. Meyer, *A World Undone: The Story of the Great War, 1914-1918* (New York: Bantam, 2015).

5 David Stone, *The Russian Army in the Great War: The Eastern Front, 1914-1918* (Lawrence: University Press of Kansas, 2021).

6 Richard Abraham, *Alexander Kerensky: The First Love of the Revolution* (New York: Columbia University Press, 1990).

7 Brackman, *The Secret File of Joseph Stalin.*

8 Ulam, *Stalin: Man Behind the Myth,* 134.

9 Service, *Lenin: A Biography,* 333.

10 Ulam, *Stalin: Man Behind the Myth,* 140.

11 Ibid., 140–1.

12 Slusser, *Stalin in October,* 87–95.

13 Ibid., 107.

14 Joel Carmichael, *Trotsky: An Appreciation of His Life* (New York: St. Martin's Press, 1975); Robert Service, *Trotsky: A Biography* (Cambridge, Mass.: Harvard University Press, 2009); Robert Payne, *The Life and Death of Trotsky* (New York: Lume, 2019); Allan Todd, *Trotsky: The Passionate Revolutionary* (London: Pen and Sword, 2022).

15 Milovan Djilas, *The New Class* (New York: Frederick Praeger, 1957), 50.

16 Volkogonov, *Stalin,* 104.

17 Service, *Trotsky,* 110.

18 Medvedev, *Let History Judge,* 559.

19 Ulam, *Stalin: Man Behind the Myth,* 149.

20 Ibid., 154.

21 Service, *Trotsky,* 190.

22 Rabinovitch, *Bolsheviks Come to Power,* 294.

23 Ibid., 272.

24 Service, *Lenin: A Biography,* 311.

25 Leon Trotsky, *Trotsky's Diary in Exile, 1935* (Cambridge, Mass.; Harvard University Press, 1958), 293.

26 For histories of the Soviet Union, see: Bertram Wolfe, *Communist Totalitarianism: Keys to the Soviet System* (Boston: Beacon Press, 1956); Stephen Cohen, *Rethinking the Soviet Experience: Politics and History Since 1917* (New York: Oxford University Press, 1985); Geoffrey Hosking, *A History of the Soviet Union, 1917-1991* (London: Fontana Press, 1992); Martin Malia, *The Soviet Tragedy: A History of Socialism, 1917-2000* (New York: Free Press, 1995); Dmitri Volkogonov, *The Rise and Fall of the Soviet Empire: Political Leaders from Lenin to Gorbachev* (London: HarperCollins, 1999); Michael Kort, *The Soviet Colossus: History and Aftermath* (New York: Routledge, 2019).

27 Service, *Lenin: A Biography*, 350.

28 Ibid., 334.

29 Ibid., 349.

30 Ibid., 316.

31 Figes, *Revolutionary Russia*, 107.

32 Leon Trotsky, *Terrorism and Communism: A Reply to Kautsky* (New York: Verso, 2017), 63.

33 Service, *Trotsky*, 267.

34 James Harris, *The Great Fear: Stalin's Terror of the 1930s* (New York: Oxford University Press, 2016), 29.

35 Paul Gregory, ed., *The Economics of Forced Labor: The Soviet Gulag* (Palo Alto, Calif.: Hoover Institute Press, 2003); Anne Applebaum, *Gulag: A History of the Soviet Concentration Camps* (New York: Anchor, 2004); Alexander Solzhenitsyn, *The Gulag Archipelago: An Experiment in Literary Investigation* (New York: Harper Perennial, 2007); Steven Rosefield, *Red Holocaust* (New York: Routledge, 2009).

36 Evan Mawdsley, *The Russian Civil War* (Boston: Allen and Unwin, 1987), 191; Steven Rosefield, *Red Holocaust* (New York: Routledge, 2009), 67.

37 Mawdsley, *Russian Civil War*; Bruce Lincoln, *Red Victory: A History of the Russian Civil War* (New York: Simon and Schuster, 1989); Jonathan Smele, *The 'Russian' Civil Wars, 1916-1926: Ten Years That Shook the World* (New York: Oxford University Press, 2017).

38 Mawdsley, *Russian Civil War*, 6.

39 Both quotes from ibid., 48, 45.

40 Damien Wright, *Churchill's Secret War with Lenin: British and Commonwealth Intervention in the Russian Civil War* (New York: Helion Press, 2022); Anne Reid, *A Nasty Little War: The Western Intervention into Russia's Civil War* (New York: Basic Books, 2024).

41 Mawdsley, *Russian Civil War*, 144, 167.

42 Francesco Benvenuti, *The Bolsheviks and the Red Army, 1918-1922* (New York: Cambridge University Press, 1988).

43 Service, *Trotsky*, 232.

44 *Stalin Works*, 4:249.

45 Service, *Trotsky*, 223.

46 Montefiore, *Stalin: Court of the Red Tsar*, 33.

47 Norman. Davies, *White Eagle, Red Star: The Polish-Soviet War, 1919-1920* (London: Pimlico, 2003); Peter Whitewood, *The Soviet-Polish War and Its Legacy: Lenin's Defeat and the Rise of Stalinism* (New York: Bloomsbury, 2023).

48 Roy Medvedev, *On Stalin and Stalinism* (New York: Oxford University Press, 1979), 21.

49 Medvedev, *Let History Judge*, 128–9.

50 Craig Nation, *Black Earth, Red Star: A History of Soviet Security Policy* (Ithaca, N.Y.: Cornell University Press, 1992), 1.

51 Adam Ulam, *Expansion and Coexistence: Soviet Foreign Policy, 1917-1973* (New York: Praeger, 1974); Craig Nation, *Black Earth, Red Star: A History of Soviet Security Policy* (Ithaca, N.Y.: Cornell University Press, 1992); Gabriel Gradetsky, *Soviet Foreign Policy, 1917-1991: A Retrospective* (New York: Routledge, 1994); Frederic Fleron, Erik Hoffman and Robbin Laird, eds, *Soviet Foreign Policy, 1917-1991: Classics and Contemporary Issues* (New York: Routledge, 2018).

52 Helmut Gruber, *Soviet Russia Masters the Comintern: International Communism in the Era of Stalin's Ascendency* (New York: Anchor Books, 1974); Kevin McDermott and Jeremy Agnew, *The Comintern: A History of International Communism from Lenin to Stalin* (New York: St. Martin's Press, 1997).

53 Service, *Trotsky*, 250.

54 McDermott, *Comintern*, 21–2.

55 Mawdsley, *Russian Civil War*, 285–7. Peter Juviler, 'Contradictions of Revolution: Juvenile Crime and Rehabilitation,' in *Bolshevik Culture* (Bloomington: University of Indiana Press, 1985), 264.

56 Harold Fisher, *The Famine in Soviet Russia, 1921-1923: The Operations of the America Relief Administration* (New York: Macmillan, 1927); Henry Beeuwkes, *American Medical and Sanitary Relief in the Russian Famine, 1921-1923* (New York: Legare Street Press, 2022).

Chapter 3: Power Struggle

1 Khrushchev, *Remembers*, 17.

2 Victor Serge, *Memoirs of a Revolutionary, 1901-1941* (New York: Oxford University Press, 1978), 94.

3 Mawdsley, *Russian Civil War*, 287–9.

4 Alec Nove, *An Economic History of the USSR* (New York: Penguin, 1990), 86, 94.

5 Louis Fisher, *The Life of Lenin* (New York: Harper and Row, 1964), 524.

6 Souvarine, *Stalin*, 216, 302, 303; Deutscher, *Stalin*, 234.

7 Conquest, *Great Terror*, 3.

8 Khrushchev, *Remembers*, 20.

9 Montefiore, *Stalin: Court of the Red Tsar*, 44.

10 Vyacheslav Molotov, *Molotov Remembers: Inside Kremlin Politics* (Chicago: Ivan Dee, 1993); Geoffrey Roberts, *Molotov: Stalin's Cold Warrior* (Washington D.C.: Potomac Books, 2011).

11 Montefiore, *Stalin: Court of the Red Tsar*, 39.

12 Ulam, *Stalin: Man Behind the Myth*, 216.

13 'Khrushchev Secret Speech,' Khrushchev, *Remembers*, 563.

14 Khrushchev, *Remembers*, 44.

15 Ibid., 46.

16 Catherine Merridale, *Moscow Politics and the Rise of Stalin: The Communist Party in the Capital, 1925-32* (London: Macmillan, 1990).

17 Volkogonov, *Stalin*, 57.

18 Trotsky, *My Life*, 485.

19 McNeal, *Stalin*, 101.

20 Tucker, *Stalin as Revolutionary*, 130.

21 Service, *Lenin: A Biography*, 463, 469.

22 Volkogonov, *Stalin*, 94.

23 *Stalin Works*, 6:357.

24 Volkogonov, *Stalin*, 109.

25 McNeal, *Stalin*, 95–6.

26 Volkogonov, *Stalin*, 60.

27 Ulam, *Stalin: Man Behind the Myth*, 273–4.

28 Volkogonov, *Stalin*, 182.

29 Ulam, *Stalin: Man Behind the Myth*, 269.

30 Medvedev, *Let History Judge*, 183.

31 Ibid., 132.

32 Ulam, *Stalin: Man Behind the Myth*, 359.

Chapter 4: Stalinism

1 Robert Daniels, ed., *The Stalin Revolution: Foundations of Soviet Totalitarianism* (Lexington, Mass.: D.C. Heath, 1972); Anton Antonov-Ovseenko, *The Time of Stalin: Portrait of a Tyranny* (New York: Harper and Row, 1981); Robert Tucker, *Stalin in Power: The Revolution from Above*

(New York: W.W. Norton, 1990); John Channon, ed., *Politics, Society and Stalinism in the USSR* (New York: St. Martin's Press, 1998); Robert Tucker, ed., *Stalinism: Essays in Historical Interpretation* (New Brunswick, N.J.: Rutgers University Press, 2000); Christopher Reed, ed., *The Stalin Years: A Reader* (New York: Red Globe, 2002).

2 Alan Bullock, *Hitler and Stalin: Parallel Lives* (New York: Vintage, 1993), 416.

3 Peter Deriabin, *Inside Stalin's Kremlin: An Eyewitness Account of Brutality, Duplicity and Intrigue* (Lincoln: University of Nebraska Press, 1998).

4 Lewis Steigelbaum and Ronald Suny, eds, *Making Soviet Workers: Power, Class and Identity* (Ithaca, N.Y.: Cornell University Press, 1994); E.A. Rees, *Stalinism and Soviet Rail Transport* (New York: St. Martin's Press, 1995); David Shearer, *Industry, State and Society in Stalin's Russia, 1926-1932* (Ithaca, N.Y.: Cornell University Press, 1996); Kenneth Straus, *Factory and Community in Stalin's Russia: The Making of an Industrial Working Class, 1928-1933* (Pittsburgh: University of Pittsburgh Press, 1998).

5 *Stalin Works*, 11:248.

6 Mikhail Morukov, 'The White Sea Canal,' in Gregory, ed., *Economics of Forced Labour*, 151–62; Applebaum, *Gulag*, 79.

7 Stephen Kotkin, *Magnetic Mountain: Stalinism as a Civilization* (Berkeley: University of California Press, 1995); G.T. Ritterspoon, *Stalinist Simplifications and Soviet Complications: Social Tensions and Political Conflicts in the USSR, 1933-53* (Philadelphia: Harwood Academic, 1991); Sheila Fitzpatrick, *Everyday Stalinism: Ordinary Life in Extraordinary Times* (New York: Oxford University Press, 2000); Lewis Siegelbaum and Andrei Sokolov, eds, *Stalinism as a Way of Life: A Narrative in Documents* (New Haven, Conn.: Yale University Press, 2003).

8 David Dallin, 'The Return of Inequality,' in Daniels, ed., *Stalin Revolution*, 110.

9 Nicolas Werth, 'Stalin's System during the 1930s,' in Henry Rousso, ed., *Stalinism and Nazism: History and Memory Compared* (Lincoln: University of Nebraska Press, 2004), 37.

10 Ulam, *Stalin: Man Behind the Myth*, 322–3, 332.

11 Nicolas De Witt, *Education and Professional Employment in the USSR* (Washington D.C.: National Science Foundation, 1961), 783; Shiela Fitzpatrick, 'Cultural Revolution as Class War', in Sheila Fitzpatrick, ed., *Cultural Revolution in Russia, 1928-1932* (Bloomington: University of Indiana Press, 1984), 33; Moshe Lewin, 'Society, State and Ideology during the First Five-Year Plan,' in Fitzpatrick, ed., Cultural Revolution in Russia, 53; David Dallin, 'The Return of Inequality', in Daniels, ed., *Stalin Revolution*, 113–14.

12 Medvedev, *Let History Judge*, 212.

13 Nicolas Werth, 'Forms of Autonomy in 'Socialist Society', in Rousso, ed., *Stalinism and Nazism*, 120.

14 Montefiore, *Stalin: Court of the Red Tsar*, 46.

15 Medvedev, *Let History Judge*, 227, 243; Alec Nove, 'Economics and Personality', in Daniels, ed., *The Stalin Revolution*, 64.

16 Robert Conquest, *The Harvest of Sorrow: Soviet Collectivization and the Terror-Famine* (New York: Oxford University Press, 1986); Sheila Fitzpatrick, *Stalin's Peasants: Resistance and Survival in the Russian Village* (New York: Oxford University Press, 1994); Lynne Viola, *Peasant Rebels Under Stalin: Collectivization and the Culture of Peasant Resistance* (New York: Oxford University Press, 1996); Andrea Graziosa, *The Great Soviet Peasant War: Bolsheviks and Peasants, 1917-1933* (Cambridge, Mass.: Harvard University Press, 1996).

17 Medvedev, *Let History Judge*, 244; Conquest, *Great Terror*, 20.

18 Winston Churchill, *Memoirs of the Second World War: An Abridgement of the Six Volumes of The Second World War* (Boston: Houghton Mifflin, 1987), 633.

19 Lewin, 'Society, State and Ideology, in Fitzpatrick, ed., *Cultural Revolution in Russia*, 66.

20 Khrushchev, *Remembers*, 19.

21 *Stalin Works*: 13:38–39.

22 Ibid., 13:42.

23 Volkogonov, *Stalin*, 186.

24 Ulam, *Stalin: Man Behind the Myth*, 349.

25 Rosamond Richardson, *The Long Shadow: Inside Stalin's Family* (Boston: Little, Brown, 1993).

26 Khrushchev, *Remembers*, 292.

27 Alliluyeva, *Only One Year*, 141–2.

28 Montefiore, *Stalin: Court of the Red Tsar*, 12.

29 Alliluyeva, *Only One Year*, 145.

30 Montefiore, *Stalin: Court of the Red Tsar*, 108.

31 Ibid., 119.

Chapter 5: Communist Culture

1 For Soviet culture, see: Sheila Fitzpatrick, ed., *Cultural Revolution in Russia, 1928-1931* (Bloomington: University of Indiana Press, 1978); Abbott Gleason, Peter Kenez and Richard Stites, eds, *Bolshevik Culture: Experiment and Order in the Russian Revolution* (Bloomington: University of Indiana Press, 1985); Sheila Fitzpatrick, *The Cultural Front: Power and Culture in Revolutionary Russia* (Ithaca, N.Y.: Cornell University

Press, 1992); Vladimir Brovkin, *Russia After Lenin: Politics, Culture and Society, 1921-1929* (New York: Routledge, 1998); Jeffrey Brooks, *Thank You, Comrade Stalin! Soviet Public Culture from Revolution to Cold War* (Princeton, N.J.: Princeton University Press, 2001); Caterina Clark and Evgeny Dobrenko, *Soviet Culture and Power* (New Haven, Conn.: Yale University Press, 2007); Isaiah Berlin, *The Soviet Mind: Russian Culture under Communism* (Washington D.C.: Brookings Institute Press, 2011); Nicholas Rzhevsky, ed., *The Cambridge Companion to Modern Russian Culture* (New York: Cambridge University Press, 2012).

2 Medvedev, *Let History Judge*, 129.

3 Sheila Fitzpatrick, 'Cultural Revolution as Class War', in Fitzpatrick, ed., *Cultural Revolution in Russia*, 8.

4 Gail Lapidus, 'Educational Strategies and Cultural Revolution: The Politics of Soviet Development', in Fitzpatrick, ed., *Cultural Revolution in Russia*, 84.

5 Edward Brown, 'The Mobilization of Culture', in Daniels, ed., *Stalin Revolution*, 130.

6 Ibid., 133.

7 Brooks, *Thank You, Comrade Stalin!*, 108.

8 Volkogonov, *Stalin*, 130.

9 Richard Stites, 'Iconoclastic Currents in the Russian Revolution: Destroying and Preserving the Past', in Gleason, Kenez and Stites, eds, *Bolshevik Culture*, 17.

10 Brown, 'Mobilization of Culture', in Daniels, ed., *Stalin Revolution*, 131.

11 Leon Trotsky, 'Art and Politics in Our Epoch', *Partisan Review*, vol. 5, no. 3, August–September 1938, 4.

12 Brown, 'Mobilization of Culture', in Daniels, ed., *Stalin Revolution*, 131.

13 Ibid., 134.

14 Jeffrey Brooks, 'The Breakdown in Production and Distribution of Printed Material, 1917-1927', in Gleason, Kenez and Stites, eds, *Bolshevik Culture*, 166.

15 Ibid.

16 Ibid., 153.

17 Conquest, *Great Terror*, 300.

18 Montefiore, *Stalin: Court of the Red Tsar*, 95.

19 Ibid.

20 Ibid., 133.

21 Ibid., 136.

22 Richard Taylor, 'The Birth of Soviet Cinema', in Gleason, Kenez and Stites, eds, *Bolshevik Culture*, 190.

23 Ibid., 193.

24 Medvedev, *Let History Judge*, 832.

25 Ibid., 98.

26 Conquest, *Great Terror*, 306.

27 Alliluyeva, *Only One Year*, 390.

28 Ibid., 23.

29 Stephen White, 'Stalinism and the Graphic Arts', in Channon, ed., *Politics, Society and Stalinism in the USSR*, 155.

30 Pyotr Malevsky-Malevitch, ed., *Russia U.S.S.R.: A Complete Handbook* (New York: William Farquhar Payson, 1933), 665; Fitzpatrick, *Stalin's Peasants*, 225–6, 363.

31 Sheila Fitzpatrick, 'Stalin and the Making of a New Elite, 1928-1939', *Slavic Review*, vol. 38, no. 3 (September 1979), 378.

32 Sheila Fitpatrick, *Education and Social Mobility in the Soviet Union, 1921-1934* (Cambridge: Cambridge University Press, 1979); Kendall Bailes, *Technology and Society under Lenin and Stalin: The Origins of Soviet Technical Intelligentsia, 1917-1941* (Princeton, N.J.: Princeton University Press, 1978); Nicolas Lampert, *The Technical Intelligentsia and the Soviet State* (New York: Oxford University Press 1979).

33 Gail Lapidus, 'Educational Strategies and Cultural Revolution: The Politics of Soviet Development', in Fitzpatrick, ed., *Cultural Revolution in Russia*, 101.

34 Nicolas De Witt, *Education and Professional Employment in the USSR* (Washington D.C.: National Science Foundation, 1961), 783; Shiela Fitzpatrick, 'Cultural Revolution as Class War', in Fitzpatrick, ed., *Cultural Revolution in Russia*, 33; Moshe Lewin, 'Society, State and Ideology during the First Five-Year Plan', in Fitzpatrick, ed., *Cultural Revolution in Russia*, 53; David Dallin, 'The Return of Inequality,' in Daniels, ed., *Stalin Revolution*, 113–14.

35 Nicolas Werth, 'Stalin's System during the 1930s', Rousso, ed., *Stalinism and Nazism*, 50.

36 Conquest, *Great Terror*, 293, 295, 297.

37 Robert Conquest, *The Nation Killers: The Soviet Deportation of Nationalities* (London: Macmillan, 1970).

38 Conquest, *Great Terror*, 229, 232.

39 Isaac Deutscher, *The Prophet Outcast: Trotsky, 1929-1940* (New York: Verso, 2003), 369.

40 Applebaum, *Gulag*, xx.

41 H.G. Wells, *Experiment in Autobiography* (New York: Macmillan, 1934), 684–9.

42 Gleason, *Totalitarianism*, 59.

43 Paul Kengor, *Dupes: How America's Adversaries Have Manipulated Progressives for a Century* (New York: Simon and Schuster, 2018).

44 Joseph Davies, *Mission to Moscow* (New York: Simon and Schuster, 1941), 269, 272, 280.

45 Wendell Willkie, *One World* (New York: Simon and Schuster, 1943), 85–6.

46 Conquest, *Great Terror*, 469.

47 John Gaddis, *The United States and the Origins of the Cold War, 1941-1947* (New York: Columbia University Press, 1972), 37.

48 Frank Warren, *Liberals and Communism: The 'Red Decade' Revisited* (Bloomington: Indiana University Press, 1966).

49 Warren, *Liberals and Communism*, 213.

50 Gaddis, *United States and the Origins of the Cold War*, 44.

51 Darin Stephanov, *Ruler Personality Cults from Empire, Nation-States and Beyond in Symbolic Patterns and International Dynamics* (New York: Routledge, 2020); Frank Dikotter, *How to Be a Dictator: The Cult of Personality in the Twentieth Century* (New York: Bloomsbury, 2022).

52 Kevin Morgan, *International Communism and the Cult of the Individual: Leaders and Martyrs under Lenin and Stalin* (New York: Palgrave Macmillan, 2017).

53 Nina Tumarkin, *Lenin Lives: The Lenin Cult in Soviet Russia* (Cambridge, Mass.: Harvard University Press, 1997).

54 Alec Nove, ed., *The Stalin Phenomenon* (London: Trafalgar Square Press, 1993); Jan Plamper, *The Stalin Cult: A Study in the Alchemy of Power* (New Haven, Conn.: Yale University Press, 2012); Anita Pisch, *The Personality Cult of Stalin in Soviet Posters, 1929-1953* (Canberra: University of Australia Press, 2016).

55 Medvedev, *Let History Judge*, 325.

56 Khrushchev, *Remembers*, 47.

57 McNeal, *Stalin*, 150–1.

Chapter 6: Terror

1 Montefiore, *Stalin: Court of the Red Tsar*, 129–30.

2 McNeal, *Stalin*, 151–2.

3 Ulam, *Stalin: Man Behind the Myth*, 373.

4 Khrushchev, *Remembers*, 572–3.

5 Roy Medvedev, *Let History Judge: The Origins and Consequences of Stalinism* (New York: Columbia University Press, 1989); Robert Conquest, *The Great Terror: A Reassessment* (New York: Oxford University

Press, 1990); James Harris, *The Great Fear: Stalin's Terror of the 1930s* (New York: Oxford University Press, 2016).

6 Robert Conquest, *Stalin and the Kirov Murder* (New York: Oxford University Press, 1989); Amy Knight, *Who Killed Kirov?: The Kremlin's Greatest Mystery* (New York: Hill and Wang, 1999).

7 John Getty, *Origins of the Great Purges: The Soviet Communist Party Reconsidered, 1933-1938* (New York: Cambridge University Press, 1985); Robert Conquest, *Inside Stalin's Secret Police: NKVD Politics, 1936-39* (Stanford, Calif.: Stanford University Press, 1985); John Getty and R.T. Manning, eds, *Stalinist Terror: New Perspectives* (New York: Cambridge University Press, 1993); John Getty and Oleg Naumov, *The Road to Terror: Stalin and the Self-Destruction of the Bolsheviks, 1932-1939* (New Haven, Conn.: Yale University Press, 1999).

8 Montefiore, *Stalin: Court of the Red Tsar*, 162; Conquest, *Stalin and the Kirov Murder*, 67.

9 Volkogonov, *Stalin*, 247.

10 Montefiore, *Stalin: Court of the Red Tsar*, 185.

11 Ulam, *Stalin: Man Behind the Myth*, 413–14.

12 Conquest, *Great Terror*, 115, 119.

13 Lee, *Stalin and the Soviet Union*, 32.

14 Ulam, *Stalin: Man Behind the Myth*, 425.

15 Volkogonov, *Stalin*, 63–4.

16 Montefiore, *Stalin: Court of the Red Tsar*, 211.

17 Ibid., 274.

18 Conquest, *Great Terror*, 252.

19 Ulam, *Stalin: Man Behind the Myth*, 434.

20 Medvedev, *Let History Judge*, 202.

21 Roy Medvedev, *All Stalin's Men: Six Who Carried Out the Bloody Purges* (New York: Anchor, 1985).

22 Montefiore, *Stalin: Court of the Red Tsar*, 236.

23 Amy Knight, *Beria: Stalin's First Lieutenant* (Princeton, N.J.: Princeton University Press, 1994).

24 Montefiore, *Stalin: Court of the Red Tsar*, 76, 294.

25 Khrushchev, *Remembers*, 352.

26 Montefiore, *Stalin: Court of the Red Tsar*, 214.

27 Tucker, *Stalin in Power*, 407.

28 Montefiore, *Stalin: Court of the Red Tsar*, 228–9, 249, 250, 271.

29 Nicolas Werth, 'Stalin's System during the 1930s', in Rousso, ed., *Stalinism and Nazism*, 43–4.

30 Daniel Diller, *Russia and the Independent States* (Washington D.C.: Congressional Quarterly, 1994), 162–4.

31 Montefiore, *Stalin: Court of the Red Tsar*, 232; Conquest, *Great Terror*, 427.

32 Peter Whitewood, *The Red Army and the Great Terror: Stalin's Purge of the Military* (Lawrence: University of Kansas Press, 2015).

33 Conquest, *Great Terror*, 204.

34 Ibid., 450, 297.

35 William Chase, *Enemies within the Gates?: The Comintern and the Stalinist Repression, 1934-39* (New Haven, Conn.: Yale University Press, 2001).

36 Isaac Deutscher, *The Prophet Outcast: Trotsky, 1929-1940* (New York: Verso, 2003).

37 Isaac Levine, *The Mind of an Assassin* (New York: Farrar, Straus and Cudahy, 1959).

38 Ibid., 188.

39 Conquest, *Great Terror*, 275, 290, 330–1, 484–6.

Chapter 7: World War

1 Stanley Payne, *A History of Fascism, 1914-1945* (Madison: University of Wisconsin Press, 1995); Robert Paxton, *The Anatomy of Fascism* (New York: Vintage, 2004).

2 R.J.B. Bosworth, *Mussolini* (London: Arnold, 2002).

3 Alan Tasman, ed., *The Culture of Japanese Fascism* (Durham, N.C.: Duke University Press, 2009); Walter Skya, *Japan's Holy War: The Ideology of Radical Shinto Ultranationalism* (Durham, N.C.: Duke University Press, 2009); Yoshiki Yoshimi, *Grassroots Fascism: The War Experience of the Japanese People* (New York: Columbia University Press, 2016).

4 Brendan Simms, *Hitler: A Global Biography* (New York: Basic Books, 2001); Ian Kershaw, *Hitler: 1889-1936, Hubris* (New York: W.W. Norton, 2000); Ian Kershaw, *Hitler: 1936-1945, Nemesis* (New York: W.W. Norton, 2001); Volker Ulrich, *Hitler: Ascent, 1889-1939* (New York: Vintage, 2017); Volker Ullrich, *Hitler: Downfall, 1939-1945* (New York: Vintage, 2021).

5 Michael Burleigh, *The Third Reich: A New History* (New York: Hill and Wang, 2001); William Shirer, *The Rise and Fall of the Third Reich* (1959) (New York: Simon and Schuster, 2011); Thomas Childers, *The Third Reich: A History of Nazi Germany* (New York: Simon and Schuster, 2018).

6 Conquest, *Great Terror*, 196.

7 Montefiore, *Stalin: Court of the Red Tsar*, 491–2.

8 Jonathan Haslam, *The Soviet Union and the Struggle for Collective Security in Europe, 1933-1939* (New York: St. Martin's Press, 1984); Geoffrey

Roberts, *The Soviet Union and the Origins of the Second World War: Russo-German Relations, 1933-1941* (New York: Red Globe, 1995).

9 W.G. Beasley, *Japanese Imperialism, 1984-1945* (Oxford: Clarendon Press, 1991); S.C.M. Payne, *The Japanese Empire: Grand Strategy from the Meiji Restoration to the Pacific War* (New York: Cambridge University Press, 2017).

10 Basil Liddell Hart, *The History of the Second World War* (New York: Konecky and Konecky, 1970); Donald Miller, *The Story of World War II* (New York: Simon and Schuster, 2002); Martin Gilbert, *The Second World War* (New York: Henry Holt, 2004); Evan Mawdsley, *The Story of World War II* (New York: Simon and Schuster, 2020); Victor Davis, *The Second World Wars: How the First Global Conflict Was Fought and Won* (New York: Basic Books, 2020).

11 William Nester, *World of War: A History of American Warfare from Jamestown to the War on Terror* (New York: Stackpole Books, 2024).

12 William Nester, *Franklin Roosevelt and the Art of Leadership: Battling the Great Depression and the Axis Powers* (London: Frontline Books, 2024).

13 Robert Dalleck, *Franklin D. Roosevelt and American Foreign Policy, 1932-1945* (New York: Oxford University Press, 1979).

14 Alan Bullock, *Hitler and Stalin: Parallel Lives* (New York: Vintage, 1993), 525.

15 Richard Thornton, *The Comintern and the Chinese Civil War, 1926-1931* (Seattle: University of Washington Press, 1969); Edward Carr, *The Twilight of Comintern, 1930-1935* (New York: Pantheon Books, 1982).

16 Kevin McDermott and Jeremy Agnew, *The Comintern: A History of International Communism from Lenin to Stalin* (New York: St. Martin's Press, 1997), 137.

17 Edward Carr, *The Comintern and the Spanish Civil War* (New York: Pantheon Books, 1984); Dan Richardson, *Comintern Army: The International Brigades in Spain's Civil War* (Lexington: University of Kentucky Press, 2014).

18 Antony Beevor, *The Battle for Spain: The Spanish Civil War, 1936-1939* (New York: Penguin, 2006).

19 Medvedev, *Let History Judge*, 726.

20 E.R. Hooton, *Stalin's Claws: From the Purges to the Winter War: Red Army Operations before Barbarossa* (New York: Tattered Flag, 2013).

21 Rana Miller, *Forgotten Ally; China's World War II, 1937-1945* (New York: Mariner Books, 2014).

22 Iris Chang, *The Rape of Nanking* (New York: Basic Books, 2012).

23 Kui Kwang Shum, *The Chinese Communist Road to Power: The Anti-Japanese National United Front* (New York: Oxford University Press, 1988).

24 Alvin Coox, *Nomonhan: Japan Against Russia, 1939*, 2 vols (Stanford, Calif.: Stanford University Press, 1985); Stuart Goldman, *Nomonhan: The Red Army's Victory that Shaped World War II* (Annapolis: Naval Institute Press, 2012).

25 Volkogonov, *Stalin*, 353.

26 Ibid., 354–5.

27 Anthony Read and David Fisher, *The Deadly Embrace: Hitler, Stalin and the Nazi-Soviet Pact, 1939-1941* (New York: W.W. Norton, 1989); Anthony Read and David Fisher, *The Deadly Embrace: Hitler, Stalin and the Nazi-Soviet Pact* (New York: W.W. Norton, 1989).

28 Montefiore, *Stalin: Court of the Red Tsar*, 310–11.

29 Brackman, *The Secret File of Joseph Stalin*, 285.

30 Khrushchev, *Remembers* 128.

31 Roger Moorhouse, *Poland 1939: The Outbreak of World War II* (New York: Basic Books, 2020); David Williamson, *Poland Betrayed: The Nazi-Soviet Invasions of 1939* (London: Pen and Sword, 2020).

32 William Trotter, *Frozen Hell: The Russo-Finish Winter War of 1939-1940* (New York: Algonquin Books, 2000); Alexander Churbanyan and Harold Shukman, eds, *Stalin and the Soviet-Finnish War, 1939-40* (London: Frank Cass, 2002).

33 Pavel Aptekov and Olga Dudorova, 'Peace and Statistics of Losses, Unheeded Warning and Winter War', *Slavic Military Studies*, vol. 10, no. 1 (March 1997), 200–09; Read and Fisher, *The Deadly Embrace*, 401–17.

34 Khrushchev, *Remembers*, 154.

35 Montefiore, *Stalin: Court of the Red Tsar*, 330.

36 Khrushchev, *Remembers*, 152.

37 Charles Bohlen, *Witness to History, 1929-1969* (New York: W.W. Norton, 1973), 60.

38 Montefiore, *Stalin: Court of the Red Tsar*, 334, 705.

39 François Kersaudy, *Norway 1940* (Lincoln: University of Nebraska Press, 1998).

40 Julian Jackson, *The Fall of France: The Nazi Invasion of 1940* (New York: Oxford University Press, 2004); Alistair Horne, *To Lose a Battle: France 1940* (New York: Penguin, 2009).

41 James Holland, *The Battle of Britain: Five Months that Changed the World, May to October 1941* (New York: St. Martin's Griffin Press, 2012); Stephen Bungay, *The Most Dangerous Enemy: A History of the Battle of Britain* (New York: Aurum Press, 2016).

42 Andrew Williams, *The Battle of the Atlantic: The Allied Submarine Fight against Hitler's Gray Wolves of the Sea* (New York: Basic Books, 2004);

Jonathan Dimbleby, *The Battle of the Atlantic: How the Allies Won the War* (New York: Oxford University Press, 2018).

43 Both quotes, Nester, *Roosevelt*, 114.

44 Warren Kimball, *The Most Unsordid Act: Lend-Lease, 1939-1941* (Baltimore: Johns Hopkins University Press, 1969); George Herring, *Aid to Russia, 1941-1947: Strategy, Diplomacy and the Origins of the Cold War* (New York: Columbia University Press, 1973); Leon Martel, *Lend-Lease, Loans and the Coming of the Cold War: A Study of the Implementation of Foreign Policy* (Boulder, Colo.: Westview, 1979).

45 Nester, *Roosevelt*, 115.

46 Jane Rogoyska, *Surviving Katyn: Stalin's Polish Massacre and the Search for Truth* (New York: Simon and Schuster, 2021).

47 Volkogonov, *Stalin*, 374.

48 Evan Mawdsley, *Thunder in the East: The Nazi-Soviet War, 1941-1945* (New York: Hodder Arnold, 2005), 213–14; David Glantz, *Colossus Reborn: The Red Army at War, 1941-1943* (Lawrence: University Press of Kansas, 2005), 538, 588.

49 Mawdsley, *Thunder in the East*, 30; Glantz, *Colossus Reborn*, 159, 538.

50 Glantz, *Colossus Reborn*, 189, 218–19.

51 Steve Zaloga, *Soviet Tanks and Combat Vehicles of World War Two* (London: Arms and Armor Press, 1989); David Porter, *Soviet Tank Units, 1939-45* (London: Amber Books, 2020).

52 Mawdsley, *Thunder in the East*, 198.

53 Volkogonov, *Stalin*, 368; Glantz, *Colossus Reborn*, 467.

54 Dwight Eisenhower, *Crusade in Europe* (Garden City, N.Y.: Doubleday, 1948), 467–8.

55 Montefiore, *Stalin*, 331.

56 Mawdsley, *Thunder in the East*, 38.

57 Georgi Zhukov, *The Memoirs of Marshal Zhukov* (New York: Delacorte Press, 1971); William Spahr, *Zhukov: the Rise and Fall of a Great Captain* (Novato, Calif.: Presidio Press, 1993); Otto Chaney, *Zhukov* (Norman: University of Oklahoma Press, 1996).

58 Chaney, *Zhukov*, 166.

59 Mawdsley, *Thunder in the East*, 19, 30, 32–3.

60 David Doyle, *The Complete Guide to German Armored Vehicles* (New York: Skyhorse, 2019; David Porter, *German Tanks in World War II* (London: Amber Books, 2020).

61 Mawdsley, *Thunder in the East*, 85.

62 Ibid., 26.

63 Ibid., 49.

64 Ibid., 50–1.

65 Volkogonov, *Stalin*, 418.

66 Mawdsley, *Thunder in the East*, 185.

67 Ibid., 43.

68 John Barber and Mark Harrison, eds, *The Soviet Defense-Industry Complex from Stalin to Khruschev* (New York: Macmillan, 2000), 100.

69 Ibid.

70 Mawdsley, *Thunder in the East*, 202.

71 Glantz, *Colossus Reborn*, 135.

72 Jonathan Dimbleby, *Operation Barbarossa: The History of a Cataclysm* (New York: Oxford University Press, 2021).

73 Gabriel Gorodetsky, *Grand Delusion: Stalin and the German Invasion of Russia* (New Haven, Conn.: Yale University Press, 1999).

74 Mawdsley, *Thunder in the East*, 18.

75 Ibid., 36–7.

76 Montefiore, *Stalin: Court of the Red Tsar*, 354.

77 Ibid., 358.

78 Jozo Tomasevich, *War and Revolution in Yugoslavia, 1941-1945* (Stanford, Calif.: Stanford University Press, 2002); James Burgwyn, *Empire on the Adriatic: Mussolini's Conquest of Yugoslavia, 1941-1943* (New York: Enigma Books, 2005).

79 Jeffrey Plowman, *Greece 1941: The Death Throes of Blitzkrieg* (London: Pen and Sword, 2019).

80 For the Eastern Front, see: Alan Clark, *Barbarossa: The Russian-German Conflict, 1941-45* (New York: Quill, 1985); Evan Mawdsley, *Thunder in the East: The Nazi-Soviet War, 1941-1945* (New York: Hodder Arnold, 2005); Gantz, *Colossus Reborn*; Christian Hartman, *Nazi Germany's War in the East, 1941-1945* (New York: Oxford University Press, 2018).

81 For the war's first half-year, see: David Stahel, *Operation Barbarossa and Germany's Defeat in the East* (New York: Cambridge University Press, 2011); Christer Bergstrom, *Operation Barbarossa 1941: Hitler against Stalin* (New York: Casemate, 2018); James Ellman, *Hitler's Great Gamble: A New Look at German Strategy, Operation Barbarossa and the Axis Defeat in World War II* (New York: Stackpole, 2019); Robert Kershaw, *War without Garlands: Operation Barbarossa 1941-1942* (New York: Goodall, 2020); Jonathan Dimbleby, *Operation Barbarossa: the History of a Catastrophe* (New York: Oxford University Press, 2021).

82 Mawdsley, *Thunder in the East*, 85–6.

83 Ibid., 58–9.

84 Jane Degras, ed., *Soviet Documents on Foreign Policy*, 5 vols (Oxford: Oxford University Press, 1953), 3:490–1.

85 Zhukov, *Memoirs*, 235.

86 For Stalin's war leadership, see: Albert Seaton, *Stalin as Military Commander* (New York: Praeger, 1998); Geoffrey Roberts, *Stalin's Wars: From World War to Cold War, 1939-1953* (New Haven, Conn.: Yale University Press, 2006); Sean McMeekin, *Stalin's War: A New History of World War II* (New York: Basic Books 2022). For relations among Stalin and his generals, see: Bialer Seweryn, ed., *Stalin and His Generals: Soviet Military Memoirs of World War II* (New York: Pegasus, 1969); Harold Shukman, ed., *Stalin's Generals* (London: Grove Press, 1993); Albert Axell, *Stalin's War Through the Eyes of His Commanders* (London: Arms and Armour, 1997); William Spahr, *Stalin's Lieutenants: A Study of Command under Duress*, (Novato, Calif.: Presidio Press, 1997).

87 Djilas, *Conversations*, 62.

88 Khrushchev, *Remembers*, 169.

89 *Stalin Works*, 1:404.

90 Harrison Salisbury, *900 Days: The Siege of Leningrad* (New York: Da Capo Press, 2003); Anna Reid, *Leningrad: The Tragedy of a City under Siege, 1941-44* (New York: Bloomsbury, 2012).

91 Chaney, *Zhukov*, 154.

92 Mawdsley, *Thunder in the East*, 136.

93 Ibid., 134–6.

94 Volkogonov, *Stalin*, 456.

95 Zhukov, *Memoirs*, 339–40.

96 Mawdsley, *Thunder in the East*, 121.

97 Chaney, *Zhukov*, 201.

98 William Nester, *Winston Churchill and the Art of Leadership* (London: Frontline, 2020); Nester, *Roosevelt*.

99 William Averell Harriman, *Special Envoy to Churchill and Stalin, 1941-1946* (New York: Random House, 1975), 77, 170.

100 Churchill, *Memoirs of the Second World War: Abridged*, 469–71.

101 Ellman, *Hitler's Great Gamble*, 103.

102 Steven Miner, *Between Churchill and Stalin: The Soviet Union, Great Britain and the Origins of the Grand Alliance* (Chapel Hill: University of North Carolina Press, 1988), 147.

103 Miner, *Between Churchill and Stalin*; Martin Folly, Geoffrey Roberts and Oleg Rzheshevsky, *Churchill and Stalin: Comrades-in-Arms during the Second World War* (London: Pen and Sword, 2020).

104 *Stalin's Correspondence*, 11–12.

105 Mark Stoler, *The Politics of the Second Front: American Military Planning and Coalition Warfare, 1941-1943* (Westport, Conn.: Greenwood, 1977).

106 Miner, *Between Churchill and Stalin*, 150–1.

107 *Stalin's Correspondence*, 16.

108 Andrew Rawson, *Organizing Victory: The War Conferences, 1941-1945* (New York: Spellmount Publishers, 2013).

109 *Stalin's Correspondence*, 18.

110 Vojtech Mastny, *Russia's Road to the Cold War: Diplomacy, Warfare and the Politics of Communism, 1941-1945* (New York: Columbia University Press, 1979), 45.

111 Glantz, *Colossus Reborn*, 249, 251, 323, 442.

112 Chaney, *Zhukov*, 203–04.

113 Mawdsley, *Thunder in the East*, 144, 146.

114 Ibid., 147.

115 Ibid., 149.

116 Churchill, *Memoirs of the Second World War, Abridged*, 618–10.

117 Ibid., 621–2, 624.

118 *Stalin's Correspondence*, 60–1.

119 Ibid., 61–3.

120 Churchill, *Memoirs of the Second World War, Abridged*, 627.

121 David O'Keefe, *One Day in August: The Untold Story Behind Canada's Tragedy at Dieppe* (New York: Vintage, 2014).

122 Rick Atkinson, *An Army at Dawn: The War in North Africa, 1942-1943* (New York: Henry Holt, 2007); Martin Kitchen, *Rommel's Desert War: Waging World War II in North Africa, 1941-1943* (New York: Cambridge University Press, 2009).

123 *Stalin's Correspondence*, 132.

124 Ibid., 133.

125 Mawdsley, *Thunder in the East*, 151.

126 Antony Beevor, *Stalingrad: The Fateful Siege, 1942-1943* (New York: Penguin, 1999).

127 Mawdsley, *Thunder in the East*, 185, 186.

128 Ibid.

129 David Glantz, *The Battle of Kursk* (New York: Basic Books, 1999); Lloyd Clark, *The Battle of Tanks: Kursk, 1943* (New York: Grove Press, 2012).

130 Mawdsley, *Thunder in the East*, 228.

131 Matthew Cooper, *The Phantom War: The German Struggle against Soviet Partisans, 1941-44* (London: Macdonald and Janes, 1979); Leonard

Grenkevich and David Glantz, *The Soviet Partisan Movement, 1941-1944: A Critical Historiographical Analysis* (New York: Routledge, 1999); Alexander Hill, *The War Behind the Eastern Front: Soviet Partisans in North West Russia, 1941-44* (New York: Routledge, 2004); Ben Shepherd, *War in the Wild East: The German Army and Soviet Partisans* (Cambridge, Mass.: Harvard University Press, 2004).

132 Mawdsley, *Thunder in the East*, 232.

133 Cooper, *Phantom War*, 169.

134 Volkogonov, *Stalin*, 486.

135 *Stalin's Correspondence*, 120–1.

136 Ibid., 121–2.

137 Ibid., 124–5.

138 Rick Atkinson, *The Day of Battle, 1943-1944: The War in Sicily and Italy* (New York: Henry Holt, 2008).

139 Andrew Sangster and Pier Battistelli, *Flawed Commanders and Strategy in the Battles for Italy, 1943-45* (New York: Casemate, 2023).

140 Keith Sainsbury, *The Turning Point: Roosevelt, Stalin, Churchill and Chiang Kai-Shek, 1943: The Moscow, Cairo and Teheran Conferences* (New York: Oxford University Press, 1985).

141 Susan Butler, ed., *Dear Mr. Stalin: The Complete Correspondence of Franklin D. Roosevelt and Joseph V. Stalin* (New Haven, Conn.: Yale University Press, 2008); Susan Butler, *Roosevelt and Stalin: Portrait of a Partnership* (New York: Vintage, 2016).

142 *Stalin's Correspondence*, 175.

143 Harriman, *Special Envoy*, 273–4.

144 Ibid., 278.

145 Montefiore, *Stalin: Court of the Red Tsar*, 500.

146 Djilas, *Conversations*, 73.

147 Harriman, *Special Envoy*, 282.

148 Alliluyeva, *Only One Year*, 370.

149 Volkogonov, *Stalin*, 151–2.

150 James Greensmith, *In the Mind of Stalin* (London: Pen and Sword, 2023), 89.

151 Martin Walker, *The Cold War: A History* (New York: Henry Holt, 1993), 12.

152 *Stalin's Correspondence*, 242.

153 Ibid., 254.

154 Ibid.

155 Ibid., 255.

156 Rick Atkinson, *The Guns at Last Light: The War in Western Europe, 1944-1945* (New York: Henry Holt, 2013).

157 Gaddis, *United States and the Origins of the Cold War*, 18.

158 Davies, *Mission to Moscow*.

159 Gaddis, *United States and the Origin of the Cold War*, 84–5.

160 Both quotes from ibid., 54, 64.

161 Mastny, *Russia's Road to the Cold War*, 212–13.

162 Ibid., 232.

163 Churchill, *Memoirs of the Second World War, Abridged*, 885–6.

164 *Stalin's Correspondence*, 289–92.

165 Michael Dobbs, *Six Months in 1945: FDR, Stalin, Churchill and Truman—from World War to Cold War* (New York: Alfred Knopf, 2012), 198.

166 Djilas, *Conversations*, 110.

167 Mawdsley, *Thunder in the East*, 217.

168 Ibid., 394.

169 Toland, *Last 100 Days*, 41.

170 Diane Shaver Clemens, *Yalta* (New York: Oxford University Press, 1970); Athan Theoharis, *The Yalta Myth: An Issue in U.S. Politics 1945-1955* (Columbia: University of Missouri Press, 1970); Russell Buhite, *Decisions at Yalta: An Appraisal of Summit Diplomacy* (Wilmington, Del.: Scholarly Resources, 1986); S.M. Plokhy, *Yalta: The Price of Peace* (New York: Viking, 2010).

171 Dobbs, *Six Months in 1945*, 23–5.

172 Ibid., 31–2.

173 Toland, *Last 100 Days*, 60–1, 87.

174 Ibid., 93.

175 Ibid., 108.

176 William Leahy, *I Was There: The Personal Story of the Chief of Staff to Presidents Roosevelt and Truman* (New York: Whittlesey House, 1950), 315–16

177 Both quotes from Toland, *Last 100 Days*, 87.

178 Montefiore, *Stalin: Court of the Red Tsar*, 470.

179 Ibid., 483.

180 Robert Sherwood, *Roosevelt and Hopkins: An Intimate History* (New York: Harper Brothers, 1948), 344.

181 Anthony Eden, *The Reckoning* (Boston: Houghton Mifflin, 1965), 593.

182 Dobbs, *Six Months in 1945*, 65–6.

183 Ibid., 139.

184 Stephen Ambrose, *Eisenhower and Berlin, 1945: The Decision to Halt at the Elbe* (New York: W.W. Norton, 1967).

185 Toland, *Last 100 Days*, 325.

186 Martin Blumenson, ed., *The Patton Papers, 1940-1945* (New York: Da Capo, 1996), 685.

187 Toland, *Last 100 Days*, 308, 329.

188 Both quotes from ibid., 326.

189 Ibid., 328.

190 Seweryn Bialer, ed., *Stalin and His Generals: Soviet Military Memoirs of World War II* (New York: Pegasus, 1969), 516–20.

191 Both quotes from Harriman, *Special Envoy*, 437–48.

192 Ibid., 441.

193 Butler, ed., *Dear Mr. Stalin*, 23.

194 *Stalin's Correspondence*, 320.

195 Alonzo Hamby, *Man of the People: A Life of Harry S. Truman* (New York: Oxford University Press, 1995).

196 Gaddis, *United States and the Origins of the Cold War*, 199.

197 Hamby, *Man of the People*, 270.

198 Harry Truman, *Memoirs of Harry S. Truman: 1945, Year of Decisions* (New York: Doubleday, 1955) 79–82.

199 Antony Beevor, *The Fall of Berlin, 1945* (New York: Penguin, 2003).

200 Zhukov, *Memoirs*, 622.

201 Bialer, ed., *Stalin and His Generals*, 557–8.

202 Zhukov, *Memoirs*, 627–8.

203 Gleason, *Totalitarianism*, 68.

204 Harriman, *Special Envoy*, 474.

205 Arnold Offner, *Another Such Victory: President Truman and the Cold War, 1945-1953* (Sanford, Calif.: Stanford University Press, 2002), 41.

206 Herbert Feis, *Between War and Peace: The Potsdam Conference* (Princeton, N.J.: Princeton University Press, 1960); Charles Mee, *Meeting at Potsdam* (London: M. Evans, 1975); Michael Neiberg, *Potsdam: The End of World War II and the Remaking of Europe* (New York: Basic Books, 2015).

207 Kuromiya, *Stalin*, 204.

208 Michael Neiberg, *Potsdam: The End of World War II and the Remaking of Europe* (New York: Basic Books, 2015), 62.

209 Gar Alperovitz, *Atomic Diplomacy: Hiroshima and Potsdam* (New York: Random House, 1965); Herbert Feis, *The Atomic Bomb and the End of World War II* (Princeton, N.J.: Princeton University Press, 1966).

210 Churchill, *Memoirs of the Second World War, Abridged*, 980–1.

211 Ibid., 985.

212 Andrei Gromyko, *Memoirs* (New York: Doubleday, 1990), 109.

213 John Ellis, *World War II: A Statistical Survey for All the Combatants* (New York: Facts On File, 1993), 253–4.

214 Glantz, *Colossus Reborn*, 535, 588, 620.

215 Mawdsley, *Thunder in the East*, 102–05.

216 Ibid., 238.

217 Alexander Dallin, *German Rule in Russia, 1941-1945: A Study of Occupation Policies* (Boulder, Colo.: Westview Press, 1981).

218 Michael Parrish, *The Lesser Terror: Soviet State Security, 1939-1945* (Westport, Conn.: Praeger, 1996).

219 Montefiore, *Stalin: Court of the Red Tsar*, 441, 472–3.

220 E.A. Rees, 'Stalinism: The Primacy of Politics,' in Channon, ed., *Politics, Society and Stalinism in the USSR*, 61; Glantz, *Colossus Reborn*, 544; Montefiore, *Stalin*, 395; Mawdsley, *Thunder in the East*, 215; Volkogonov, *Stalin*, 446.

221 Robert Conquest, *Stalin: Breaker of Nations* (New York: Penguin, 1992).

222 Nicolas Werth, 'Strategies of Violence in Stalinist USSR', in Rousso, ed., *Stalinism and Nazism*, 87.

223 Mawdsley, *Thunder in the East*, 231–2.

224 Zhukov, *Memoirs*, 652–4.

Chapter 8: Cold War

1 For overviews of the Cold War, see: John Gaddis, *The Long Peace: Inquiries in the History of the Cold War* (New York: Oxford University Press, 1987); Walter LaFeber, *America, Russia and the Cold War, 1945-1990* (New York: McGraw-Hill, 1991); Martin Walker, *The Cold War: A History* (New York: Henry Holt, 1993); Bruce Brager, *The Iron Curtain: The Cold War in Europe* (New York: Chelsea House, 2004); John Gaddis, *Strategies of Containment: A Critical Appraisal of Postwar American National Security Policy* (New York: Oxford University Press, 2005); Odd Westad, *The Cold War: A World History* (New York: Hachette, 2017). For the origins of the Cold War, see: Herbert Feis, *From Trust to Terror: The Onset of the Cold War, 1945-1950* (New York: W.W. Norton, 1970); Pierre de Senarclens, *From Yalta to the Iron Curtain: The Great Powers and the Origins of the Cold War* (New York: Berg, 1995); Michael Dobbs, *Six Months in 1945: FDR, Stalin, Churchill and Truman from World War*

to Cold War (New York: Alfred Knopf, 2012); Martin McCauley, *The Origins of the Cold War, 1941-1949* (New York: Routledge, 2021). For American perspectives and policies in the early Cold War, see: John Gaddis, *The United States and the Origins of the Cold War, 1941-1947* (New York: Columbia University Press, 1972); Joyce and Gabriel Kolko, *The Limits of Power: The World and the United States Foreign Policy, 1945-1954* (New York: Harper and Row, 1972); Daniel Yergin, *Shattered Peace: The Origins of the Cold War and the National Security State* (Boston: Houghton Mifflin, 1977); Terry Anderson, *The United States, Great Britain and the Cold War, 1944-1947* (Columbia: University of Missouri Press, 1981); Robert Hathaway, *Ambiguous Partnership: Britain and America, 1944-1947* (New York: Columbia University Press, 1981); Robert Messer, *The End of an Alliance: James E. Brynes, Roosevelt, Truman and the Origins of the Cold War* (Chapel Hill: University of North Carolina Press, 1982); Henry Ryan, *The Vision of Anglo-America: The U.S.-U.K. Alliance and the Emerging Cold War, 1943-1946* (Cambridge: Cambridge University Press, 1986); Randall Woods and Howard Jones, *Dawning of the Cold War: The United States Quest for Order* (Athens; University of Georgia Press, 1991); Arnold Offner, *Another Such Victory: President Truman and the Cold War, 1945-1953* (Stanford, Calif.: Stanford University Press, 2002). For Soviet perspectives and policies in the early Cold War, see: William McCraig, *Stalin Embattled, 1943-1948* (Detroit: Wayne State University Press, 1978); Vojtech Mastny, *Russia's Road to the Cold War: Diplomacy, Warfare and the Politics of Communism, 1951-1945* (New York; Columbia University Press, 1979); William Taubman, *Stalin's American Policy: From Entente to Détente to Cold War* (New York: W.W. Norton, 1982); Vladislav Zubok and Constantine Peshakov, *Inside the Kremlin's Cold War: From Stalin to Khrushchev* (Cambridge, Mass.: Harvard University Press, 1996); Geoffrey Roberts, *Stalin's Wars: From World War to Cold War, 1939-1953* (New Haven, Conn.: Yale University Press, 2006); Timothy Snyder and Ray Brandon, eds, *Stalin and Europe: Imitation and Domination* (New York: Oxford University Press, 2014).

2 Djilas, *Conversations*, 114.

3 *Stalin Works*, 3:7.

4 Ivo Banac, ed., *The Diary of George Dimitrov, 1933-1949* (New Haven, Conn.: Yale University Press, 2008), 258.

5 Churchill, *Memoirs of the Second World War, Abridged*, 767.

6 John Gimbel, *The American Occupation of Germany: Politics and the Military, 1945-1949* (Sanford, Calif.: Stanford University Press, 1968); Bruce Kuklick, *American Policy and the Division of Germany: The Clash with Russia Over Reparations* (New York: Cornell University Press, 1972); Tony Sharp, *The Wartime Alliance and the Zonal Division of Germany* (Oxford: Clarendon, 1975); John Backer, *The Decision to Divide Germany: American Foreign Policy in Transition* (Durham, N.C.: Duke University Press,

1978); Giles Macdonough, *After the Reich: The Brutal History of the Allied Occupation* (New York: Basic Books, 2009).

7 Dobbs, *Six Months in 1945*, 275.

8 Ibid., 321.

9 Zubok and Peshakov, *Inside the Kremlin's Cold War*, 147.

10 Dobbs, *Six Months in 1945*, 314, 321.

11 Joseph Persico, *Nuremburg: Infamy on Trial* (New York: Penguin, 1995); Paul Roland, *The Nuremberg Trials: The Nazis and Their Crimes Against Humanity* (New York: Chartwell Books, 2010).

12 Suzanne Pepper, *Civil War in China: The Political Struggle, 1945-1949* (New York: Rowman and Littlefield, 1999); Diane Lary, *China's Civil War: A Social History, 1945-1949* (New York: Cambridge University Press, 2019); Parkes Coble, *The Collapse of Nationalist China: How Chiang Kai-Shek Lost China's Civil War* (New York: Cambridge University Press, 2023).

13 Diller, ed., *Russia and the Independent States*, 58.

14 Figes, *Revolutionary Russia*, 240.

15 Volkogonov, *Stalin*, 307; Vadim Rogovin, *Stalin's Terror of 1947-1948: Political Genocide in the USSR* (New York: Mehring Books, 2008).

16 Nicolas Werth, 'Forms of Autonomy in "Socialist Society"', in Rousso, ed., *Stalinism and Nazism*, 120–3.

17 Wood and Jones, *Dawning of the Cold War*, 55.

18 Medvedev, *Let History Judge*, 770.

19 Zubok and Peshakov, *Inside the Kremlin's Cold War*, 88.

20 John Baron, *KGB: The Secret World of Soviet Secret Agents* (New York: Reader's Digest Press, 1974); Brian Freemantle, *Inside the KGB: The World's Largest Intelligence Organization* (New York: Henry Holt, 1984); Christopher Andrew and Oleg Gordievsky, *KGB: The Inside Story of Its Foreign Operations from Lenin to Gorbachev* (New York: Harper Collins, 1990); Christopher Andrew, *The Sword and the Shield: The Mitrokhin Archive and the Secret History of the KGB* (New York: Basic Books, 2001).

21 Yuri Modin, *My 5 Cambridge Friends: Burgess, Maclean, Philby, Blunt and Cairncross* (New York: Farrar, Straus and Giroux, 1995); Andrew Lownie, *Stalin's Englishman: The Inside Story of the Cambridge Spy Ring* (New York: Lume, 2023).

22 Joseph Albright and Marcia Kunstel, *Bombshell: The Secret Story of America's Unknown Atomic Spy Conspiracy* (New York: Times Books, 1997).

23 Chrisopher Lash, *The Agony of the American Left* (New York: Random House, 1969); Mary Sperling McAuliffe, *Crisis on the Left: Cold War Politics and American Liberals, 1947-1954* (Amherst: University of

Massachusetts Press, 1978); William O'Neil, *A Better World: The Great Schism: Stalinism and the American Intellectuals* (New York: Simon and Schuster, 1982); Theodore Draper, *American Communism and Soviet Russia* (New York: Routledge, 2004).

24 David Caute, *The Great Fear: The Anti-Communist Purge Under Truman and Eisenhower* (New York: Simon and Schuster, 1978); Ella Schrecter, *Many Are the Crimes: McCarthyism in America* (Princeton, N.J.: Princeton University Press, 1999).

25 Peter Coleman, *The Liberal Conspiracy: The Congress for Cultural Freedom and the Struggle for the Mind of Postwar Europe* (New York: Free Press, 1989).

26 George Orwell, 'Politics and the English Language', in George Orwell and Ian Angus, eds, *Collected Essays, Journalism and Letters of George Orwell: In Front of Your Nose, 1945-1950* (New York: Mariner Books, 1971), 4:136.

27 Fraser Harbutt, *The Iron Curtain: Churchill, America and the Origins of the Cold War* (New York: Oxford University Press, 1986).

28 Churchill, *Memoirs of the Second World War, Abridged*, 996–8.

29 Greg Herken, *The Winning Weapon: The Atomic Bomb in the Cold War, 1945-1950* (New York: Alfred Knopf, 1980); Harry Borowski, *A Hollow Threat: Strategic Air Power and Containment before Korea* (Westport, Conn.: Greenwood, 1982); Richard Rhodes, *The Making of the Atomic Bomb* (New York: Simon and Schuster, 1986).

30 Churchill, *Memoirs of the Second World War, Abridged*, 1006.

31 Gaddis, *United States and the Origins of the Cold War*, 268.

32 John Gaddis, *George Kennan: An American Life* (New York: Penguin, 2012).

33 The Long Telegram [Original] from George Kennan in Moscow to the Secretary of State, 22 February 22 1945, *National Security Archive*, website; Mr. X, 'The Sources of Soviet Conduct', *Foreign Affairs*, vol. 25, no. 4, (July 1947), 566–82; George Kennan, *Memoirs, 1925-1950* (Boston: Little, Brown, 1967).

34 Winston Churchill, *The Gathering Storm: The Second World War, Volume 1* (New York: Houghton Mifflin Harcourt, 1948), 404.

35 George Kennan, *Memoirs, 1925-1950* (Boston: Little, Brown and Company, 1967), 528–9.

36 Ibid., 526.

37 For America's reconstruction of West Europe, see: Thomas Patterson, *Soviet-American Confrontation: Postwar Reconstruction and the Origins of the Cold War* (Baltimore: Johns Hopkins University Press, 1973); Alan Milward, *The Reconstruction of Western Europe, 1945-51* (London: Methuen, 1984); David Ellwood, *Rebuilding Europe: Western Europe,*

America and Postwar Reconstruction (New York: Routledge, 2017). For America's reconstruction of Japan, see: Michael Schaller, *The American Occupation of Japan: The Origins of the Cold War in Asia* (New York: Oxford University Press, 1987); Theodore Cohen, *Remaking Japan: The American Occupation as New Deal* (New York: Free Press, 1987): John Dower, *Embracing Defeat: Japan in the Wake of World War II* (New York: W.W. Norton, 2000).

38 Bruce Kuniholm, *The Origins of the Cold War in the Near East: Great Power Conflict and Diplomacy in Iran, Turkey and Greece* (Princeton, N.J.: Princeton University Press, 1980).

39 Gaddis, *United States and the Coming of the Cold War*, 351.

40 Immanuel Wexler, *The Marshall Plan Revisited: The European Recovery in Economic Perspective* (Westport, Conn.: Greenwood, 1983); Charles Mee, *The Marshall Plan: The Launching of the Pax Americana* (New York: Simon and Schuster, 1984); Michael Hogart, *The Marshall Plan: America, Britain and the Reconstruction of Western Europe, 1947-1952* (Cambridge: Cambridge University Press, 1987); Charles Kindleberger, *Marshall Plan Days* (Boston: Allen and Unwin, 1987); Greg Behrman, *The Most Noble Adventure: The Marshall Plan and the Reconstruction of Post-War Europe* (New York: Aurum Press, 2008).

41 Manuel Gottlieb, *The German Peace Settlement and the Berlin Crisis* (New York: Paine-Whitman, 1960); Jean Smith, *The Defense of Berlin* (Baltimore: Johns Hopkins University Press, 1963); Daniel Nelson, *The Wartime Origins of the Berlin Dilemma* (Tuscaloosa: University of Alabama Press, 1978); Avi Shlaim, *The United States and the Berlin Blockade, 1948-1949: A Study of Decision-Making* (Berkeley: University of California Press, 1983); Ann and John Tusa, *The Berlin Airlift: The Cold War Mission to Save a City* (New York: Skyhorse, 2019).

42 Wood and Jones, *Dawning of the Cold War*, 191.

43 Ibid., 215.

44 Herken, *The Winning Weapon*, 241, 263.

45 Shlaim, *United States and the Berlin Blockade*, 254–6.

46 Timothy Ireland, *Creating the Entangling Alliance: The Origins of the North Atlantic Treaty Organization* (Westport, Conn.: Greenwood, 1981); Lawrence Kaplan, *The United States and NATO: The Formative Year*, Lexington: University of Kentucky Press, 1984); John Gillingham and Francis Heller, eds, *NATO: The Founding of the Atlantic Alliance and the Integration of Europe* (New York: Palgrave Macmillan, 1992).

47 Volkogonov, *Stalin*, 537.

48 David Holloway, *Stalin and the Bomb: The Soviet Union and Atomic Energy, 1939-1956* (New Haven, Conn.: Yale University Press, 1994).

49 Djilas, *Conversations*, 132.

50 Alan Ulam, *Tito and the Cominform* (Cambridge, Mass.: Harvard University Press, 1952); Jozc Pirjevec, *Tito and His Comrades* (Madison: University of Wisconsin Press, 2018).

51 Archie Brown, *The Rise and Fall of Communism* (New York: Random House, 2009), 207.

52 Josip Broz Tito, 'The First Breach; The Excommunication of Yugoslavia', in Ali, ed., *The Stalinist Legacy*, 215, 216.

53 Roy Medvedev, *On Stalin and Stalinism* (New York: Oxford University Press, 1979), 145.

54 Jian Chen, *Mao's China and the Cold War* (Chapel Hill: University of North Carolina Press, 2001).

55 Mao Zedong, *On Guerilla Warfare* (New York: Martino's Fine Books, 2017).

56 Maurice Meisner, 'Iconoclasm and Cultural Revolution in Russia and China', in Abbott Gleason, Peter Kenez and Richard Stites, eds, *Bolshevik Culture: Experiment and Order in the Russian Revolution* (Bloomington: University of Indiana Press, 1985), 282.

57 Maurice Meisner, *Mao Zedong: A Political and Intellectual Portrait* (New York: Polity, 2006); Julia Lovell, *Maoism: A Global History* (New York: Alfred Knopf, 2019).

58 William Stueck, *The Road to Confrontation: American Foreign Policy toward China and Korea, 1947-1950* (Chapel Hill: University of North Carolina Press, 1981).

59 Ernest May, *American Cold War Strategy: Interpreting NSC 68* (New York: St. Martin's Press, 1993); Curt Cardwell, *NSC 68 and the Political Economy of the Early Cold War* (New York: Cambridge University Press, 2015).

60 Ulam, *Stalin: Man Behind the Myth*, 695.

61 Sergei Goncharov, John Lewis and Xue Litai, *Uncertain Partners: Stalin, Mao and the Korean War* (Stanford, Calif.: Stanford University Press, 1993).

62 Burton Kaufman, *The Korean War: Challenges in Crisis, Credibility and Command* (New York: McGraw Hill, 1986); Bruce Cumings, *The Korean War* (New York: Modern Library, 2011).

63 LaFeber, *America, Russia and the Cold War*, 105.

64 Zubok and Peshakov, *Inside the Kremlin's Cold War*, 71.

65 Michael Schaller, *The American Occupation of Japan: The Origins of the Cold War in Asia* (New York: Oxford University Press, 1987); John Dower, *Embracing Defeat: Japan in the Wake of World War II* (New York: W.W. Norton, 2000); Dayna Barnes, *Architects of Occupation: American Experts and Planning for Postwar Japan* (Ithaca, N.Y.: Cornell University Press, 2018).

66 Ulam, *Stalin: Man Behind the Myth*, 435.

67 Alexander Solzhenitsyn, *The First Circle* (New York: Harper and Row, 1968), 91, 120.

68 Khrushchev, *Remembers*, 299.

69 Ibid., 276–7.

70 Georges Bortoli, *The Death of Stalin* (New York: Praeger, 1975); Joshua Rubinstein, *The Last Days of Stalin* (New Haven, Conn.: Yale University Press, 2017).

71 Ulam, *Stalin: Man Behind the Myth*, 6.

Chapter 9: Afterlife

1 Robert Tucker, *The Soviet Political Mind: Stalinism and Post-Stalin Change* (New York: W.W. Norton, 1971); Tariq Ali, ed., *The Stalinist Legacy: The Impact on Twentieth Century World Politics* (Boulder: Lynne Rienner, 1984); Yuri Glazov, *The Russian Mind Since Stalin's Death* (New York: Springer, 1985).

2 Nicolas Werth, 'Strategies of Violence in the Stalinist USSR', in Rousso, ed., *Stalinism and Nazism*, 91.

3 LaFeber, *America, Russia and the Cold War*, 144.

4 Gaddis, *Strategies of Containment*, 129.

5 Offner, *Another Such Victory*, 419–20.

6 Su-Kyoung Hwang, *Korea's Grievous War* (Philadelphia: University of Pennsylvania Press, 2016); U.S. Military Spending, 1946-2009, Center for Defense Information, website.

7 Gaddis, *Strategies of Containment*, 131.

8 Matthew Ridgway, *The Korean War* (Garden City, N.Y.: Doubleday, 1967), vi.

9 Khrushchev, *Remembers*, 344.

10 Ibid., 17–18.

11 'Khrushchev Speech,' ibid., 559.

12 Ibid., 567.

13 Ibid., 347.

14 Medvedev, *Let History Judge*, 839–40.

15 Conquest, *Great Terror*, 477.

16 Robert Desjardins, *The Soviet Union through French Eyes: 1945-1985* (New York: St. Martin's Press, 1988); Tony Judt, *Past Imperfect: French Intellectuals, 1944-1956* (Berkeley: University of California Press, 1992); Andrew Sobaret, *Generation Stalin: French Writers, the Fatherland and the Cult of Personality* (Bloomington: Indiana University Press, 2018).

17 Raymond Aaron, *The Opium of the Intellectuals* (Garden City, N.Y.: Doubleday, 1957), xviii, 14.

18 Quotes from Gleason, *Totalitarianism*, 143, 147.

19 Friedrich and Brzezinski, *Totalitarian Dictatorship*, 43, 288–9.

20 Figes, *Revolutionary Russia*, 267–8.

21 Vaclav Havel, *Power of the Powerless: Citizens against the States in Central Eastern Europe* (New York: Routledge, 1985), 30–1.

22 Daniel Diller, ed., *Russia and the Independent States* (Washington D.C.: Congressional Quarterly, 1993), 144.

23 Ibid., 299.

24 William Taubman, *Gorbachev: His Life and Times* (New York: W.W. Norton, 2017).

25 Diller, *Russia and the Independent States*, 105.

26 Medvedev, *Let History Judge*, 6.

27 Richard Sakwa, *Russian Politics and Society* (New York: Routledge, 2008), 12.

28 Timothy Colton, *Yeltsin: A Life* (New York: Basic Books, 2008).

29 Diller, *Russia and the Independent States*, 119.

30 Sakwa, *Russian Politics and Society*, 22.

31 Ibid., 22–3.

32 Diller, *Russia and the Independent States*, 215.

33 William Nester, *Putin's Virtual War: Russia's Subversion and Conversion of America, Europe and the World Beyond* (London: Frontline Books, 2019).

34 Ibid., ix.

35 Sakwa, *Russian Politics and Society*, 359.

36 World Fact Book, Country Profiles, cia.gov.

37 Ibid.

Chapter 10: Appraisals

1 Khrushchev, *Remembers*, 279.

2 Ibid., 210, 564.

3 Harriman, *Special Envoy*, 536.

4 Marshall Shulman and Robert Legvold, *Stalin's Foreign Policy Reappraised* (New York: Routledge, 2019).

5 Harriman, *Special Envoy*, 536.

6 Medvedev, *Let History Judge*, 712.

7 Sarah Davies, 'The Leader Cult: Propaganda and Its reception in Stalin's Russia,' in Channon, ed., *Politics, Society and Stalinism in the USSR*, 124.

8 Alliluyeva, *Only One Year*, 142–3.

9 For Stalin's war leadership, see: Albert Seaton, *Stalin as Military Commander* (New York: Praeger, 1998); Geoffrey Roberts, *Stalin's Wars: From World War to Cold War, 1939-1953* (New Haven, Conn.: Yale University Press, 2006); Sean McMeekin, *Stalin's War: A New History of World War II* (New York: Basic Books 2022).

10 Mawdsley, *Thunder in the East*, 207.

11 Volkogonov, *Stalin*, 474.

12 Khrushchev, *Remembers*, 160, 592.

13 Stephanie Courtois et al., *The Black Box of Communism: Crimes, Terror, Repression* (Cambridge, Mass.: Harvard University Press, 1999).

14 Alliluyeva, *Only One Year*, 182.

15 Friedrich and Brzezinski, *Totalitarian Dictatorship*, 105.

16 Tormey, *Making Sense of Tyranny*, 169, 171–2.

17 Leszek Kolakowski, *The Main Currents of Marxism: Its Rise, Growth and Dissolution, The Breakdown* (New York: Oxford University Press, 1981), 97.

18 Khrushchev, *Remembers*, 258, 307.

19 Ibid., 7.

20 Djilas, *Conversations*, 187–8.

21 Khrushchev, *Remembers*, 76.

22 Montefiore, *Stalin: Court of the Red Tsar*, 231.

23 Djilas, *Conversations*, 106.

24 Bohlen, *Witness to History*, 338–9.

25 Ulam, *Stalin: Man Behind the Myth*, 433.

26 McNeal, *Stalin*, 182–3.

27 For comparison of Communism and Nazism, see: Ian Kershaw and Moshe Lewin, eds, *Stalinism and Nazism: Dictatorship in Comparison* (New York: Cambridge University Press, 1997); François Furet and Ernst Nolte, *Fascism and Communism* (Lincoln: University of Nebraska Press, 2001); Henry Rousso, ed., *Stalinism and Nazism: Theory and Memory Compared* (Lincoln: University of Nebraska Press, 2004); Paul Corner, ed., *Popular Opinion in Totalitarian Regimes: Fascism, Nazism, Communism* (New York: Oxford University Press, 2009); Vladimir Tisamaneanu, *The Devil in History: Communism, Fascism and Some Lessons of the Twentieth Century* (Berkeley: University of California Press, 2012); Klaus-Goran Karlsson, *Perspectives on the Entangled History of Communism and Nazism* (New York: Lexington Books, 2015). For comparisons of Stalin and Hitler, see: Alan Bullock, *Hitler and Stalin: Parallel Lives* (New York: Vintage, 1993);

Laurence Rees, *Hitler and Stalin: The Tyrants and the Second World War* (New York: Penguin, 2020).

28 Bullock, *Hitler and Stalin*, 501–02, 804.

29 Tinatin Japaridze, *Stalin's Millennials: Nostalgia, Trama and Nationalism* (New York: Lexington, 2024).

30 'Stalin Is More Popular Than Ever in Russia Survey Shows', *U.S. News and World Report*, 9 May 2019; 'Putin Plummets, Stalin Stays on Top in Russians' Ranking of "Notable" Historic Figures—Poll', *Moscow Times*, 21 June 2021.

31 Yevgeni Yevtushenko, 'The Heirs of Stalin,' in Ali, ed., *The Stalinist Legacy*, 548.

BIBLIOGRAPHY

Primary Sources

Alliluyeva, Svetlana, *Only One Year: A Memoir*, New York: Harper and Row, 1969.

Axell, Albert, *Stalin's War Through the Eyes of His Commanders*, London: Arms and Armour, 1997.

Banac, Ivo, ed., *The Diary of George Dimitrov, 1933-1949*, New Haven, Conn.: Yale University Press, 2008.

Beria, Sergo, *Beria, My Father: Inside Stalin's Kremlin*, London: Duckworth Publishers, 2001.

Bialer, Seweryn, ed., *Stalin and His Generals: Soviet Military Memoirs of World War II*, New York: Pegasus, 1969.

Blumenson, Martin, ed., *The Patton Papers, 1940-1945*, New York: Da Capo, 1996.

Bohlen, Charles, *Witness to History, 1929-1969*, New York: W.W. Norton, 1973.

Brandt, Conrad, Benjamin Swartz and John Fairbank, eds, *A Documentary History of Chinese Communism*, Cambridge, Mass.: Harvard University Press, 1952.

Butler, Susan, ed., *Dear Mr. Stalin: The Complete Correspondence of Franklin D. Roosevelt and Joseph V. Stalin*, New Haven, Conn.: Yale University Press, 2008.

Churchill, Winston, *The Gathering Storm: The Second World War, Volume 1*, New York: Houghton Mifflin Harcourt, 1948.

Churchill, Winston, *Memoirs of the Second World War: An Abridgement of the Six Volumes of The Second World War*, Boston: Houghton Mifflin, 1987.

Davies, Joseph, *Mission to Moscow*, New York: Simon and Schuster, 1941.

Degras, Jane, ed., *Soviet Documents on Foreign Policy*, 5 vols, Oxford: Oxford University Press, 1953.

Deriabin, Peter, *Inside Stalin's Kremlin: An Eyewitness Account of Brutality, Duplicity and Intrigue*, Lincoln: University of Nebraska Press, 1998.

Djilas, Milovan, *Conversations with Stalin*, New York: Harcourt, Brace and World, 1962.

Dobrynin, Anatoly, *In Confidence: Moscow's Ambassador to Six Cold War Presidents*, Seattle: University of Washington Press, 2001.

Duranty, Walter, *Duranty Reports Russia*, New York: Viking, 1934.

Eden, Anthony, *The Reckoning*, Boston: Houghton Mifflin, 1965.

Eisenhower, Dwight, *Crusade in Europe*, New York: Doubleday, 1948.

Gromyko, Andrei, *Memoirs*, New York: Doubleday, 1990.

Harriman, William Averell, with Elie Abel, *Special Envoy to Churchill and Stalin, 1941-1946*, New York: Randon House, 1975.

Hull, Cordell, *The Memoirs of Cordell Hull*, New York: Macmillan, 1948.

Kennan, George, *Memoirs, 1925-1950*, Boston: Little, Brown, 1967.

Khrushchev, Nikita, *Khrushchev Remembers*, Boston: Little, Brown and Company, 1970.

Leahy, William, *I Was There: The Personal Story of the Chief of Staff to Presidents Roosevelt and Truman*, New York: Whittlesey House, 1950.

Ministry of Foreign Affairs, *Correspondence between the Chairman of the Council of Ministers of the U.S.S.R and the Presidents of the U.S.A and the Prime Ministers of Great Britain during the Great Patriotic War of 1941-1945*, New York: Capricorn Books, 1965.

Molotov, Vyacheslav, *Molotov Remembers: Inside Kremlin Politics*, Chicago: Ivan Dee, 1993.

Reed, Christopher, ed., *The Stalin Years: A Reader*, New York: Red Globe, 2002.

Ridgway, Matthew, *The Korean War*, Garden City, N.Y.: Doubleday, 1967.

Serge, Victor, *Memoirs of a Revolutionary, 1901-1941*, New York: Oxford University Press, 1978.

Sherwood, Robert, *Roosevelt and Hopkins: An Intimate History*, New York: Harper Brothers, 1948.

Smith, Walter Bedell, *My Three Years in Moscow*, New York: J.B. Lippincott Company, 1948.

Stalin, Joseph, *Selected Writings*, Westport, Conn.: Greenwood, 1970.

Stalin, Joseph, *The Works of Joseph Stalin*, vols 1–13, Moscow: Foreign Language Publication House, 1954.

Trotsky, Leon, *My Life: An Attempt at an Autobiography*, New York: Charles Scribners' Sons, 1930.

Trotsky, Leon, *Trotsky's Diary in Exile, 1935*, Cambridge, Mass., Harvard University Press, 1958.

Trotsky, Leon, *Terrorism and Communism: A Reply to Kautsky*, New York: Verso, 2017.

Truman, Harry, *Memoirs of Harry S. Truman: 1945, Year of Decisions*, New York: Doubleday, 1955.

Wells, H.G., *Experiment in Autobiography*, New York: Macmillan, 1934.

Willkie, Wendell, *One World*, New York: Simon and Schuster, 1943.

Zhukov, Georgi, *The Memoirs of Marshal Zhukov*, New York: Delacorte Press, 1971.

Secondary Sources

Aaron, Raymond, *The Opium of the Intellectuals*, Garden City, N.Y.: Doubleday, 1957.

Abraham, Richard, *Alexander Kerensky: The First Love of the Revolution*, New York: Columbia University Press, 1990.

Abramovitch, Ralph, *The Soviet Revolution, 1917-1939*, New York: International Universities Press, 1962.

Adorno, Theodor, Else Frenkel-Brunswick, Daniel Levinson and Nevitt Stanford, *The Authoritarian Personality*, New York: Harper, 1950.

Albright, Joseph and Marcia Kunstel, *Bombshell: The Secret Story of America's Unknown Atomic Spy Conspiracy*, New York: Times Books, 1997.

Ali, Tariq, ed., *The Stalinist Legacy: The Impact on Twentieth Century World Politics*, Boulder: Lynne Rienner, 1984.

Alperovitz, Gar, *Atomic Diplomacy: Hiroshima and Potsdam*, New York: Random House, 1965.

Altemeyer, Bob, *The Authoritarian Specter*, Cambridge, Mass.: Harvard University Press, 1996.

Ambrose, Stephen, *Eisenhower and Berlin, 1945: The Decision to Halt at the Elbe*, New York: W.W. Norton, 1967.

Anderson, Terry, *The United States, Great Britain and the Cold War, 1944-1947*, Columbia: University of Missouri Press, 1981.

Andrew, Christopher, *The Sword and the Shield: The Mitrokhin Archive and the Secret History of the KGB*, New York: Basic Books, 2001.

Andrew, Christopher and Oleg Gordievsky, *KGB: The Inside Story of the Its Foreign Operations from Lenin to Gorbachev*, New York: Harper Collins, 1990.

Antonov-Ovseenko, Anton, *The Time of Stalin: Portrait of a Tyranny*, New York: Harper and Row, 1981.

Applebaum, Anne, *Gulag: A History of the Soviet Concentration Camp*, New York: Anchor, 2004.

Applebaum, Anne, *The Twilight of Democracy: The Seductive Lure of Authoritarianism*, New York: Knopf Doubleday, 2020.

Arendt, Hannah, *The Origins of Totalitarianism*, New York: Harcourt, Brace, Janovich, 1973.

Armour, Ian, *A History of Eastern Europe, from 1918 to the Present*, New York: Bloomsbury, 2021.

Ascher, Abraham, *The Revolution of 1905: Russia in Disarray*, Stanford, Calif.: Stanford University Press, 1988.

Atkinson, Rick, *An Army at Dawn: The War in North Africa, 1942-1943*, New York: Henry Holt, 2007.

Atkinson, Rick, *The Day of Battle, 1943-1944: The War in Sicily and Italy*, New York: Henry Holt, 2008.

Atkinson, Rick, *The Guns at Last Light: The War in Western Europe, 1944-1945*, New York: Henry Holt, 2013.

Babone, Salvatore, *The New Authoritarianism: Trump, Populism and the Tyranny of Experts*, New York: Polity, 2018.

Backer, John, *The Decision to Divide Germany: American Foreign Policy in Transition*, Durham, N.C.: Duke University Press, 1978.

Bailes, Kendall, *Technology and Society under Lenin and Stalin: The Origins of the Soviet Technical Intelligentsia, 1917-1941*, Princeton, N.J.: Princeton University Press, 1978.

Barber, John and Mark Harrison, eds, *The Soviet Defence-Industry Complex from Stalin to Khruschev*, New York: Macmillan, 2000.

Barnes, Dayna, *Architects of Occupation: American Experts and Planning for Postwar Japan*, Ithaca, N.Y.: Cornell University Press, 2018.

Barron, John, *KGB: The Secret World of Soviet Secret Agents*, New York: Reader's Digest Press, 1974.

Beasley, W.G., *Japanese Imperialism, 1984-1945*, Oxford: Clarendon Press, 1991.

Beeuwkes, Henry, *American Medical and Sanitary Relief in the Russian Famine, 1921-1923*, New York: Legare Street Press, 2022.

Beevor, Antony, *Stalingrad: The Fateful Siege, 1942-1943*, New York: Penguin, 1999.

Beevor, Antony, *The Fall of Berlin, 1945*, New York: Penguin, 2003.

Beevor, Antony, *The Battle for Spain: The Spanish Civil War, 1936-1939*, New York: Penguin, 2006.

Beevor, Antony, *Russia: Revolution and Civil War, 1917-1921*, New York: Viking, 2022.

Behrman, Greg, *The Most Noble Adventure: The Marshall Plan and the Reconstruction of Post-War Europe*, New York: Aurum Press, 2008.

Ben-Ghiat, Ruth, *Strongmen: Mussolini to the Present*, New York: W.W. Norton, 2021.

Benvenuti, Francesco, *The Bolsheviks and the Red Army, 1918-1922*, New York: Cambridge University Press, 1988.

Bergstrom, Christer, *Operation Barbarossa 1941: Hitler against Stalin*, New York: Casemate, 2018.

Berlin, Isaiah, *The Soviet Mind: Russian Culture under Communism*, Washington D.C.: Brookings Institute Press, 2011.

Billington, James, *The Icon and the Axe: An Interpretive History of Russian Culture*, New York: Vintage, 1970.

Borowski, Harry, *A Hollow Threat: Strategic Air Power and Containment before Korea*, Westport, Conn.: Greenwood, 1982.

Bortoli, Georges, *The Death of Stalin*, New York: Praeger, 1975.

Bosworth, R.J.B., *Mussolini*, London: Arnold, 2002.

Brackman, Roman, *The Secret File of Joseph Stalin: A Hidden Life*, New York: Routledge, 2000.

Brager, Bruce, *The Iron Curtain: The Cold War in Europe*, New York: Chelsea House, 2004.

Brooke, Alan, *War Diaries, 1939-1945: Field Marshal Lord Alanbrooke*, New York: Phoenix Press, 2002.

Brooks, Jeffrey, *Thank You, Comrade Stalin! Soviet Public Culture from Revolution to Cold War*, Princeton, N.J.: Princeton University Press, 2001.

Brovkin, Vladimir, *Russia After Lenin: Politics, Culture and Society, 1921-1929*, New York: Routledge, 1998.

Brown, Archie, *The Rise and Fall of Communism*, New York: Random House, 2009.

Brown, Wendy, Peter Gordon and Max Pensky, *Authoritarianism: Three Inquires in Critical Theory*, Chicago: University of Chicago Press, 2018.

Buhite, Russell, *Decisions at Yalta: An Appraisal of Summit Diplomacy*, Wilmington, Del.: Scholarly Resources, 1986.

Bullock, Alan, *Hitler and Stalin: Parallel Lives*, New York: Vintage, 1993.

Bungay, Stephen, *The Most Dangerous Enemy: A History of the Battle of Britain*, New York: Aurum Press, 2016.

Burgwyn, James, *Empire on the Adriatic: Mussolini's Conquest of Yugoslavia, 1941-1943*, New York: Enigma Books, 2005.

Burleigh, Michael, *The Third Reich: A New History*, New York: Hill and Wang, 2001.

Bushkovitch, Paul, *A Concise History of Russia*, New York: Cambridge University Press, 2011.

Butler, Susan, *Roosevelt and Stalin: Portrait of a Partnership*, New York: Vintage, 2016.

Cardwell, Curt, *NSC 68 and the Political Economy of the Early Cold War*, New York: Cambridge University Press, 2015.

Carmichael, Joel, *Trotsky: An Appreciation of His Life*, New York: St. Martin's Press, 1975.

Carr, Edward, *The Bolshevik Revolution, 1917-1923*, 3 vols, London: Macmillan, 1950–2.

Carr, Edward, *The Twilight of Comintern, 1930-1935*, New York: Pantheon Books, 1982.

Carr, Edward, *The Comintern and the Spanish Civil War*, New York: Pantheon Books, 1984.

Caute, David, *The Great Fear: The Anti-Communist Purge Under Truman and Eisenhower*, New York: Simon and Schuster, 1978.

Chaney, Otto, *Zhukov*, Norman: University of Oklahoma Press, 1996.

Chang, Iris, *The Rape of Nanking*, New York: Basic Books, 2012.

Channon, John, ed., *Politics, Society and Stalinism in the USSR*, New York: St. Martin's Press, 1998.

Chase, William, *Enemies within the Gates?: The Comintern and the Stalinist Repression, 1934-39*, New Haven, Conn.: Yale University Press, 2001.

Chen, Jian, *Mao's China and the Cold War*, Chapel Hill: University of North Carolina Press, 2001.

Childers, Thomas, *The Third Reich: A History of Nazi Germany*, New York: Simon and Schuster, 2018.

Churbanyan, Alexander and Harold Shukman, ed., *Stalin and the Soviet-Finnish War, 1939-40*, London: Frank Cass, 2002.

Claeys, Gregory, *Marx and Marxism*, New York: Bold Type Books, 2018.

Clark, Alan, *Barbarossa: The Russian-German Conflict, 1941-45*, New York: Quill, 1985.

Clark, Caterina and Evgeny Dobrenko, *Soviet Culture and Power*, New Haven, Conn.: Yale University Press, 2007.

Clark, Lloyd, *The Battle of Tanks: Kursk, 1943*, New York: Grove Press, 2012.

Clemens, Diane Shaver, *Yalta*, New York: Oxford University Press, 1970.

Coble, Parkes, *The Collapse of Nationalist China: How Chiang Kai-Shek Lost China's Civil War*, New York: Cambridge University Press, 2023.

Cohen, Stephen, *Rethinking the Soviet Experience: Politics and History Since 1917*, New York: Oxford University Press, 1985.

Cohen, Theodore, *Remaking Japan: The American Occupation as New Deal*, New York: Free Press, 1987.

Coleman, Peter, *The Liberal Conspiracy: The Congress for Cultural Freedom and the Struggle for the Mind of Postwar Europe*, New York: Free Press, 1989.

Conquest, Robert, *The Nation Killers: The Soviet Deportation of Nationalities*, London: Macmillan, 1970.

Conquest, Robert, *Inside Stalin's Secret Police: NKVD Politics, 1936-39*, Stanford, Calif.: Stanford University Press, 1985.

Conquest, Robert, *The Harvest of Sorrow: Soviet Collectivization and the Terror-Famine*, New York: Oxford University Press, 1986.

Conquest, Robert, *Stalin and the Kirov Murder*, New York: Oxford University Press, 1989.

Conquest, Robert, *The Great Terror: A Reassessment*, New York: Oxford University Press, 1990.

Conquest, Robert, *Stalin: Breaker of Nations*, New York: Penguin, 1992.

Cooper, Matthew, *The Phantom War: The German Struggle against Soviet Partisans, 1941-44*, London: Macdonald and Janes, 1979.

Coox, Alvin, *Nomonhan: Japan Against Russia, 1939*, 2 vols, Stanford, Calif.: Stanford University Press, 1985.

Corner, Paul, ed., *Popular Opinion in Totalitarian Regimes: Fascism, Nazism, Communism*, New York: Oxford University Press, 2009.

Courtois, Stephanie, et al., *The Black Box of Communism: Crimes, Terror, Repression*, Cambridge, Mass.: Harvard University Press, 1999.

Cumings, Bruce, *The Korean War*, New York: Modern Library, 2011.

Dalleck, Robert, *Franklin D. Roosevelt and American Foreign Policy, 1932-1945*, New York: Oxford University Press, 1979.

Dallin, Alexander, *German Rule in Russia, 1941-1945: A Study of Occupation Policies*, Boulder, Colo.: Westview Press, 1981.

Daniels, Robert, ed., *The Stalin Revolution: Foundations of Soviet Totalitarianism*, Lexington, Mass.: D.C. Heath, 1972.

Davies, Norman, *White Eagle, Red Star: The Polish-Soviet War, 1919-1920*, London: Pimlico, 2003.

Davis, Victor, *The Second World Wars: How the First Global Conflict Was Fought and Won*, New York: Basic Books, 2020.

De Witt, Nicolas, *Education and Professional Employment in the USSR*, Washington D.C.: National Science Foundation, 1961.

Demmet, Mattias, *The Psychology of Totalitarianism*, New York: Chelsea Green, 2016.

Desjardins, Robert, *The Soviet Union through French Eyes: 1945-1985*, New York: St. Martin's Press, 1988.

Deutscher, Isaac, *Stalin: A Political Biography*, New York: Oxford University Press, 1949.

Deutscher, Isaac, *The Prophet Outcast: Trotsky, 1929-1940*, New York: Verso, 2003.

Diamond, Larry and Marc Plattner, *Authoritarianism Goes Global: The Challenge to Democracy*, Baltimore: Johns Hopkins University Press, 2016.

Dikotter, Frank, *Dictators*, New York: Bloomsbury, 2020.

Diller, Daniel, ed., *Russia and the Independent States*, Washington D.C.: Congressional Quarterly, 1993.

Dimbleby, Jonathan, *The Battle of the Atlantic: How the Allies Won the War*, New York: Oxford University Press, 2018.

Dimbleby, Jonathan, *Operation Barbarossa: The History of a Cataclysm*, New York: Oxford University Press, 2021.

Dobbs, Michael, *Six Months in 1945: FDR, Stalin, Churchill and Truman from World War to Cold War*, New York: Alfred Knopf, 2012.

Dower, John, *Embracing Defeat: Japan in the Wake of World War II*, New York: W.W. Norton, 2000.

Doyle, David, *The Complete Guide to German Armored Vehicles*, New York: Skyhorse, 2019.

Draper, Theodore, *American Communism and Soviet Russia*, New York: Routledge, 2004.

Eastman, Max, *Great Companions: Critical Memoirs of Some Famous Friends*, New York: Farrar, Straus and Cudahy, 1959.

Ellman, James, *Hitler's Great Gamble: A New Look at German Strategy, Operation Barbarossa and the Axis Defeat in World War II*, New York: Stackpole, 2019.

Ellwood, David, *Rebuilding Europe: Western Europe, America and Postwar Reconstruction*, New York: Routledge, 2017.

Engelstein, Laura, *Russia in Flames: War, Revolution and Civil War, 1914-1921*, New York: Oxford University Press, 2017.

Erikson, Erik, *Childhood and Society*, New York: W.W. Norton, 1950.

Feis, Herbert, *Between War and Peace: The Potsdam Conference*, Princeton, N.J.: Princeton University Press, 1960.

Feis, Herbert, *The Atomic Bomb and the End of World War II*, Princeton, N.J.: Princeton University Press, 1966.

Feis, Herbert, *From Trust to Terror: The Onset of the Cold War, 1945-1950*, New York: W.W. Norton, 1970.

Ferguson, Niall, *The Pity of War: Explaining World War I*, New York: Basic Books, 1999.

Figes, Orlando, *A People's Tragedy: The Russian Revolution, 1891-1924*, New York: Penguin, 1998.

Figes, Orlando, *Natasha's Dance: A Cultural History of Russia*, New York: Henry Holt, 2002.

Figes, Orlando, *Revolutionary Russia, 1891-1991*, New York: Henry Holt, 2014.

Figes, Orlando, *The Story of Russia*, New York: Metropolitan Books, 2023.

Fisher, Harold, *The Famine in Soviet Russia, 1921-1923: The Operations of the America Relief Administration*, New York: Macmillan, 1927.

Fisher, Louis, *The Life of Lenin*, New York: Harper and Row, 1964.

Fitpatrick, Sheila, *Education and Social Mobility in the Soviet Union, 1921-1934*, Cambridge: Cambridge University Press, 1979.

Fitzpatrick, Sheila, ed., *Cultural Revolution in Russia, 1928-1931*, Bloomington: University of Indiana Press, 1984.

Fitzpatrick, Sheila, *The Cultural Front: Power and Culture in Revolutionary Russia*, Ithaca, N.Y.: Cornell University Press, 1992.

Fitzpatrick, Sheila, *Stalin's Peasants: Resistance and Survival in the Russian Village*, New York: Oxford University Press, 1994.

Fitzpatrick, Sheila, *Everyday Stalinism: Ordinary Life in Extraordinary Times*, New York: Oxford University Press, 2000.

Fitzpatrick, Sheila, *The Russian Revolution, 1917-1921*, New York: Oxford University Press, 2017.

Fleron, Frederic, Erik Hoffman and Robbin Laird, eds, *Soviet Foreign Policy, 1917-1991: Classics and Contemporary Issues*, New York: Routledge, 2018.

Folly, Martin, Geoffrey Roberts and Oleg Rzheshevsky, *Churchill and Stalin: Comrades-in-Arms during the Second World War*, London: Pen and Sword, 2020.

Forti, Simona, *Totalitarianism: A Borderline Idea*, Palo Alto, Calif.: Sanford University Press, 2024.

Frantz, Eric, *Authoritarianism: What Everyone Needs to Know*, New York: Oxford University Press, 2019.

Freemantle, Brian, *Inside the KGB: The World's Largest Intelligence Organization*, New York: Henry Holt, 1984.

Freeze, Gregory, *Russia: A History*, New York: Oxford University Press, 2009.

Friedrich, Carl and Zbigniew Brzezinski, *Totalitarian Dictatorship and Autocracy*, Cambridge, Mass.: Harvard University Press, 1956.

Fromm, Erich, *The Escape from Freedom*, New York: Farrar and Rinehart, 1941.

Furet, François and Ernst Nolte, *Fascism and Communism*, Lincoln: University of Nebraska Press, 2001.

Gaddis, John, *The United States and the Origins of the Cold War, 1941-1947*, New York: Columbia University Press, 1972.

Gaddis, John, *The Long Peace: Inquiries in the History of the Cold War*, New York: Oxford University Press, 1987.

Gaddis, John, *Strategies of Containment: A Critical Appraisal of Postwar American National Security Policy*, New York: Oxford University Press, 2005.

Gaddis, John, *George Kennan: An American Life*, New York: Penguin, 2012.

Getty, John, *Origins of the Great Purges: The Soviet Communist Party Reconsidered, 1933-1938*, New York: Cambridge University Press, 1985.

Getty, John and R.T. Manning, eds, *Stalinist Terror: New Perspectives*, New York: Cambridge University Press, 1993.

Getty, John and Oleg Naumov, *The Road to Terror: Stalin and the Self-Destruction of the Bolsheviks, 1932-1939*, New Haven, Conn.: Yale University Press, 1999.

Geyer, Michael and Sheila Fitzpatrick, eds, *Beyond Totalitarianism: Stalinism and Nazism Compared*, New York: Cambridge University Press, 2008.

Gilbert, Martin, *The Second World War*, New York: Henry Holt, 2004.

Gillingham, John and Francis Heller, eds, *NATO: The Founding of the Atlantic Alliance and the Integration of Europe*, New York: Palgrave Macmillan, 1992.

Gimbel, John, *The American Occupation of Germany: Politics and the Military, 1945-1949*, Sanford, Calif.: Stanford University Press, 1968.

Glantz, David, *The Battle of Kursk*, New York: Basic Books, 1999.

Glantz, David, *Colossus Reborn: The Red Army at War, 1941-1943*, Lawrence: University Press of Kansas, 2005.

Glazer, Amelia and Stephen Lee, eds, *Comintern Aesthetics*, Toronto: University of Toronto Press, 2020.

Glazov, Yuri, *The Russian Mind Since Stalin's Death*, New York: Springer, 1985.

Gleason, Abbott, Peter Kenez and Richard Stites, eds, *Bolshevik Culture: Experiment and Order in the Russian Revolution*, Bloomington: University of Indiana Press, 1985.

Gleason, Abbott, *Totalitarianism: The Inner History of the Cold War*, New York: Oxford University Press, 2001.

Goldman, Stuart, *Nomonhan: The Red Army's Victory that Shaped World War II*, Annapolis: Naval Institute Press, 2012.

Goldstone, Jack, ed., *Revolutions: Theoretical, Comparative and Historical Studies*, New York: Centage, 2002.

Goldstone, Jack, Leonid Grinin and Andrey Korotayev, eds, *The Handbook of Revolutions in the 21st Century*, New York: Springer, 2022.

Goncharov, Sergei, John Lewis and Xue Litai, *Uncertain Partners: Stalin, Mao and the Korean War*, Stanford, Calif.: Stanford University Press, 1993.

Gorodetsky, Gabriel, *Grand Delusion: Stalin and the German Invasion of Russia*, New Haven, Conn.: Yale University Press, 1999.

Gottlieb, Manuel, *The German Peace Settlement and the Berlin Crisis*, New York: Paine-Whitman, 1960.

Gradetsky, Gabriel, *Soviet Foreign Policy, 1917-1991: A Retrospective*, New York: Routledge, 1994.

Graziosa, Andrea, *The Great Soviet Peasant War: Bolsheviks and Peasants, 1917-1933*, Cambridge, Mass.: Harvard University Press, 1996.

Gray, Philip, *Totalitarianism: The Basics*, New York: Routledge, 2013.

Greensmith, James, *In the Mind of Stalin*, London: Pen and Sword, 2023.

Gregor, James, *Marxism, Fascism and Totalitarianism: Chapters in the Intellectual History of the Twentieth Century*, Palo Alto, Calif.: Stanford University Press, 2008.

Gregory, Paul, ed., *The Economics of Forced Labor: The Soviet Gulag*, Palo Alto, Calif.: Hoover Institute Press, 2003.

Grenkevich, Leonard and David Glantz, *The Soviet Partisan Movement, 1941-1944: A Critical Historiographical Analysis*, New York: Routledge, 1999.

Gruber, Helmut, *Soviet Russia Masters the Comintern: International Communism in the Era of Stalin's Ascendency*, New York: Anchor Books, 1974.

Hamby, Alonzo, *Man of the People: A Life of Harry S. Truman*, New York: Oxford University Press, 1995.

Harbutt, Fraser, *The Iron Curtain: Churchill, America and the Origins of the Cold War*, New York: Oxford University Press, 1986.

Harper, Alan, *The Politics of Loyalty: The White House and the Communist Issue, 1946-1952*, Westport, Conn.: Greenwood Press, 1969.

Harris, James, *The Great Fear: Stalin's Terror of the 1930s*, New York: Oxford University Press, 2016.

Hartman, Christian, *Nazi Germany's War in the East, 1941-1945*, New York: Oxford University Press, 2018.

Haslam, Jonathan, *The Soviet Union and the Struggle for Collective Security in Europe, 1933-1939*, New York: St. Martin's Press, 1984.

Hathaway, Robert, *Ambiguous Partnership: Britain and America, 1944-1947*, New York: Columbia University Press, 1981.

Havel, Vaclav, *Power of the Powerless: Citizens against the States in Central Eastern Europe*, New York: Routledge, 1985.

Haycock, Dean, *Tyrannical Minds: Psychology, Profiling, Narcissism and Dictatorship*, New York: Pegasus, 2021.

Hayek, Friedrich von, *The Road to Serfdom*, Chicago: University of Chicago Press, 1944.

Herken, Greg, *The Winning Weapon: The Atomic Bomb in the Cold War, 1945-1950*, New York: Alfred Knopf, 1980.

Herring, George, *Aid to Russia, 1941-1947: Strategy, Diplomacy and the Origins of the Cold War*, New York: Columbia University Press, 1973.

Hetherington, Marc and Jonathan Weiler, *Authoritarianism and Polarization in American Politics*, New York: Cambridge University Press, 2009.

Hill, Alexander, *The War Behind the Eastern Front: Soviet Partisans in North-west Russia, 1941-44*, New York: Routledge, 2004.

Hogart, Michael, *The Marshall Plan: America, Britain and the Reconstruction of Western Europe, 1947-1952*, Cambridge: Cambridge University Press, 1987.

Holland, James, *The Battle of Britain: Five Months that Changed the World, May to October 1941*, New York: St. Martin's Griffin Press, 2012.

Holloway, David, *Stalin and the Bomb: The Soviet Union and Atomic Energy, 1939-1956*, New Haven, Conn.: Yale University Press, 1994.

Hooton, E.R., *Stalin's Claws: From the Purges to the Winter War: Red Army Operations before Barbarossa*, New York: Tattered Flag, 2013.

Horne, Alistair, *To Lose a Battle: France 1940*, New York: Penguin, 2009.

Horney, Karen, *New Ways in Psychoanalysis*, New York: W.W. Norton, 1939.

Horney, Karen, *Our Inner Conflicts*, New York: W.W. Norton, 1945.

Horney, Karen, *Neurosis and Human Growth*, New York: W.W. Norton, 1950.

Hosking, Geoffrey, *A History of the Soviet Union, 1917-1991*, London: Fontana Press, 1992.

Hoskins, Geoffrey, *Russia and the Russians*, Cambridge, Mass.: Belnap Press, 2011.

Hwang, Su-Kyoung, *Korea's Grievous War*, Philadelphia: University of Pennsylvania Press, 2016.

Ireland, Timothy, *Creating the Entangling Alliance: The Origins of the North Atlantic Treaty Organization*, Westport, Conn.: Greenwood, 1981.

Jackson, Julian, *The Fall of France: The Nazi Invasion of 1940*, New York: Oxford University Press, 2004.

Judt, Tony, *Past Imperfect: French Intellectuals, 1944-1956*, Berkeley: University of California Press, 1992.

Kaplan, Lawrence, *The United States and NATO: The Formative Years*, Lexington: University of Kentucky Press, 1984.

Karlsson, Klaus-Goran, *Perspectives on the Entangled History of Communism and Nazism*, New York: Lexington Books, 2015.

Kengor, Paul, *Dupes: How America's Adversaries Have Manipulated Progressives for a Century*, New York: Simon and Schuster, 2018.

Kersaudy, François, *Norway 1940*, Lincoln: University of Nebraska Press, 1998.

Kershaw, Ian, *Hitler: 1889-1936, Hubris*, New York: W.W. Norton, 2000.

Kershaw, Ian, *Hitler: 1936-1945, Nemesis*, New York: W.W. Norton, 2001.

Kershaw, Ian and Moshe Lewin, eds, *Stalinism and Nazism: Dictatorship in Comparison*, New York: Cambridge University Press, 1997.

Kershaw, Robert, *War without Garlands: Operation Barbarossa 1941-1942,* New York: Goodall, 2020.

Kimball, Warren, *The Most Unsordid Act: Lend-Lease, 1939-1941,* Baltimore: Johns Hopkins University Press, 1969.

Kindleberger, Charles, *Marshall Plan Days,* Boston: Allen and Unwin, 1987.

Kitchen, Martin, *Rommel's Desert War: Waging World War II in North Africa, 1941-1943,* New York: Cambridge University Press, 2009.

Knight, Amy, *Beria: Stalin's First Lieutenant,* Princeton, N.J.: Princeton University Press, 1994.

Knight, Amy, *Who Killed Kirov?: The Kremlin's Greatest Mystery,* New York: Hill and Wang, 1999.

Kolko, Joyce and Gabriel, *The Limits of Power: The World and the United States Foreign Policy, 1945-1954,* New York: Harper and Row, 1972.

Kolakowski, Leszek, *The Main Currents of Marxism: Its Rise, Growth and Dissolution, The Breakdown,* New York: Oxford University Press, 1981.

Kort, Michael, *The Soviet Colossus: History and Aftermath,* New York: Routledge, 2019.

Kotkin, Stephen, *Magnetic Mountain: Stalinism as a Civilization,* Berkeley: University of California Press, 1995.

Kotkin, Stephen, *Stalin: Volume 1, Paradoxes of Power, 1878-1928,* New York Penguin, 2015.

Kotkin, Stephen, *Stalin: Volume 2, Waiting for Hitler, 1929-1941,* New York: Penguin, 2018.

Kreusz, Tomas, *Revolutionary Lenin: An Intellectual Biography,* New York: Monthly Review Press, 2018.

Kuklick, Bruce, *American Policy and the Division of Germany: The Clash with Russia Over Reparations,* New York: Cornell University Press, 1972.

Kuniholm, Bruce, *The Origins of the Cold War in the Near East: Great Power Conflict and Diplomacy in Iran, Turkey and Greece,* Princeton, N.J.: Princeton University Press, 1980.

Kuromiya, Hiroaki, *Stalin: Profiles in Power,* New York: Routledge, 2013.

LaFeber, Walter, *America, Russia and the Cold War, 1945-1990,* New York: McGraw-Hill, 1991.

Lampert, Nicolas, *The Technical Intelligentsia and the Soviet State,* New York: Oxford University Press 1979.

Lary, Diane, *China's Civil War: A Social History, 1945-1949,* New York: Cambridge University Press, 2019.

Lash, Christopher, *The Agony of the American Left,* New York: Random House, 1969.

Lee, Stephen, *Stalin and the Soviet Union,* New York: Routledge, 2005.

Levering, Ralph, *American Opinion and the Russian Alliance, 1939-1945,* Chapel Hill: University of North Carolina Press, 1976.

Levine, Isaac, *The Mind of an Assassin,* New York: Farrar, Straus and Cudahy, 1959.

Levitsky, Steven and Daniel Ziblatt, *How Democracies Die*, New York: Broadway Books, 2018.

Liddell Hart, Basil, *The History of the Second World War*, New York: Konecky and Konecky, 1970.

Lincoln, Bruce, *Red Victory: A History of the Russian Civil War*, New York: Simon and Schuster, 1989.

Lovell, Julia, *Maoism: A Global History*, New York: Alfred Knopf, 2019.

Lownie, Andrew, *Stalin's Englishman: The Inside Story of the Cambridge Spy Ring*, New York: Lume, 2023.

Macdonough, Giles, *After the Reich: The Brutal History of the Allied Occupation*, New York: Basic Books, 2009.

Malevsky-Malevitch, P., ed., *Russia U.S.S.R.: A Complete Handbook*, New York: William Farquhar Payson, 1933.

Malia, Martin, *The Soviet Tragedy: A History of Socialism, 1917-2000*, New York: Free Press, 1995.

Martel, Leon, *Lend-Lease, Loans and the Coming of the Cold War: A Study of the Implementation of Foreign Policy*, Boulder, Colo.: Westview, 1979.

Mastny, Vojtech, *Russia's Road to the Cold War: Diplomacy, Warfare and the Politics of Communism, 1951-1945*, New York; Columbia University Press, 1979.

Mawdsley, Evan, *The Russian Civil War*, Boston: Allen and Unwin, 1987.

Mawdsley, Evan, *Thunder in the East: The Nazi-Soviet War, 1941-1945*, New York: Hodder Arnold, 2005.

Mawdsley, Evan, *The Story of World War II*, New York: Simon and Schuster, 2020.

May, Ernest, *American Cold War Strategy: Interpreting NSC 68*, New York: St. Martin's Press, 1993.

Mayer, Arno, *The Furies: Violence and Terror in the French and Russian Revolutions*, Princeton, N.J.: Princeton University Press, 2000.

McAuliffe, Mary Sperling, *Crisis on the Left: Cold War Politics and American Liberals, 1947-1954*, Amherst: University of Massachusetts Press, 1978.

McCauley, Martin, *The Origins of the Cold War, 1941-1949*, New York: Routledge, 2021.

McCraig, William, *Stalin Embattled, 1943-1948*, Detroit: Wayne State University Press, 1978.

McDermott, Kevin and Jeremy Agnew, *The Comintern: A History of International Communism from Lenin to Stalin*, New York: St. Martin's Press, 1997.

McMeekin, Sean, *To Overthrow the World: The Rise and Fall of Communism*, New York: Basic Books, 2024.

McNeal, Robert, *Stalin: Man and Ruler*, New York: New York University Press, 1988.

Medvedev, Roy, *On Stalin and Stalinism*, New York: Oxford University Press, 1979.

Medvedev, Roy, *Khrushchev*, New York: Columbia University Press, 1983.

Medvedev, Roy, *All Stalin's Men: Six Who Carried Out the Bloody Purges*, New York: Anchor, 1985.

Medvedev, Roy, *Let History Judge: The Origins and Consequences of Stalinism*, New York: Columbia University Press, 1989.

Mee, Charles, *Meeting at Potsdam*, London: M. Evans, 1975.

Mee, Charles, *The Marshall Plan: The Launching of the Pax Americana*, New York: Simon and Schuster, 1984.

Meisner, Maurice, *Mao Zedong: A Political and Intellectual Portrait*, New York: Polity, 2006.

Menze, Ernest, ed., *Totalitarianism Reconsidered*, Port Washington, N.Y.: Kennikat, 1981.

Merloo, Joost, *The Rape of the Mind: The Psychology of Thought Control, Menticide and Brainwashing*, New York: Martino Publishing, 2015.

Merridale, Catherine, *Moscow Politics and the Rise of Stalin: The Communist Party in the Capital, 1925-32*, London: Macmillan, 1990.

Merridale, Catharine, *Night of Stone: Death and Memory in Russia*, New York: Viking, 2001.

Messer, Robert, *The End of an Alliance: James E. Brynes, Roosevelt, Truman and the Origins of the Cold War*, Chapel Hill: University of North Carolina Press, 1982.

Meyer, G.J., *A World Undone: The Story of the Great War, 1914-1918*, New York: Bantam, 2015.

Milburn, Michael and Sheree Conrad, *Raised to Rage: The Politics of Anger and the Roots of Authoritarianism*, Cambridge, Mass.: MIT Press, 2016.

Miller, Donald, *The Story of World War II*, New York: Simon and Schuster, 2002.

Miller, Rana, *Forgotten Ally; China's World War II, 1937-1945*, New York: Mariner Books, 2014.

Milward, Alan, *The Reconstruction of Western Europe, 1945-51*, London: Methuen, 1984.

Miner, Seven, *Between Churchill and Stalin: The Soviet Union, Great Britain and the Origins of the Grand Alliance*, Chapel Hill: University of North Carolina Press, 1988.

Modin, Yuri, *My 5 Cambridge Friends: Burgess, Maclean, Philby, Blunt and Cairncross*, New York: Farrar, Straus and Giroux, 1995.

Montefiore, Simon, *Stalin: The Court of the Red Tsar*, New York: Alfred Knopf, 2004.

Montefiore, Simon, *Young Stalin*, New York: Vintage, 2009.

Moorhouse, Roger, *Poland 1939: The Outbreak of World War II*, New York: Basic Books, 2020.

Morgan, Kevin, *International Communism and the Cult of the Individual: Leaders and Martyrs under Lenin and Stalin*, New York: Palgrave Macmillan, 2017.

Nation, Craig, *Black Earth, Red Star: A History of Soviet Security Policy*, Ithaca, N.Y.: Cornell University Press, 1992

Neiberg, Michael, *Potsdam: The End of World War II and the Remaking of Europe*, New York: Basic Books, 2015.

Nelson, Daniel, *The Wartime Origins of the Berlin Dilemma*, Tuscaloosa: University of Alabama Press, 1978.

Nester, William, *Putin's Virtual War: Russia's Subversion and Conversion of America, Europe and the World Beyond*, London: Frontline Books, 2019.

Nester, William, *Winston Churchill and the Art of Leadership*, London: Frontline, 2020.

Nester, William, *World of War: A History of American Warfare from Jamestown to the War on Terror*, New York: Stackpole Books, 2024.

Nester, William, *Franklin Roosevelt and the Art of Leadership: Battling the Great Depression and the Axis Powers*, London: Frontline Books, 2024.

Nove, Alec, *An Economic History of the USSR*, New York: Penguin, 1990.

Nove, Alec, ed., *The Stalin Phenomenon*, London: Trafalgar Square Press, 1993.

O'Brien, Paul, *Total State: Totalitarianism and How We Can Resist It*, New York: Wordwell, 2023.

Offner, Arnold, *Another Such Victory: President Truman and the Cold War, 1945-1953*, Stanford, Calif.: Stanford University Press, 2002.

O'Neil, William, *A Better World: The Great Schism: Stalinism and the American Intellectuals*, New York: Simon and Schuster, 1982.

Orwell, George and Ian Angus, eds, *Collected Essays, Journalism and Letters of George Orwell: In Front of Your Nose, 1945-1950*, New York: Mariner Books, 1971.

Panne, Jean-Louis et al, *The Black Book of Communism: Crimes, Terror, Repression*, Cambridge, Mass.: Harvard University Press, 1999.

Parrish, Michael, *The Lesser Terror: Soviet State Security, 1939-1945*, Westport, Conn.: Praeger, 1996.

Patterson Thomas, *Soviet-American Confrontation: Postwar Reconstruction and the Origins of the Cold War*, Baltimore: Johns Hopkins University Press, 1973.

Pauley, Bruce, *Hitler, Stalin and Mussolini: Totalitarianism in the Twentieth Century*, New York: Wiley Blackwell, 2014.

Paxton, Robert, *The Anatomy of Fascism*, New York: Vintage, 2004.

Payne, Robert, *The Life and Death of Trotsky*, New York: Lume, 2019.

Payne, S.C.M., *The Japanese Empire: Grand Strategy from the Meiji Restoration to the Pacific War*, New York: Cambridge University Press, 2017.

Payne, Stanley, *A History of Fascism, 1914-1945*, Madison: University of Wisconsin Press, 1995.

Pepper, Suzanne, *Civil War in China: The Political Struggle, 1945-1949*, New York: Rowman and Littlefield, 1999.

Perrie, Maureen, *The Cult of Ivan the Terrible in Stalin's Russia*, New York: Palgrave Macmillan, 2001.

Persico, Joseph, *Nuremburg: Infamy on Trial*, New York: Penguin, 1995.

Pipes, Richard, *The Formation of the Soviet Union: Communism and Nationalism*, Cambridge, Mass.: Harvard University Press, 1964.

Pipes, Richard, *Communism: A History*, New York: Modern Library, 2003.

Pirjevec, Jozc, *Tito and His Comrades*, Madison: University of Wisconsin Press, 2018.

Pisch, Anita, *The Personality Cult of Stalin in Soviet Posters, 1929-1953*, Canberra: University of Australia Press, 2016.

Plamper, Jan, *The Stalin Cult: A Study in the Alchemy of Power*, New Haven, Conn.: Yale University Press, 2012.

Plokhy, S.M., *Yalta: The Price of Peace*, New York: Viking, 2010.

Plowman, Jeffrey, *Greece 1941: The Death Throes of Blitzkrieg*, London: Pen and Sword, 2019.

Porter, David, *Soviet Tank Units, 1939-45*, London: Amber Books, 2020.

Porter, David, *German Tanks in World War II*, London: Amber Books, 2020.

Priestfield, David, *The Red Flag: A History of Communism*, New York: Grove Press, 1999.

Rabinovitch, Alexander, *The Bolsheviks Come to Power: The Revolution of 1917 in Petrograd*, New York: Haymarket Books, 2017.

Radzinsky, Edvard, *Stalin*, New York: Anchor, 1996.

Rawson, Andrew, *Organizing Victory: The War Conferences, 1941-1945*, New York: Spellmount Publishers, 2013.

Rancour-Laferreriere, Daniel, *The Mind of Stalin*, New York: Ardis, 1988.

Read, Anthony and David Fisher, *The Deadly Embrace: Hitler, Stalin and the Nazi-Soviet Pact, 1939-1941*, New York: W.W. Norton, 1989.

Rees, E.A., *Stalinism and Soviet Rail Transport*, New York: St. Martin's Press, 1995.

Rees, Laurence, *Hitler and Stalin: The Tyrants and the Second World War*, New York: Penguin, 2020.

Reid, Anna, *Leningrad: The Tragedy of a City under Siege, 1941-44*, New York: Bloomsbury, 2012.

Reid, Anna, *A Nasty Little War: The Western Intervention into Russia's Civil War*, New York: Basic Books, 2024.

Rhodes, Ben, *After the Fall: The Rise of Authoritarianism in the World We've Made*, New York: Random House, 2022.

Rhodes, Richard, *The Making of the Atomic Bomb*, New York: Simon and Schuster, 1986.

Richardson, Dan, *Comintern Army: The International Brigades in Spain's Civil War*, Lexington: University of Kentucky Press, 2014.

Richardson, Rosamond, *The Long Shadow: Inside Stalin's Family*, Boston: Little, Brown, 1993.

Ritterspoon, G.T., *Stalinist Simplifications and Soviet Complications: Social Tensions and Political Conflicts in the USSR, 1933-53*, Philadelphia: Harwood Academic, 1991.

Roberts, Geoffrey, *The Soviet Union and the Origins of the Second World War: Russo-German Relations, 1933-1941*, New York: Red Globe, 1995.

Roberts, Geoffrey, *Stalin's Wars: From World War to Cold War, 1939-1953*, New Haven, Conn.: Yale University Press, 2006.

Roberts, Geoffrey, *Molotov: Stalin's Cold Warrior*, Washington D.C.: Potomac Books, 2011.

Rogovin, Vadim, *Stalin's Terror of 1947-1948: Political Genocide in the USSR*, New York: Mehring Books, 2008.

Rogoyska, Jane, *Surviving Katyn: Stalin's Polish Massacre and the Search for Truth*, New York: Simon and Schuster, 2021.

Roland, Paul, *The Nuremberg Trials: The Nazis and Their Crimes Against Humanity*, New York: Chartwell Books, 2010.

Rosefield, Steven, *Red Holocaust*, New York: Routledge, 2009.

Rousso, Henry ed., *Stalinism and Nazism: Theory and Memory Compared*, Lincoln: University of Nebraska Press, 2004.

Rubinstein, Joshua, *The Last Days of Stalin*, New Haven, Conn.: Yale University Press, 2017.

Ryan, Henry, *The Vision of Anglo-America: The U.S.-U.K. Alliance and the Emerging Cold War, 1943-1946*, Cambridge: Cambridge University Press, 1986.

Rzhevsky, Nicholas, ed., *The Cambridge Companion to Modern Russian Culture*, New York: Cambridge University Press, 2012.

Sablinsky, Walter, *The Road to Bloody Sunday: Father Gapon and the St. Petersburg Massacre of 1905*, Princeton, N.J.: Princeton University Press, 1976.

Sainsbury, Keith, *The Turning Point: Roosevelt, Stalin, Churchill and Chiang Kai-Shek, 1943: The Moscow, Cairo and Teheran Conferences*, New York: Oxford University Press, 1985.

Salisbury, Harrison, *Black Nights, White Snow: Russia's Revolutions, 1905-1917*, New York: Da Capo, 1981.

Salisbury, Harrison, *900 Days: The Siege of Leningrad*, New York: Da Capo Press, 2003.

Sanderson, Stephen, *Revolutions: A Worldwide Introduction to Social and Political Contention*, New York: Routledge, 2010.

Sangster, Andrew and Pier Battistelli, *Flawed Commanders and Strategy in the Battles for Italy, 1943-45*, New York: Casemate, 2023.

Schaller, Michael, *The American Occupation of Japan: The Origins of the Cold War in Asia*, New York: Oxford University Press, 1987.

Schlesinger, Arthur, *The Vital Centre: The Politics of Freedom*, Boston: Houghton Mifflin, 1949.

Schmeman, Alexander, *The Foundations of Russian Culture*, New York: Holy Trinity Seminary Press, 2024.

Schrecter, Ella, *Many Are the Crimes: McCarthyism in America*, Princeton, N.J.: Princeton University Press, 1999.

Seaton, Albert, *Stalin as Military Commander*, New York: Praeger, 1998.

Sebestyn, Victor, *Lenin: The Man, Dictator and the Master of Terror*, New York: Vintage, 2018.

Senarclens, Pierre de, *From Yalta to the Iron Curtain: The Great Powers and the Origins of the Cold War*, New York: Berg, 1995.

Service, Robert, *The Bolshevik Party in Revolution: A Study in Organizational Change, 1917-1923*, London: Macmillan, 1979.

Service, Robert, *Lenin: A Political Life*, 3 vols, Bloomington: University of Indiana Press, 1985, 1991, 1995.

Service, Robert, *A History of 20th Century Russia*, Cambridge, Mass.: Harvard University Press, 1998.

Service, Robert, *Lenin: A Biography*, Cambridge, Mass.: Harvard University Press, 2000.

Service, Robert, *Stalin: A Biography*, London: Macmillan, 2004.

Service, Robert, *Trotsky: A Biography*, Cambridge, Mass.: Harvard University Press, 2009.

Service, Robert, *Comrades: A History of Communism*, Cambridge, Mass.: Harvard University Press, 2010.

Service, Robert, *The Last of the Tsars: Nicholas II and the Russian Revolution*, New York: Macmillan, 2017.

Shapiro, Leonard, *The Communist Party of the Soviet Union*, New York: Random House, 1970.

Shapiro, Leonard, *Totalitarianism*, New York: Praeger, 1972.

Sharp, Tony, *The Wartime Alliance and the Zonal Division of Germany*, Oxford: Clarendon, 1975.

Shearer, David, *Industry, State and Society in Stalin's Russia, 1926-1932*, Ithaca, N.Y.: Cornell University Press, 1996.

Shepherd, Ben, *War in the Wild East: The German Army and Soviet Partisans*, Cambridge, Mass.: Harvard University Press, 2004.

Shirer, William, *The Rise and Fall of the Third Reich* (1959), New York: Simon and Schuster, 2011.

Shlaim, Avi, *The United States and the Berlin Blockade, 1948-1949: A Study of Decision-Making*, Berkeley: University of California Press, 1983.

Shukman, Harold, ed., *Stalin's Generals*, London: Grove Press, 1993.

Shulman, Marshall, and Robert Legvold, *Stalin's Foreign Policy Reappraised*, New York: Atheneum, 1969.

Shum, Kui Kwang, *The Chinese Communist Road to Power: The Anti-Japanese National United Front*, New York: Oxford University Press, 1988.

Siegelbaum, Lewis and Andrei Sokolov, eds, *Stalinism as a Way of Life: A Narrative in Documents*, New Haven, Conn.: Yale University Press, 2003.

Simms, Brendan, *Hitler: A Global Biography*, New York: Basic Books, 2001.

Skocpol, Theda, *States and Social Revolutions*, New York: Cambridge University Press, 2015.

Skya, Walter, *Japan's Holy War: The Ideology of Radical Shinto Ultranationalism*, Durham, N.C.: Duke University Press, 2009.

Slusser, Robert, *Stalin in October: The Man Who Missed the Revolution*, Baltimore: Johns Hopkins Press, 1987.

Smele, Jon and Anthony Heywood, *The Russian Revolution of 1905: Centenary Perspectives*, New York: Routledge, 2005.

Smele, Jonathan, *The 'Russian' Civil Wars, 1916-1926: Ten Years That Shook the World*, New York: Oxford University Press, 2017.

Smith, Gaddis, *American Diplomacy during the Second World War*, New York: Alfred Knopf, 1985.

Smith, Jean, *The Defence of Berlin*, Baltimore: Johns Hopkins University Press, 1963.

Snyder, Timothy, *On Tyranny: Twenty Lessons from the Twentieth Century*, New York: Crown, 2017.

Snyder, Timothy and Ray Brandon, eds, *Stalin and Europe: Imitation and Domination*, New York: Oxford University Press, 2014.

Solzhenitsyn, Alexander, *The First Circle*, New York: Harper and Row, 1968.

Solzhenitsyn, Alexander, *The Gulag Archipelago: An Experiment in Literary Investigation*, New York: Harper Perennial, 2007.

Souvarine, Boris, *Stalin*, Stanford, Calif.: Hoover Institute Press, 1964.

Spahr, William, *Zhukov: the Rise and Fall of a Great Captain*, Novato, Calif.: Presidio Press, 1993.

Spahr, William, *Stalin's Lieutenants: A Study of Command under Duress*, Novato, Calif.: Presidio Press, 1997.

Stahel, David, *Operation Barbarossa and Germany's Defeat in the East*, New York: Cambridge University Press, 2011.

Steigelbaum, Lewis and Ronald Suny, eds, *Making Soviet Workers: Power, Class and Identity*, Ithaca, N.Y.: Cornell University Press, 1994.

Steinberg, Mark, *The Russian Revolution, 1905-1921*, New York: Oxford University Press, 2017.

Stephanov, Darin, *Ruler Personality Cults from Empire, Nation-States and Beyond in Symbolic Patterns and International Dynamics*, New York: Routledge, 2020.

Stoler, Mark, *The Politics of the Second Front: American Military Planning and Coalition Warfare, 1941-1943*, Westport, Conn.: Greenwood, 1977.

Stone, David, *The Russian Army in the Great War: The Eastern Front, 1914-1918*, Lawrence: University Press of Kansas, 2021.

Straus, Kenneth, *Factory and Community in Stalin's Russia: The Making of an Industrial Working Class, 1928-1933*, Pittsburgh: University of Pittsburgh Press, 1998.

Stueck, William, *The Road to Confrontation: American Foreign Policy toward China and Korea, 1947-1950*, Chapel Hill: University of North Carolina Press, 1981.

Sunstein, Cass, ed., *Can It Happen Here?: Authoritarianism in America*, New York: Dey Street Books, 2018.

Tasman, Alan, ed., *The Culture of Japanese Fascism*, Durham, N.C.: Duke University Press, 2009.

Taubman, William, *Stalin's American Policy: From Entente to Détente to Cold War*, New York: W.W. Norton, 1982.

Taubman, William, *Khrushchev: The Man and His Era*, New York: W.W. Norton, 2004.

Taubman, William, Sergei Khrushchev and Abbott Gleason, *Nikita Khrushchev*, New Haven, Conn.: Yale University Press, 2000.

Taylor, F. Flagg, *The Great Lie: Classic and Recent Appraisals of Ideology and Totalitarianism*, New York: Regnery Gateway, 2023.

Theoharis, Athan, *The Yalta Myth: An Issue in U.S. Politics 1945-1955*, Columbia: University of Missouri Press, 1970.

Thornton, Richard, *The Comintern and the Chinese Civil War, 1926-1931*, Seattle: University of Washington Press, 1969.

Tisamaneanu, Vladimir, *The Devil in History: Communism, Fascism and Some Lessons of the Twentieth Century*, Berkeley: University of California Press, 2012.

Todd, Allan, *Trotsky: The Passionate Revolutionary*, London: Pen and Sword, 2022.

Toland, John, *The Last 100 Days*, New York: Random House, 1966.

Tomasevich, Jozo, *War and Revolution in Yugoslavia, 1941-1945*, Stanford, Calif.: Stanford University Press, 2002.

Tormey, Simon, *Making Sense of Tyranny: Interpretations of Totalitarianism*, Manchester, U.K.: Manchester University Press, 1995.

Trotter, Wiliam, *Frozen Hell: The Russo-Finish Winter War of 1939-1940*, New York: Algonquin Books, 2000.

Tucker, Robert, *The Soviet Political Mind: Stalinism and Post-Stalin Change*, New York: W.W. Norton, 1971.

Tucker, Robert, *Stalin as Revolutionary, 1879-1929: A Study in History and Personality*, New York: W.W. Norton, 1973.

Tucker, Robert, *Stalin in Power: The Revolution from Above, 1928-1941*, New York: W.W. Norton, 1990.

Tucker, Robert, ed., *Stalinism: Essays in Historical Interpretation*, New Brunswick, N.J.: Rutgers University Press, 2000.

Tumarkin, Nina, *Lenin Lives: The Lenin Cult in Soviet Russia*, Cambridge, Mass.: Harvard University Press, 1997.

Tusa, Ann and John, *The Berlin Airlift: The Cold War Mission to Save a City*, New York: Skyhorse, 2019.

Ulam, Adam, *Tito and the Cominform*, Cambridge, Mass.: Harvard University Press, 1952.

Ulam, Adam, *Stalin: The Man and His Era*, New York: Viking, 1973.

Ulam, Adam, *Expansion and Coexistence: Soviet Foreign Policy, 1917-1973*, New York: Praeger, 1974.

Ulam, Adam, *Stalin: The Man Behind the Myth*, New York: Viking 1982.

Ulrich, Volker, *Hitler: Ascent, 1889-1939*, New York: Vintage, 2017.

Ullrich, Volker, *Hitler: Downfall, 1939-1945*, New York: Vintage, 2021.

Venturi, Franco, *The Roots of Revolution: A History of the Populist and Socialist Movements in 19th Century Russia*, New York: Legare Street Press, 2023.

Viola, Lynne, *Peasant Rebels Under Stalin: Collectivization and the Culture of Peasant Resistance*, New York: Oxford University Press, 1996.

Volkogonov, Dmitri, *Stalin: Triumph and Tragedy*, New York: Grove Weidenfeld, 1991.

Volkogonov, Dmitri, *The Rise and Fall of the Soviet Empire: Political Leaders from Lenin to Gorbachev*, London: HarperCollins, 1999.

Walker, Martin, *The Cold War: A History*, New York: Henry Holt, 1993.

Warren, Frank, *Liberals and Communism: The 'Red Decade' Revisited*, Bloomington: Indiana University Press, 1966.

Westad, Odd, *The Cold War: A World History*, New York: Hachette, 2017.

Wexler, Immanuel, *The Marshall Plan Revisited: The European Recovery in Economic Perspective*, Westport, Conn.: Greenwood, 1983.

Whitewood, Peter, *The Red Army and the Great Terror: Stalin's Purge of the Military*, Lawrence: University of Kansas Press, 2015.

Whitewood, Peter, *The Soviet-Polish War and Its Legacy: Lenin's Defeat and the Rise of Stalinism*, New York: Bloomsbury, 2023.

Whitfield, Stephen, *The Culture of the Cold War*, Baltimore: Johns Hopkins University Press, 1991.

Williams, Andrew, *The Battle of the Atlantic: The Allied Submarine Fight against Hitler's Gray Wolves of the Sea*, New York: Basic Books, 2004.

Williamson, David, *Poland Betrayed: The Nazi-Soviet Invasions of 1939*, London: Pen and Sword, 2020.

Wintr, Jerzy, ed., *The New Authoritarianism: Challenges to Democracy in the 21st Century*, New York: Verlag Barbara Budrich, 2019.

Wolfe, Bertram, *Communist Totalitarianism: Keys to the Soviet System*, Boston: Beacon Press, 1956.

Worsley, Peter, *Marx and Marxism*, New York: Routledge, 2002.

Woods, Randall and Howard Jones, *Dawning of the Cold War: The United States Quest for Order*, Athens; University of Georgia Press, 1991.

Wright, Damian, *Churchill's Secret War with Lenin: British and Commonwealth Intervention in the Russian Civil War*, New York: Helion Press, 2022.

Yergin, Daniel, *Shattered Peace: The Origins of the Cold War and the National Security State*, Boston: Houghton Mifflin, 1977.

Yoshimi, Yoshiki, *Grassroots Fascism: The War Experience of the Japanese People*, New York: Columbia University Press, 2016.

Zaloga, Steve, *Soviet Tanks and Combat Vehicles of World War Two*, London: Arms and Armour Press, 1989.

Zubok, Vladislav and Constantine Pleshakov, *Inside the Kremlin's Cold War: From Stalin to Khrushchev*, Cambridge, Mass.: Harvard University Press, 1996.

Articles

Aptekov, Pavel and Olga Dudorova, 'Peace and Statistics of Losses, Unheeded Warning and Winter War', *Slavic Military Studies*, vol. 10, no. 1 (March 1997), 200–09.

Fitzpatrick, Sheila, 'Stalin and the Making of a New Elite, 1928-1939', *Slavic Review*, vol. 38, no. 3 (September 1979), 377–402.

Kennan, George, The Long Telegram [Original] from George Kennan in Moscow to the Secretary of State, 22 February 1945, *National Security Archive*, website.

Kennan, George, Mr. X, 'The Sources of Soviet Conduct', *Foreign Affairs*, vol. 25, no. 4 (July 1947), 566–82.

Savushkin, Robert, 'In the Tracks of a Tragedy: On the 50th Anniversary of the Start of the Great Patriotic War', *Journal of Soviet Military History*, vol. 4, no. 2 (June 1991), 213–51.

Trotsky, Leon, 'Art and Politics in Our Epoch', *Partisan Review*, vol. 5, no. 3 (August-September 1938), 3–10.

INDEX